New Perspectives on the House of Representatives

New Perspectives on the House of Representatives

THIRD EDITION

Robert L. Peabody
The Johns Hopkins University

and

Nelson W. Polsby
The University of California, Berkeley

Rand McNally College Publishing Company / Chicago

77 78 79 10 9 8 7 6 5 4 3 2 1

Preface

    This third edition of *New Perspectives* arrives at a time when information about the House of Representatives is at flood tide. Where our first edition could include nearly all the best scholarly work then available on the House, today it would take a book many times this size to do a similar job. Consequently, the task of the editors has grown over the years. Our goal for this edition is to give students a sense of the changes that are going on in the House of Representatives and at the same time to provide a sample of the varied approaches that scholars have used in studying the House.

    There is still no substitute, in our opinion, for close and detailed observation as a technique of inquiry, and most of the selections herein continue to pay tribute to the fruitfulness of that approach. As scholars have developed a consensus about what is happening to the contemporary House, however, they have pressed their inquiries back into history, where direct observation is impossible and where, therefore, inferences have to be made on the basis of newspaper accounts, diaries, contemporary studies, and such time-series data as scholars have been able to reconstruct.

    Readers will also note the use of "hard" data, such as roll calls and election returns, in more recent studies. Likewise, attitude surveys, a data generating method that has been so important in other branches of political science, has also left its mark on Congressional studies.

While bringing the book up to date we have tried, nevertheless, to remind readers that the House still embodies considerable continuity with past practices. Students will be well advised to check their daily newspapers for accounts of institutional change in the House. With this book in hand, we hope it will be possible to make better sense out of the headlines and to come away with a deeper understanding of how the House works.

Washington, D.C.   RLP
Berkeley, California   NWP
June, 1976

Contents

Part One |

CONGRESSMEN
AND THEIR
CONSTITUENTS

1

The Representative and His District

Lewis Anthony Dexter

I

We talk frequently of a representative or senator "represent-ing" or "failing to represent" his constituents. This is shorthand. The fact is the congressman represents his image of the district or of his

Reprinted (modified) from *Human Organization* 16 (Spring, 1957) by per-mission of the author. Copyright 1957 by Lewis Anthony Dexter. The present analysis is based upon about 650 interviews conducted from 1953 through 1957 (420 of them by the author) with politicians, businessmen, trade-union leaders, and departmental officials about the influences impinging upon the formulation of policy. More than one hundred of those interviewed were members of Congress and forty were executive assistants on Capitol Hill. Four hundred of the interviews utilized dealt with formation of policy or communication of preference on the Reciprocal Trade Extension Acts of 1953, 1954, and 1955, and it is around these that the analysis was chiefly organized. An article by Frank Bonilla, "When Is Petition Pressure?" in *Public Opinion Quarterly* 1956, is based upon the same set of interviews. Considerable use has been made of my own participation in politics in, for example, the state government of Massachusetts from September 1956 to August 1957, in the Stevenson primary campaign of 1956, and in an effort to arouse public interest in a civil defense bill.

The interviews referred to have been made part of the Archives of Elite Inter-views at Johns Hopkins University, which is designed to collect interviews with persons who were important political leaders in North America in the years 1950 to 1970.

In its present form, this article is chapter 8 of L. A. Dexter's *Sociology and Politics of Congress* (Chicago: Rand McNally, 1960), and is presented as part of a theory of marginal attention introduced in chapters 6 and 7 of that book.

constituents (or fails to represent his, or our, image of them). How does he get this image? Where does it come from?

ON NUMEROUS IMPORTANT POLICY MATTERS, HE HEARS NOTH-
ING FROM HIS CONSTITUENCY. But whether he hears anything on an issue, what he hears, whom he hears from, and how he interprets what he hears all *vary* depending upon the kind of person he is, the kind of associations he has had and has now in the constituency and in Washington, the public image of his interests and concerns, and the background information or misinformation he possesses. An editorial summary of an earlier draft of this paper said: "Congressmen make choices about which people communicate with them." In large part this is also a manner of speaking. It would be more precise to say that the people, in electing a congressman, have chosen one sort of recording instrument or another, and that while one instrument may be adjusted to catch and hear one sort of communication, another will hear a different sort, and so on. Although congressmen do, to a small degree, consciously choose what they shall hear, it is probably more significant that in large measure their personalities, careers, and public images make them choose what they hear and how they interpret it.

A good many congressmen believe that their districts feel very strongly on this, that, or the other issue, and that they are constrained therefore to vote a certain way. The more sophisticated realize, of course, that legislative procedures and processes are so complex that it is more often than not possible to go through the motions of conforming to such views without helping to enact them when they believe the public preference to be wrong. On most issues, out of a desire to serve the district or from indifference, many congressmen do go along with any view they believe "the district" holds strongly. When the chips are down and they have to declare themselves, *some* will vote against their convictions and for their constituents' (presumed) preferences.

This situation has led to a series of classical utterances on the moral problem of the representative: *Should he sacrifice his judgment to his constituents' inclinations as he conceives them or not?* It would be more accurate to emphasize the ways in which representatives' beliefs about constituent preference are functions of the channels of communication and the special processes of transaction between constituents and representatives rather than of anything else.

If this is in fact so, more students of representation and representatives would concur with Congressman Herman P. Eberharter's interpretation of the representative-constituent picture. He had for years been at the center of the legislative issues that have provoked the most comments by critics of "pressure," and he told me early in my study of reciprocal trade (1953): "You know, I am sure you will find out a congressman can do pretty much what he decides to do, and he doesn't have to bother too much about criticism. I've seen plenty of cases since I've been up here where a guy will hold one economic or political position and get along all right; and then he'll die or resign and a guy comes in who holds quite a different economic or political position, and he gets along all right too. That's the fact of the matter."

II

THE FIRST DIFFERENCE BETWEEN SOME CONGRESSMEN AND OTHERS IS HOW (CONSCIOUSLY OR UNCONSCIOUSLY) THEY DEFINE THEIR RESPONSIBILITIES. Many of the congressmen interviewed about both tariff and defense matters referred to a personal conception of what they owed their jobs, of what in some circles would be called "professional obligation." A few had explicit and many apparently held implicit theories of representation. [So far as I could tell,] these theories of representation were not, except in a few instances, *directly* derived from philosophical or academic sources. They resulted from the experiences of men facing the actual moral complexities of a job.

Some members spoke of their obligation to select the right course regardless of the views of their constituents. For instance, Congressman Noah Mason for a good many years represented a district that (according to interviews with business interests in the district and from an economic analysis of its industrial situation) was inclined to favor the reciprocal trade program. Nevertheless he said, "Oh, knowing my stubborn characteristics, no one ever thinks he can change me, you know. . . . Some of my people say, 'You may not agree with this man Mason, but you know where he stands.'" Mr. Mason agreed that if fate were to select as his successor a Clarence Randall–type "free trader," such a man would be able to vote for a reciprocal trade program without much difficulty, but Mason interrupted an effort to probe this point further by declaring: "That's because they [my constituents] do not really understand the matter. During the twenty-one years reciprocal trade has been in effect, it has had . . . [and he named various alleged or actual consequences that he regarded as evil]. There isn't any use trying to change me!"

[On the other hand, another congressman, whom I shall call Mr. Emphatic,] voted the same way as Mr. Mason on the Reciprocal Trade Extension Act of 1955 partly because of a different definition of his responsibility. He said: "My first duty is to get reelected. I'm here to represent my district. . . . This is part of my actual belief as to the function of a congressman. . . . What is good for the majority of districts is good for the country. What snarls up the system is these so-called statesmen—congressmen who vote for what they think is the country's interest. . . . Let the senators do that. . . . They're paid to be statesmen; we aren't." (This was said sarcastically, but without humorous intent.)

A congressman we may call Mr. Leader, as strong a supporter of reciprocal trade as Mr. Mason is an opponent of it, comes fairly close to Mr. Mason in his attitude toward constituent opinion. Said Leader: "You're not identifying me on this, of course? It's strictly confidential? Always bear in mind there are those in Congress who lead their districts and those who are led by them. . . . It makes a lot of difference. . . . The ruanga growers of my district never opposed *me* on reciprocal trade. . . . I think I have convinced these men that a program of high tariffs would not assist them and I think my viewpoint has gained general acceptance from them."

Several times he spoke of himself as having "straightened out" people who had seen the matter "wrongly." In another interview during the same session, but dealing with an unrelated piece of legislation in which he had also played a prominent part, Mr. Leader showed his conception of his role on this matter to be very similar. The reciprocal trade issue is so well known, the origin of Mr. Leader's views so deeply based, and his technical knowledge of the field so considerable that he is almost certainly right in his contemptuous dismissal of the possibility that any lobbying or pressure could change his position. However, regarding the moving-picture tax, it is entirely probable that a public relations campaign did manipulate *the facts* that came to his attention and to the attention of some of his colleagues, much as Mr. Fourth, as I shall call him, was influenced on the reciprocal trade issue.

Mr. Fourth represents a district in which there is vociferous anti-reciprocal-trade sentiment. This district also has strong economic reasons for supporting reciprocal trade and a particularly influential number of intellectuals predisposed toward reciprocal trade. Mr. Fourth showed how a portion of the district can influence a man when he said, "My impulses when I came down here were in favor of trade, not aid, until I started to hear all sorts of things from my district. . . . So actually, when you stack all these things together, well, you're in favor of trade, not aid, but goodness, there comes a time . . . If trade means wholesale layoffs in your district . . . I've got any number of letters against it. Carpets, imported rugs . . . There's been around thre-hundred layoffs in a local bicycle plant. Textiles, chemicals, electrical equipment, glass salesmen . . . It's difficult to get figures. I assume the Randall Commission report has them. I haven't had time to read it. I don't know. . . . I assume that the people I hear from exaggerate the seriousness of the situation, but still that it is serious."

Mr. Fourth ultimately voted against reciprocal trade on the key votes; the decisive factor appears to have been his unwillingness to separate himself from several members from his state, also of junior status, who were more certain in their opposition to reciprocal trade. Mr. Fourth, according to his colleagues, was wavering as late as two hours before the vote. Had the chairman of his state delegation (who strongly supported the reciprocal trade bill for party reasons) personally requested his support, he might well have voted the other way. But he was obviously uncertain, *on the reciprocal trade issue*, whether to adopt the role of servant of his district (as he conceived its desires) or to think in terms of the ideology implied by the phrase "trade, not aid." How he would vote was therefore completely unpredictable. Had he stumbled into any one of three congressmen with strong pro-reciprocal-trade views in the lobby or the corridors just before the vote, he might have voted the other way.

Congressman Fourth's vote was unpredictable because on this particular issue he did not have a clear conception of what his obligations were. On some issues—flood control or taxes affecting the major agricultural product of the district—one could predict that he would see his responsibility as being almost exclusively to the district. On others—particularly those under consideration by the very important subcommittee of which he is a member—he would be strongly inclined to emphasize national interest in some form as against district concern; on that subcommittee, national defense often enters in.

III

CONGRESSMEN TEND TO SEE THEIR OBLIGATIONS AS BEING EITHER TO THE NATION OR TO THEIR CONSTITUENCY. Other equally possible obligations are seemingly not considered.

Obligation seemed to be conceived as national interest versus district interest (district interest was often, as in the case of Mr. Emphatic, related to reelection, and therefore to self-interest). No congressman interviewed indicated any feeling of moral obligation to our allies or to any other country, although our allies are regarded instrumentally as means. This is contrary to a theory sometimes expressed that Americans tend to adopt some favorite foreign country as "theirs." Also, reference to representing a region (the South, the West, New England) was very slight.

THE CONGRESSMAN'S DEFINITION OF NATIONAL INTEREST AND RESPONSIBILITY ON A PARTICULAR ISSUE DEPENDS IN LARGE MEASURE UPON HIS UNDERSTANDING OF THE FACTS OF A PARTICULAR ISSUE. Both Congressman Leader and Congressman Mason were quite clear on what they believed were the facts of the reciprocal trade question, and they had no doubt about the effects of the legislation (although their facts were to a great extent contradictory and their conclusions opposite). Congressman Fourth, on the other hand, was susceptible to influence from either side because he lacked any clear idea of what reciprocal trade legislation means or entails. His sympathy for the phrase "trade, not aid" came from a diffuse and generalized acceptance of a *slogan* rather than from an understanding of facts or consequences. He was really uncertain what, if any, difference his vote on reciprocal trade would make to the national welfare. Thus he [could], much more easily than Mr. Leader or Mr. Mason, see the matter as one of simply performing a service for discontented people in his district. It is far less likely that he would, in the absence of external stimuli, feel any strong need to learn the facts. On *service* matters—and much of a congressman's job is service—most congressmen are willing to go along with those constituents who seem to know what service they want performed and how it is to be performed (provided, of course, nothing irregular is requested). But if, for instance, Mr. Fourth were a New Deal "intellectual"—and his district is one that in my judgment might easily elect such a person—he would have interpreted the same situation quite differently. And if he were a *politically astute* New Deal "intellectual," he would have seen that the major agricultural crop of the district is exported, that several large industries in the area depend on foreign trade, and so forth.

A CONGRESSMAN'S CONCEPTION OF HIS DISTRICT CONFIRMS ITSELF, TO A CONSIDERABLE EXTENT, AND MAY CONSTITUTE A SORT OF SELF-FULFILLING PROPHECY. Remember Congressman Eberharter's words: "You know, I am sure you will find out a congressman can do pretty much what he decides to do, and he doesn't have to bother too much about criticism." Within the limits of the morally and sociologically conceivable (no congressman from Alabama in 1942 could have advocated integration, for instance), a congressman has a very wide range of choices on any given issue *so far as his constituency is concerned*. His relationships in the House or Senate and with his party leadership, of course, limit these choices severely. It is a fact, however, that there is no district viewpoint *as such* to be represented on the overwhelming majority of issues. A few will care one way and a few the other, but the issue will be insignificant or unknown to the great majority. Indeed, in many districts, only a fraction of the voters know the name of their congressman, let alone how he voted on a particular issue.

A congressman of my acquaintance took about a hundred letters that he received on a particular issue and checked the registration of the writers. He found that almost three-quarters of them were not registered in his district. What difference, then, would their views make with respect to his prospects for reelection? Mr. Emphatic, who insisted that he was representing his district's desires, was nevertheless led by my questions to admit that more than likely none of the workers presumably represented by him actually knew how he had voted. "Not a single one of them," he complained, "wrote in to thank me, though hundreds had written asking me to vote their way." He attributed this in large measure to the allegation that the largest newspaper in the district was anti-Emphatic. However, since newspapers published outside the district which gave front-page publicity to his stand had far greater circulation in the district than the anti-Emphatic local paper, this seems an unsound explanation.

Actually, most of the letters Mr. Emphatic received and most of the comments he heard originated in three large plants in the district, and they represented less than 7 percent of the voters of the district. These plants were organized by national unions, which, in chalking up Mr. Emphatic's score in 1956, were (ironically enough), inclined to regard his vote against reciprocal trade as an anti-labor vote. Fortunately for him, his stand on other matters and his personal contacts offset this factor. Of the groups in the district, only members of the League of Women Voters wrote to him in favor of reciprocal trade. "They aren't," he averred, "God knows, a potent political force; and all their letters are damn stilted, right out of the same handbook." Actually, however, it was likely that the League members would remember in 1956, and perhaps again in 1958, how he voted. And because of the ethnic and academic composition of the district, League members may have had some influence outside their own membership. It would have been perfectly possible for Mr. Emphatic to take the reverse position, favoring reciprocal trade, and still to regard himself as representing his district—particularly since the area also had a strong port interest.

A congressman has great difficulty in deciding what the viewpoint of the district is even on such an issue as reciprocal trade. Most persons with an interest or belief in the tariff will have interests or beliefs in other issues as well. Thus the most effective representation of their overall interests may necessitate concessions on some matters in order to get along with party leadership, colleagues, or prominent committee members in the Congress. "Joe Martin and Charlie Halleck, in their heart of hearts," said Representative Richard Simpson, "certainly go along with us, not with the White House, on this; and they can swing twenty-five votes, at least, any time they want. We lost by less than twenty-five votes, so they beat us." Martin was the Republican leader, Halleck his likely successor. Is a congressman doing a better job of representing his district when he keeps in the good graces of such powerful men (and thereby helps to get a bridge or a new post office or a dam for his district) or when he opposes them on an issue, the details of which no one will remember six months later? Mr. Simpson was one of the most persistent enemies of reciprocal trade in the party, and he was probably the most effective in a quiet way. He was opposed to reciprocal trade in part because of its "harmful" effect on his district. However, he cheerfully admitted, "It wouldn't make any difference what I do on this matter" insofar as his reelection was concerned. Afterward he qualified this by saying that perhaps the incumbent ought not to stick his neck out strongly *for* reciprocal trade, but there was no call for activity of any kind. (Of course, Simpson was personally so powerful that he did not need to worry much about crossing Martin or Halleck.)

IV

A CONGRESSMAN HEARS MOST OFTEN FROM THOSE WHO AGREE WITH HIM. A congressman's relationships with his district tend to be maintained through a small group of people he knew before he was elected, or through a group that has since then worked closely with him. Generally speaking, the views of those whom he knew prior to his election tend to be more like his than do the views of the "average" voter; it is a well-known fact that we tend to be like the people with whom we associate and vice versa. Also, most of the people who have worked closely with the congressman since his election—because he is a congressman—have a particular ax to grind. They will naturally tend therefore to stress agreement with him on issues about which they are not concerned, just as salesmen typically do not disagree with their customers on politics. For several years I wondered about the unfavorable references congressmen frequently made to the League of Women Voters and several times to delegations from labor unions. Ultimately it occurred to me that these two groups are probably the only ones that seriously, on a face-to-face basis, year after year go over with a congressman a series of issues on which they disagree with him. Because their efforts cannot be entirely discounted as "politics," they make congressmen uncomfortable.

Congressmen may also have a few close supporters upon whom they rely who tend to become "their" men, and who shift as they shift. This is not always just a matter of holding on to a job, but may represent confidence in a man, prestige gained by association with him, or an unwillingness to sacrifice an investment in good will that may be utilized for better public or personal purposes in the future. Such supporters are likely to couch any criticism in tactical terms, and ultimately to follow the leader. Speaking as a formerly somewhat active politician myself, I am pretty sure that the men I choose to follow would be *right* from my standpoint on basic issues of international agreement, national defense, civil rights, and public safety and police about which I particularly care. That is why I am for them. Consequently I can imagine few instances when I would seriously object to or criticize a stand they might take on some other and to me less important matter. This is true in spite of the fact that I am much more issue-oriented than most active supporters and campaigners.

SOME MEN AUTOMATICALLY INTERPRET WHAT THEY HEAR TO SUPPORT THEIR OWN VIEWPOINT. Senator Green of Rhode Island did not think he heard much about foreign imports. Congressman Forand, also from Rhode Island, said, "It's either the first or second most important issue with me. Unemployment is the other. And, of course, they're really the same thing."

The last sentence is the clue to why Mr. Forand heard so much more than Mr. Green about foreign imports. When Mr. Green heard about unemployment, he heard just about unemployment, or just about the declining industries of the area, or just about the invidious differential effect that accelerated amortization and certain other tax provisions had had on industry in the area. In fact, when I talked to him about the tariff, he advised me that I really ought to study accelerated amortization. Mr. Forand, however, interpreted almost any statement about unemployment as a plea for relief from foreign imports. Sometimes it was, but sometimes it wasn't. So, seeing the same men and hearing the same things said, Mr. Forand "heard" about tariff matters, Mr. Green did not.

The difference between Messrs. Green and Forand was illustrated at a dinner held by a joint labor-management committee from their area. The speaker who represented the trade association was really eloquent when he spoke for protection and against reciprocal trade. He hardly mentioned regional competition. The union executive who followed him sounded as though he were giving a courtesy speech of no importance when he attacked foreign imports; but when he attacked the southern states, which in his view were "robbing the North of jobs and keeping wage rates down," he changed in manner and appearance to a deeply earnest man. Mr. Green turned to the representative of the trade association and asked a searchingly critical question that implied that the latter really knew nothing about foreign trade and its effect on the economy. Mr. Forand, however, stood up to take the bows when another colleague, Anton N. Sadlak from the adjoining state of Connecticut, assured those present: "Forand and I, you can be sure, will do everything to protect our industries against foreign competition. We will be right in there fighting for you." Almost certainly, Forand actually "heard" strongly held views against reciprocal trade on this occasion, whereas Green did not.

IN MORE GENERAL TERMS, WHAT CONGRESSMEN HEAR AND HOW THEY INTERPRET WHAT THEY HEAR DEPENDS ON WHO THEY ARE. Conventional discussion of the relationship between congressmen and constituents assumes that the kind of man the congressman is has no bearing on what he hears from the district, and that the question is whether he follows or contravenes district sentiment. The notion of the congressman representing "the" district at least needs restatement *in terms of a particular congressman* who represents what he hears from the district as he interprets it. And his interpretation results from his being the particular kind of person he is and is reputed to be.

Of course, congressmen will hear many of the same things. The similarity is very great, since there are common factors in the careers of American politicians and since congress is a continuing social group where habits and attitudes are likely to persist. The old hands (staff, lobbyists, and active constituents as well as members) teach the younger ones. Furthermore, and not surprisingly, within any given district the balance of forces may continue so that several successive congressmen will belong to the same politico-social group (sometimes even when they are members of different parties). The real test of how successfully the district exerts an inescapable pressure upon the congressmen comes when, without any sharp shift in population characteristics in the district, the congressman comes from a different social grouping than most of his constituents.

Students of comparative politics have, however, much more manageable ways of exploring this problem than by studying the activities of congressmen from the same district at different times. For instance, even in terms of our focus upon substantive issues, if I had realized the significance of knowing how a congressman's interpretation of what he hears is affected by his perception of the job, the constituency, and the facts, I could have tried to find out how senators of the same party and from the same state (but representing different factions and obviously looking at the world differently) understood the reciprocal trade question. It is hardly credible that Alexander Wiley, Republican of Wisconsin, and Joseph McCarthy, Republican of Wisconsin, could have heard the same messages on domestic security and international relations. It would have been interesting, therefore, to find out whether Wiley was as sympathetic as McCarthy was to the "need" for protecting Wisconsin's fur-bearing-mammal breeders and trappers against foreign competition. A. Willis Robertson and Harry Byrd of Virginia, Lyndon Johnson and Price Daniel of Texas, J. Glenn Beall and John Butler of Maryland, Ed Martin and James Duff of Pennsylvania, Norris Cotton and Styles Bridges of New Hampshire, [and] Wayne Morse and Richard Neuberger of Oregon all would have made interesting studies from this standpoint. As it happened, I did most of my interviewing with representatives simply because senators' schedules are so much more complex and it is harder to get to see them. (A first-term senator may serve on as many as fourteen subcommittees, something unimaginable in the House.)

V

TRANSACTION RATHER THAN INTERACTION. As long as we think of the relationship between a member and a district as *inter*actional —one pressing on the other in a kind of billiard-ball psychology—I suspect that we will have considerable difficulty in describing or understanding exactly what goes on. The *trans*actional mode of analysis, as developed by John Dewey and Arthur Bentley,[1] supplies us with a leading hypothesis in terms of which political communications can be understood.

HOW A CONGRESSMAN WAS "INFLUENCED" BY HIS DISTRICT: A TRANSACTIONAL RELATIONSHIP. Mr. Serious-Consideration provides a very good case study of how a particular constellation of factors in the district may lead to a particular vote. The vote cannot be understood unless we recognize that both a congressman, as a personality and at a particular time, and the district, as he understands it, are variables.

During the spring of 1954, my old friend Mr. Straightforward did considerable canvassing in the district with a view to running for Congress in the primary against Mr. Serious-Consideration. Mr. Straightforward, incidentally, had held public office in the area several times

1. John Dewey and Arthur Bentley, *The Knowing and the Known* (Boston: Beacon, 1949); and Bentley, *An Inquiry into Inquiries* (Boston: Beacon, 1954).

before. He told me, in effect, "There's practically no interest in trade or tariff matters in the district. If you're thinking [as we were] of interviewing businessmen and labor leaders about it, don't bother. None of them know anything about it. It just doesn't bulk large in their sight." Mr. Serious-Consideration, however, reported in the same year that in his view it was the most significant or certainly one of the three most significant issues to his constituents.

Why the difference? It can be explained, I think, partly by the fact that Mr. Serious-Consideration was, consciously or unconsciously, lookink for ways in which he could appeal to local labor without offending local business. Protection again "low-wage foreign imports" is, as trade association executives pointed out to us, an excellent issued for *uniting* labor and management in depressed or dying industries (of which there were several in the district). Mr. Straightforward, on the other hand, had a program for economic redevelopment and reform of labor legislation which deflected the attention of those whom he met, whether they agreed with him or not, from such issues as the tariff. Therefore, he probably rarely heard about the tariff as an issue. Then, too, in manner and bearing Mr. Straightforward is clearly an intellectual, and one of the popular conceptions of the intellectual is his belief in free trade, unless evidence to the contrary is supplied. Mr. Serious-Consideration is not at all of this type. Finally, Mr. Straightforward's worst fault as a politician is a rather curt dismissal of anything he regards as nonsense. Mr. Serious-Consideration, on the other hand, might justly be criticized for not being able to distinguish between more or less unmotivated grumbling and serious pleas for effective action. (Mr. Serious-Consideration is, in other words, the kind of man who could be readily persuaded that every businessman who complains about taxes is earnestly desirous of reducing armaments.)

Mr. Serious-Consideration is (rather remarkably among congressmen) a worrier. He seems genuinely to believe that we must shore up NATO by strengthening trade relations. Therefore, he called a meeting of everyone in his district who might be interested and wanted to come to discuss the problem. After this meeting, his office, which had already received a good deal of mail on the subject, was simply overwhelmed by protectionist mail. This came about because people who had attended the meeting told their friends and business acquaintances about his indecision. Mr. Serious-Consideration had called upon persons who he thought might be interested. Naturally, most of those who turned up were from protection-minded industries. It is much easier for many businessmen who seem to be in considerable economic danger from foreign imports to take a day off to attend a meeting on trade and tariffs called by a congressman than it is for businessmen who *might* benefit economically if international trade were increased in total. It is more difficult, of course, for professional and salaried people to take such time off, and it is usually quite impossible for them to charge the cost off as business expense.

So this meeting, because of the way it was called, was "stacked" in this particular district. If, on the other hand, Congressman Richard K. Lankford of the Fifth District, Maryland, had called such a meeting, it might well have been stacked the other way. His district is a big tobacco-growing area that is well aware of its dependence on sales to Switzerland, and there had been Swiss threats to cut off purchases unless the U.S. withdrew its trade barriers to Swiss watches. Congressman Serious-Consideration or even Congressman Lankford, however, by some planning could have gotten a more balanced attendance. A different picture would have developed if national or state leaders of those unions in the district whose headquarters favored reciprocal trade had been consulted; and if the several college professors of economics in the district and representatives of the Grange and the Farm Bureau had been invited; and if an effort had been made to get some of the nationally known supports of reciprocal trade having some ties with the district to present their viewpoints. Or several organizations could have been asked to do what the League of Women Voters has done in some areas—study the dependence of the local industries on foreign trade.

Mr. Serious-Consideration would have had to be a different kind of man to provide wider representation at his meeting. And if the agricultural commodity in which Mr. Serious-Consideration himself has had an interest were on an export basis (as it was prior to World War II), his picture of the situation might well have been altered. He would then have been hearing from his own associates in his own trade association. (The only reason that the commodity was not exported during 1953 to 1955 was that the American market consumed all that was then produced.)

Mr. Serious-Consideration finally decided to vote against the party leadership on the key votes on reciprocal trade. He justified himself by objecting to various procedural aspects of the legislation—for instance, the so-called gag rule under which the bill was brought to the floor. But he had not objected to this gag rule, which is familiar parliamentary practice, in other cases where it was invoked. He continued to regard himself as a strong advocate of reciprocal trade.

WHEN A CONGRESSMAN WAS NOT MUCH INFLUENCED BY HIS DISTRICT. Representative Herbert B. Warburton (R., Del., 1953–1955) provided a particularly clear example of the way in which a congressman may select the kind of communications he hears. In answer to a question from me, he said to his secretary, "Am I right? We haven't received mail from more than five people on this tariff business." I looked somewhat astounded and she replied, "Yes, except of course for the pressure groups." The congressman had instructed her to segregate all recognized pressure-group mail. And he added, quite offhandedly, that he would discount, "because of his self-interest," one of the five people who had written him about the tariff. His attitude may, in part at least, explain why the chemical companies and other industries in the state had never given him "any particular specifications" on the tariff. It certainly clarifies his assertion that his approach to the problem of communications had "choked off" pressure-group mail.

Such an approach is relatively easy in Delaware, where Du Pont, because of its tremendous size and consciousness of its own vulnerability, has developed a practice and to some extent a doctrine of self-restraint. In a sense, Congressman Warburton's procedure[2] was made much easier because of the effect upon Du Pont of the munitions investigations of thirty-odd years ago, and the company's subsequent earnest effort never, never, never to get into that sort of trouble again. Thus it could happen [that], when a prominent Delaware Democrat was asked why Du Pont had not put on a campaign in regard to tariff matters (if, as it was reported, Du Pont was hostile to the Reciprocal Trade Extension Act), he said in a genuinely shocked voice, "Oh, the company would never allow that, two or three letters at the most."

A CONGRESSMAN'S REPUTATION AMONG THOSE WHO MIGHT WANT TO INFLUENCE HIM DETERMINES IN LARGE MEASURE WHAT ACTUALLY IS SAID TO HIM. Most lobbyists appear to follow the principle of going to see only those who already agree with them. "Work with your friends, but don't stir up your enemies" is a principle fairly widely held by Capitol Hill lobbyists. (Since each congressman has his own office and can be approached separately, this is fairly easy. However, in those state capitols where members of a committee, even though they may disagree on a particular issue, nevertheless hang around a lot

2. Congressman Warburton followed the same procedure on other matters. He was, it is true, rather badly beaten in his try for the Senate in 1954 by the incumbent Democrat, J. Allen Frear, but there is no reason to suppose his handling of communications had anything to do with the outcome. Far more significant political factors, such as the downstate opposition to integration, probably explain that.

For background on Warburton's district, see "Delaware: Where the Elephant Fears to Dance Among the Chickens," in Raymond A. Bauer, Ithiel de Sola Pool, and Lewis A. Dexter, *American Business and Public Policy: The Politics of Foreign Trade* (New York: Atherton, 1963), pp. 265–76; reprinted in, among others, *American Governmental Institutions*, ed. Aaron Wildavsky and Nelson W. Polsby (Chicago: Rand McNally, 1968), pp. 463–72.

together, it is reportedly more difficult. Here the lobbyists may use a different technique.) There is a reason for this prudence. Most investigations of lobbying and of particular lobbyists seem to have been started by congressmen who were annoyed at being continually approached by lobbyists with whom they disagreed. There is also another possible reason: it makes the job easy for the lobbyist. Representatives of the League of Women Voters and of labor-union councils, who do not follow this principle, make themselves unpopular in some quarters.

The tendency to abstain from trying to influence those whom you believe to be against you affects the districts back home as well as professional Capitol Hill lobbyists. The Farm Bureaus in Congressman Mason's district, like most Farm Bureaus, were definitely committed to the reciprocal trade program. Nevertheless, when a delegation went to see him it made no effort to talk in favor of reciprocal trade (although delegations from neighboring bureaus from similar districts did reportedly do so when talking to *their* congressmen). Our correspondent in Mr. Mason's district inquired of Farm Bureau representatives why they made no such effort, and he summarized their attitude this way: "The farmers deliberately avoided mention of tariffs. When I asked one of them why he didn't beard old Mason in his high-tariff den, he replied, 'Nothing in the world will change his thinking on tariffs, so why bother? He knows how we feel and can't help but feel a little nervous about the situation. So we can take that nervousness and get him to go along with us on things he isn't so dead set against.' " The probability is that they didn't *change* him on anything, but they may have influenced him to take a more aggressive and effective part on an issue of importance to them—an issue on which he did not disagree, but which he considered less important than they did.

In another instance, the congressmen from a certain area were inclined to be rather blunt and not to rely on any indirection. Before the 1955 vote on reciprocal trade, the Farm Bureau sent representatives in to talk with these congressmen. One of them, whom I shall call Congressman Ridge, told me that the farmers said, "National asked us to pass the word along that we're in favor of reciprocal trade—but we shan't be mad if you vote against it." Then, according to Mr. Ridge, one of the congressmen asked the Farm Bureau men if any one of them really favored reciprocal trade. Anyone who knows the congressmen present can be sure that at least two of them would look ready to slay on the spot any farmer bold enough to say yes. Apparently no one did say yes, and the reason may have been similar to that advanced by the Farm Bureau member from Mr. Mason's district. So Mr. Ridge, who was not so strongly opposed to reciprocal trade as some of his colleagues, was pushed to this conclusion: Everybody in my state is against reciprocal trade. The only ones for it would be the ultrainternationalists.

Of course, if Mr. Ridge were a devoted supporter of reciprocal trade, or if he were a really sophisticated analyst of interpersonal relations, he might well have felt that the conclusion was not that easy. But he is neither of these, and so he allied himself entirely to his colleagues' opposition to the reciprocal trade program.

Several congressmen told me that they tell their constituents, in effect, "I want a letter of such-and-such a kind, or I won't pay any attention to it." One of the most dedicated opponents of reciprocal trade in the country was a man who had often pointed out that reciprocal trade is really an invention of Karl Marx himself, designed to "make us captives of the Kremlin," developed and implemented by Harry Dexter White. This congressman stated that he told his constituents that he was interested only in "factual, thoughtful" letters, nothing mass-produced or propagandistic. He also told me that in three months he had not received one single letter opposing his views on reciprocal trade, whereas he had received over 2,000 supporting his position, 1,750 of which were definitely individually composed letters. The very extremity of his position apparently led those who might have disagreed with him to feel, "Oh, what's the use?" Senators who make statements of this kind, however, may simply not know what mail they get, since the mail clerks handle it. Most members of the House do have a fairly good idea of what is coming in to them. Of course, protectionist mail was mass-produced in a way in which reciprocal trade mail was not, and it is far more likely that a protectionist congressman would receive nothing in opposition to his stand rather than the reverse. (Oil interests on the Atlantic seaboard did mass-produce mail protesting the fuel-oil quota.)

We need more knowledge of the image of a person to whom a communication is sent as it appears in the mind of the sender. By and large, I strongly suspect that the bulk of political communications in the United States today tends to be addressed to those believed most likely to be sympathetic. Exceptions may occur when an issue becomes one of great involvement (as reciprocal trade did *not*, from 1953 to 1955) or of interest to persons politically very unsophisticated who have no image of specific political figures. (Occasionally, too, a writer may regard his request as one for a personal service, but in the recipient's view it may involve an issue. A sympathetic response is expected, of course, to a request for a personal service.)

SOME COMMUNICATIONS TEND TO BE UNCLEAR IN THEIR MEANING. A good deal of so-called lobbying by constituents tends to be nothing more than a social visit and a general discussion. One senator's assistant said, "You know, many of these guys who come in here from back home never talk about issues at all. I've seen lots of them supposedly lobbying. Now, Roughie [the senator] takes me to lunch with them and we go out to lunch, but they don't necessarily talk about anything. Roughie just knows a good guy may be going out of business because he doesn't get more trade or so. It's the spirit that influences him." Interestingly enough, some weeks later I found that this particular assistant was completely ignorant of the quite strong feelings (verbalized in other quarters) on tariff matters of an important industry in the state. This is an industry whose representatives had visited him and the senator, and in whose behalf he personally had spent many hours performing other chores in administrative agencies.

Mr. Personal, as I shall call him, represented a district very much like Rhode Island, and he was home every weekend. He was professedly strongly opposed to reciprocal trade, but when I questioned him, he said he really did not know whether people had talked about the tariff with him or not. At first it seemed as though this might be because of his schedule, which was so heavy that most men could not have stood it and as a result he must have been always fatigued. But the real point appears to be that Mr. Personal's attention in oral conversations back home was focused on requests for personal services. He was the archetype of the errand-boy congressman, and the only things he seemed attuned to hear were requests for personal services. He shunted comments on issues to one side or regarded them as preliminaries to requests for favors. When Mr. Forand heard someone talk about unemployment caused by foreign imports, he regarded it as a request to fight reciprocal trade. Mr. Green regarded it as nonsense, although possibly nonsense of which he should be cognizant. But Mr. Personal paid only vague attention to it except insofar as it led or might lead to a request for him to perform a service. In this he may well have been correct, for very few constituents talk about an issue with a congressman just to talk about the issue. I spent about twenty days in the winter of 1956 acting as comanager of a candidate in a congressional primary campaign, and about half of this time I was actually with the candidate. During the entire twenty days only four people raised any national or international issues whatsoever with him or me. Others who worked for him at the same time and in the same area had similar reports to make, and I have had similar experiences in other campaigns.[3]

3. There is a sharp difference between one's experience when handling public relations and mail from interest groups at campaign headquarters and observations when accompanying candidates in the field. In the former case, a good many questions are asked about issues; in the latter, very few.

VI

IMPORTANT INSTANCES WHEN CONGRESSMEN WERE CHANGED BY THEIR DISTRICTS. In the two statistically notable shifts on reciprocal trade in 1955 as compared with previous year, (1) southern Congressmen, mostly representing textile manufacturing districts, for the first time voted against the Hull reciprocal trade program in spite of a traditional veneration for free trade in the South; and (2) farm belt congressmen from districts where isolationist sentiment had been fairly strong, supported reciprocal trade on the key votes for the first time. The latter were presumably influenced by the organized efforts of national Farm Bureau leaders to get their local leaders to understand the (actual or alleged) dependence of farm prosperity upon international trade and the (actual or alleged) values of a program of trade, not aid. But those who were influenced were not, so far as is known, men to whom the issue mattered much one way or another. There is no way of sorting out the relative weight of the constituency's concern from that of the influence of the leadership of the Republican party, President Eisenhower, and Minority Leader Martin.

In the case of the southern congressmen the matter is clearer. Here "pressure education"—agitation in the district—worked. They broke with the southern tradition and the tradition of Cordell Hull, the father of reciprocal trade. They challenged and to some degree pressured that highly respected southern senator, Walter George, on his long-standing pro-reciprocal-trade position. And they gave, in this case, a weapon to Herman Talmadge, George's potential opponent in the senatorial primary of 1956, in spite of the fact that practically none of them would have preferred Talmadge to George. This breaking with precedent was chiefly the result of the communications they received from their districts, largely from textile interests. Some southern congressmen received more mail on the reciprocal trade question in a few weeks than they normally did in months on all issues combined. That the mail was more or less synthetic and stimulated is shown by the fact that some congressmen, whose positions were known to be unchangeable, received not a single letter! For these southern congressmen, such a flood of mail was apparently like the first engagement in a war for inexperienced troops. They had never seen anything of the sort before. The result: most of the Georgia delegation opposed reciprocal trade on the key votes. Hugh Alexander, successor to Muley Doughton, who as leader of Ways and Means had year after year pushed reciprocal trade through committee and the House much as

Cordell Hull wanted it, voted against the program of Hull and Doughton.

This does not controvert what has been said before, except in one respect. Most of these men, although traditionally free traders, cared very little about the issue one way or the other. If industry and the workers in their district were convinced that reciprocal trade would hurt them, they were willing enough to go along—just as most of them would go along with their farmers if the latter wanted new soil-conservation legislation. In either case, they would regard themselves simply as serving their constituents.

VII

PRESSURE IS HOW YOU SEE IT. "Pressure" and "pressure politics" are regarded by most "sophisticated" people today as explaining a great deal that happens. But it was frequently impossible to find any admission of or apparently any awareness of pressure. That was not because shrewd and worldly politicians were concealing what really went on from this naive and innocent interviewer and his naive and innocent colleagues.

The reason is explained by an assistant of a senator I shall call Mr. Service: "There are very few people actually pressuring us, even if you count all we hear about all issues. Seriously, the sense of being pressured is a matter of reaction. Other people who get no more mail than we do in this office would say, 'See how much pressure is on me.' We don't feel it. Sure, you get mail. It's just that so-and-so makes more phone calls than somebody else. The result is purely physical. It isn't a representation of what or how or when people are going to vote in elections. . . . My personal opinion is that members of most organizations make up their minds on what they read in the papers without reference to organizations."

With this theory of voting behavior, Senator Service's assistant naturally will not be too much worried by a good deal of effort to get him or his boss to change policies; he simply will not regard it as pressure.

Congressman Widesight amusingly illustrated the point made by Service's assistant. Mr. Widesight has moods when he reaches way out into left field looking for things to worry about, things that might possibly defeat him. One day, discussing reciprocal trade, he said that things were very bad indeed. His reason was that he was getting "so much" mail against it. "I, whom they never used to bother at all!" When I checked with his secretary later, I found he couldn't possibly have received more than fifty letters (representing glass, electrical equipment, and two or three bicycle firms) opposing reciprocal trade. This was only a fraction of the mail Senator Service received on the same matter. It was also a fraction of what Congressman Widesight himself had several times received on other matters, such as postal pay increases. However, Widesight was accustomed to communications on that issue, and he wasn't accustomed to them on the reciprocal trade issue.

As a matter of fact, on the reciprocal trade issue most of the congressmen interviewed reported that no one had come to see them. Several of them expressed the wish that someone would make the issue clear. (This does not mean, of course, that they were not approached, but simply that they had forgotten the approach or had not realized its purpose.) Some of them tried to question me about the matter in what I think was a serious effort to get some guidance. Generally, as good interviewing technique requires, I maintained complete neutrality. However, in two conversations (after the vote, when it could make no difference) I think I convinced members that a strengthened escape clause results in the worst of both worlds.[4] This is a position I do hold, although I was of necessity neutral on the major

4. Perhaps I should explain this. Escape-clause provisions permit U.S. producers who feel themselves handicapped in certain ways by competition from foreign imports, presumably admitted under reciprocal trade agreements, to appeal to the Tariff Commission. If they can "prove injury" the Tariff Commission can and is then presumably morally obligated to suspend the harm-producing portions of the relevant agreements. That is, if squeegee manufacturers can show that a reciprocal trade agreement with Ruritania by which the duty on Ruritanian squeegees has been reduced from ten cents a pound to six cents a pound has led to a critical invasion of the U.S. market by Ruritanian-made squeegees and driven good New England squeegee manufacturers into a desperate situation, the Tariff Commission supposedly will take action to suspend that particular portion of the Ruritanian agreement. Of course, the Ruritanian government then has the right to suspend some equivalent portion of the agreement, to the disadvantage of U.S. producers—so perfectly innocent manufacturers of squodunks in Baltimore may suddenly find that the Ruritanian government, to balance the U.S. escape-clause action against Ruritanian squeegees, has raised its tariff rate on squodunks. The net result is that Baltimore squodunk manufacturers and Ruritanian squeegee manufacturers, having presumably invested time and effort in establishing a marketing division abroad and perhaps increased their actual production facilities because of the foreign marketing possibilities, suddenly find themselves forced to cut back.

As a matter of fact, it is generally thought—and was and is thought by me—that the escape-clause provision does discourage many manufacturers abroad from trying to market in the United States. In actual practice, the Tariff Commission has been extremely conservative about admitting proof of injury, and few manufacturers abroad have really been hurt by such actions; but how is a firm that might spend thousands or millions on developing a market to know it won't be the unlucky victim? Even if in the end its operations are not harmed, threats

substantive issue. It was perfectly clear that no one had ever really explained to the two members I talked to why there is objection to the strong escape-clause procedure, in spite of the fact that one of the two key votes on the issue revolved around this. (Since the key votes were decided by seven or fewer members, every vote counted.)

Even when there is a considerable amount of what the outsider would consider pressure, the point made by Senator Service's assistant is entirely valid. What you call pressure, or what you feel to be pressure, depends on how thick your skin is. To many men in politics, threats alone represent the only real pressure, because they know very well that few votes are actually lost on any one issue such as reciprocal trade. But, of course, what is a threat to one man is not a threat to another. (For comparison, we should have studied some explosive issues like McCarthyism or humane slaughtering or perhaps some issues in which the profit-and-loss relationship is clearer, like the question of pay increases for postal employees.)

The most strongly felt kind of pressure on the reciprocal trade issue came, apparently, from Speaker Sam Rayburn and the Democratic leadership against the potentially recalcitrant Democrats. Speaker Rayburn attended a breakfast for freshman congressmen shortly before the vote and said, in effect, that he'd discovered that those who go along get along. One new member regarded this as pressure—a threat. Another new member, actually probably more vulnerable because of his factional position and his position within the delegation, did not. Both of them failed to go along. Aside from this speech, most of the pressure on the doubtful members seems to have come through the grapevine *or from their own apprehensions as to what might happen if they bolted the party leadership* (the "law" of anticipated reaction).

One reason why fairly few members seem to have felt pressure on this matter is to be explained by reference to their background and associations in local politics. In many states, pressure on matters like highway contracts or patronage or even for or against gubernatorial programs must be relatively heavy—that is, threats are far more common at the state level than they are in Washington. Many congressmen come from such a background, and a good many are still involved

---

of escape-clause action may drag on for years, and during all this time foreign manufacturers who might otherwise enter the U.S. market will hesitate to do so.

My particular objection to the escape-clause provision is twofold: (*a*) it increases instability in governmental action on foreign trade, when trade is encouraged above everything else by the ability of suppliers to be sure what government will do; and (*b*) the possibility of retaliatory action (as against squodunkers in Baltimore) creates an economically and morally quite unfair hazard to trade development.

in local conflicts about patronage, contracts, and so on. As a result, Washington to them seems very mild.

Nagging may also be called pressure, whether it is done by mail or in person. When a congressman has definitely announced his stand and does not intend to switch it, he resents being bothered by avoidable pleas (pressures) to change. The resentment point, obviously, is highly individual, so one man's pressure is another man's routine.

It should never be forgotten that most congresmen respect—although in an inarticulate or almost subconscious way—the right of petition. They have a general feeling that everyone should have a right to talk or write to them about any public issue. That's what they're there for. But they aren't as worried about each communication as college professors might expect. They generally feel they have an equal right to disregard the petitioner's point, once it has been courteously received and acknowledged. Until a congressman definitely makes up his mind, it isn't pressure—it's communication or information. Much of what Mr. Fourth, for instance, believes about reciprocal trade he learned from his mail.

VIII

OPPORTUNISM IS ALSO WHERE YOU SEE IT. Outsiders, nonpoliticians, tend to attribute many political decisions to opportunism. Also, opponents in politics sometimes attribute the decisions of the other party or faction to opportunism. However, in the interviews I conducted, few congressmen attributed their friends' decisions or their own to opportunism. When friends differ on a particular issue, each may consider that the heat is on the other. It is certainly true that in these interviews many men were amazingly—and often embarrassingly—frank about events, relationships, and personal opinions. But insofar as the acknowledged pictures they have of themselves are concerned, at least as portrayed in their interviews with me, opportunism has little part. Even the congressman who related his obligation to his district directly to his chances for reelection spoke of his "duty" to get reelected. No one used a systematically opportunistic vocabulary of motives to explain himself or his actions. Perhaps a different type of interview, some sort of "depth interviewing," would bring out a hidden set of self-images at variance with this surface picture. However, I have no evidence to that effect and am inclined to doubt it.

This report is in contrast, as far as overt self-picturing is concerned, to the views of local politicians whom I have known, notably in Massachusetts and Kansas City, Missouri, many of whom (I am speaking of local Democrats in the 1950s) were far more ready to picture themselves as opportunists than the congressmen interviewed in these studies. (In Massachusetts there has been some alteration in this regard in the 1960s; I have had no recent contact with local Kansas City politics.)

2

Congressional Elections

David R. Mayhew

Of the electoral instruments voters have used to influence American national government, few have been more important than the biennial "net partisan swing" in United States House membership. Since Jacksonian times, ups and downs in party seat holdings in the House have supplied an important form of party linkage.

The seat swing is, in practice, a two-step phenomenon. For a party to register a net gain in House seats there must occur (a) a gain (over the last election) in the national proportion of popular votes cast for House candidates of the party in question. That is, the party must be the beneficiary of a national trend in popular voting for the House.[1] But there must also occur (b) a translation of popular vote gains into seat gains.[2] Having the former without the latter might be interesting but it would not be very important.

The causes of popular vote swings have only recently been traced with any precision. There is voter behavior that produces the familiar

Reprinted by permission of the author and publisher from David R. Mayhew, "Congressional Elections: The Case of the Vanishing Marginals," *Polity* 6:3 (1974):295–317. Originally presented at the Spring, 1973, New England Political Science Association meetings.

1. To put it yet another way, voting for House candidates must have a "national component" to it. See Donald E. Stokes, "Parties and the Nationalization of Electoral Forces," ch. 7 in William N. Chambers and Walter D. Burnham, *The American Party Systems* (New York: Oxford University Press, 1967).

2. The best analysis of translation formulas is in Edward R. Tufte, "The Relation Between Seats and Votes in Two-Party Systems," *American Political Science Review* 67 (June, 1973):540–54.

mid-term sag for parties in control of the presidency.[3] There is the long-run close relation between changes in economic indices and changes in the House popular vote.[4] There are doubtless other matters that can give a national cast to House voting, including wars.[5]

The consequences of partisan seat swings (built on popular vote swings) have been more elusive but no less arresting. As in the case of the Great Society Congress (1965–1966), House newcomers can supply the votes to pass bills that could not have been passed without them. Presidents with ambitious domestic programs (Woodrow Wilson, Franklin Roosevelt, Lyndon Johnson) have relied heavily on the votes of temporarily augmented Democratic House majorities. No clear argument can be made, of course, that a bill-passing binge like that of 1965 to 1966 offers a direct conversion of popular wishes into laws. The evidence is more ambiguous. At the least a House election like the one of 1964 produces a rotation of government elites that has policy consequences; at the most there is some detectable relation between what such temporarily empowered elites do and what popular wishes are. Over time the working of the seat swing has sometimes given a dialectical cast to national policy-making, with successive elites making successive policy approximations. A case in point is the enactment of the Wagner Act in the Democratic Seventy-fourth Congress followed by its Taft-Hartley revision in the Republican Eightieth. Because of all the translation uncertainties the House seat swing has been a decidedly blunt voter intrument, but it has been a noteworthy instrument nonetheless.

The foregoing is a preface to a discussion of some recent election data. The data, for the years 1956 to 1972, suggest strongly that the House seat swing is a phenomenon of fast declining amplitude and therefore of fast declining significance. The first task here will be to lay out the data—in nearly raw form—in order to give a sense of their shape and flow. The second task will be to speculate about causes of the pattern in the data, the third to ponder the implications of this pattern.

I

[The data are presented in Figure 2–1, an array of 22 bar graphs arranged across two pages in three columns of nine, nine, and

3. Angus Campbell, "Surge and Decline: A Study in Electoral Change," ch. 3 in Campbell et al., *Elections and the Political Order* (New York: Wiley, 1966).

4. Gerald H. Kramer, "Short-Term Fluctuations in U.S. Voting Behavior, 1896–1964," *American Political Science Review* 65 (1971):131–43.

5. Ibid., p. 140.

Figure 2-1. Frequency Distributions of Democratic Percentages of the Two-Party Vote in House Districts

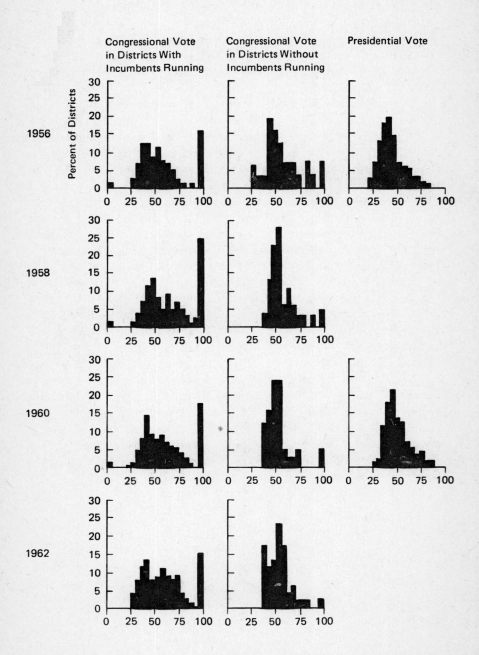

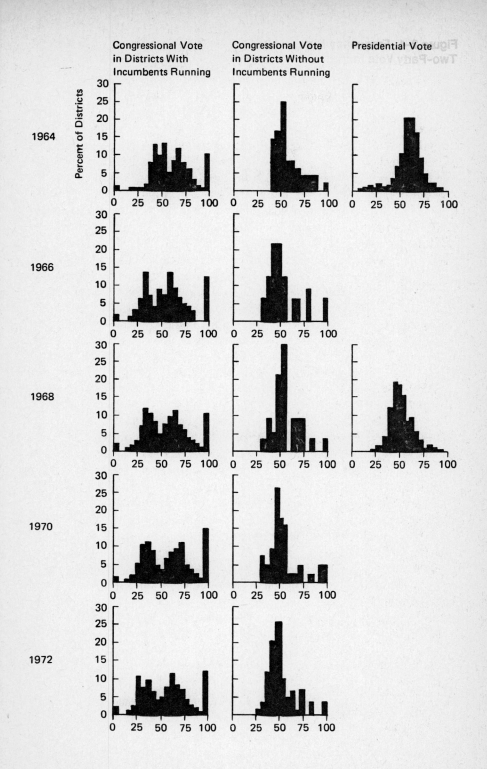

four.] It will be useful to begin with an examination of the four graphs in the right-hand column.

Each of the four right-hand graphs is a frequency distribution in which congressional districts are sorted according to percentages of the major-party presidential vote cast in them in one of the four presidential elections of the years 1956 to 1968.[6] The districts are cumulated vertically in percentages of the total district set of 435 rather than in absolute numbers. The horizontal axis has column intervals of 5 percent, ranging from a far-left interval for districts where the Democratic presidential percentage was 0 to 4.9 to a far-right interval where the percentage was 95 to 100. Thus the 1956 graph shows that the Stevenson-Kefauver ticket won 50 to 54.9 percent of the major-party vote in about 7 percent of the districts (actual district $N = 30$) and a modal 40 to 44.9 percent of the vote in about 20 percent of the districts (actual $N = 87$).

In themselves these presidential graphs hold no surprises; they are presented for the purpose of visual comparison with the other data. The presidential mode travels well to the left of the 50 percent mark in 1956 and well to the right in 1964, but the four distributions are fundamentally alike in shape—highly peaked, unimodal, not far from normal.

The center and left columns give frequency distributions, organized on the same principles as the four presidential graphs, in which House districts are sorted according to percentages of the major-party House vote cast in them in each of the nine congressional elections in the years 1956 to 1972. But for each House election there are two graphs side by side. For each year the graph in the left column gives a distribution of returns for all districts in which an incumbent congressman was running, the center column a set of returns for districts with no incumbents running.[7]

The center graphs, the "open seat" distributions, are erratically shaped because the N's are small. The number of House districts without incumbents running averages forty-three (about a tenth of the membership) and ranges from thirty-one (in 1956) to fifty-nine (in 1972); there is no discernible upward or downward trend in the series.

6. At the time of writing no comparable figures were yet available for the 1972 election. Dealing with the 1968 returns by calculating percentages of the major-party vote poses obvious problems—especially in the South—but so does any alternative way of dealing with them. Congressional district data used in Figure 2–1 and following tables and figures were taken from *Congressional Quarterly* compilations.

7. An incumbent is defined here as a congressman who held a seat at the time he was running in a November election, even if he had first taken the seat in a recent by-election.

With allowances made for erratic shape these nine "open seat" distributions are much alike. All are highly peaked and centrally clustered. In 1958 and 1968 nearly 30 percent of the readings appear in the modal interval (in both cases the 50-to-54.9-percent-Democratic interval). Over the set of nine elections the proportion of "open seat" outcomes falling in the 40-to-59.9-percent area ranges from 54.8 percent to 70.2 percent, the proportion in the 45-to-54.9-percent area from 29.0 percent to 50.1 percent. All of which imparts the simple and obvious message that House elections without incumbents running tend to be closely contested.

The nine graphs in the left-hand column give distributions for districts with incumbents running.[8] Thus in 1956 about 9 percent of districts with incumbents running yielded returns in the 45-to-49.9-percent-Democratic interval. In some of these cases the incumbents were Democrats who thereby lost their seats; in any of these nine graphs the election reading for a losing incumbent will appear on what was, from his standpoint, the unfortunate side of the 50 percent line. In an Appendix the nine data sets are disaggregated to show where in fact incumbents lost.

Immediately visible on each of these incumbency graphs is the isolated mode in the 95-to-100-percent interval, recording the familiar phenomenon of uncontested Democratic victories—mostly in the South. But, if these right-flush modes can be ignored for a moment, what has recently been happening in the contested range is far more interesting. In 1956 and 1960 the distributions in the contested range are skewed a little to the right, but still not far from normal in shape. In the 1958 and 1962 midterm years the distributions are somewhat flatter and more jagged.[9] In 1964 and 1966 they appear only tenuously normal. In 1968, 1970, and 1972 they have become emphatically bimodal in shape. Or, to ring in the uncontested Democratic seats again, the shape of incumbency distributions has now become strikingly trimodal. Thus in the 1972 election there was a range of reasonably safe Republican seats (with the 25-to-29.9-percent and 35-to-39.5-

8. The center graphs cover districts with no incumbents, the left-hand graphs districts with one incumbent. This leaves no place in the diagram for districts with two opposite-party incumbents running against each other. There were 16 of these throw-in cases over the period: seven in 1962, one in 1966, four in 1968, one in 1970, three in 1972. Republicans won in ten of them.

9. On balance it can be expected that distributions will be more centrally clustered in presidential than in midterm years, for the reason that presidential elections enroll expanded electorates in which disproportionate numbers of voters violate district partisan habits in their congressional voting. See Harvey Kabaker, "Estimating the Normal Vote in Congressional Elections," *Midwest Journal of Political Science* 13 (1969):58–83.

percent intervals most heavily populated), a range of reasonably safe Democratic seats (peaked in the 60-to-64.9-percent interval), and a set of forty-four uncontested Democratic seats.

The title of this paper includes the phrase, "The Case of the Vanishing Marginals." The "vanishing marginals" are all those congressmen whose election percentages could, but now do not, earn them places in the central range of these incumbency distributions. In the graphs for the most recent elections the trough between the "reasonably safe" Republican and Democratic modes appears in the percentage range that we are accustomed to calling "marginal." Figure 2–2 captures the

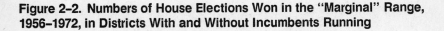

Figure 2–2. Numbers of House Elections Won in the "Marginal" Range, 1956–1972, in Districts With and Without Incumbents Running

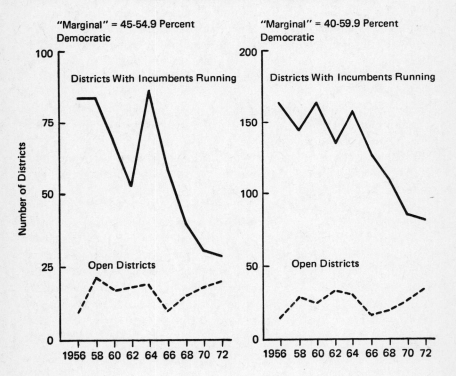

point, with time series showing how many incumbent congressmen have recorded percentages in the "marginal" range in each election from 1956 through 1972.[10] The lower series on the two Figure 2–2

10. Again, the sixteen throw-in cases are not included. It should be recalled here that some of these incumbents in the marginal range moved across the 50

graphs show, for comparative purposes, the number of "open seat" outcomes in the marginal range. In one graph, marginality is defined narrowly (45 to 54.9 Democratic percentage of the major-party vote), in the other broadly (40 to 59.9 percent). By either definition the number of incumbents running in the marginal zone has roughly halved over the sixteen-year period.[11] For some reason, or reasons, it seems to be a lot easier now than it used to be for a sitting congressmen to win three-fifths of the November vote.

II

Why the decline in incumbent marginality? No clear answer is available.[12] Adding complexity to the problem is the fact that the proportion of House seats won in the marginal range has been slowly declining for over a century.[13] Whatever mix of causes underlies the long-run change could account for much of the rapid current change as well. On the assumption that the contemporary decline is not ephemeral, perhaps the most useful thing to do here is to set out some hypotheses which may singly or in combination account for it. Five hypotheses are offered below. Some have a more persuasive ring than others; none is wholly implausible. The first has to do with district line-drawing, the next three with congressmen's actions designed to attract votes, the last with voter behavior not inspired by congressmen's actions.

(1) The line-drawing explanation is easy to reach for. In the last decade of chronic redistricting, the possibility of building districts to profit incumbents has not been lost on House members or others acting in their interest. With county lines less sacred than they once were, ingenious districts can be and have been drawn. And there are good examples of cross-party districting deals among congressmen of large

---

percent mark and lost their seats. (See the Appendix.) Of the 198 incumbents who lost elections to opposite-party challengers in the 1956-to-1972 period, only four plummeted far enough to fall outside the broadly defined (40–59.9 percent) marginal range.

11. The decline has come in spite of Republican inroads in southern House districts. One reason here is that, once they have gotten their seats, southern Republican incumbents tend to win elections handily; sixteen of twenty-two of them won with over 60 percent of the major-party vote in 1970, eighteen of twenty-two in 1972.

12. Albert D. Cover is conducting research at Yale on incumbency and marginality in the 1960s.

13. I owe this point to Walter D. Burnham. On long-run decline in House turnover see Charles O. Jones, "Inter-Party Competition for Congressional Seats," *Western Political Quarterly* 17 (1964):461–76.

state delegations.[14] But the problem with the line-drawing hypothesis is that it seems not to explain very much. Manipulation of the aggregate national data does not yield an impressive relation between redistricting and electoral benefit.[15] Moreover, if voters are being partitioned into safe House districts it can be argued that bimodal patterns ought to appear sooner or later in presidential and "open seat" distributions of the sort displayed in Figure 2–1. Of bimodalism the relevant Figure 2–1 graphs give no trace, although it must be said that the evidence is inconclusive. The evidence on redistricting generally is incomplete and inconclusive. But the odds are that it will not explain very much. If all 435 congressmen were suddenly to retire in 1974, and if elections to replace them were conducted in the 1972 district set, the odds are that a distribution of new member percentages would look like a presidential or an evened out "open seat" distribution—unimodal and roughly normal, though perhaps still with a modest isolated mode for uncontested Southerners.

The next four hypotheses hinge on the assumption that House incumbency now carries with it greater electoral advantages than it has in the past. There is evidence that it does.[16] One way to try to find out is to look at what happens to party fortunes in districts where congressmen die, retire, or lose primaries—to compare the last November percentages of veteran incumbents with the percentages of their successor nominees. Table 2–1 does this for the six elections in the years 1962 to 1972. Figures are given for transitions in which the retirees were at least two-term veterans and where the bracketing elections were both contested by both parties. It is hard to tease conclusions out of these data; the universes for the six elections are small, the districts in each interelection set vary widely in their change percentages, national trends affect Democrats and Republicans differently, and there is the redistricting problem throughout. But these are all of the data there are on the point. Most of the columns in the table include figures on districts with line changes. Including these raises the obvious problem that redistricting itself can affect party per-

14. Some strategies and examples are discussed in David R. Mayhew, "Congressional Representation: Theory and Practice in Drawing the Districts," ch. 7 in Nelson W. Polsby, ed., *Reapportionment in the 1970s* (Berkeley: University of California Press, 1971), pp. 274–84.

15. On the 1966 election see Robert J. Erikson, "Malapportionment, Gerrymandering, and Party Fortunes in Congressional Elections," *American Political Science Review* 66 (1972):1238.

16. Robert Erikson estimates that incumbency status was worth about 2 percent of the vote in the 1950s and early 1960s, but about 5 percent in 1966 and thereafter. Erikson, "The Advantage of Incumbency in Congressional Elections," *Polity* 3 (1971):395–405. Erikson, "Malapportionment, Gerrymandering, and Party Fortunes in Congressional Elections," op. cit., p. 1240.

Table 2-1. Change in Party Percentage in House Districts Where Incumbents Have Retired, Died, or Lost Primaries

| | Districts Without Line Changes | | | | | | Districts With Line Changes | |
| | Democratic Districts | | Republican Districts | | All Districts | | All Districts | |
	N	Mean	N	Mean	N	Mean	N	Mean
1962	(4)	−5.2	(4)	−0.2	(8)	−2.7	(9)	+1.3
1964	(12)	+5.5	(13)	−8.2	(25)	−1.6		
1966	(3)	−6.2	(3)	−2.5	(6)	−4.3	(7)	−7.7
1968	(4)	+1.1	(3)	−14.9	(7)	−5.8	(12)	−8.6
1970	(15)	−4.9	(17)	−7.9	(32)	−6.5	(4)	−5.7
1972	(2)	−26.7			(2)	−26.7	(25)	−9.5

Districts With and Without Line Changes

| | Democratic Districts | | Republican Districts | | All Districts | | All Districts | | All Districts | |
	N	Mean	N	Mean	N	Mean	N	Weighted Mean	N	Median
1962	(5)	−6.0	(12)	+1.8	(17)	−0.5	(17)	−2.1	(17)	−3.1
1964	(12)	+5.5	(13)	−8.2	(25)	−1.6	(25)	−1.3	(25)	−3.1
1966	(8)	−8.9	(5)	−1.8	(13)	−6.2	(13)	−5.4	(13)	−8.2
1968	(10)	−1.4	(9)	−14.5	(19)	−7.6	(19)	−8.0	(19)	−4.7
1970	(19)	−5.1	(17)	−7.9	(36)	−6.4	(36)	−6.0	(36)	−5.6
1972	(12)	−13.1	(15)	−9.0	(27)	−10.8	(27)	−11.1	(27)	−10.2

centages. But there is some justification for the inclusion. For one thing, no systematic difference appears here between what happens electorally in redrawn and untouched districts. For another, it is impossible to get any reading at all on the 1972 election without inspecting the redrawn districts; twenty-five of the twenty-seven "succession nominations" occurred in 1972 in districts with line changes. If handled carefully the altered districts can yield information. Redrawn districts are covered here if they were treated in the press as being more or less "the same" as districts preceding them; thus, for example, Paul Cronin is commonly regarded as Bradford Morse's successor in the fifth Massachusetts district, although Cronin's 1972 boundaries are somewhat different from Morse's old ones.

What to look for in Table 2–1 is whether switches in party nominees bring about drops in party percentages. The bigger the drop the higher the putative value of incumbency. Interelection changes in party percentage are calculated here by comparing party shares of the total congressional district vote in the bracketing elections.[17] The first three columns in the table give data only on districts without line changes. Thus in 1962 there were four Democratic retirements (or deaths, etc.) in districts with 1960 lines intact; the Democratic share of the total vote fell an average of 5.2 percent in these four districts between 1960 and 1962. In the four Republican retirement districts in 1962 the Republican share of the total vote fell an average of 0.2 percent. In 1964 there was an understandable party gain in the Democratic retirement districts, and an especially heavy mean loss in the Republican set. Fortuitously, the numbers of retirement districts for the two parties are almost identical in each of the five elections in 1962 through 1970, so it makes sense to calculate mean change values for all retirement districts regardless of party in each year in order to try to cancel out the effects of election-specific national trends. This is done in the third column, a list of cross-party percentage change means for the six elections. (Thus in 1964 the average change in the twenty-five retirement seats was a negative 1.6 percent even though the average party values were far apart; Republicans generally lost more in their transitions than Democrats gained in theirs.) Here there emerges some fairly solid evidence. Mean drops in percentage were higher in 1966, 1968, and 1970 than in 1962 and 1964. (1972, with its N of 2, can be ignored.) The best evidence is for 1964 and 1970, with their large N's. Loss of incumbents cost the parties a mean of 1.6 percent in 1964, a mean of 6.5 percent in 1970.

17. Figures 2–1 and 2–2 are built on candidate percentage of the major-party vote, Table 2–1 on percentages of the total vote.

In the fourth column, figures on transitions in redrawn districts are introduced. The values are mean changes for redrawn retirement districts by year regardless of party. It will be seen that these values differ in no systematic way from the values for undisturbed districts in the third column. There is the same general trend toward bigger drops in percentage. Especially striking is the 1972 value of minus 9.5 percent, lower than any other reading in the list of values for redrawn districts. The fifth, sixth, and seventh columns of the table give mean values by year, respectively, for Democratic, Republican, and all retirement districts, with no distinctions being made between altered and unaltered districts. The eighth column gives a weighted mean for each year, a simple average of the party averages. Finally the ninth column gives a median value for the set of all readings in each year.

These readings, tenuous as they are, all point in the same direction. Incumbency does seem to have increased in electoral value, and it is reasonable to suppose that one effect of this increase has been to boost House members of both parties out of the marginal electoral range. If incumbency has risen in value, what accounts for the rise? The second, third, and fourth hypotheses below focus on electorally useful activities that House members may now be engaging in more effectively than their predecessors did ten or twenty years ago.

(2) House members may now be advertising themselves better. Simple name recognition counts for a lot in House elections, as the Survey Research Center data show.[18] A name perceived with a halo of good will around it probably counts for more. If House members have not profited from accelerated advertising in the last decade, it is not from want of trying. The time series in Figure 2–3 shows, in millions of pieces, how much mail was sent out from the Capitol (by both House and Senate members) in each year from 1954 through 1970.[19] The mail includes letters, newsletters, questionnaires, child-care pamphlets, etc., some of them mailed to all district box-holders. Peak mailing months are the Octobers of evennumbered years. Mail flow more than sextupled over the sixteen-year period, with an especially steep increase between 1965 and 1966. In fact the mail-flow curve matches well any incumbency-advantage curve derivable from the data in Table 2–1. There is no letup in sight; one recent estimate has it that House members will send out about 900,000 pieces of mail per

18. Donald E. Stokes and Warren E. Miller, "Party Government and the Saliency of Congress," ch. 11 in Angus Campbell, et al., *Elections and the Political Order* (New York: Wiley, 1966), pp. 204–9.
19. Data supplied by Albert D. Cover.

Figure 2–3. Franked Mail Sent out by House and Senate Members, in Millions of Pieces, 1954–1970

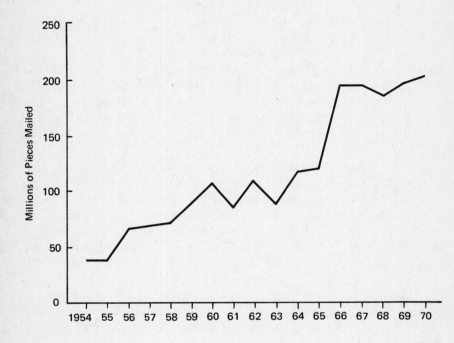

Source: U.S. Congress, House Committee on Appropriations, *Hearings Before a Subcommittee of the Committee on Appropriations, Legislative Branch Appropriations for 1970*, 91st Cong., 1st sess., 1969, p. 501 has 1954 to 1968 data. Subsequent annual hearings update estimated franking use.

member in 1974, at a total public cost of $38.1 million.[20] So the answer to the incumbency advantage question could be a remarkably simple one: the more hundreds of thousands of messages congressmen rain down on constituents the more votes they get. Whether all this activity has significantly raised the proportion of citizens who know their congressmen's names is uncertain. There are some Gallup readings showing that the share of adults who could name their congressmen rose from 46 to 53 percent between 1966 and 1970.[21]

(3) Another possibility is that House members may be getting more political mileage out of federal programs. The number of grant-in-aid

20. Norman C. Miller, "Yes, You Are Getting More Politico Mail; And It Will Get Worse," *Wall Street Journal* (March 6, 1973).
21. Gallup survey in *Washington Post* (September 20, 1970).

programs has risen in the last decade at something like the rate of Capitol mail flow. The more programs there are, the more chances House members have to claim credit ostentatiously for the local manifestations of them—housing grants, education grants, anti-pollution grants, etc.

(4) Yet another possibility is that House members have become more skilled at public position-taking on "issues." The point is a technological one. If more congressmen are commissioning and using scientific opinion polls to plumb district sentiment, then House members may have become, on balance, more practiced at attuning themselves to district opinion.[22] There is a possibility here, however hard it is to try to measure. There may be a greater general sophistication today about polling and its uses. In 1964, forty-nine Republican House members running for reelection signed a preconvention statement endorsing Senator Goldwater. It was claimed that Goldwater's nomination would help the party ticket. The forty-nine suffered disproportionately in November.[23] In 1972 there was no comparable rush among House Democrats to identify themselves with Senator McGovern.

(5) The fifth and last hypothesis has to do with changes in voter behavior not inspired by changes in incumbent activities. It is possible that incumbents have been profiting not from any exertions of their own but from changes in voter attitudes. A logic suggests itself. Voters dissatisfied with party cues could be reaching for any other cues that are available in deciding how to vote. The incumbency cue is readily at hand. This hypothesis assumes a current rise in discontent with parties; it assumes nothing about changes in the cues voter have been receiving from congressmen.

There is no point in speculating further here about causes. But it is important that the subject be given further treatment, if for no other reason than that some of the variables can be legally manipulated. The congressional franking privilege comes first to mind.

III

If fewer House members are winning elections narrowly, and if the proportion of "open seats" per election is not rising, it ought to follow that congressional seat swings are declining in amplitude. The

22. There is a discussion of roll-call position-taking and its electoral effects in Robert Erikson, "The Electoral Impact of Congressional Roll Call Voting," *American Political Science Review* 65 (1971):1018–32.

23. Robert A. Schoenberger, "Campaign Strategy and Party Loyalty: The Electoral Relevance of Candidate Decision-Making in the 1964 Congressional Elections," *American Political Science Review* 63 (1969):515–20.

argument requires no assumption that national swings in the House popular vote are changing in amplitude—and indeed there is no evidence in the contemporary data that they are. It does require the assumption that a congressman's percentage showing in one election supplies information on his strength as he goes into the next. That is, a House member running at the 60 percent level is less likely to be unseated by an adverse 5 percent party trend next time around than one running at the 54 percent level. It is easy to predict that a popular voting trend will cut less of a swath through a set of congressmen whose last-election percentages are arrayed like those in the 1968, 1970, and 1972 incumbency graphs of Figure 2–1 than through a set whose percentages are centrally and normally distributed.

There is evidence suggesting that the flight from marginality is having its posited effect. Edward Tufte has found that a "swing ratio"—a rate of translation of votes into seats—built on data from the 1966, 1968, and 1970 elections yields an exceptionally low value when compared with ratios for other election triplets over the last century.[24] The figures in Table 2–2 point in the same direction. Supplied here are

Table 2–2. House Vote Swings and Seat Swings, 1956–1972

	Change in National Popular Vote Over Last Election (percent)	Net Partisan Seat Swing Over Last Election	Incumbent Losses to Opposite Party Challengers		
			D	R	Total
1956	1.5 D	2 D	8	7	15
1958	5.1 D	49 D	1	34	35
1960	1.1 R	20 R	22	3	25
1962	2.2 R	2 R	9	5	14
1964	4.7 D	36 D	5	39	44
1966	6.2 R	47 R	39	1	40
1968	0.4 R	5 R	5	0	5
1970	3.3 D	12 D	2	9	11
1972	1.4 R	12 R	6	3	9

data on popular vote swings, net partisan seat swings, and incumbency defeats for each and both parties in the election years from 1956 through 1972.[25] It is worth noting that the large seat swings of 1958,

24. Op. cit., pp. 549–50.
25. The incumbency defeat figures cover only loses to opposite-party challengers. Thus once again the sixteen throw-in cases are disregarded. Also ignored are

1964, and 1966 were heavily dependent upon defeats of incumbents. Very few incumbents have lost since 1966. (Almost all the 1972 losers were victims of line changes.) Especially interesting are the figures for 1970, a year in which the popular vote swing was a fairly sizable 3.3 percent. Yet only nine incumbents of the disfavored party lost and the net swing over 1968 was only twelve—of which three changed over in 1969 by-elections. Part of the explanation here is doubtless that the disfavored party had relatively few incumbents in the vulnerable range to protect. Only forty-seven Republicans running in 1970 had won under the 60 percent mark in 1968, whereas there had been eighty-two comparably exposed Republicans running in 1958, seventy-six Republicans in 1964, and seventy-nine Democrats in 1966.

What general conclusions can be drawn? If the trends hold we are witnesses to the blunting of a blunt instrument. It may be too soon to say that seat swings of the 1958 or 1964 variety can be consigned to the history books, but it is hard to see how they could be equaled in the newer electoral circumstances. There is probably another manifestation here of what Walter Dean Burnham calls "electoral disaggregation"—a weakening of the peculiar links that party has supplied between electorate and government.[26] There is a concomitant triumph for the Madisonian vision; a Congress less affected by electoral tides is, on balance, one less susceptible to presidential wiles. But there is a long-run danger that a Congress that cannot supply quick electoral change is no match for a presidency that can.

Appendix

The columns of figures in Table 2–3 are frequency distributions of Democratic percentages of the November two-party House vote recorded in districts with incumbents of either (but not both) of the parties running, in biennial elections from 1956 through 1972, with

---

the November loses of two highly visible Democrats—Brooks Hays (1958) and Louise Day Hicks (1972)—to independents who thereupon enrolled as Democrats themselves in Washington. It might be added here that some incumbents do after all lose their primaries. The figures for losses to primary challengers are: six in 1956, four in 1958, five in 1960, eight in 1962, five in 1964, five in 1966, three in 1968, nine in 1970, eight in 1972. The figures for losses where redistricting has thrown incumbents into the same primary: five in 1962, three in 1964, three in 1966, one in 1968, one in 1970, six in 1972. Whatever their qualitative effects, primaries have not rivaled the larger November swings in turnover leverage.

26. "The End of American Party Politics," *Trans-Action* 7 (December, 1969): 18–20.

Table 2-3. Number of Districts Casting Democratic Percentages of the Two-Party Vote, by Year and Party of Incumbent

Democratic Percentage of Vote	Number of Districts																	
	1956		1958		1960		1962		1964		1966		1968		1970		1972	
	D	R	D	R	D	R	D	R	D	R	D	R	D	R	D	R	D	R
0– 4.9		3		1		3		1				4		9		5		7
5– 9.9																		
10– 14.9																		
15– 19.9																		
20– 24.9						1				1								2
25– 29.9		13		1		3		11		1		3		1		2		7
30– 34.9		28		11		16		24		7		8		3		5		38
35– 39.9		54		27		33		39	2	25	1	24		6		15		27
40– 44.9		54		44	3	56		45	2	47	8	53		25		40		36
45– 49.9	8	28	1	50	19	19	2	19	1	38	30	26	5	47	2	41	2	22
50– 54.9	40	6	4	27	28	3	7	4	14	35	28	6	26	39	8	34	4	10
55– 59.9	28	1	11	7	36		23	1	18	4	53	3	38	31	20	7	15	2
60– 64.9	28		33		27		36		35		34	1	43	10	28	1	27	1
65– 69.9	21		19		26		32		45		26		24		35		40	
70– 74.9	10		26		21		27		29		20		22		42		30	
75– 79.9	7		17		16		31		24		13		12		15		26	
80– 84.9	2		10		11		11		13		9		10		12		16	
85– 89.9	4		1		4		4		4				4		4		9	
90– 94.9	1		5		3		2		2				1		1		7	
95–100.0	68		95		72		56		40		51		41		56		44	

separate columns for each year for districts harboring Democratic and Republican incumbents. Thus in 1956 there were twenty-eight districts with Republican incumbents running in which Democratic percentages were in the 45-to-49.9-percent range. There were also eight districts with Democratic incumbents running in which Democratic percentages were in the 45-to-49.9-percent range; these eight Democrats thereby lost their seats. Values for incumbents who lost seats to opposite-party challengers are indicated by boldface type.

3

Congressional Recruitment and Representation

Leo M. Snowiss

This is a study of the relationship between local political organization, candidate recruitment, and representation in the United States House of Representatives. It seeks to ascertain the effects which different systems of recruitment have upon the kinds of men who enter public life and the public policies they espouse. A case study of metropolitan Chicago is used to demonstrate the utility of this kind of analysis. The objective is to distinguish distinct systems of recruitment in the Chicago area, describe the factors associated with each, and note the consequences of each for representation in Congress.

Recruitment and Organization

Political recruitment is the process by which public officials attain office. The study of recruitment and the study of representation are complementary. Knowledge of representative institutions gives

Reprinted by permission of the author and publisher from Leo M. Snowiss, "Congressional Recruitment and Representation," *American Political Science Review* 60:3 (1966):627–39. This is a revised version of a paper delivered at the annual meeting of the American Political Science Association, Washington, D.C., September, 1965. The original version was written while the author was a Fellow at the Brookings Institution. Additional assistance was provided by the Institute of Government and Public Affairs at the University of California, Los Angeles. The author gratefully acknowledges the helpful comments made by Gerald Bender, Martin Edelman, James Guyot, Duncan MacRae, Jr., John Manley, Stephen V. Stephens, and Raymond E. Wolfinger.

direction to analyses of recruitment; in turn, knowledge of factors affecting recruitment may explain much about the behavior of legislative bodies.

THE NECESSITY OF ORGANIZATION. Congressional recruitment is essentially a problem of organization. Congressional districts, with populations generally in excess of 400,000, are typified by social diversity and the dispersion of politically relevant power. The concentration of sufficient power for the nomination and election of candidates for Congress is a difficult problem. Congressional districts are rarely "natural" political units, neatly corresponding to local governmental lines or to concentrations of particular population groups and interests. Local politicians generally do try to establish relatively homogeneous districts in which there are favorable concentrations of politically relevant power. But demographic homogeneity and concentration of power are not optimally achieved even in the most favorable circumstances, such as those found in the relatively compact districts of central Chicago. While the population of a central city district may be relatively homogeneous in terms of some relevant variables (e.g., income and home ownership), its population may show signs of diversity and conflict with regard to others (e.g., race and ethnicity); it may contain potentially conflicting units of state and local governmental power (e.g., wards and state assembly districts); and it will very likely have numerous politically interested and potentially conflicting organizations (e.g., party factions, unions, ethnic and service clubs).[1]

SYSTEMS OF RECRUITMENT. The organization of effective power for recruitment is not unstructured or haphazard. To the extent that distinct processes of concentrating power can be isolated, patterns of recruitment and their consequences for representation can be classified and analyzed. A *system* of recruitment is a complex of variables affecting the organization of constituency power in a way which produces identifiable types of legislators. A system of recruitment is essentially a system of organization.

I have utilized five major variables in analyzing the organization of power for recruitment in the Chicago area:

(1) SOCIAL BASES OF ORGANIZATION. Social structures set the parameters for political systems. This is certainly manifest in the well-

1. Even Adolph Sabath (d., 1952), dean of the House and Chairman of its Rules Committee, was not immune to political attack by various party factions. On several occasions high-ranking national leaders, acting through Mayors Kelly and Kennelley, had to intervene to save his seat from ward committeemen anxious to displace him in the name of their own ethnic communities. Even within the well-disciplined Democratic party, only strong leadership could maintain unity.

documented correlations between key socioeconomic variables and both party identification and electoral support.[2] However, insofar as the systematic organization of power for recruitment is concerned, it is the primary electorates which are crucial. They provide the most active party workers, the most dependable electoral support, and the major sources of intraparty factionalism and competition. This distinction is important because primary electorates do not simply mirror the social structure of general electorates. On the contrary, primary turnouts tend to distort and exaggerate the social bases of partisan support which are manifest in general elections.[3]

(2) ORGANIZATIONAL RESOURCES. If primary electorates provide the social bases for organization support, the availability and suitability of particular resources affect the actual exploitation of those bases. Distinct systems of recruitment tend to be associated with the extent to which types of material or nonmaterial incentives (patronage or issues, respectively) are applied to particular kinds of primary electorates.[4]

(3) ORGANIZATIONAL STRUCTURE. The utilization of particular kinds and quantities of resources largely determines the character of organizational authority and the capacity of organizations to resist external influence. The use of material incentives tends to be associated with party organizations which are relatively hierarchic (evincing centralized leadership, discipline, and unity) and impermeable (resisting external influences upon their decision-making processes), while reliance on nonmaterial incentives tends toward dispersed authority and permeable decision-making structures.

(4) ORGANIZATIONAL ETHOS. The dominant resources and prevailing structures tend to promote characteristic organizational values. Materially-oriented party organizations with elaborate structures of authority tend to promote certain skills (such as bargaining and com-

2. For a summary of the relevant literature, see Nelson W. Polsby and Aaron B. Wildavsky, *Presidential Elections* (New York: Charles Scribner's Sons, 1964), chs. 1 and 3.

3. A general discussion of the effects of the primary on the party system is found in V. O. Key, Jr., *American State Politics: An Introduction* (New York: Alfred A. Knopf, 1956), chs. 4–6. The social bases of party organization in Los Angeles are analyzed in Dwaine Marvick and Charles R. Nixon, "Recruitment Contrasts in Rival Campaign Groups," in Dwaine Marvick (ed.), *Political Decision-Makers* (Glencoe: The Free Press, 1961), ch. 5.

4. The effects of material and nonmaterial resources upon organizations are treated in Peter B. Clark and James Q. Wilson, "Incentive Systems: A Theory of Organizations," *Administrative Science Quarterly* 6 (September, 1961):129–66.

promise) among their personnel, while issue-oriented party organizations are more inclined to emphasize ideological commitment.[5]

(5) ORGANIZATIONAL CONTROL. If congressional recruitment is essentially a process of organizing power, it is imperative to ascertain the extent to which particular organizations can control their electoral environments in both primary and general elections. In the Chicago area, the regular party organizations control recruitment with varying degrees of success, depending on their internal structure, the extent of electoral competition, and the character of organized nonparty counter-elites in the primary electorates. Party organizations which are faction-ridden and/or confronted with well-organized and readily available nonparty opposition in primaries tend to lose control over recruitment at the nominating stage. In districts where general elections tend to be highly competitive (irrespective of the primary situation), the regular party organizations may not actually lose control over recruitment, but deliberately tend to recruit from sources outside the party organizations. Insofar as the regular party organizations tend toward internal recruitment, organizational ethos has a decisive impact on the character of the men who run for Congress. Where external recruitment prevails, party organizational ethos is less important and the character of nonparty elites takes on greater significance.

Metropolitan Chicago: Three Types of Districts

The fundamental character of postwar representation in Congress from the Chicago area was established by the Apportionment Act of 1947, the first congressional redistricting in Illinois since 1901. The new apportionment delineated three systems of political recruitment among the districts allotted to Cook County. These have been five safely Democratic *inner-city* "machine" districts, five (four after the apportionment of 1961) *outer-city* swing districts, and three Republican-oriented *suburban* districts. The three areas are relatively distinct in regard to their socioeconomic characteristics and divisions of partisan sentiment. These differences are summarized in Tables 3-1 and 3-2.

5. Ibid.; James Q. Wilson, *The Amateur Democrat* (Chicago: University of Chicago Press, 1962); James Q. Wilson, "The Economy of Patronage," *The Journal of Political Economy* 69 (August, 1961):360-80.

Table 3–1. Indices of Socioeconomic Status, by Type of District, 1960

	Percentages		
	Inner City	Outer City	Suburban
Family Income Under $5,000	37	26	16
Family Income Over $10,000	14	26	33
Minority Groups (Negroes plus foreign stock)	65	55	36
High School Graduates	25	42	50
Home Ownership, single family	14	26	62
Home Ownership, total	29	36	72
White Collar	32	49	53

Source: Compiled from U.S. Bureau of the Census, *U.S. Census of Population and Housing: 1960 Census Tracts,* Final Report PHC (1)-26. (Washington, D.C., U.S. Government Printing Office, 1962). The districts are for the apportionment of 1947. The reapportionment of 1961 did not alter these figures significantly.

Table 3–2. Metropolitan Chicago Congressional Voting Trends: Averages by Type of District

District Type	Percent Democratic								
	1948	1950	1952	1954	1956	1958	1960	1962	1964
Inner City	71	65	66	74	63	76	74	71	77
Outer City	51	46	47	56	51	62	58	55	62
Suburban	42	35	36	40	35	42	40	35	41

Sources: *The Congressional Quarterly Almanac* 13 (Washington, D.C., 1957:180-81; ibid., 17 (1961):1039-40; *The Congressional Quarterly Weekly Report,* Part 1 (April 5, 1963):482, and ibid., Part 1 (March 26, 1965):477.

I. The Inner City Districts

The apportionment of 1947 created five congressional districts in the center of Chicago (the First, Fifth, Sixth, Seventh, and Eighth). They cut a wide swath through the city from Lake Michigan in the east out along the slum wards adjoining the Chicago River and Sanitary Canal, and westward into mixed residential and industrial areas. This area is the least affluent in Cook County and has always been heavily populated by ethnic and racial minorities.

INNER-CITY DEMOCRATIC ORGANIZATION. The inner-city districts are the domain of the Democratic party organization. The basic character of the organization throughout Cook County has been molded here, where its most extensive electoral support lies. This organization is a classic political "machine," a kind of party organization which relies primarily upon material incentives for its ward and precinct workers and supplies local services for its voter constituents. Nonmaterial rewards, for workers or voters, generally are not needed or used.[6] With large stocks of patronage available from city, county, and state offices, and with relatively centralized control over the distribution of those stocks, the organization is both massive and disciplined. This is especially true in the inner-city wards of Chicago, where the low socioeconomic status of the people is conducive to a materially-oriented organization.

Six attributes of the Democratic organization have decisively affected inner-city congressional recruitment:

(1) Although party structure is formally based upon ward-level organization, party leaders have been able to centralize the distribution of patronage and maintain a relatively hierarchic structure of authority throughout the city and county.

(2) The centralization of patronage has enabled party leaders to ensure unity among ward and township organizations. Committeemen cannot oppose the organization slate of candidates with impunity in either primary or general elections.

(3) Unity and hierarchy have made organization decision-making relatively impervious to the influences of rival nonparty groups, associations, and elites in the primary electorate. Although the preferences of external groups (e.g., unions and ethnic associations) are considered, the slating of candidates for Congress is controlled entirely by the party leaders.

(4) The predominance of material incentives and the need to maintain the unity of a rather complex organization have contributed to an ethos which tends to inhibit the use of issues for obtaining either personnel or public support. The organization is able to maintain unity through intricate bargaining over the allocation of patronage. Issues, on the other hand, are deemed irrelevant at best and dangerously

6. The early formation and contemporary operation of the Democratic organization in Chicago have been described and analyzed so often elsewhere that the analysis here need not go beyond a few summary remarks. For detailed treatments, see Edward C. Banfield, *Political Influence* (Glencoe: The Free Press, (1961); Edward C. Banfield and James Q. Wilson, *City Politics* (Cambridge: Harvard University Press, 1963), ch 9; Harold F. Gosnell, *Machine Politics, Chicago Model* (Chicago: The University of Chicago Press, 1937); Martin Meyerson and Edward C. Banfield, *Politics, Planning and the Public Interest* (Glencoe: The Free Press, 1955), chs. 3 and 11 James Q. Wilson, *Negro Politics* (Glencoe: The Free Press, 1960), ch. 3.

divisive at worst. Under such conditions, skills at bargaining, negotiation, and compromise are fostered and rewarded.

(5) The availability of important local offices as the major sources of patronage and of prestigious career objectives has produced a strong local orientation in the organization and among its personnel. The office of congressman is not highly regarded because it has no patronage worth mentioning and no apparent influence upon local politics. High city, county, or statewide offices, with relatively broader jurisdictions, considerable administrative responsibilities, and greater visibility, are more eagerly sought than seats in Congress.

(6) Since the inner-city organization is in large part an alliance of numerous ward-based ethnic, racial, and religious groups, such affiliations have become important criteria for determining the distribution of patronage and elective office—in effect, the allocation of power within the organization.

INNER-CITY RECRUITMENT. The recruitment of congressmen from the inner-city districts has been an internal affair of the Democratic party organization during the last thirty years. Massive, hierarchic, unified, impervious to external pressure, and without serious Republican opposition, the Democratic organization has been able to exercise absolute control over the nomination and election of inner-city congressmen. Long-standing membership in the organization has been the single most important criterion of selection. The congressmen have been chosen by party regulars from among party regulars.[7] They have risen through the party apparatus following career lines shaped by the distribution of power and the existence of established traditions. The party tends to funnel certain racial, ethnic, and religious groups to specific organizational and public positions. A given office may be reserved for Irishmen, or particular ward organizations may by tradition be awarded specified offices or patronage jobs. And offices are traded as patronage in bargains among different factions within the party. In this manner, prospective careers are determined and paths to Congress established.

Internal recruitment has had certain pronounced effects upon the character of inner-city representation in Congress:

(1) Reflecting the material ethos of the organization, inner-city

7. The fifteen men who have represented the inner city between 1932 and 1964 have owed much to the local organization. Seven of the congressmen had been slated by the organization and elected to legislative positions (in the State Assembly or the City Council) before going to Congress and two others had been elected to local executive offices. Four of the others had held high patronage positions in Chicago. Six of the fifteen were ward committeemen.

congressmen have been well schooled in and appreciate the value of quiet bargaining, negotiation, and compromise—virtues amply rewarded in the House. But few are skilled orators or advocates. Such abilities are not often needed in the House, but when they are, the inner-city congressmen are handicapped.

(2) The local, nonideological orientation of the organization generally has not been conducive to the recruitment of men who know much about questions of national policy. The nature of organization business has given few the time or incentive to prepare themselves for an office of national stature.

(3) Democrats who have risen through the disciplined and unified local party organization are well aware of the virtues of party unity. Local experience has taught them that in unity there is power. Chicago Democratic congressmen, particularly those from the inner city, value party cohesion as a positive good in need of little or no justification.

(4) Inner-city Democrats abjure personality politics. Since recruitment is entirely controlled by the organization, there is little incentive for individuals to cultivate personal publicity or personal followings among the electorate. Inner-city congressmen tend to resent individuals who consciously attempt to attract personal publicity. There is even some inclination to regard those who frequently make policy pronouncements as somewhat opportunistic and sensationalistic. Politics tends to be viewed as a cooperative, organizational enterprise.

(5) Inner-city Democrats tend to be relatively old when they go to Congress. The elaborate structure of the organization usually entails a lengthy tenure and ascent through the hierarchy of organization-controlled offices. Since 1932, all but two of the fifteen inner-city congressmen have been at least forty-five years old when first elected. Ten were over fifty, and one was seventy-eight. Although its utility to the organization is low, the office is not without its glamor and has tended to become a reward for long and loyal service.[8]

II. The Suburban Districts

The three suburban districts (the Fourth, Tenth, and Thirteenth) have been the most safely Republican in metropolitan Chi-

8. For comparative data, see Tables 3–3 and 3–4. Even the youngest man ever elected to Congress from an inner-city district, Dan Rostenkowski, had considerable experience within the organization. His father was a Democratic committeeman. Mr. Rostenkowski grew up in the organization, served two terms in the State General Assembly, was elected Treasurer of the Cook County Young Democrats, and was elected to Congress in 1958 at the age of thirty. He became a party committeeman when his father was appointed to a federal job in 1961.

cago.[9] Three features of suburban society have decisively affected suburban organization for recruitment. First, as Table 3–1 indicates, these are the most affluent districts in the area. There are, however, numerous suburbs with large working class populations, concentrations of heavy industry, and pockets of poverty—a fact of decisive importance for Democratic township organization. Secondly, with thirty townships and over 100 municipalities, the dispersion of power and population is especially great.[10] Thirdly, there is a widely shared political ethic which is antagonistic to, if not incompatible with, organization politics. This ethic is manifest in the nonpartisan local governments of most suburban municipalities, which deny to the parties potentially large stocks of patronage.[11]

SUBURBAN REPUBLICAN ORGANIZATION. Just as the Democratic organization in metropolitan Chicago takes its characteristic form in central Chicago, the archetype of the Republican organization is found in the suburbs, where its voting support is most secure. Republican party organization and recruitment here have been shaped by the inadequacy and ineffectiveness of patronage in the suburban political milieu. Because the districts are so large, with dispersed populations living in individual homes, effective precinct work requires very large corps of party workers. The patronage needed is much greater than the supplies available from suburban sources. Moreover, the relatively high socioeconomic status of the people and the ethic antagonistic to the use of patronage severely limit the utility of that which is available. The Republican township organizations encounter these conditions and beliefs more than the suburban Democratic party organizations and in exaggerated form. The Republicans must appeal to those more affluent country towns and townships where the suburban ethic is strongest and the middle and upper classes largest. This is true for the general and especially for the primary electorate.

Republican township leaders have had to make extensive use of

9. Only four Democratic candidates received as much as 45 percent of the vote in individual suburban districts between 1948 and 1964. No Republican candidate for Congress has received a comparable percentage of the inner-city vote during this period.

10. District densities vary from 1,556 (Fourth Congressional District) to 5,164 (Tenth Congressional District) persons per square mile. In the city of Chicago, densities range from 9,880 (Second Congressional District) to 30,600 (Ninth Congressional District). Source: U.S. Bureau of the Census, *Congressional Distirct Data Book (Districts of the Eighty-eighth Congress)*—A Statistical Abstract Supplement (Washington, D. C.: U.S. Government Printing Office, 1963), pp. 128 and 135.

11. For an extensive treatment of the use of patronage in suburban Cook County, see David McCoy, "Patronage in Suburbia" (Unpublished Ph.D. dissertation, Department of Political Science, University of Chicago, 1963).

issue-oriented volunteer workers as the fundamental basis of party organization in the suburbs. The result in each of the three districts has been an organization which is nonmaterially oriented, under-manned, undisciplined if not disunited, decentralized, and easily penetrated by external elites from the primary electorate. The fact that the Republican committeemen have little useable patronage is of decisive importance. Without it they lack the resources to attract sufficient campaign workers and have no effective sanctions with which to discipline their organizations. In primary elections, township committeemen cannot rely on their volunteer precinct captains to work for the entire organization slate. Congressional district caucuses cannot even rely upon individual committeemen to adhere to caucus-endorsed candidates for Congress. Even when the organization is united, it cannot assure a safe primary vote, because nonpatronage volunteers do not work their precincts all year and cannot build per-sonal ties with their constituents.

The character of the major Republican counter-elites in the primary electorate has also affected the structure of the party organization. Generally speaking, although the party depends upon the good will and support of the business community in general elections, businessmen have had a rather disruptive influence on the party structure in pri-mary elections. The party simply does not know when a prosperous businessman will decide to embark upon a political career or support a nonorganization Republican for some office. If the Republican pri-maries were controlled by strong party organizations this would not be possible. On the other hand, the presence of prosperous businessmen who finance their own or help to finance someone else's campaign is an independent factor which damages already precarious organization control of the Republican primaries. Public-spirited businessmen have upset regular Republican organization expectations on all levels of government in Illinois—from the ward or township to the governor-ship. In primary elections for public offices, it is not uncommon for a segment of the regular party to ally itself with some businessman and oppose other elements in the regular party who have endorsed some other candidates.

SUBURBAN REPUBLICAN RECRUITMENT. In sharp contrast to the inner-city Democratic pattern, suburban Republican recruitment gen-erally has not been from within the party organization.[12] The non-hierarchic, highly permeable structure of Republican organization has

12. Since the creation of the three suburban districts in 1947, only one of the seven Republicans elected had previously held a party organization position of any consequence. Given the uncertainty of the primaries, few committeemen have sought the nomination.

compelled Republican candidates for Congress to rely upon personal initiative and personal resources. The system tends to foster extreme sensitivity to the character of the primary electorate, which candidates must scrupulously cultivate.

External recruitment has had the following concrete effects upon the character of suburban congressmen and representation:

(1) These Republican congressmen have tended to be issue-oriented conservatives. They have had to cultivate primary electorates which are generally among the most prosperous and traditionally conservative in the entire county. From these primary electorates they have had to enlist large numbers of volunteer workers[13] (to supplement or combat the weak regular party organizations, as the case may be), solicit financial contributions, and obtain whatever support they can from prestigious businessmen. The primary constituency has set certain broad limits to the process of recruitment, while the influence of the business community and issue-oriented volunteers, drawn from among the more activist Republican elements in the primary electorate, have further influenced the process.

(2) Insofar as the Republicans elected to Congress have been issue-oriented and ideologically inclined, they have tended to put less emphasis on skills of bargaining or negotiation and more on oratory and public advocacy. The contrast with the inner-city Democrats is particularly great.[14]

(3) In the absence of adequate organizational control, suburban Republican congressmen must engage in personality politics. They have either begun their congressional careers with relatively well-known names (two of the seven were school-district superintendents) or have made every honorable effort to publicize their names and cultivate personal followings.

(4) Suburban Republican congressmen seem to place considerably less value on party cohesion for its own sake than do inner-city Democrats. The Republican recruitment process is hardly conducive to traditions of unity and even less to any capacity to enforce it.[15]

13. In some cases personal organizations have been exceptionally large. This has been particularly true of the Thirteenth Congressional District, where the last two representatives could rely on well over 1,000 volunteers in primary or general elections.

14. Speeches and insertions in the *Congressional Record* are a helpful (albeit inadequate) index to the differences between the two groups in this regard. On the whole, suburban Republicans have shown a greater propensity for oratory and on a wider range of issues than have the inner-city Democrats.

15. During the postwar period under study, Illinois Republican congressmen have not caucused with anything approaching the regularity of the Democratic

(5) Suburban candidates of both parties tend to be the youngest in Cook County. The seven suburban Republican congressmen who have served since 1949, the products of the most open, unstructured and uncertain system of recruitment in metropolitan Chicago, have averaged about forty-seven years of age when first elected to Congress.[16]

SUBURBAN DEMOCRATIC ORGANIZATION. Democratic recruitment is very different from its Republican counterpart in the suburbs. Because the Democratic organization in Cook County is relatively centralized, it has access to stocks of patronage in a variety of offices outside of the suburbs and can distribute them in townships where they are scarce. Many township committeemen themselves have patronage jobs controlled by the central committee. In each of the three suburban districts, Democratic party organization is characterized by the patronage-service concept with hierarchic, unified leadership not easily permeated by external elites. The Democratic party has been able to build township organizations of this type because its primary electorate is largely composed of lower-status groups who are amenable to the nonissue service appeals associated with patronage-oriented organizations. While it is true that the size of this electorate is sharply restricted in relation to the general electorate in most townships, it has been adequate to give the organization firm control over primary elections.

This control is facilitated by the structure of the potential counter-elites in that electorate—the labor unions. Labor cannot wheel into Democratic primary politics the way businessmen can enter Republican primaries. While businessmen can act as individual entrepeneurs, unions must act as collective entities—they are bureaucracies whose political decisions must be bureaucratic, not individual. The labor movement and the Democratic party in Cook County are both relatively centralized. Union leaders must think of the long-term effects and ramifications of opposition to a centralized and powerful Democratic political organization. They must also consider how best to

---

delegation, which has consciously sought to maintain high cohesion on roll-call votes. Unity among Illinois Republicans is much less deliberately cultivated.

16. The nine outer-city Republicans who have served in Congress during this same period have averaged fifty-three years of age when first elected. No Republicans have been elected from inner-city districts since 1934. Although Republican candidates are nominated in all five inner-city districts, the action is perfunctory because the election is viewed almost invariably as an impossible cause by party officials and nominees alike. Moreover, since the Republicans are patronage-poor, the nomination cannot even be used as a qualification for obtaining some other office. The analysis of recruitment is not an especially fruitful enterprise under these circumstances.

allocate the limited political resources of their organizations. These officials are not individualistic entrepeneurs free to spend their own fortunes. Consequently, the suburban Democratic primaries are highly structured—the party organizations are strong and disciplined and the only source of countervailing power is weaker and disinclined to risk adventuresome political fliers.

SUBURBAN DEMOCRATIC RECRUITMENT. In each of the three suburban townships the Democratic organization is strong enough to control its own internal affairs, including the recruitment of candidates for public office. This strength, however, is built upon a severely restricted primary electorate. In general elections, where the public at large must be solicited, patronage-based Democratic organizations are much less effective. Not only are they too small for the task; they are the wrong kind of organization for the suburban milieu. The very factors which give the Democratic organization control over primary elections hurt their effectiveness in general elections. Then, when Democratic candidates must broaden their appeal to the wider general electorate, the ideals of the suburban ethic or "political culture" come into conflict with the image projected by the Democratic township organizations. The use of patronage, closed primaries, and central committee influence in the township political organizations are not viewed with favor in the middle class suburbia which decides the outcome of the general elections.

Although Democratic recruitment is internally controlled, Republican predominance in the general electorate has decisively affected the recruitment of Democratic candidates. Because there is no presumption of victory in the general elections (the Democrats have won only one suburban election since 1948), old-line organization stalwarts have not valued the nomination. On the contrary, it has been sought by ambitious young men, mostly lawyers, seeking to establish themselves politically or professionally. The committeemen, in turn, tend to use the power of endorsement as a kind of incentive to induce aspirants to join their township organizations and serve for some time prior to receiving the nomination. Twenty-six organization-backed candidates were nominated in the three suburban districts between 1948 and 1964; seventeen, or about two-thirds, were attorneys, compared to one-third of the inner-city congressmen during the same period. These divergent patterns are an indication of the relative professionalization of career expectations in the inner-city organization, where the probability of recruiting candidates from an independent profession is less likely than in the suburbs.

The disadvantageous competitive situation in general elections has affected internal recruitment in other important aspects. The average age of the suburban nominees has been forty-four years, some six years younger than the average for the inner-city congressmen when first elected. (Of the seventeen suburban lawyers, eight were under forty when nominated.) The fact that suburban nominees have not had to rise through the Democratic party hierarchy largely accounts for their relative youth. Moreover, the candidates tend to be issue-oriented and are, like their Republican opponents, compelled to indulge in personality politics.[17]

III. The Outer City Districts

Nowhere in metropolitan Chicago is the influence of organization upon recruitment more evident than in the outer-city districts (the second, third, ninth, eleventh, and former twelfth). The heterogeneous and intermediate socioeconomic status of the people in these districts has provided ample social bases for the organizations of the two parties in their characteristic forms. The extremes of poverty and affluence are more evenly divided in this area than in either of the other two sets of districts. (See Table 3–1.) Neither party is compelled to build its outer-city organization on severely attenuated primary electorates. Nor has either party had to face almost certain defeat in general elections throughout the entire period under study, as has been the case in the suburbs and inner city. At the same time, there have been gradual changes in the demographic and political environments within which the organizations must function. While the organizational structures have remained relatively stable in form, the districts have evolved from marginally Republican to marginally (and in some cases safely) Democratic.[18] (See Table 3–2.) Analysis of these districts over time reveals the variable influences of party organization and constituency upon candidate recruitment.

17. Since, with a single exception, these candidates were not elected, it was not possible to ascertain their orientation toward party unity and the utilization of particular skills in concrete legislative situations. Issue-orientation and personality politics were evident in their campaigns and in interviews. Not infrequently, these propensities among suburban Democratic candidates created strains between them and the non-issue-oriented organizations which nominated them.

18. Population trends since the apportionment of 1947 have contributed greatly to the increasing outer city Democratic pluralities shown in Table 3–2. The principal sources of the trend have been the expansion of the Negro ghetto, especially into a few wards in the Second and Third Congressional Districts, and the outmigration of Jews from the west side into some wards in the Second, Ninth, and old Twelfth Congressional Districts.

OUTER-CITY REPUBLICAN ORGANIZATION AND RECRUITMENT. Like Republican organizations throughout Cook County, those in the outer city are poorly disciplined, understaffed, and readily permeated by external elites because they have little patronage and must rely heavily on volunteer workers. Again the most important consequence of party organizational weakness is the enhanced influence of the primary electorate in the recruitment process. As in the suburbs, the system has tended to produce conservative candidates who have been issue-oriented, inclined (if not actually compelled) to cultivate personal followings and personal volunteer organizations, and disinclined to treat party unity as a cardinal virtue.

The influence of the Republican primary electorate has been more evident in the outer-city districts than in the suburbs, where the dispersion of the electorate has tended to diffuse the influence of particular townships, municipalities, and population groups. On the other hand, a Republican legislature created the outer-city districts with specific, traditionally Republican, areas of support at the heart of each. These communities are pockets of prosperity which serve as sources of money, volunteer personnel, and candidates in congressional elections. The founding of the districts in 1947 actually helped to structure power and recruitment in the primary constituency. As long as these communities have remained intact, they have dominated a recruitment process which has culminated in the nomination of outspokenly conservative candidates for Congress. This has been especially evident in the Third and Eleventh Districts. In each case, the candidates have come from a single ward dominated by long-established communities. In the case of the Third Congressional District, that community is formally organized into an association which has exercised considerable influence over the weak, disunited Republican party organization in the key Republican ward. In the Second Congressional District two wards generally dominated, while in the Ninth Congressional District it was the Lake Shore Gold Coast area in general.

But changes in outer-city social structure and party competition during the last decade have promoted deviations in the old patterns of recruitment in a number of districts:

(1) When population changes have altered the balance of party competition and the composition of Republican primary electorates, significant changes in candidate recruitment have occurred. This has been most evident in the Lake Shore districts, which have had a large immigration of Jews. By the late 1950s these districts (especially the Second and old Twelfth) were beginning to slate avowedly liberal candidates for Congress. Where the effective primary electorate changed, so too did the available and influential elites, the personnel

of the ward organizations, and eventually the kind of candidates recruited.[19]

(2) Where population changes have altered party competition but have not affected the structure of the Republican primary electorate, recruitment patterns have tended to remain relatively stable. Republican party leaders have known for some time that population trends were fundamentally altering the balance of partisan support in the outer city. But in districts with stable primary electorates, the party has not nominated candidates who could appeal to the new general electorates. This has been true particularly in the Third and Eleventh Districts, where the balance of partisan sentiment has been least unfavorable to the Republicans and the primary electorates have been the most stable.

(3) As the outer-city have become increasingly Democratic, Republican candidates have tended to become younger. The average age of outer-city Republican nominees from 1950 through 1956 was fifty-two years; since 1958 the average has dropped to about forty-six years.

OUTER-CITY DEMOCRATIC ORGANIZATION AND RECRUITMENT. The Democratic organizations in the outer-city wards are patronage and service-oriented, disciplined, hierarchic, and relatively impervious to external influences upon recruitment. Although the socioeconomic conditions of the outer city are not ideal for this form of organization, considerable patronage has been invested there and organizations thoroughly capable of controlling primary elections and of appreciably influencing general elections have been created. Two factors have contributed to the success of outer-city Democratic organizations. First, population changes have made some outlying wards very much like wards found in central Chicago. Secondly, the large electoral base which the Democrats have in the poor areas of "mixed" wards gives them power to exert considerable influence in the more affluent areas of those wards—by distributing the prestigious patronage and emoluments to which a ruling party has access and by recruiting volunteers with practical interests in joining the ruling party of the wards and city. Republican committeemen complain that some of their best captains are enticed into the enemy camp.

Although the Democratic organizations are strong enough to control

19. The permeability of the Republican party organization has admitted a number of liberal Republican committeemen, many of them Jewish. This is particularly true in the northern Lake Shore wards, where the largest numbers of Jewish people have moved in the last decade. With only one exception, the highly structured Democratic organizations in these same wards have remained in the hands of Irish Catholics.

the outer-city primary electorate, the marginality of the general elec-
orate has compelled candidates to seek organized support beyond that
which the party can supply. Notwithstanding this dependence on outside groups, particularly labor, recruitment has not been affected.
Labor's hierarchic organizational ties to the Democratic party in the
city as a whole are such that bolting the ticket (in primaries or general
elections) in these districts could not be done without risking too much
elsewhere in the city.

Nevertheless, electoral marginality has had a decisive impact on
outer-city Democratic recruitment. Although the process is internal,
marginality has tended to divert the recruitment process away from
old-line politicians of the type sent to Congress from the inner-city
districts. Most Democratic candidates and congressmen from the outer
city have not held important party positions. In these districts, the kind
of candidate slated for Congress has depended upon the party committeemen's assessments of the electoral situation at a given time. When
the prospects of victory have seemed remote, the candidates chosen
have been outsiders with tenuous links to the organization, or loyal
men being rewarded with the candidacy or being groomed for more
important (i.e. local) offices.[20]

Information is available on nineteen of the twenty-one Democrats
who have been nominated in the outer city area since 1932 (the
Second, Third, and Ninth Districts) and 1947 (when the Eleventh
and Twelfth Districts were created). The average age of the nineteen candidates when first slated is forty-seven years. Table 3–3 com-

**Table 3–3. Age of Democratic Candidates when
First Nominated, 1932–1964**

District Type	Average Age	Percent Under 40	Total Cases[a]
Inner City	50	13	15
Outer City	47	37	19
Suburban	44	44	26

[a] Two outer-city districts (11th and 12th) and two suburban districts (4th and 10th) were
created in 1947, so information dates from 1948.

20. In the Third Congressional District, for example, the seat was marginal
during the 1940s and early 1950s, moving with national trends. But a large influx of Negroes gradually changed the partisan balance and, in 1958, an
organization committeeman, William Murphy, decided the time was ripe to send
himself to Congress and did so.

pares the averages of the three district categories in this regard. The fact that the outer-city average falls between the other averages is a useful indicator of the overall differences between the three district categories. Where the party organization is highly structured and entrenched, and where electoral security is most certain, candidates tend to be recruited internally from among organization men who have served the party for many years. Where the opposite conditions prevail, younger men with tenuous ties to the organization are recruited. The political significance of these age differentials must be emphasized. It is the men who come from the marginal and unsafe districts who tend to be young enough to acquire seniority and with it power and leadership potential in Congress. But it is precisely these men who have the least chance of electoral survival.

The age differential is by no means the most important consequence of the different recruitment patterns in the inner- and outer-city districts. Like the suburban candidates, outer-city Democrats have not been systematically socialized into norms which have become second nature for typical inner-city congressmen. The differences are obvious and important for understanding the operation of the Chicago Democratic delegation in Congress. It is the outer-city congressmen who have been the most inclined to seek personal publicity, least committed to the intrinsic value of party unity, most articulate, and most issue-oriented.

Chicago Democrats In Congress

For the past decade, Democrats have dominated the Chicago delegation in the House. Although Democratic candidates have failed to carry a suburban district since the election of 1948, they won every congressional election in the inner city since 1934 and in the outer city since 1958. The impact which different systems of recruitment have upon representation can be evaluated by examining the means utilized by the Democratic delegation in exploiting the principal sources of influence in the House: the seniority and committee systems, bloc voting, and the skills and knowledge of individual members.

THE SENIORITY AND COMMITTEE SYSTEMS. When they were first elected to Congress, the average age of the twenty-one Democrats who have represented Chicago since 1949 has been fifty years (median fifty-three). The eleven from the inner city averaged fifty-two, while those from the outlying districts averaged forty-eight. Only five (24 percent) were under forty when first elected—four of them having come from unsafe outer-city districts which were marginally Republican when they were first elected.[21] During this same period, House Democrats who have served as committee chairmen have averaged forty-one years of age (median forty) when first elected to Congress. The Chicago delegation has been under a considerable handicap in achieving senior committee rank.[22]

BLOC VOTING. Leadership of the delegation has perforce accrued to the safe inner-city members with close ties to the local party organization. Without adequate important committee or subcommittee chairmanships during most of the postwar period, delegation leaders have had to be concerned with the cultivation of personal friendships among congressional leaders, a willingness to go along with the requests of others, and the promotion of delegation cohesion as a bargaining instrument. Long experienced in the practical political arts, the inner-city members have been well trained for such tasks. Under their leadership, the delegation has maintained extraordinary unity on roll-call votes. Since 1949, delegation leaders could rely on nine or ten sure votes, which, taken with those of a few downstate Democrats, have composed a sizeable bloc on close roll calls. These votes were readily expandable when other congressmen or delegations became indebted to the Chicago group.

The principal source of delegation unity has been the common organization background of most of the members, especially those from the inner city. They have been well aware of the utility of unity. To the organization stalwarts this is a self-evident truth which needs little explanation and no justification.

The principal source of disunity and deviant roll-call voting during the period studied almost invariably came from those outer-city congressmen who had the most tenuous ties to the organization when they were first elected. Some of these members were also prone to seek personal publicity to a degree that disturbed delegation leaders.[23] Insofar as the leaders sought to maintain group solidarity, they tried

21. Two of the four (James Murray [Third Congressional District] and Chester Chesney [Eleventh Congressional District]) were defeated after one term. A third, Sidney R. Yates (Ninth Congressional District), retired temporarily in 1962 and ran unsuccessfully for the United States Senate.

22. The problem has been especially noticeable since the death of Mr. Sabath in 1952. Generally speaking, by the time Chicago Democrats have begun to accumulate seniority and committee rank, they have been too old to enjoy the fruits of power for any length of time, if at all.

23. These habits are at least in part necessitated by the close electoral situation in these districts and the consequent need to rely on personal followings, the press, and nonparty organizations for supplementary electoral help. But the marginality of the districts is also part of the original recruitment process which tends to funnel nonorganization types to Congress in the first place.

to minimize these sources of tension emanating from outer-city recruitment.

SKILLS AND KNOWLEDGE. The recruitment process in Chicago generally has not supplied the Democratic delegation with men who have been knowledgeable about and capable of significantly contributing to the formulation of important national policies. The most articulate, interested, and best informed have almost invariably come from the outer city. But insofar as the delegation has acted in concert, the values of the inner-city representatives have prevailed. Their practical, instrumental outlook and their preoccupations with tangible, highly specific goals have helped them to acquire much of value for the city. When necessary, credits could be collected on roll-call votes in the House and even in the Senate. Pursuing limited, specific, tangible goals, they have been able to exercise considerable influence over the disposition of federal public works. In view of the recruitment patterns of the congressmen, it is not surprising that the federal projects and financing which the delegation has sought for Chicago typify the service ethos characteristic of the local political organization. Rivers and harbors, highways, and housing have been their forte. Lobbyists have complained that no one on the delegation adequately understands the complexities of new fields, particularly those relating to electronics. Moreover, inner-city congressmen rarely have initiated legislation of signal importance to the city. They generally have looked to local government and private business for requests—the highly specific kind best handled under the circumstances in the House. The justifications for these ideas and particularly the arguments for them on the floor of the House (when that was necessary) were generally left to the outer-city congressmen.

Opportunities For Future Research

The general effects of recruitment upon the functioning of the House must await systematic, extensive study of that body. The development of appropriate categories relative to the functioning of the House is clearly a prerequisite to the most useful application of recruitment analysis. Even without this knowledge, however, the variety of organizational forms in the cities throughout the nation provides an unusually large source of data for the study of political recruitment. A cursory examination of the major cities, using a very simple classification of organizational forms, is indicative of the research possibilities. Differences in the structures of the political systems within metropolitan Chicago suggest great differences between (and within some) other big cities and metropolitan areas.[24] Do these constituency differences have any systematic effects upon urban recruitment and representation in the House?

Chicago is the model of a strong, centrally-directed, patronage-oriented political organization. Labor, although relatively well-organized for political action, is relegated to a decidedly secondary position in the recruitment process. The situation in Los Angeles is very different. There, as in California generally, local parties lack effective precinct level organization, cannot control the nominating process, and have no patronage.[25] In the absence of effective local party organization, the recruitment of Democrats in Los Angeles is decisively affected by the endorsements of important groups—particularly the press, labor and the California Democratic Council, a liberal, issue-oriented, volunteer organ of the Democratic club movement.[26] In marked contrast to Chicago, local party leaders in California are primarily concerned not with local affairs, but with issues of state and national interest.[27] The general effect has been the recruitment of ideological liberals to serve in Congress. Detroit presents a third kind of political structure in which a labor union under ideologically liberal leadership has effectively dominated a weak and disunited regular Democratic party. As in Los Angeles, a local nonpartisan tradition and scarcity of patronage have crippled the Democratic party organization. But in Detroit, unlike Los Angeles, a strong, politically conscious union exists. The UAW, via its control of the local COPE organization, frequently in alliance with activist liberal or ethnic groups, has stepped into the organizational void.[28] But nowhere in Detroit has COPE been able to exercise

24. For more detailed comparisons of big cities, see the following: Charles E. Gilbert, "National Political Alignments and the Politics of Big Cities," *Political Science Quarterly* 79 (March, 1964):25–51; J. David Greenstone, "Labor Politics in Three Cities: Political Action in Detroit, Chicago, and Los Angeles," (Unpublished Ph.D. dissertation, Department of Political Science, University of Chicago, 1963); James Q. Wilson, "Politics and Reform in American Cities," in Ivan Hinderaker (ed.), *American Government Annual* (New York: Holt, Rinehart, and Winston, Inc., 1962); Wilson, *The Amateur Democrat;* Edward C. Banfield and James Q. Wilson, *City Politics* (Cambridge, Mass.: Harvard University Press, 1963); "City Bosses and Political Machines," *Annals of the American Academy of Political and Social Science* (May, 1964), entire issue. The most detailed studies are found in the series edited by Edward C. Banfield, "City Politics Reports" (Cambridge: Joint Center for Urban Studies of the Massachusetts Institute of Technology and Harvard University, 1959–1963).

25. Wilson, *Amateur Democrat,* p. 101.

26. Ibid., pp. 110–11, 118–20, 248.

27. Ibid., pp. 125, 149, 162.

28. Greenstone, op cit., ch. 2; *The Annals of the American Academy of Political and Social Science* (May, 1964):47–48; Banfield and Wilson, *City Politics,* pp. 286ff.

the degree of control over recruitment which the Democratic party organization has everywhere in Chicago. The incompleteness of organizational control by either party or labor is manifest in the importance of personality in determining the outcomes of primary elections in most Wayne County congressional districts.[29]

Other major cities more or less approximate these three types. Those with a strong, centralized, patronage-oriented Democratic party organization which can control political recruitment, as in Chicago, include Gary, Pittsburgh, and Philadelphia.[30] Other machines are weak and highly factionalized, such as those in Cleveland, Jersey City, Kansas City, and St. Louis.[31] In Boston, the Democratic organization is weak and local patronage is scarce, but state legislators do have considerable patronage and can influence the local factions.[32] There are also machines which are not city-wide. Such organizations have been strong in Baltimore and in Kings (Brooklyn) and Bronx Counties in New York City. In other areas of the city, patronage resources have been inadequate to sustain professional party organizations strong enough to dominate the political system.[33] Finally, there are cities which resemble Los Angeles or Detroit in being genuinely nonpartisan locally, with little or no patronage, and no party machines in the classic sense of the term. The major cities of this type include Milwaukee, Minneapolis, St. Paul, and San Francisco. Labor is especially well-organized and militant in San Francisco. In Minneapolis and St. Paul, labor has joined a coalition of Democratic party leaders and liberal intellectuals in the Democratic-Farmer-Labor party, which emerged as a dominant political force in 1948.[34] As we noted previously in regard to Los Angeles, the political systems in all of these cities, in marked contrast to the machine organization cities (whether centralized, factional, or partial), tend to encourage the recruitment of Democratic congressmen who are issue-oriented ideological liberals.

29. See Greenstone's discussion of the nominations of Charles Diggs, Jr. (Thirteenth), Harold Ryan (Fourteenth), John Dingell, Jr. (Fifteenth), John Lesinski, Jr. (Sixteenth), and Martha Griffiths (Seventeenth).

30. For a detailed account of the Democratic organization in Philadelphia, see Robert L. Freedman, *A Report on Politics in Philadelphia* (Cambridge: Joint Center for Urban Studies of the Massachusetts Institute of Technology and Harvard University, 1963). See also James Reichley, *The Art of Government: Reform and Organization Politics in Philadelphia* (New York: The Fund for the Republic, 1959).

31. Wilson, *American Government Annual* (1962), p. 38.

32. Ibid., p. 40; Banfield and Wilson, *City Politics*, pp. 116, 136, 152, 161, and 230.

33. This is particularly true of Queens and, lately of Manhatten, where Tammany Hall has steadily lost control. The Bronx organization has also deteriorated.

34. Banfield and Wilson, *City Politics*, pp. 285–89.

The simple classification of machine and nonmachine recruitment can be shown to have general, systematic effects in the House. We see the distinction between the ideological, issue-oriented liberal Democrats, who founded the Democratic Study Group, and the nonideological, machine liberals, who took much less interest and provided almost no leadership for the DSG during its formative years.[35] We see the distinction, too, in the different recruitment ages of northern metropolitan Democrats (Table 3–4). Irrespective of district marginality, nonmachine Democrats tend to enter Congress with a career-potential

Table 3–4. Northern Metropolitan Democrats: Age at First Election, 1953–1961, by Type of District

| Age | District Types[a] | | | | | |
| | Safe | | Unsafe | | All | |
	Machine ($N=39$)	Nonmachine (12)	Machine (28)	Nonmachine (28)	Machine (67)	Nonmachine (40)
Average	45.2	40.9	45.7	40.5	45.4	40.7
Median	44.0	40.0	44.0	40.0	44.0	40.0
Percentage Under 40	23	50	32	46	27	48

[a] Cox index of interparty competition. Edward F. Cox, "Congressional District Party Strength and the 1960 Election," *Journal of Politics* 24 (May, 1962):277-302. "Unsafe" includes three of Cox's categories: "generally" Democratic, "marginal" and "generally" Republican. Metropolitan districts are defined in *Congressional Quarterly Almanac* 12 (1956):788-791.

Machine and nonmachine categories are based on the characteristics of political organization analyzed in the discussion above. The major machine-dominated areas include: Baltimore, Boston, the Bronx, Brooklyn, Buffalo, Cleveland, Gary, Jersey City, Kansas City, Manhattan, Newark, Philadelphia, Pittsburgh, and St. Louis. A number of anti-machine congressmen have been elected in machine cities. Such men have the support of independent political organizations and are classified as nonmachine in the table. They include: Bolling (Mo.), Donovan (N.Y.), Powell (N.Y.), Roosevelt (N.Y.), and Ryan (N.Y.).

35. Mark Ferber lists twenty-seven [members of Congress] whom he calls the "inner core" of leaders in the DSG when it was organized formally during the Eighty-sixth Congress. Only three were from big cities having political machines in the traditional sense of the term, while seven were from nonmachine urban districts, which had a total of only twenty-seven Democratic representatives at that time. There were nearly twice that number of machine congressmen. For the list of DSG leaders and members during the Eighty-sixth Congress, see Mark F. Feber, "The Democratic Study Group: A Study of Intra-Party Organization in the House of Representatives" (Unpublished Ph.D. dissertation, Department of Political Science, University of California, Los Angeles, 1964). A DSG official has estimated that in the Eighty-sixth Congress only one-third of the machine Democrats in the House actually belonged to the DSG, and that many who did were there at the request of the leadership.

advantage of two to three terms. The nonmachine congressmen, however, have tended to represent districts whose electoral marginality gives the least promise of long careers in the House.

It has been pointed out that the increasing number of safe Democratic seats in the urban North and the decrease of such seats in the South portends significant changes in the distribution of power in the Democratic party in the House.[36] What kind of men will represent these urban districts? What interests and skills will they bring to the House? The decline in strength of a number of party machines and recent increases in the number of safe Democratic seats in nonmachine areas may ultimately have significant impact upon the character of the Democratic representation and leadership from the urban North.

Future analyses of recruitment need not be confined to the simple categories used for illustrative purposes here. Even the machine-nonmachine distinction can be reclassified into numerous types according to the extent of centralization, sources of resources, local goal-orientations and organizational age.

36. Raymond E. Wolfinger and Joan Heifetz, "Safe Seats, Seniority, and Power in Congress," *American Political Science Review* 59 (June, 1965):337–49. See also, Charles O. Jones, "Inter-Party Competition for Congressional Seats," *Western Political Quarterly* 17 (September, 1964):461–76.

Part Two |

GROUPS IN THE HOUSE

4

Mobilization of Liberal Strength in the House, 1955-1970: The Democratic Study Group

Arthur G. Stevens, Jr., Arthur H. Miller, and Thomas E. Mann

Introduction

Institutional arrangements devised for collective decision-making often result in biases for certain interests at the cost of others. In legislative settings, the representation of constituent interests is fundamentally affected by the processes that intervene between inputs and policy decisions. For example, reliance on committees for agenda setting and the structuring of policy alternatives results in different legislators having unequal access to important areas of decision-making. Reaction to a perceived conservative institutional bias in the U.S. House of Representatives brought a group of liberal Democrats to organize the Democratic Study Group (DSG) over a decade ago in order to counteract those factors that minimized the effect of their

Reprinted by permission of the authors and publisher, from Arthur G. Stevens, Jr., Arthur H. Miller, and Thomas E. Mann, "Mobilization of Liberal Strength in the House, 1955–1970: The Democratic Study Group," *American Political Science Review* 68:2 (1974):667–681. The authors wish to thank the Inter-University Consortium for Political Research for providing the roll-call data used in the analysis. Footnotes have been renumbered.

numbers. Factors contributing to this conservative bias and an assessment of DSG success in mobilizing its forces to counteract this bias are the subjects of this paper.

It is not difficult to picture the roadblocks in the legislative process faced in the late 1950s by the founders of the Democratic Study Group. A recitation of legislative victories of the conservative coalition during the previous two decades would go a long way toward explaining the sense of frustration felt by many liberal Democrats. The sheer number and ideological consistency of Republicans and Southern Democrats posed formidable problems for liberal efforts to legislate domestic policy. Yet what was especially grating was the failure of liberals to marshal the potential forces that they did have. Many decisions simply did not reflect the numbers they perceived to be sympathetic.

Certain institutional characteristics of the legislative process in the House provide a fruitful explanation of the liberals' dilemma. By institutional factors we mean that set of formal and informal procedures which govern everyday life within the legislative chamber. One aspect of the legislative process which emerges as relevant to the perception of a conservative bias in the House is the process of individual decision-making on roll-call votes.

There is no argument among observers of Congress that specialization is the defining characteristic of the manner in which the House conducts its business. Nor is there any disagreement over the attendant ability of individual members to exercise considerable influence within narrow policy domains. What is somewhat less settled is an understanding of how committee decisions come to be ratified by the whole House. That question is itself enormously complex and not answerable by a simple generalization appropriate for the whole range of committees in the House. What can be said, however, is that in the late 1950s the conjunction of committee leadership seniority and integration on the one hand, and the process of individual decision-making on the other, generally led to collective decisions somewhat more conservative than might otherwise have been expected.

Why is this the case? Several recent research efforts focusing on the information problems of representatives provide an interesting perspective from which to address this question.[1] An individual

1. Arthur G. Stevens, Jr., "Informal Groups and Decision-Making in the U.S. House of Representatives," (Ph.D. dissertation, University of Michigan, 1970); Donald R. Matthews and James A. Stimson, "The Decision-Making Approach to the Study of Legislative Behavior," (paper delivered at the Sixty-fifth Annual Meeting of the American Political Science Association, 1969); John S. Saloma, III, *Congress and the New Politics* (Boston: Little, Brown and Co., 1969), pp. 214–18.

representative armed with a set of policy predispositions and informed by constituent interests often is poorly prepared to cast rational votes on choices to accept, modify, or reject committee decisions. The sheer number of such decisions confronting each Congress, together with their specificity and nonideological cast, render predisposition an inadequate guide to decision-making. Information on the substantive content of the bill, its political implications, and its relationship to the representative's relevant behavior at an earlier period of time must enter into the calculus for a rational decision to be made.

The insight gained from recent research is that certain institutional forms and practices have developed in the House that provide the congressman with "shortcuts" toward gaining the information he needs. In large part, congressmen tend to rely for information on members of those committees that have jurisdiction over the legislation under consideration. As relationships with trusted sources develop, the norm is often one of cue-taking, in which only the "correct" vote direction need be communicated. As one member described the process,

> on those bills on which I have doubts, I depend on friends whose views I can trust. Sometimes when I don't know the content of a bill or an amendment, I look to see how others vote. There is an old joke about one congressman who voted "absent" because he heard another vote "present."[2]

If congressmen choose as information sources those committee members with constituencies or attitudes similar to their own, where is the slippage that might result in a bias? Part of the answer is that the member chosen as a source may not share the predispositions of the congressman seeking advice or information. As Matthews and Stimson point out,

> cue-givers in most policy areas are a biased sample of the House membership; in almost all policy areas they tend to be more senior than the average member, they tend also to be from congressional districts particularly affected by the policies in which the cue-givers specialize. Service on at least the better integrated House committees tends to socialize the specialist into an overall committee point of view which may diverge from the views of the House as a whole. . . . The policies that result from cue-taking are thus more conservative and more sensitive to the wants and needs of the immediate parties-at-interest than would be the case with fully independent decision-making.[3]

2. Stevens, pp. 58–59.
3. Matthews and Stimson, pp. 18–19.

That is, the number and strategic location of conservative-minded members make a perfect ideological matching of cue-takers and cue-givers unlikely. Of course, the likelihood of mismatch varies across committees, depending upon the extent to which the committee membership is representative of the view of the House.

Certain procedural practices in the House further complicate this information-seeking process. The dominant committee view tends to have a virtual monopoly of the most visible communication channels —committee reports and floor debate. Committee reports are frequently filed just prior to floor consideration of the legislation, making it very difficult for members to obtain relevant information, even if they had the time to do so.[4] Similarly, floor debate, managed typically by the committee or subcommittee chairman and subject to the five-minute rule on amendments, for the most part conveys information loaded in favor of the committee majority. The unanimity of cues emerging from floor debate is particularly striking when the leaders of the partisan majority and minority are in basic agreement.

Certainly these findings regarding the information problems of individual congressmen are not surprising, given our knowledge of information control in social organizations. Hierarchy and specialization generally lead to information blockage, distortion, and misrepresentation.[5]

Two other institutional factors lend credence to the liberal perception during the late 1950s of a conservative increment of strength resulting from internal processes. One was the procedure for nonrecord votes on amendments in the Committee of the Whole prior to the Ninety-second Congress. While overall attendance was low on votes in the Committee of the Whole (less than a third of all members generally participated in nonrecord votes on amendments compared to 85 to 90 percent attendance on roll calls and perfunctory quorum calls),[6] nonsouthern Democrats were notorious for their absence. They tended to represent competitive districts; hence instead of spending their time on the floor, they often were engaged in performance of constituent services or in public-relations activities. Thus conservative forces had an advantage simply as a result of the number of people on the floor.

The other disadvantage confronting liberal Democrats in the late

4. The Legislative Reorganization Act of 1970 contained a provision that requires all committee reports to be printed and available three days (excluding Saturdays, Sundays, and holidays) prior to floor consideration. Furthermore, it also stipulates that Appropriations Committee hearing transcripts be similarly available.

5. See Saloma, *Congress and the New Politics*, pp. 210–11 and the sources cited therein.

6. Democratic Study Group, Special Report, July 7, 1970.

1950s stemmed from their bargining position with the party. The seniority system had placed a number of relatively conservative southern Democrats in positions of power. Committee chairmen were free to use the powers of their official positions to implement their personal policy views regardless of whether those views were shared by a majority of their Democratic colleagues. The elected party leadership was accustomed to dealing with the southern wing of the party. And the party leadership was a deterrent to the effectiveness of liberals, especially liberals representing marginal districts, since the leadership tended to overrepresent areas of greatest Democratic strength.[7] These factors combined to make it difficult for liberals to enact their policy views.

The Democratic Study Group

Although small groups of liberals had been meeting on an ad hoc basis with increased frequency since 1953, the formal organization of the Democratic Study Group (DSG) in September 1959 marked the first sustained effort to counter the conservative coalition.[8] The organizational structure and operating strategies developed in the first few months, aimed as they were at the problems of information, attendance, and strategic bargaining, remained remarkably constant over the subsequent decade. Concerned with increasing the likelihood of liberal policy outputs, the DSG engaged in activities at every stage of the legislative process. But its major focus continued to be providing information necessary to bring some coherence to the liberal Democratic bloc.

Organization

The Democratic Study Group is a voluntary group of House Democrats with a membership roster, elected leaders, permanent staff, and a set of regularized procedures for meeting and arriving at various decisions. Membership in the DSG has ranged between 115 and 170 over the last six Congresses. It is hard to determine membership pre-

7. Barbara Hinckley, *Stability and Change in Congress* (New York: Harper and Row, 1971), p. 80.
8. The two best sources on the formation and early development of the DSG are Kenneth Kofmehl, "The Institutionalization of a Voting Bloc," *Western Political Quarterly* 17 (June, 1964):256–72; and Mark F. Ferber, "The Democratic Study Group: A Study of Intra-Party Organization in the House" (Ph.D. dissertation, University of California, Los Angeles, 1964). A more recent discussion and analysis of the effectiveness of the DSG is an excellent unpublished paper by Anne Henderson: "The Democratic Study Group: An Appraisal" (Rutgers University, 1969).

cisely because the dues-paying membership list does not necessarily mirror the whip list.[9] Occasionally an active DSG member is remiss in paying his dues, though he continues to be carried on the whip list. Similarly, it is possible for a representative who has no ideological commitment to the implicit goals of the DSG to appear as a member merely because he pays dues so as to obtain DSG information sheets.

The DSG is headed by an elected chairman and executive committee who meet regularly to exchange information and plan strategy on important legislative matters. As in other leadership groups, the size of the executive committee (eight in 1959 and fifteen in 1970) often precludes full attendance and leads to the formation of small, informal groups who work flexibly under the supervision of the chairman. Policy decisions are the responsibility of full membership meetings. On substantive issues, either the DSG position is "obvious" (e.g., civil rights), necessitating no formal decision before action is begun, or the issue is sensitive enough to divide DSG opinion (e.g., funding of the supersonic transport aircraft). Hence, generally no formal DSG positions on legislation are taken.

In practice, virtually all of DSG's activities are generated and executed by the staff, which has assumed an independent leadership role in recent years. The DSG staff ordinarily consists of approximately twelve people, four of whom engage in legislative research. The institutionalization of the DSG has left the staff director a good deal of discretion in initiating and overseeing DSG operations.

The DSG is further organized into task forces in order to complement the work of the Democratic majority on regular House committees. Their number has varied greatly during the years the DSG has been in existence, ranging from none in the Eighty-seventh Congress to eleven in the Ninety-first Congress. Task forces were intended to provide a focus of leadership thrusts articulated in DSG's formative statement of purpose. Since it early proved difficult to get substantial attendance at regular DSG meetings on issues, the task force provided a manageable group that widened participation and harnessed a chairman who typically was already an activist in the area and a member of the relevant committee. The Civil Rights and Area Redevelopment task forces were especially successful in organizing efforts that forced legislation out of committees and prevented crippling amendments on the floor. Nonetheless, activity and effectiveness have varied greatly across task forces.

9. In subsequent analysis we utilize the whip lists to identify DSG members. Special thanks are due Richard Conlon, Staff Director of the DSG, for providing these lists as well as numerous other bits of information and insight.

While a number of task forces have been viewed as successes by their members and by DSG leaders, others have not been so viewed. Several factors have worked against success: (1) staff resources apart from the task-force chairman's personal staff are limited; (2) primarily because of lack of time, participation by task-force members other than the chairman tends to be low; (3) divisions develop within task forces when the substance is outside traditional social and economic concerns; and (4) some task forces exist in areas in which legislative interest is dormant.

Activities

Within this organizational structure, the DSG engages in a series of activities designed to maximize liberal outputs throughout the legislative process. In doing so it addresses the three major difficulties identified above—information, attendance, and strategic bargaining.

A substantial portion of DSG resources are invested in meeting the information problem. Several of the staff concentrate on obtaining as much information as possible about legislation about to be reported from committees. Their sources include friendly congressmen serving on the committees, interest groups, the Administration (especially when Democratic), and DSG task-force reports. They provide this information, primarily through fact sheets and weekly legislative reports, to DSG members. The intention is to help the members avoid a mismatch between predisposition and vote by providing essential information.

A typical fact sheet is approximately five to ten pages long. It contains the legislative history of a bill, the background of the substantive problem, an outline of the major provisions of the bill, the views of the Administration, probable amendments, and arguments for and against. The dual arguments, an innovation of the last several years, reflect the desire of congressmen for complete and objective information. While in earlier years DSG leaders did not feel obliged to explicate opposing views, they always subscribed to the principle of providing members with factual information.

The DSG also distributees a weekly legislative report (originally conceived as a supplement to the weekly Democratic whip notice), briefly stating the basic provisions of bills, the position of the Administration, interest groups and affected agencies, committee action and views, anticipated amendments, and proposed terms of floor consideration. These reports, begun in 1967, obviously reflect the problem of insufficient information prevalent in the House and, more particularly, the failure of the regular party leadership to keep its followers adequately informed.

In addition to providing members with information about legislation, DSG in recent years has furnished services which involve information of different kinds. One such service is a weekly bulletin intended to aid staff of DSG members by making available such items as sample letters to constituents on current topics and bibliographies of studies done on such topics.

The DSG also provides a variety of campaign services to members and Democratic candidates for Republican seats. In addition to making financial contributions, DSG attempts to aid nonincumbent Democrats by sending them the same research reports available to members plus reports on the legislative record of their incumbent opponents and by holding seminars to give advice on campaign techniques. At the beginning of each Congress, DSG holds meetings for freshmen Democrats at which they are given advice on such matters as staffing, obtaining a desirable committee assignment, and using Library of Congress resources.

All of the above services, most of which involve providing some kind of information, are designed to increase the personal effectiveness of nonincumbent Democratic candidates and actual DSG members. Interviews indicate that such services are appreciated and in many cases provide the incentive for joining the DSG.

The DSG also has invested much effort in trying to increase the vote turnout of its members, primarily in the Committee of the Whole. One of the first actions taken by the informal group of liberals that predated the organization of the DSG was the establishment of a rudimentary whip operation. This priority persisted in the early discussions of the Democratic Study Group and led to the establishment of a whip system. The telephone whip system in which brief messages are sent to members through calls by secretaries in each DSG member's office is the simplest operation. More elaborate ad hoc whip systems are formed for specific issues by utilizing as whips those member who are already active in the particular legislative area and by including non-DSG members and excluding unsympathetic DSG members when it is advantageous to do so.

As the system evolved, special whip arrangements were developed for highly important pieces of legislation. Their most elaborate forms were those in which certain members were assigned to be responsible for others, reporting absences or "wrong" votes on tellers to contacts just off the House floor, who in turn notified lobbyists important in their districts. The 1964 Civil Rights Bill is a fine example of how the DSG whip system, in cooperation with important interest group representatives, can get members to the floor and keep them there.

Yet with the exception of a handful of important pieces of legislation, the task of increasing liberal participation on nonrecord votes in the Committee of the Whole was a frustrating one. Attendance remained relatively low, and many important votes on amendments were lost by close margins. Whatever the effect of the whip system on nonrecord votes, it was marginal compared to the increased participation arising from the rules change that allowed for record votes in the Committee of the Whole beginning in the Ninety-second Congress. (In the Ninety-second Congress, attendance on record teller votes averaged 375 compared to the 150 mean attendance on teller votes in previous years.) The DSG's awareness of the limitations of its whip system was evidenced by its leadership role in the adoption of the recorded teller.[10]

Other DSG activities fall into four classes: agenda setting, parliamentary strategy, coordination of outside groups, and institutional change.

In the early days of the DSG, the difficulty that loomed above all others was getting legislation past the Rules Committee to the House floor. Judge Smith's chamber had proved to be the burial ground of numerous pieces of domestic legislation favored by the northern liberals. In their first tactical encounters with the agenda-setting problem, the DSG was successful.[11] DSG task forces effectively organized the discharge petition on the civil rights bill and the Calendar Wednesday procedure for the area redevelopment legislation, forcing both around the Rules Committee to the House floor. Subsequently, the DSG played a major role in enlarging the Rules Committee, primarily by keeping sufficient pressure on the Speaker.

Closely related are DSG's efforts at developing optimal parliamentary strategies for legislation reported for floor consideration. The reputation of liberals for being outmaneuvered by southerners on fine points of the rules of the House was accurate. The organization of the DSG provided a focal point for harnessing what few liberal parliamentary experts existed and developing, in advance, coherent strategies for the floor.

At the same time DSG has served in an important capacity as in-house coordinator of outside lobbying groups. The tradeoff in resources has been impressive: DSG has an effective information gathering and disseminating system but little political clout; lobbies sometimes can provide the latter but are often in need of a targeted audience and

10. John F. Bibby and Roger A. Davidson, *On Capitol Hill: Studies in the Legislative Process*, 2nd ed. (Hinsdale, Ill.: Dryden Press, 1972), ch. 8.
11. Ferber, ch. 4.

general overall strategy. The marriage has worked particularly well with civil rights legislation and efforts to secure full funding of education programs.

Finally, in an effort to improve its bargaining position within the House Democratic party, the DSG has sought institutional change. It has worked within the Democratic caucus and, where necessary, the House, to modify those rules and practices largely responsible for the unresponsiveness of party leaders to the views held by a majority of their Democratic colleagues.[12] These activities are quite important to the future role of DSG within the party, and merit independent consideration.

Our theoretical discussion and description of the operations of the Democratic Study Group suggest that the formation of the DSG has led to increased turnout, especially in the Committee of the Whole, and to increased cohesion among DSG members. A concern about these dimensions of turnout and group cohesion has guided our selection of data, methodology, and analysis efforts.

Methods

Data

Several sources of data were used in this study. DSG records containing information about the organization, membership, and activities of the group were crucial. Other data sources were interviews with congressmen and records of roll-call votes. The interviews were collected at three different points in time. The first series of congressional interviews was obtained by Warren Miller and Donald Stokes in 1958 and provided initial insight into the theoretical focus of this study.[13] The second and third sets of interviews were conducted in 1969 and 1971.[14] The roll-call analysis depends upon a longitudinal set of 800 roll calls composed of a sample of 100 nonunanimous votes from

12. Roger H. Davidson, David M. Kovenock and Michael K. O'Leary, *Congress in Crisis: Politics and Congressional Reform* (Belmont, Calif.: Wadsworth Publishing Co., 1966); and Bibby and Davidson, chs. 4 and 8.

13. The interviews were obtained by Warren E. Miller and Donald E. Stokes as part of their study of the linkages between public opinion and congressional roll-call behavior. See Miller and Stokes, "Constituency Influence in Congress," *American Political Science Review* 57 (March, 1963):45–56.

14. The 1969 interviews were conducted by Arthur G. Stevens, Jr., as part of his research for the dissertation cited above. The 1971 interviews with numerous congressional staff members, DSG members and leadership, as well as some Republicans, were gathered purposely for this paper.

each of the eight Congresses between 1955 and 1970.[15] Earlier analysis utilizing the outputs of several congressional committees across five Congresses and reported elsewhere provided incentive for this paper as well as support for our findings.[16]

Analysis Techniques

Numerous methods have been developed for the study of intragroup cohesion and intergroup differentiation. The analysis methods found to be most appropriate to the concerns of this paper are based on the work of Duncan MacRae, Jr., and of Herbert Weisberg.[17] Both have been interested in the application of such dimensional techniques as factor analysis in the investigation of legislative roll-call behavior. In this framework, an interitem correlation matrix[18] for the 100 nonunanimous roll calls from each of the Congresses between 1955 and 1970 was computed and factor analyzed.[19] The results of the factor analysis, after an orthogonal rotation, are presented in Table 4–1. The importance of particular factors can easily be gauged, since the total contributions for a perfect solution are equal to the number of items analyzed—in this case, 100. The amount added to the factor contributions by the fourth and succeeding factors was generally not greater than 2 percent.[20] Thus only the first three factors were used in subsequent analysis and in the computation of factor scores, with the

15. Non-unanimous roll calls were defined as those roll calls on which at least 10 percent of the House members voted in opposition to the majority. The sample was drawn so that the number of roll calls selected is proportional to the output of the congressional committees.

16. See Stevens, and see also Arthur H. Miller, "The Impact of Committees on the Structure of Issues and Voting Coalitions: The U.S. House of Representatives, 1955–1962" (Ph.D. dissertation, University of Michigan, 1971).

17. Duncan MacRae, Jr., *Issues and Parties in Legislative Voting* (New York: Harper and Row, 1970); and Herbert F. Weisberg, "Dimensional Analysis of Legislative Roll Calls" (Ph.D. dissertation, University of Michigan, 1968).

18. The correlation coefficient used is the tetrachoric r, a measure of association that indicates the degree to which variables share a common dimension. For an excellent discussion of tetrachoric r and its applicability to dimensional analysis, see Weisberg, ch. 4, and MacRae, ch. 3.

19. The factor analysis was done with unities as the estimate of the commonalities, and an orthogonal (varimax) rotation was used to obtain the matrix of factor loadings. The solution from the orthogonal rotation was selected as optimal, since the factors were found to be uncorrelated in the oblique solution. Furthermore, the varimax solution gave the clearest pattern of loadings, i.e., an item has one large loading with much smaller remaining loadings.

20. Variance terminology is not strictly appropriate for the factor analysis of dimensioning coefficients, since such coefficients are not based on the statistical concept of covariance. The factor contributions, however, which are equal to the sum of the squared loadings for each factor, can be used as a rough measure of the relative importance of the factors.

Table 4–1. Factor Contributions from the Varimax Solution

Congress	Factor 1 [a]	Factor 2 [b]	Factor 3 [c]	Total
84th	41.16	19.26	7.14	67.56
85th	34.84	28.15	13.91	76.90
86th	44.02	28.66	13.35	86.03
87th	41.49	19.87	22.45	83.81
88th	46.34	33.05	2.64	82.03
89th	44.29	40.21	5.43	88.93
90th	47.75	29.51	–	77.26
91st	32.52	28.45	14.89	75.86

[a] These votes deal with the scope of activities performed by the federal government. Topics include regulation of waterways and power generation stations, the federal role in construction and control of public facilities, regulation of increased industrialization, farm price supports, school milk programs, and the food stamp plan.
[b] These votes seem to represent attempts to extend individual freedom and human rights. The issues include civil rights, immigration and nationality laws, criminal procedure, voting rights, subversive activities laws, minimum wages, educational loans for students, and various poverty programs.
[c] These votes deal with foreign affairs and, during the 91st Congress, limits and priorities on presidential spending.

exception of the Ninetieth Congress, for which only the first two factors were used.

Factor scores for all of the House members were then computed from the results of Table 4–1, with each congressman being assigned a factor score for each of the most important factors.[21] These scores were used to measure the degree to which congressmen voted together on roll calls defining an issue dimension. Basically, the more similarly two congressmen voted on a series of roll calls from the same issue domain, the smaller the difference in their respective scores for that factor. Thus we can use the variance of factor scores to talk about cohesion among a number of congressmen who form a voting coalition. The more similar the legislative voting behavior of the several members of the group, the smaller the variance of the factor scores assigned to those

21. The matrix of factor loadings resulting from the factor analysis of the tetrachoric *r* matrix is used to compute the factor scores. The actual computation of the scores is based on the estimation procedure suggested by Harry H. Harmon, *Modern Factor Analysis* (Chicago: University of Chicago Press, 1967), pp. 348–50. When factor analyzing tetrachoric *r*, a factor loading of unity means that the roll call falls exactly on the dimension indicated by the factor. A loading of minus one means that the item needs to be reflected (i.e., the scoring reversed) to be positively correlated with the other items on the dimension. The size of the loadings does not indicate order of the items on the dimension, only that they share a common dimension. The overwhelming majority of loadings obtained in the analysis were .8 or larger in magnitude.

members. The variance in scores for a given factor provides a measure of cohesion on the roll calls which load strongly on that factor.

Factor scores also can be used to compare voting behavior of members across a number of issue domains. This comparison is most easily accomplished by analytically treating the members as points in an n-dimensional space, where n equals the number of factors and each factor acts as an axis in a Cartesian coordinate system. Interpoint distances between the members, or between the members and the central value for the group, can then be computed from the Euclidean distance formula by using the factor scores as axis projections.[22] The mean and variance of the distances derived from these computations can be used to measure cohesion among members on a series of roll calls that come from more than one issue dimension.

Predispositions

Our central hypothesis is that the DSG communications network has had an impact on the roll-call voting of DSG members. But since the members would be expected to vote alike even in the absence of an organization,[23] how can we ascertain the impact of the group? First, longitudinal roll-call data are used, extending from the Ninety-first Congress back through two Congresses before the DSG was formed. This allows us to look at changes in DSG membership behavior across time. In so doing, treating the members *as a group* is in itself a control for predisposition; changes across time in behavior can be observed as changes on the part of a group of similarly predisposed persons. In addition, the extension backward of the file to include the Eighty-fourth and Eighty-fifth Congress allows us to examine the behavior patterns of initial DSG members before and after the group was organized and to note any change.

22. The computational formula for the squared distance between any two points in an n-dimensional space is:

$$d_{xy2} = \sum_{t=1}^{n} (x_i - y_i)^2,$$

where n is the number of dimensions (of factors), and x and y are the two different points. When mean factor scores are used to compute the distance between groups, the mean values can be readily substituted in the equation for x and y.

23. One alternative hypothesis would attribute cohesion to constituency similarity. Unfortunately, attempting to control explicitly for constituency factors would increase the complexity of the analysis far beyond the possible scope of this report.

Second, throughout the analysis the behavior of DSG members is compared with that of members of other "groups"—Republicans, southern Democrats, and nonsouthern, non-DSG Democrats. Study of the behavior of DSG members over time relative to that of nonsouthern, non-DSG Democrats enables us to compare two sets of congressmen who can be expected to share somewhat liberal predispositions. Evidence that DSG members have behaved increasingly differently from nonsouthern, non-DSG Democrats should be strongly suggestive, therefore, of "group" impact on the voting behavior of DSG members.

The behavior of Republicans and southern Democrats—the traditional adversaries of DSG—must also be traced over time. For instance, our expectation that the setting up of continuous lines of communication among liberals would lead to an improved vote performance cannot be confirmed merely by demonstrating that liberals have become more cohesive since formation of the DSG. Nor could this expectation be denied by the discovery that liberal cohesiveness has decreased. If the trend in cohesiveness among DSG members, regardless of its direction, is more favorable than that of the southern Democrats and of the Republicans—the groups the DSG was organized to counter—some support will be lent to our expectation.[24]

Findings

If the DSG communications network has had an impact on the roll-call voting behavior of DSG members, we should find traces of the following voting patterns:

(1) There will have been some increase in DSG membership turnout on roll-call votes in those cases when there was a group effort to "get out the vote." This increase will have been fairly small, however, because congressmen almost always try to vote on important legislation when the votes are recorded.

(2) The voting behavior of DSG members will have become increasingly differentiated from that of nonsouthern, non-DSG Democrats.

(3) DSG vote cohesion will have increased over time or at least will have exhibited a more positive trend than has the cohesion of Republicans or southern Democrats or both, and this trend will not have been due to recruitment of new members or to loss of old ones.

Each of these hypotheses will be investigated in turn.

24. For a more detailed explication of the measurement problems surrounding predispositions and some approaches to a solution, see Stevens, "Informal Groups and Decision-Making in the U.S. House of Representatives," pp. 42–46.

Turnout

A central concern of DSG leaders and staff has been to find means of increasing the voting participation of its members. As discussed above, an elaborate whip system was developed to notify members of important votes on the floor. In most cases, the effort has been directed toward the Committee of the Whole, where the use of non-record votes traditionally has resulted in low attendance, particularly among liberals. Occasionally the DSG whip system has been employed on roll-call votes, and it should be possible to determine the effectiveness of such efforts. (It should be noted, however, that in roll-call situations the whip system was used more to gain information about the voting intentions of congressmen than to get them to the floor.)

A measure of the DSG's impact on voting participation should differentiate votes according to whether the DSG put its whip system into operation. While this information is not available across the set of roll calls in this study, the figures in Table 4–2, collected by Anne

Table 4–2. Turnout of Key Votes, 88th–90th Congresses, by DSG Effort (percent)

Congress and Session	DSG	Nonsouthern Non-DSG Democrats	Southern Democrats	Republicans
		Intense Effort		
88–1	97.9	91.2	92.1	94.5
88–2	97.0	93.1	94.9	96.3
89–1	97.0	95.3	94.2	94.5
89–2	87.6	85.0	76.4	86.4
90–1	94.6	92.9	92.3	93.1
90–2	95.4	92.0	90.5	94.2
Mean	94.9	91.6	90.1	93.2
		No Effort		
88–1	93.9	92.1	92.4	95.2
88–2	94.1	92.7	89.5	96.6
89–1	91.4	95.3	87.9	89.5
89–2	83.6	82.9	78.1	82.0
90–1	90.4	89.6	91.2	91.7
90–2	92.6	92.0	86.3	96.0
Mean	91.0	90.8	87.6	91.8

Note: These data are taken from Anne Henderson, "The Democratic Study Group: An Appraisal," Appendix F. The author's unique position on the Hill allowed her to discern the level of DSG involvement on a set of roll call votes in the 88th–90th Congresses. She used a quasi-experimental design to study cohesion as well as turnout, and her findings on the former are generally in accord with those reported in this paper.

Henderson, provide some illustrative data. The roll calls included are those identified by *The Congressional Quarterly* as key votes. We have chosen to compare situations in which DSG mounted an intense effort with those in which it mounted none. The observed pattern of participation is consistent with our hypothesis. On intense whip efforts, DSG members participated at a higher rate than they did on roll calls with no whip efforts and at a higher rate than did members of other groups. These differences are not very impressive upon first view, but it should be noted that when turnout is approximately 91 percent without a whip effort there is little room for improvement.

DSG and Nonsouthern Non-DSG Democrats

One could legitimately question whether DSG members are different in their roll-call behavior from other Democrats who are neither southerners nor DSG members. Mean scores on each factor for each Congress were, therefore, computed for DSG members and for non-DSG nonsouthern Democrats. These factor scores were used to calculate the mean interpoint distance between these groups in the multidimensional space.[25] The resulting distances between the DSG and non-DSG nonsouthern Democrats are displayed in Figure 4–1.

In the Eighty-fourth Congress, non-DSG nonsouthern Democrats were very close to those who were to become the future DSG members,[26] particularly when compared with southern Democrats. In the Eighty-fifth Congress the distance between the DSG and the non-DSG nonsouthern Democrats grew by a multiple of 1.9, only to recede slightly in the Eighty-sixth and practically to vanish in the Eighty-seventh. The shrinkage of the distance in the Eighty-seventh is placed in perspective by examining the comparable shrinkage of the DSG–southern Democrat distance. This was the Congress just subsequent to the 1960 election, and the extremely strong tendency for *all* Democrats to close ranks in the first flush of victory (in part because of the willingness of the president to make the necessary compromises in committee) can be noted clearly. From the next Congress on, however, the distinction between the voting behavior of DSG members and other

25. The computation of the mean interpoint distance was accomplished by using the group mean on each factor as the axis location for the group; from these axis values the squared Euclidean distance between each group was obtained. (See note 22 for the formula used to compute the distance.) As the similarity in the voting behavior of the two groups increases, the distance increases. If the members of the two groups vote exactly the same on all the bills, the distance between the groups would be zero. As the two groups grow increasingly opposed to each other, the distance value also increases.

26. Future DSG members are identified as those Democratic congressmen who signed the Liberal Manifesto. For a description of that document, see Kofmehl, pp. 258–60.

Figure 4–1. Mean Interpoint Distance of Groups from the DSG

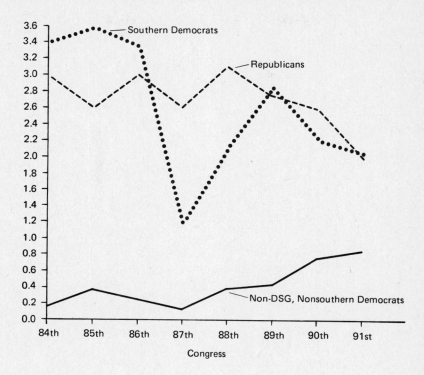

nonsouthern Democrats grew more pronounced. By the Ninety-first Congress, the distance had increased 4.9 times over what it had been in the Eighty-fourth Congress. This data array supports an argument for treating DSG members and other nonsouthern Democrats separately in roll-call analysis. It also suggests that the DSG may have had a substantial impact on its members, as the distance between them and their nonsouthern party colleagues, with whom they shared many predispositions, had widened so considerably since efforts were first made to form the DSG. Part of this distance may be due to the recruitment by the DSG of new members differing in some predispositional characteristics from the original members. A comparison of new DSG members with those already in the group will be taken up below.

Cohesion

Now we shall observe whether the data support our expectation that DSG vote cohesion has increased over time, or if it has at least exhibited a more positive trend than has that of Republicans

Figure 4–2. Distance of Congressmen from the Centroid of their Group

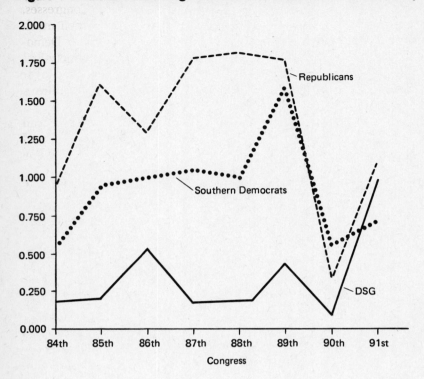

and/or southern Democrats. The centroid of the DSG membership in terms of DSG voting behavior on the major dimensions in each Congress and the distance of each member from the group center were computed.[27] The same calculations were performed separately for southern Democrats and for Republicans. Members can now be identified in terms of their distance from the centroid of their group in the multidimensional space. The mean distance of the membership from the group centroid is presented in Figure 4–2 for all three groups across the eight Congresses studied.

The amount of cohesion within the DSG on roll-call votes appears somewhat more stable than that displayed by Republicans and southern Democrats, with the exceptions of the Eighty-sixth and Ninety-first Congresses. (An explanation of the decreased cohesion shown in

27. The centroid is simply the center of the group within the hypothesized geometrical space defined by the several factors. It is found by using the mean factor scores for the group as axis projections. For example, if two factors are used, we may represent the centroid as follows:

The factor scores for each individual member (represented as a point in the two-dimensional space) are used as axis projections in computing the squared Euclid-

the Ninety-first Congress will be offered later.) These aberrations aside, there is no clear trend in DSG cohesion across Congresses. Figure 4–2 does show, however, that DSG members have been much more cohesive in each Congress than Republicans or southern Democrats (with the exception of southern Democrats in the Ninety-first Congress). Indeed, the cohesion of DSG liberals has increased over time relative to that of the southern Democrats and the Republicans (although the latter comparison is less clear than the former).

Interviews with DSG members indicate that DSG membership can be viewed in terms of a set of concentric circles. At the center is a hard core of members who almost always vote and who are very cohesive and active in DSG affairs. Most members appear to be much less involved in the DSG, with some taking very little interest in its affairs beyond receiving DSG information sheets. It is possible to identify the members of these different layers of involvement to the extent that this is reflected in roll-call voting. Table 4–3 presents the number of members falling within the different levels of cohesion as defined by arbitrarily selected cutoff points measured in multiples of one standard deviation of the distance from the DSG centroid.

Three aspect of Table 4–3 are particularly striking. First, there is a surprisingly large number of hard-core cohesive members. A bloc of 126 members who fall within 0.50 standard deviations of the DSG centroid when measured across several dimensions on 100 roll calls (as was the case in the Eighty-ninth Congress) could have considerable influence in a bargaining situation. Second, the number of hard-core voters increased dramatically and fairly steadily from the Eighty-fourth to the Ninetieth Congress, even in the Eighty-seventh Congress when the total number of members declined. This suggests that the potential impact of the DSG has soared from the early days. It demon-

---

ean distance of the individual from the group centroid. The standard deviation of the distribution of distances from the centroid is used to define the different levels of group involvement.

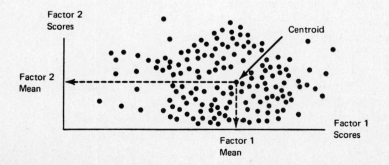

Table 4–3. Proximity on Roll-Call Votes of DSG Members to the Centroid of DSG

Standard Deviation[a]	Congress							
	84	85	86	87	88	89	90	91
1.00	57	63	110	94	106	155	124	70
0.75	50	56	97	90	102	148	115	66
0.50	41	47	74	83	93	126	99	52
0.25	24	31	45	63	71	92	65	27

Note: Each number represents the number of DSG members within the indicated distance, as measured in multiples of one standard deviation, from the DSG centroid for the indicated Congress.

[a] To facilitate comprehension, the cutoff points were translated into a statement of agreement levels by indicating the average number of roll calls on which members at the various cutoff levels differed. For example, if the core members of the DSG are defined as those lying within 0.25 standard deviations from the centroid, then we can determine, on the average, the number of roll calls on which the members lying within the various cutoff points voted differently from the core members. Results indicate that members who were beyond the core, but lying within 0.50 standard deviations, differed from the core on 5.5 percent of the roll calls; members within 0.75 standard deviations differed on 8.2 percent; and those within 1.00 standard deviations differed on 11.2 percent of the roll calls. Thus in the Nintieth Congress, for example, ninety-nine members of the DSG voted the same way on at least 94.5 percent of the roll calls.

strates that the core of the DSG has not only multiplied in numbers but also become more cohesive. Third, once again the figures for the Ninety-first Congress constitute a striking reversal of a trend.

As the above figures tend to vary with the size of the DSG, Table 4–4 presents the proportions of the membership falling within each cutoff range. It now seems apparent that the reversal of the trend toward an increasingly large cohesive core of members appearing in the Ninetieth Congress is due primarily to electoral forces in the 1966 campaign; the DSG lost approximately forty members in that election. Until the Ninety-first Congress the proportion of the membership which led solidly together increased fairly steadily. Over most of the Congresses, this phenomenon occurred at the same time that membership was increasing. Since a large proportion of new members tend to be freshman congressmen, this fact testifies to the impact of the DSG on the socialization of freshmen.

We can easily identify the members who frequently break ranks with the DSG majority. Throughout the history of the DSG these members have represented primarily rural districts—unlike the majority of their colleagues—and the few southern DSG members have tended to be among their number. This is not to say that no large-city Democrats

Table 4–4. Proximity on Roll-Call Votes of DSG Members to the Centroid of DSG

Standard Deviation[a]	Congress							
	84	85	86	87	88	89	90	91
1.00	.850	.787	.839	.817	.854	.871	.885	.500
0.75	.746	.700	.740	.782	.822	.822	.821	.471
0.50	.611	.587	.564	.721	.750	.700	.707	.371
0.25	.358	.387	.343	.547	.572	.505	.464	.192

Note: Each number represents the proportion of the DSG members within the indicated distance, as measured in multiples of one standard deviation, from the DSG centroid for the indicated Congress.
[a] See Table 4-3, note a.

were among the group that deviated most from the core DSG; indeed, several can be so labeled.

In Figure 4–2 we detected a weak tendency for the DSG to become more cohesive over time relative to southern Democrats and to the Republicans when cohesion was measured in terms of the average distance from the group centroid. In Tables 4–3 and 4–4 we noted that the proportion of DSG members relatively close to the group centroid clearly has increased over the years. One might question whether this increase in cohesion could be due to recruitment of new DSG members whose voting behavior placed them closer to the center of the group than those members present in the previous Congress. If this were so, then the favorable trend in cohesion demonstrated by the DSG could not be attributed to the impact of the DSG communication network on members already there. In order to test this alternative hypothesis, the average distance from the DSG centroid for new members and for returning members was calculated for each Congress. These figures are presented in Figure 4–3.

As Figure 4–3 demonstrates, in every Congress after the formation of the DSG the new members were farther away, on the average, from the center of the group than were returning members. This is a definite reversal of the behavior of the individuals whom we labeled new members in the Eighty-fifth Congress: those signers of the Liberal Manifesto in the Eighty-fifth Congress who were serving their first terms in Congress. It appears obvious that the maintenance or increase of DSG cohesion across any two Congresses has occurred *in spite of* the recruitment of new members. Examination of the behavior of members who dropped out of the DSG indicates that, on the whole, they were no farther away from the centroid of the group than were those who remained. Any increases in DSG cohesion could not, there-

Figure 4–3. Distance of New and Returning Members from the DSG Centroid

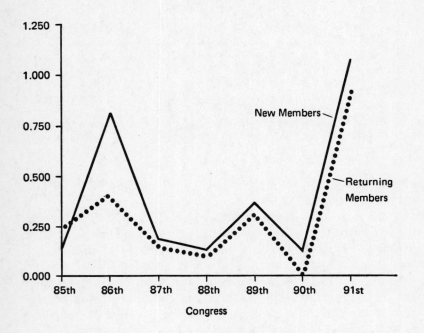

fore, have been due to loss of membership. The overwhelming majority of cases of membership loss has been due either to defeat at the polls or to retirement. The few members motivated to withdraw voluntarily were farther from the group center, in their last Congress of DSG membership, than was the average DSG member.

As established from Figure 4–3, DSG members tend to detract from the cohesion of the group during their first term of membership. Since the number of new members has varied substantially across Congresses, mainly owing to the shifts in electoral tides, another time series of cohesion figures for the DSG, Republicans, and southern Democrats should be examined. In this instance, we have labeled as members of each group only those who had also been members in the preceding Congress. (It should be noted that new southern Democrats and new Republicans, unlike new DSG members, show no tendency to be "off the reservation" in their first Congress of membership; indeed, more often than not, they are closer to the center of their respective groups during this period than is the average returning member.)

Figure 4–4. Distance of Returning Members from the Centroid of their Group

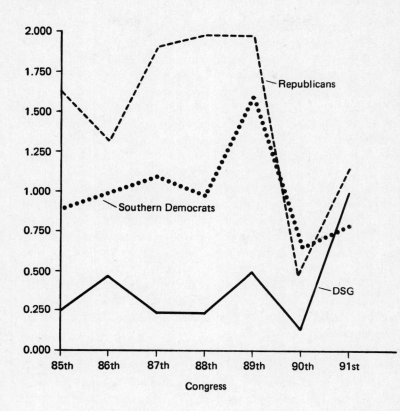

In Figure 4–4 an emerging trend toward increased cohesiveness on the part of the DSG can be observed between the Eighty-fifth and the Ninetieth Congresses even without comparison to southern Democrats and Republicans. These figures are more in accord with the message of Tables 4–3 and 4–4 than were those of Figure 4–2 in which new members were treated similarly in compilation to those longer exposed to communications within their respective groups.

We have presented evidence relating to each of the voting patterns to be expected if the setting up of continuous lines of communication among liberal Democrats did indeed lead to improved liberal performance on roll-call votes. In each case the expected pattern has been found—usually rather clearly. We cannot safely conclude that the organization of the DSG alone is responsible for this improved liberal performance without collecting and analyzing interview data on the subject, but this does seem to be an entirely reasonable inference.

Reversals of Trends in the Ninety-First Congress

At a number of points in this paper, we have noted startling reversals of trends occurring in the Ninety-first Congress. Interviews with our congressional respondents disclosed that that Congress had witnessed an unusually large amount of DSG dissension, most of it related to the Indochina war and the related questions of the balance of powers between president and Congress and the matter of national priorities. Indeed, a minority of DSG members in the Ninetieth Congress had organized as a subgroup to press for U.S. withdrawal from Indochina. Labeling themselves "the Group," these fifteen or so members had by the beginning of the Ninety-first Congress contributed substantially to the growing visibility of the priorities issue in the House—at no small cost to the internal harmony of the DSG. A glance at the factor score variance of DSG members on the three major factors underlying voting in the Ninety-first Congress discloses unequivocally that their lack of cohesiveness relative to previous years was due almost entirely to the third factor. DSG variance on the three factors was .04720, 15782, and .74717, respectively. Indeed, when factor scores are recalculated on the basis of the first two dimensions only, the entries which would appear for the DSG in Figures 4–2 to 4–4 no longer appear aberrant.

Inspection of the factor analyses for the Ninety-first and previous Congresses makes it clear that this third factor, which accounts for 15 percent of the total variance, was unique to the Ninety-first Congress. The nature of the roll calls loading heavily on Factor 3 substantially accords with our expectations: They occurred on bills dealing with placing limits on presidential spending, with military assistance to the Republic of China, and with national policy in relation to Vietnam. Factor analysis of the roll-call votes on bills emanating from the Foreign Affairs Committee documents the growth in the Ninetieth and Ninety-first Congresses of separate factors related to military spending and Southeast Asia policy. These war-related bills and resolutions from the Foreign Affairs Committee apparently evoked cleavages in the Ninety-first Congress similar to those appearing on other matters concerning national priorities.

Examination of the factor-score variance of members of other groups on this factor shows that the DSG was far less cohesive on these votes than was any other group studied (see Table 4–5). The evidence strongly indicates that, inasmuch as normal cleavages were undisturbed for everyone except DSG members, the growth of this separate "national priorities" dimension can be attributed primarily to members of the Democratic Study Group. The growing numbers of congressmen questioning U.S. involvement in Southeast Asia and its effects on domestic programs have come largely from the ranks of the DSG, although Republicans and non-DSG Democrats plus additional DSG members seem to be joining this dissent in substantial numbers in the Ninety-second Congress. The differences in direction of positions taken by members of the various groups on this factor in the Ninety-first Congress are also indicated in Table 4–5.

Of perhaps vital importance to the continuing effectiveness of the DSG is the future of the third dimension of alignment, which gained importance at the roll-call stage of the congressional process in the Ninety-first Congress. As we have seen, this dimension has very strong foreign affairs overtones, but it also includes such matters as funding for the SST. Will the relative importance of this dimension continue to increase? If so, does this mean that the DSG will have difficulty maintaining even the degree of overall cohesion which it displayed in the Ninety-first Congress? The answer to the latter question depends on at least two factors. The first has to do with the substantive composition of this dimension, specifically the proportion of related roll calls which are more or less purely in the realm of foreign affairs, as opposed to items such as funding for the SST. The second determinant has to do with shifting opinion on this set of issues within the DSG, and hence involves some mention of the role played by physical replacement of DSG membership.

Our factor analyses disclose that in the last two Congresses, Foreign Affairs Committee bills increasingly have been differentiated according to whether their content was primarily of a technical or a military nature. And, on the latter dimension, DSG members, badly split in the Ninety-first Congress, since that time seem to have become increasingly united in opposition to U.S. military involvement abroad, especially in Southeast Asia.

If the cohesion of the DSG is indeed increasing on roll calls dealing

Table 4–5. Factor-Score Variances of Groups on Factor 3, 91st Congress

Group	Variance on Factor 3	Mean Score
DSG	.74717	.26198
Non-DSG Nonsouthern Democrats	.28293	−.56830
Southern Democrats	.16027	−.66446
Republicans	.33455	.13606

with military aspects of foreign affairs, this is partially due to the physical replacement of DSG members. Unfortunately, the number of persons involved is so small that not much can be said about them systematically.

Conclusion

Our findings pertaining to cohesion indicate that for the most part DSG cohesion has increased relative to that of other groups and that the positions taken on issues by DSG members usually are easily distinguishable from those of nonmembers. More important, however, the evidence is unmistakable that the Democratic Study Group members are, on most issues, quite united and that they constitute a formidable bloc. The number and proportion of members comprising the cohesive core has increased rather steadily as the DSG has widened the scope of its research and communications network. The dissension in the DSG over matters pertaining to the war and national priorities appears not to have reversed this trend on issues within the major dimensions of conflict in the House, and there is some evidence that, even on roll-call voting, turnout of DSG members has been increased by DSG efforts.

The Democratic Study Group has been shown to be quite cohesive on most votes; even on the new third dimension, if the above argument is correct, DSG cohesion is increasing rapidly. Where, then, does the DSG go from here, in winning roll-call votes? This is a crucial question because the DSG in the Ninety-second Congress, even with increased numbers, has lost several votes by very small margins. The optimal DSG strategy would appear to be to try harder to replace incumbent congressmen not identified with the DSG with freshmen likely to join. Just a few new members might make a great difference in vote outcomes. DSG leadership is not blind to this potential and, as indicated in our introductory comments, is increasingly emphasizing electoral activities.

5

The Conservative
Coalition in Congress

John F. Manley

"Nothing renders Congress less capable of action than the need for it," according to Richard Harris (1968:56), and numerous students of American political institutions agree. Even when the necessary allowances are made for the hyperbole of catchy phrases, the fact remains that Congress is a ponderous decision-making body, more adept at delaying and diluting legislative proposals than taking clear-cut, decisive action. A policy-making institution composed of 535 diverse individuals is not, in Nelson Polsby's words, "designed to be fast on its 1,070 feet" (1971:13).

If crises are severe enough, such as those of 1933 and 1941, Congress can act swiftly, but in normal times the legislative process takes time. One reason is, of course, structural: Congress is large and complex. But a more fundamental cause is political. In Congress there are lots of conflicting opinions and objectives to be reconciled, and no underlying base of agreement that allows a congressional majority to govern with parliamentary ease. In the absence of an overwhelming consensus on either the need for or the precise form of federal action, conflicts

Reprinted by permission of the author and Sage Publications, Inc., from John F. Manley, "The Conservative Coalition in Congress," *American Behavioral Scientist* 17:2 (1973):223–47. Copyright © 1973 by Sage Publications, Inc. This essay is part of the author's larger study of the Conservative Coalition being supported by the Brookings Institution. The conclusions expressed are those of the author and do not necessarily represent those of the trustees, the officers, or other staff members of the Brookings Institution.

over policy are represented in the congressional parties, splitting them
into blocs and factions that have to be accommodated before Congress
can make any decisions at all. Majorities are built in Congress, not
elected to it; hence congressional politics is coalition politics.

To say that congressional politics is coalition politics is not to deny
that party affiliation is important in congressional decisions. It is,
rather, to emphasize the coalitional nature of the parties and to direct
attention toward cross-party coalitions as basic elements of congressional policy-making. Party identification may be the best single
predictor of congressional voting, as several roll-call studies conclude,
but it is also true that on many issues party defections determine the
results. Moreover, even if party lines hold firm the reason often lies
in the bargains and compromises forced by the influential blocs that
constitute the parties. Much of the substance of policy made by
Congress hinges on these bargains and compromises; they account for
why and how blocs become majority coalitions.

The Conservative Coalition

Since the time of Franklin Roosevelt, one of the most endur-
ing and consequential alliances in Congress has existed between conservative Republicans and conservative Democrats, mostly from the
South. At times, the Conservative Coalition has dominated national
policy-making by passing conservative legislation and/or stalemating
liberal bills (the Eightieth Congress, 1947 to 1948); and at times it
has been so outnumbered that all it could do was raise a faint voice
of protest against extending the scope of federal intervention in the
nation's life (the Eighty-ninth Congress, 1965 to 1966). In general,
however, the coalition has been a potent force behind conservative
interests. When the Conservative Coalition joins the issue, it wins far
more than it loses.

This essay examines three questions about the Conservative Coalition. First, in what sense is it accurate to say that there is a Conservative Coalition in Congress? Attention to the question is necessitated
by the frequent denials inside Congress that such a coalition exists,
and by the possibility that in dealing with roll-call votes one is dealing
with nothing more than a statistical artifact: simply because southern
Democrats and Republicans vote alike in opposition to northern Democrats does not necessarily prove that the coalition is anything more
than a group of like-minded individuals voting the same way. Second,
how often has the coalition appeared and how successful has it been
in Congress since 1933? Third, how has the coalition behaved under

the presidency of Richard Nixon, and what can one expect of the coalition in the years ahead if the Republican Party continues to make electoral headway in the South?

The Conservative Coalition: Collusion, Consensus, or Both?

One of the first and most vitriolic debates over the Conservative Coalition occurred toward the end of the 1939 session of the Senate when Senator Claude Pepper of Florida took the floor to denounce those who had undercut Roosevelt's program (*Congressional Record* 1939). It is not clear from the debate precisely who Pepper meant to include in the "pharisaical alliance," but the Florida liberal's outburst incensed many of his conservative colleagues.

According to Pepper, the 1939 session of Congress showed that a "willful alliance" was bent on withholding "aid and meager succor from the unemployed and the aged of America, in the hope that in their mad misery they might raise their hand against a president and an administration who have tried to restore them to the dignity and the opportunity of American citizens." Pepper, who had reached the Senate with FDR's backing in the 1936 landslide, accused the "designing alliance" of "having prostituted their power to serve the United States Chamber of Commerce, the Manufacturers' Association, and the beneficiaries of special privilege, who hate in their hearts the man who has tried to lighten the burden of toil on the back of labor." The implication was that a group of senators—a "scheming alliance"—had conspired against the working man; but when called upon by Walter George of Georgia to name names, Pepper refused. Senator Josiah Bailey of North Carolina took Pepper's remarks personally and asked if it would be in order to characterize them as "cowardly and mendacious?" Bailey closed the colloquy by informing the Senate that he would relay his views to Pepper privately.

Pepper's target was unclear. He did not charge any individual senators with conspiracy nor did he refer explicitly to southern Democrats and Republicans. He did refer to the opposition to the Fair Labor Standards Act as an example of conservative efforts on behalf of employers, and that Act had been fought by Republicans and southern Democrats. But Pepper evidently was content to vary the pejorative adjective before "coalition" and let individual senators speculate on exactly who fit the odious description.

Still, Pepper's remarks came at the time described by the leading historian of the emergence of the Conservative Coalition as the coalition's "zenith" (Patterson 1967: ch. 9), and it was probably quite clear to his listeners that he was referring to George, Byrd, Glass, Bailey, and their Republican associates. In any event, the debate touched off by Pepper's comments revealed the open rupture in the Democratic party between such all-out New Deal supporters as Pepper and the southern conservatives.

A second discussion of the Conservative Coalition, complete with denials as to its existence, occurred on the Senate floor a few years after the 1939 exchange. Senator Harry Byrd, one of the first and most consistent defectors from FDR's New Deal, took the floor in 1943 to denounce charges made by Pennsylvania Senator Joseph Guffey that northern Republicans and southern Democrats had conspired to deprive members of the armed forces of their voting rights (*Congressional Record* 1943). As quoted by Byrd, Guffey referred to the alliance which passed the voting bill as the "most unpatriotic and unholy alliance that has occurred in the United States Senate since the League of Nations for peace of the world was defeated in 1919." Here was an explicit charge against the southerners and Republicans made by a senator who at the time was chairman of the Democratic Senatorial Campaign Committee.

More interesting than Byrd's categorical denial of the charge is that on this occasion Josiah Bailey expressed what must have been widely held sentiments among southern Democrats as to what it was like to be a Democrat from the South. Expressing his pride in being a southern Democrat, Bailey reminded his colleagues that in the dark days before 1932—"when it [the Democratic party] was not permitted to serve around the altars which our fathers had made holy"—the party had been kept alive in the South. As Bailey noted:

> Down yonder across the Potomac, and the James, and all the way to the Gulf, and beyond the Mississippi, we kept the fires burning upon the altars of our fathers and of our country, and when there was nobody else to vote in the electoral college for the Democratic candidate, southern Democrats were sending 144 votes to the electoral college; and for that we are scornfully referred to as southern Democrats.

For this, Bailey felt, the southern Democrats deserved better than scorn from their northern brethren.

What concerned Bailey was not the unfair distribution of Democratic patronage. Southern Democrats, he observed, "know where the patronage goes in the day of victory, and they know who leads the way to the trough where the pigs feed and the swill is poured out. We know we are not in that number." Not patronage but disparagement upset the southern Democrat; especially obnoxious was the word "unholy." For himself, Bailey was proud not to be part of a holy alliance including Joseph Guffey of Pennsylvania, and he warned that if such attacks continued the Democratic party would be destroyed:

> Mr. President, I will be through in a moment. I merely want to say another word, and very solemnly. They can drive us out; yes they can drive us out. There can be an end of insults, there can be an end of toleration, there can be an end of patience. We can form a southern Democratic party and vote as we please in the electoral college, and we will hold the balance of power in this country.
>
> We can throw the election into the House of Representatives and cast the votes of 16 states.

The presidency of Franklin Roosevelt was, as Bailey's speech makes clear, a mixed blessing to some southern Democrats. FDR's political base included the South, and he normally took pains not to alienate the South, but his national strength weakened the power of the South in the Democratic party at the same time that his domestic policies increasingly violated traditional southern politcal values. Yet the South had been Democratic so long and the ties binding the southern and northern wings of the party were so strong that it is small wonder that talk of unholy bipartisan alliances with Republicans would upset —indeed infuriate—Democrats like Byrd and Bailey. Interestingly, the Republican half of the alliance has been just as quick to defend their party integrity as the threatened southerners.

"Now I have to say something which all of us know," Paul Douglas of Illinois told the Senate in 1961, "although we seldom speak about it: I refer to the bipartisan, unholy alliance which exists in this body, and also in the House of Representatives, between the conservative Republicans and the conservative Democrats of the South" (*Congressional Record* 1961:38, 80–86). Douglas got no further before he was interrupted by Minority Leader Everett Dirksen: "Mr. President, that is the sheerest nonsense I have ever heard spouted on the floor of the Senate." Dirksen's response touched off some laughter in the Senate and when it subsided Douglas opined that he "thought that would stir up the alliance. But statement is true." Dirksen called Douglas's charge an "untruth" and offered to submit to the discipline of the Senate if his choice of words violated Senate rules. "This business of talking about unholy alliances," Dirksen said, "is the sheerest 'stuff.' "

Again laughter came from the Senate but Douglas persisted.

When challenged by John Marshall Butler that the country could use a little more of the benefits of the unholy alliance Douglas tried to get Butler to admit that such an alliance was real, but Butler refused the bait. Bush of Connecticut—who denied that he was a member of the alliance and said he knew no one who was—wanted to know why it was called unholy. Capehart of Indiana wondered which part of the coalition, the conservative Republicans or the conservative Democrats, was unholy. Douglas replied that the alliance was unholy because it thwarted the will of the people as registered in presidential elections, and he argued that it was "the chemical combination" that was unholy. "Although individually they may be very fine persons, when they are put together they have a chemical effect which is not good. . . ."

Essentially similar arguments concerning the coalition were made by a Republican in the House of Representatives the year before Douglas's charge. Reacting to press accounts that House Republicans were refusing to sign a discharge petition on the 1960 civil rights bill as payment for southern votes on the 1959 Landrum-Griffin labor bill, Representative Thomas B. Curtis (Mo.) pointed to the coalitional character of the Democratic party and claimed that the real coalition in Congress consisted of northern and southern Democrats, not southerners and Republicans (*Congressional Record* 1960b:700–704). In Curtis's view, the Democratic coalition was a coalition for power: control of the House. The unholy alliance among the Democrats therefore explained why the civil rights bill was held up. As he explained it, the fact that Republicans usually join the northern Democrats on civil rights bills refuted the charge that the Conservative Coalition was responsible for the current delay. In the absence of a quid pro quo binding the Republicans and southern Democrats in the same way that northern and southern Democrats were bound by sharing organizational control of the House, the Republican–southern Democratic coalition was fictitious. Curtis's challenge to the Democratic party was to show the same kind of cohesion on civil rights that it showed when electing the Speaker and organizing the congressional committees, a challenge which everyone, including Curtis, knew was impossible.

The Missouri Republican's call for southern and northern Democrats to cooperate on civil rights was answered by Representative Frank Thompson (D., N.J.), a leading member of the liberal House Democratic Study Group (*Congressional Record* 1960a:1440–44). Thompson, citing the "impartial" *Congressional Quarterly* and its studies of Conservative Coalition voting in Congress, argued that the coalition did indeed exist. "The operation of the coalition is a matter of record," Thompson said, "and has been most successful on legislation such as education, social welfare, public housing, immigration, taxes, labor antitrust, civil rights, public works, and resource development." He thereupon inserted in the *Congressional Record* a brief history of the coalition from 1937 to 1959 which outlined the ups and downs—mostly ups—of the coalition.

The basic reason behind the conflicting opinions on the coalition is that the coalition is an informal organization which, given its existence in the no-man's-land between the two major political parties, operates in subtle, hard-to-observe ways. In denying the existence of the coalition, Dirksen rested his case on the argument that "I have yet to see the time when there has been formalized, on the floor or off the floor, a meeting of Senators on this side of the aisle and a meeting of Senators on that side of the aisle" (*Congressional Record* 1961:3883).

At the same time that he made this argument, however, Dirksen also acknowledged that something—agreement on policy—does unite conservatives in Congress:

> The term "alliance" is now used instead of the old, hackneyed phrase "coalition." But whether either one is used, it presupposes some concerted action, and that is derived from the fact that either we see eye to eye with some of our distinguished colleagues on the other side of the aisle, or they see eye to eye with us. However, we can only draw the inference that there is an unholy alliance or that there is a coalition. I have said before, and I shall repeat it, that I reject that kind of inference on every possible kind of occasion.

"Two souls with but a single thought," replied Douglas.

Simple policy agreement may be the single most important element holding the Conservative Coalition together, but the claim that the coalition is no more than an accidental meeting of minds is excessive. There is substantial evidence of joint planning on the part of coalition leaders, and coalition observers have detected a number of cases of overt bipartisan cooperation among conservatives. In the face of this evidence, the fact that no regular formal caucuses of conservatives are held, and the fact that Republicans sometimes vote with northern Democrats against the southern Democrats, are insufficient to support the claim that the coalition is purely accidental. The coalition is, in fact, many times a consciously designed force in the legislative process, and this is true for both the committee stage and the floor stage of that process.

Important testimony on the existence and nature of the Conservative Coalition was gathered in an interview (August 19, 1970) with Howard W. ("Judge") Smith who, until his 1966 primary defeat, was the leading spokesman and strategist for southern Democrats in the House. Judge Smith was first elected to the House in 1931 and, together with

Eugene Cox of Georgia, became a leading foe on the House Rules Committee of liberal legislation. When Cox died in 1952, Smith took over as the informal head of the southern Democrats. In the 1950s and 1960s Smith and the Republican leaders Joseph W. Martin and Charles A. Halleck headed the Conservative Coalition in the House. Recalling the early years of the coalition, Smith observed:

> Joe Martin was a very powerful, very partisan leader. He and Eugene Cox worked together on many issues. Our group—we called it our "group" for want of a better term—was fighting appropriations. We did not meet publicly. The meetings were not formal. Our group met in one building and the conservative Republicans in another, on different issues. *Then Eugene Cox, Bill Colmer, or I would go over to speak with the Republicans, or the Republican leaders might come to see us. It was very informal.* Conservative southerners and Republicans from the northern and western states. A coalition did exist in legislation. But we met in small groups. There were no joint meetings of conservative Republicans and southern Democrats.

When asked if it is fair to say that a Conservative Coalition existed in the House in the sense that on some issues there was explicit cooperation between southern Democrats and Republicans, Smith replied: "It's fair, sure, but never in a formal way." No formal meetings were necessary because, as Smith said of Halleck's predecessor as minority leader, Joseph W. Martin, "I'd see Joe Martin every half-hour on the floor." On one occasion, so close did House conservatives work together, that John Taber (R., N.Y.), a leading conservative on the Appropriations Committee, lent Smith one of his staff men to assist the Judge in finding ways of reducing federal expenditures.

Judge Smith's testimony on the workings of the coalition is complemented by that of his late partner in coalition politics, Joe Martin. Martin, who became House Republican leader in 1939 and held that post until defeated by Halleck in 1959, recalls how the coalition operated:

> In any case when an issue of spending or of new powers for the president came along, I would go to Representative Howard W. Smith of Virginia, for example, and say, "Howard, see if you can't get me a few Democratic votes here." Or I would seek out Representative Eugene Cox of Georgia, and ask, "Gene, why don't you and John Rankin and some of your men get me some votes on this?"

> Cox was the real leader of the southerners in the House. He was a good speaker and wielded considerable influence. He and I came to

Congress the same year, and we became friends while serving together on the Rules Committee. After I was chosen leader he and I were the principal points of contact between the northern Republicans and the southern Democratic conservatives. A bushy-haired Georgia lawyer, Cox was a typical old-fashioned southern leader, who fought tirelessly for states' rights. His opposition to the New Deal was much more in-grown than mine, and he was ready to fight to any lengths to keep further power out of the hands of Franklin Roosevelt. In these circumstances, therefore, it was unnecessary for me to offer any quid pro quo for conservative southern support. It was simply a matter of finding issues on which we saw alike [Martin 1960:84–85].

Halleck's turn to be deposed as minority leader came in 1965 when Gerald R. Ford replaced him. Among the reasons for Ford's victory was a widespread feeling among Republicans that they should more actively seek alternatives to Democratic policy proposals, and not simply rest content voting "no." The Halleck-Ford contest was less a contest between ideological opposites than a battle between policy activists and negativists; the former, grouped around Ford, were defined by a diffuse sense that something was wrong with their party rather than by a clear-cut platform for the future. Two years after his ascendancy Ford declared the Republican party's independence from conservative Democrats and announced, as he called it, a new "Southern Strategy" for House Republicans. As Ford defined it:

The strategy is to drive southern Democrats in the House into the arms of the administration—where they belong—on votes that will hurt them in their home congressional districts.

This strategy runs exactly counter to the old pattern of a southern Democrat–Republican coalition that often prevailed over administration forces in the House in years past.

But I think it is far better to lose a few legislative battles and win the next election. Besides, in following my Southern Strategy we Republicans in the House are staking out positions in which we believe— responsible, constructive positions.

There will be times when Republicans will win in the Ninetieth Congress. We won't win as many legislative fights as we could if we resorted to the *old coalition tactics* but it's the Big Prize that counts, and that's what we're after.

The Big Prize is control of at least one House of Congress and control of the White House. We want that prize not because we relish power for the sake of power but because we sincerely believe that our course,

our program, is a better way than LBJ [*Congressional Record* 1967:
45407–9; emphasis added].

Ford's apparent break with conservative Democrats no doubt upset
many members of his own party; but the other half of the coalition
was even more disturbed. Omar Burleson (D., Tex.), the chairman of
the southern Democratic caucus in the House (dubbed "Boll Weevils"
by the press), responded to Ford's threat by pointing out that far from
driving the southern Democrats anywhere, Ford was likely to have
his hands full taking care of the twenty or so Republican liberals and
those Republican conservatives who "put the good of this country
ahead of party."

The Ford-Burleson exchange exposes the complex relationships
among blocs in the House. Burleson, who denied that any surreptitious
coalition of conservatives exists in the House, but admitted that conservative Democrats frequently meet to "determine tactics for offering
certain amendments," pleaded for the maintenance of what he called
"rapport" between his group and the Republicans. By and large Ford
stuck to his independent course; but he let the southerners know that
although the Republican party would chart its own course on policy,
it welcomed whatever Democratic support it could get. Seeing an
opportunity to foment dissension within the Conservative Coalition, the
House Democratic whip, Hale Boggs, joined the debate by pointing
out that, as he learned early in his House career, Republicans are un-
trustworthy allies who seek to defeat Democrats, not work with them.
Two days after the debate a majority of southern Democrats and Republicans banded together against the majority of northern Democrats
to defeat rent supplements, a major plank in Lyndon Johnson's Great
Society program.[1]

Conservatives in the House and Senate are bonded together primarily by agreement on policy. Sharing a common outlook on policy,
they do not need an elaborate organization to hold them together; as
Joe Martin said, the major task is finding issues on which they agree
and, once this is accomplished, coalescence is to some extent automatic.
Under these conditions the task of conservative leaders is twofold:
first, shaping issues on which conservatives can act together; second,
applying whatever prods are necessary to a united joint effort. For this
task an informal organization with some internal lines of communication and with some central direction by recognized leaders is all that

1. At the same time, however, defections from the Coalition led to the defeat of
a Republican motion removing all but planning money from the Model Cities
program; see *Congressional Quarterly Weekly Report* (1967:825).

is required. And this is precisely what the Conservative Coalition is: an informal, bipartisan bloc of conservatives with leaders who jointly discuss strategy and line up votes.

Coalition Voting in Congress

Congressional conservatives have exerted great influence on public policy through their control of some of the most important committees in Congress. At various times since the New Deal, a bipartisan group of conservatives has largely controlled the decisions of such Senate committees as Armed Services, Finance, Appropriations, and Judiciary. Similarly, conservatives have dominated strategic House committees for long periods of time, including Rules, Ways and Means, Appropriations, Armed Services, Education and Labor, Un-American Activities, and the District of Columbia Committee. In short, powerful committees in both chambers have often been dominated by conservatives while other branches of the government, most notably the presidency, have been in liberal hands.

Conservative strength in committee is matched by conservative strength on the floor, and it is the floor stage of the legislative process that provides the best overview of conservative power. Two questions about coalition voting will be answered here: (1) how often does the coalition appear in Congress on roll-call votes; and (2) when the coalition appears, how does it do?[2]

One of the first political scientists to be concerned with coalition voting was V. O. Key. Key devoted two chapters of his classic *Southern Politics* to southern Democratic strength and voting in Congress. He found that on 275 contested House roll-call votes during the years 1933, 1937, 1941, and 1945, a majority of southern Democrats joined a majority of Republicans in opposition to the northern Democrats only 28 times (10.2 percent) (Key 1949:374). In the Senate, Key studied 598 contested votes in the seven odd-numbered years between 1933 and 1945. The Conservative Coalition appeared on only 54 of these votes (9 percent) (Key 1949:355). In addition, rarely did 70 percent or more of the southern Democrats defect to the Republican party. Key (1949:355) reached the conclusion that the "report of the southern Democratic–Republican congressional coalition has been not a little exaggerated."

2. The "Conservative Coalition" appears when a majority of voting southern Democrats and a majority of voting Republicans oppose a majority of voting northern Democrats. "The South" is defined as the eleven former Confederate states.

Figure 5-1. Percentage of all Contested House Roll Calls on Which the Conservative Coalition Appeared, and Won, 73rd-92nd Congresses (1933-1972)

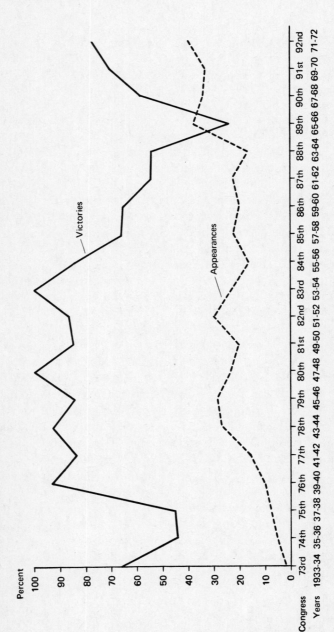

Note: ["Contested" where the] minority is greater than 10 percent of the majority.

Figure 5-2. Percentage of all Contested Senate Roll Calls on Which the Conservative Coalition Appeared, and Won, 73rd-92nd Congresses (1933–1972)

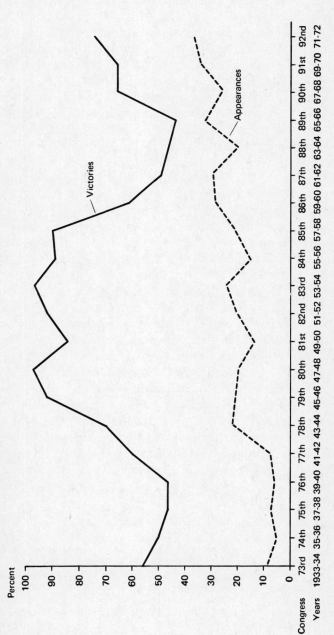

Note: ["Contested" where the] minority is greater than 10 percent of the majority.

A more complete picture of coalition voting in the House and Senate since 1933 is provided in Figures 5–1 and 5–2. In addition, the figures show the won/loss record of the coalition during these years, a question Key did not go into.[3]

As can be seen from Figure 5–1, the coalition in the House did appear on a rather small percentage of contested votes during the years Key studied. Less then 10 percent of the roll calls were coalition votes during Roosevelt's first three Congresses (1933–1939), and coalition voting did not exceed 20 percent until the Seventy-eighth Congress (1943–1944). Since 1943, however, the coalition has almost always exceeded the 20 percent mark, and in the late 1960s, over 30 percent of the votes were coalition roll calls. From 1946 to 1969 the Conservative Coalition appeared on 544 House roll calls, or about 26 percent of the 2053 votes. Clearly the House coalition has been more salient in the postwar years than it was during the period studied by Key.

Figure 5–2 shows that, like the House, the coalition did not appear on more than 20 percent of the contested votes in the Senate until the 1943-to-1944 Congress, but that since that time 20 to 30 percent of the roll calls have been coalition votes.[4] From the Truman years to Nixon, the coalition appeared on 900, or 23 percent, of the 3894 contested roll calls in the Senate. Again, the Senate coalition emerges as a more common voting pattern after World War II than when Key examined it.

Figures 5–1 and 5–2 also show the ups and downs of the coalition's success since 1933. Three distinct periods stand out. In both the House and Senate, the 1930s are marked by the relative infrequency of coalition voting and by its comparatively low batting average when it does appear. Beginning in 1939 in the House, however, and in 1941 for the Senate, the coalition wins a large majority of the votes on which it appears. Throughout the 1940s and well into the 1950s, the coalition wins 70 percent or more of the votes in both chambers. In the Senate, the coalition's batting average drops significantly beginning with 1959 (the 1958 Senate elections resulted in a seventeen-seat Democratic gain), and it never climbs back to its earlier levels. In the House,

3. Following Key, these figures exclude "hurrah" votes on which the minority is less than ten percent. This has the effect of showing a greater percentage of coalition roll calls than reported by *Congressional Quarterly* in its yearly studies. *CQ* also includes Kentucky and Oklahoma in its definition of the South. Eliminating nearly unanimous votes gives a more accurate picture of the incidence of coalition voting than that presented by *CQ*. In 1972, for example, *CQ* shows the coalition appearing on 25 percent of the roll calls in the House, and 28 percent of the Senate votes. My figures show 37 percent of the contested roll calls in the House as coalition votes, and 38 percent for the Senate.

4. Figure 5–2 is drawn largely from Margolis (1973). I am grateful to Professor Margolis for his excellent description of coalition voting in the Senate.

the coalition's batting average drops below 70 percent starting in 1957 and stays in the 50 to 60 percent range throughout the 1960s (save for the Eighty-ninth Congress when it hit an all-time low of 24 percent). The coalition's win rate in the House for 1957 to 1968 was 55 percent compared to the 1939 to 1956 average of 91 percent.

Figures 5–1 and 5–2 are based on roll-call votes and therefore provide only a rough guide to the power of conservatives in the House and Senate. For example, although the coalition pattern appears on a minority of all contested votes, it regularly includes many of the most consequential issues decided by Congress. These figures do not show how much legislation was watered down or compromised to keep the northern and southern wings of the Democratic party together. These data take into account neither those issues, such as medical care for the aged, that were bottled up for years in committee, nor those issues, such as national health insurance for all Americans, that have yet to see the light of day.

Still, it is significant that the Conservative Coalition, born in the 1930s, has persisted as a relatively common and potent voting alliance for forty years. In both chambers, the coalition was less successful in the late 1950s and in the 1960s than it was earlier, but as the record of the Ninetieth Congress (1967–1968) shows, the coalition was anything but a paper tiger as the 1970s dawned. In that Congress, just prior to Richard Nixon's Presidency, the coalition won 65 percent of Coalition votes in the Senate, and 59 percent in the House. With a Republican in the White House, liberals in Congress feared the worst. And, with exceptions, they got it.

The Conservative Coalition and The Nixon Presidency

In 1968 and 1972 Richard Nixon proved that he was a far more acceptable presidential candidate to the South than the nominee of the Democratic party.[5] The so-called "solid South" had been shaking for many years before Nixon's election, but his strength in this traditionally Democratic area far surpassed that of his mentor, Dwight D. Eisenhower. Hubert Humphrey carried only Texas in 1968. Nixon carried five southern states over both Humphrey and George Wallace: Florida, North Carolina, South Carolina, Tennessee, and Virginia. Wallace won the remaining five states: Alabama, Arkansas, Georgia,

5. In 1960, John Kennedy outpolled Nixon in eight of the eleven southern states—all save Florida, Tennessee, and Virginia.

Louisiana, and Mississippi. Moreover, in the five states that voted for Wallace, two (Arkansas and Georgia) preferred Nixon to Humphrey. In 1972, with Wallace out of the race and George McGovern as the Democratic candidate, all eleven southern states followed the national trend for Nixon.

Given Nixon's appeal in the South, a resurgence of Conservative Coalition voting in Congress was to be expected, and the coalition members did not disappoint. Figures 5–1 and 5–2 show that during Nixon's first term, in both the House and Senate, the coalition's appearance reached all-time highs, and coalition victories approached the high levels of the 1940s and 1950s.[6] In the House in the Ninety-second Congress (1971–1972), the coalition appeared on 40 percent of the contested votes, and won almost eight out of ten. Thirty-seven percent of the contested votes in the Senate during 1971 to 1972 were coalition roll calls, and 75 percent of them were won by the coalition. Thus, a fourth period emerges from Figures 5–1 and 5–2: Nixon's first term in which the coalition was a dominant force in both chambers, more dominant than it had been for several years.

On the plus side for the Senate coalition during Nixon's first term were votes on the Safeguard ABM, closing Job Corps centers, granting governors veto power over legal services programs, military aid to Greece, cutting $292.1 million from OEO, the defeat of the Hatfield-McGovern amendment limiting U.S. troops in Vietnam, modification of the filibuster rule, the Lockheed loan, confirmation of William Rehnquist to the Supreme Court, uniform school desegregation standards for the entire nation, defeat of efforts to strengthen the enforcement powers of the Equal Employment Opportunity Commission, killing the Family Assistance Plan, confirmation of Richard Kleindienst as Attorney General, and twenty of twenty-seven amendments dealing with tax reform. In the House, the coalition won votes on the Safeguard ABM, limiting federal authority in the area of school desegregation, the Cooper-Church amendment barring U.S. troops in Cambodia, authorization of the supersonic transport (SST), strong anti-busing legislation, the Lockheed loan, several amendments to end the Vietnam war, diluting a minimum wage bill, and establishing a $250 billion ceiling on federal spending complete with item veto power for the President.

6. For 1969 to 1972, I have relied on *CQ*'s base to get comparable figures on coalition appearances. Since *CQ* includes Kentucky and Oklahoma as southern states, these data are not exactly the same as one gets for the 1933-to-1968 part of the graphs, but it is felt that whatever differences there are they are of minor significance to the interpretation that follows. For *CQ*'s studies, see *Congressional Quarterly Weekly Report* (1970, 1972a, 1972b).

The list of coalition victories is impressive, but the coalition does not win all the time. The coalition lost votes in the Senate on the nomination of Clement Haynsworth and Harrold Carswell to the Supreme Court, the Cooper-Church amendment limiting the use of troops in Cambodia, the SST, expansion of the food-stamp program, providing twenty-six additional weeks of unemployment compensation payments to unemployed workers, various amendments to set a time-table for withdrawal of U.S. troops from Vietnam, and a liberal fili-buster against strong anti-busing legislation passed by the House. In the House, the coalition lost votes dealing with Adam Clayton Powell, voting rights, continuation of the SST, a plan for a comprehensive child-development program, prohibition of food stamps to families of striking workers, and a proposal allowing the president to restrict the travel of U.S. citizens to countries with which the United States is in armed conflict. Coalition successes overshadow defeats, but it should be noted that conservative defections and high cohesion among liberals can, and sometimes do, determine the outcome on major issues, even with a Republican in the White House.[7]

Speculations

Enough variations exist in congressional coalition politics to warn against speculating about future developments, but some factors that may shape the future are fairly clear and deserve special men-tion. First, the power of the southern Democrats in the House and Senate Democratic caucuses has been declining steadily for several years. Second, House Speaker Carl Albert has increasingly sided with liberals against the conservative Democrats. Third, there is renewed talk, particularly in the House, of a southern Democratic bolt to the Republican party—realignment of the parties from the top. Should these forces continue in their current direction, radical changes will follow in Congress. An incautious observer might say that we are currently living through a crucial transitional period in American politics, and such a prediction may well prove accurate.

In 1960, seven Republicans were elected to the House of Representa-tives from the South. Twelve years later there were 34, and the total number of southern Democrats had dropped from 99 to 74. As they decline in numbers, the conservative southern Democrats decline in

7. Of course, President Nixon's position was not always the same as the Con-servative Coalition's. In the Ninety-second Congress (1971–1972), the President stated a position on 46 House coalition roll calls, agreeing with the coalition on 40 of them. He agreed with the Senate coalition 40 out of 43 times that he took a position. See *Congressional Quarterly Weekly Report* (1972a, 1972b).

influence vis-à-vis the northern wing of the party. In addition, the southerners have been losing key leaders and leadership positions (Judge Smith, William Colmer, Carl Vinson, and others are gone from the House). Northern liberals gained ascendancy in the Senate following the 1958 and subsequent elections, and such long-time Senate leaders as Richard Russell no longer skillfully direct the southern cause. As the Republican party gained seats in the South, the ties binding the northern and southern wings of the Democratic party together have been placed under enormous stress. And, further aggravating the southern Democratic decline, House liberals have become increasingly well-organized (though still imperfectly organized) through the Democratic Study Group. There are still enough inconsistencies among northern Democrats, and enough conservative southern Democrats, to prevent absolute liberal control of the Democratic caucus, but the trend is in this direction.

A related development in the House is an important change in the role of the Democratic leadership. In the old days under Sam Rayburn, the leadership served effectively as the balance wheel of the Democratic party. Rayburn, with the support of southern and northern Democrats, played a delicate balancing role in the House. When the DSG was launched in the late 1950s, Rayburn's tacit blessing was essential to the liberals; he held the pivotal position in the House. John McCormack tried to follow the Rayburn script in the 1960s but strong liberal pressures made his Speakership increasingly difficult. Carl Albert, caught in the same dilemma that faced McCormack, has with increasing frequency responded positively to the demands of the liberal wing of the party. Democratic liberals have not yet toppled senior conservative leaders, but they have forced votes to decide committee chairmanships, they helped pave the way for numerous important reforms in the House, and they have used the caucus for such unusual actions as directing the Democratic members of the Foreign Affairs Committee to report anti-war legislation.

The House Democratic party is not what it used to be; neither is the party leadership. Richard Bolling made headlines in 1967 when he called for McCormack's removal as Speaker. Today Bolling, who lost a 1962 bid for the majority leadership to Albert, is one of the Speaker's closest advisors. Changes such as these are reflective of the basic undercurrents changing, and challenging, the House Democratic party.

If conservative southern Democrats can no longer function effectively within the party, and if they see the party leaders as captives of the DSG, they may seriously consider a formal alliance with the Republicans that would allow the coalition to organize the House. Under

Rayburn, such an idea would have appeared far-fetched; today, the informal leader of the southern Democrats, Representative Joe Waggonner of Louisiana, talks openly about doing it.

Some southern Democrats, like John Connally, have switched parties but Waggonner (quoted in Miller 1973) has suggested another course: "Don't be too surprised if eventually some efforts are made to take control of the majority in the House through a coalition that wouldn't require change in party registration." Southern conservatives, in other words, could continue to run as Democrats but vote with the Republicans to elect a Republican Speaker and, presumably, organize the committees with Republican majorities. "You wouldn't have left your old Democratic friends back home," Waggonner points out, "you'd have brought them some more influence, instead."

Waggonner's talk may be nothing more than a ploy to scare his liberal colleagues into treating the conservatives with a bit more respect, but if it is more than this it could lead to changes in the House rivaling those of 1910 to 1911 when Joe Cannon lost much of his power. What is interesting about Waggonner's threat is how plausible it seems when placed in the context of growing party competition in the South.

At the moment, Waggonner and other conservative House Democrats are attempting to improve their position in the Democratic caucus. Previous threats to the Democratic party from disaffected elements have not amounted to much. But as the data show, since 1965 southern Democrats and Republicans have been voting together with greater regularity than ever before. When House Republican leaders need votes, they contact Waggonner, and vice-versa. Are the internal and external pressures toward party realignment within the House rising? If so, will they lead to a formal cross-party alliance that will allow the Republican party to gain what it has failed to gain electorally, control of the House?

No one, of course, can tell. But the factors pointing in this direction are clear, and may be irreversible. It is not only possible for southern Democrats to become Republicans, many have done it and more will in the future. When William Colmer of Mississippi, chairman of the Rules Committee, retired in 1972, his Administrative Assistant, Trent Lott, ran for the seat and won it—as a Republican. Realignments of this sort will no doubt continue in the South, and they bode ill for the traditional coalition that is the Democratic party.

Inside the House, the southern Democratic response to their declining influence will be partially decided by the response of the Republican party. When Gerald Ford made his 1967 speech declaring independence from the southern Democrats, he did so for electoral reasons: he wanted Republican control of the House and he felt that the party could no longer afford to write off the South (personal interview, September 8, 1972). Ford, like his predecessor, Charles Halleck, has not been choosy about where he searches for votes among the Democrats, and his 1967 speech did not lead to any major changes in the relationship between Republicans and southern Democrats. Given the difficulty of defeating entrenched southern Democrats, Ford decided to work with them on a daily basis and await the openings southern retirements and deaths would bring. In other words, the working relationships between Ford and the southern Democrats have been good enough so that Waggonner's threat might work. What effects the Watergate scandal may have on these questions remain to be seen, but the situation in the House and in the South makes the possibility of a realignment a real one.[8]

The current situation in the House is a paradox, and how this paradox is resolved will profoundly affect future House—and American—politics. As congressional liberals gain power in the Democratic caucus, they run the risk of losing Democratic control of the House. As the southern Democrats have lost power in the Democratic caucus, they have also voted more and more with the Republicans and won more and more of the votes. As a final rebuke to the party that once dominated their region, and which they themselves once dominated, the conservative southern Democrats could in a tight situation tip the balance of power to the Republicans, and thereby help bring to fruition some of the hopes of those who desire party realignment in the United States. Liberals inside and outside Congress might be less than happy with the consequences of this action, but at least the parties would be a little less confounding. As for the liberals, they might look back on the old days with a certain degree of nostalgia, unless, of course, the American people take a large unexpected turn to the left. At this writing, a realignment and consolidation of conservative power, though a risky prediction, seems more likely than a massive liberal revival.

8. Such a move would no doubt hasten shifts in the opposite direction, such as those of Donald Riegle and Ogden Reid from the Republican party to the Democratic. If all or nearly all of the conservative southern Democrats bolted the party, however, it is doubtful that liberal Republican shifts could fully compensate for the loss to the Democratic party. At present, there are simply not enough Riegles and Reids to make up the difference. Similar forces are at work in the Senate, though less clearly. When, in 1972, it appeared that the Republicans might come close to a Senate majority, there was talk of some conservative Democratic Senators (e.g., James Eastland) switching parties, but nothing came of it.

References

Congressional Quarterly Weekly Report (1972a) November 18.
———— (1972b) January 15.
———— (1971) January 29.
———— (1970) January 16.
———— (1967) May 19.
Congressional Record (1967) May 15.
———— (1961) March 14.
———— (1960a) January 27.
———— (1960b) January 18.
———— (1943) December 7.
———— (1939) August 5.
Harris, R. 1968. "If you love your guns." *New Yorker* (April 20).
Key, V. O. 1949. *Southern Politics*. New York: Random House-Vintage.
Margolis, J. 1937. "The conservative coalition in the U.S. Senate." Ph.D. dissertation, University of Wisconsin.
Martin, J. 1960. *My First Fifty Years in Politics*. New York: McGraw-Hill.
Miller, N. C. 1973. "Rep. Joe Waggonner is a Democrat, but Nixon finds him a loyal ally." *Wall Street Journal.* (April 13).
Patterson, J. T. 1967. *Congressional Conservatism and the New Deal*. Lexington, Ky.: Univ. of Kentucky Press.
Polsby, N. W. 1971. *Congress and the Presidency*. Englewood Cliffs, N.J.: Prentice-Hall.

6

State Party Delegations in the U.S. House of Representatives: A Comparative Study of Group Cohesion

Barbara Deckard

Congressional scholars, in recent years, have shown an increasing interest in state party delegations in the House of Representatives. David Truman's[1] findings concerning voting cohesion among the members of state party delegations have been confirmed in recent studies by Donald Matthews and James Stimson[2] and by Aage Clausen.[3] While differing in approach and method, these studies show that many state party delegations display considerable voting cohesion,

Reprinted by permission of the author and publisher from Barbara Deckard, "State Party Delegations in the U.S. House of Representatives: A Comparative Study of Group Cohesion," *Journal of Politics* 34:1 (1972):199–222. This article is based upon the author's Ph.D. dissertation, "State Party Delegations in the House of Representatives," (University of Rochester, 1970). Special thanks are due to Richard F. Fenno for his help and encouragement at every stage in the research project.

1. David B. Truman, "The State Delegation and the Structure of Voting in the United States House of Representatives," *The American Political Science Review* 50 (December, 1956):1023–45.
2. Donald R. Matthews and James A. Stimson, "Decision-Making by U.S. Representatives: A Preliminary Model," in *Political Decision-Making*, ed. Sidney Ulmer (New York: Van Nostrand, 1970), pp. 14–43.
3. Aage R. Clausen, "Home State Influences on Congressional Behavior" (paper delivered at the sixty-sixth annual meeting of the American Political Science Association, Los Angeles, Calif., September 2–6, 1970).

and the authors all infer that this cohesion is, in part, the result of interaction and cue-giving within the delegation. Using data obtained from interviews and observation, Alan Fiellin[4] and John Kessel[5] showed that the delegations they studied, the New York Democratic delegation and the Washington delegation respectively, are, in fact, face-to-face groups in which the members serve as sources of information and as allies for one another. Work by Charles Clapp[6] and by Randall Ripley[7] also indicates that some state party delegations are sociological groups that influence the behavior of their members.

These studies suggest that some state party delegations, through the effect they have on their members' behavior, do influence the political process in the House. The studies also indicate that delegations vary considerably in voting cohesion and in the extent to which they function as face-to-face groups. The purpose of this paper is to explore this latter variation and attempt an explanation. An explanation of this variation in group cohesiveness should clarify the role of delegations in the House and increase our understanding of political behavior in Congress. The existence of the delegation as a categorical group is purely a function of electoral outcomes; its existence as a sociological group is, however, dependent upon the decisions of its members.

Hypotheses

The basic framework of analysis is derived from small-group theory. The limitations of the data prohibit a use of the more sophisticated ideas and theoretical relations of that literature. A few basic principles will be used to suggest hypotheses, but no attempt will be made to use or test all of the possible small-group findings that might in fact be relevant to our task. This is an exploratory study, and the author's interest centers on the politically significant behavioral indicators and consequences of cohesiveness, not on cohesiveness as a theoretical notion.

4. Alan Fiellin, "The Functions of Informal Groups: A State Delegation," in *New Perspectives on the House of Representatives,* [First Edition], ed. Robert L. Peabody and Nelson W. Polsby (Chicago: Rand McNally and Co., 1963), pp. 59–78.

5. John H. Kessel, "The Washington Congressional Delegation," *Midwest Journal of Political Science* 8 (February, 1964):1–21.

6. Charles L. Clapp, *The Congressman: His Work as He Sees It* (Garden City, N.Y.: Doubleday and Co., Inc., 1964), pp. 41–50.

7. Randall B. Ripley, *Party Leaders in the House of Representatives* (Washington, D.C.: The Brookings Institution, 1967), pp. 169–75.

Cohesiveness is the central concern of small-group theory. "Theoretically, cohesiveness is the essential small-group characteristic. This 'stick togetherness' or member attraction at once characterizes a small group and differentiates it from other social units."[8] While the literature it too voluminous to review,[9] there is general agreement that cohesiveness is a function of the attractiveness of the group to its members. The characteristics of the group and the characteristics of the member together determine attractiveness. The attractiveness of many informal groups derives from the psychological and social rewards they provide their members. But, because of the time pressures under which the congressman works, it seems reasonable to assume that a group must also provide him with political benefits if it is to be worth the time it costs him.

Previous studies provide considerable information on the problems the congressman faces.[10] The freshman congressman must learn a complex new job before he can become an effective participant in the political process in the House. Getting a good committee assignment—one that will help him win reelection or prestige in the House and preferably both—is an extremely important step in the congressman's House career. Whether he is a freshman or a several-term member who wants to change committees, he must have someone to speak for him in his party's committee on committees. All congressmen, the most senior as well as the freshmen, are faced with a perpetual need for information at as cheap a cost in time as possible. Even a senior man has a direct share in the making of only a small fraction of all House decisions. Allies can give a member a voice in committees other than his own. In bargaining with committee or party leaders or with the executive branch, allies are helpful to the senior man and essential to the junior member. The only task that delegations have been assigned is that of channeling their members' committee preferences to the party committee on committees. Fiellin's and Kessel's studies show that some delegations also help their members with the problems of socialization, information, and allies.

Delegations can perform a number of useful functions for their members. But, since attractiveness depends upon the characteristics of the member as well as on those of the group, the value placed upon the

8. Robert T. Golembiewski, *The Small Group* (Chicago and London: The University of Chicago Press, 1962), p. 149. Also see Darwin Cartwright and Alvin Zander, eds., *Group Dynamics: Research and Theory* (Evanston, Ill. and Elmsford, N.Y.: Row, Peterson, and Co., 1960), p. 72.

9. See Golembiewski, *Small Group,* and Cartwright and Zander, *Group Dynamics.* Also T. M. Newcomb, R. H. Turner, and P. E. Converse, *Social Psychology: The Study of Human Interaction* (New York: Holt, Rinehart, and Winston, 1965).

10. See among others Clapp, *The Congressman.*

aid the delegation can provide may vary among congressmen. While all congressmen do need allies and a cheap source of information and thus will find very useful a delegation that provides these aids, this usefulness must be weighed against the time cost of participation. The congressman is most likely to perceive the benefits of participation as greater than the costs if the functions the delegation can perform are directly related to his primary political goals. To the man who aspires to a position of influence in the House, the functions a state party delegation can perform are central. Even after he has learned the ways of the House and has obtained a good committee assignment, he still needs a cheap source of information and allies. Both are essential for the attainment and effective use of a position of influence. If, however, the congressman's goal is higher office, the delegation can do little to help him directly. He must satisfy the demands of the desired office's constituents. These demands come from outside the House and much of the behavior required to satisfy them must take place in the constituency of the desired office. Because the congressman must apportion his limited time so as to maximize the probability of attaining his primary goal, he may well consider the time cost of group membership prohibitive. Furthermore, the delegation may contain a number of potential rivals.

Since the value of a cohesive delegation is a function of the congressman's goals, the first hypothesis concerns the distribution of goals within the delegation: *The greater the proportion of delegation members interested in making the House their career, the more likely it is that the delegation will act as a group.* The second hypothesis concerns the stability of the delegation: *The more stable the delegation—that is, the lower the rate of membership turnover—the more likely it is to act as a group.* The importance of stability has been overwhelmingly demonstrated in small-group and organizational studies,[11] so little need be said in explanation or justification. High turnover increases the cost of delegation membership for senior members by increasing the time that must be spent in the socialization of new members. Further, it directly reduces the benefits since new members, lacking expertise, influence, and friends, can initially contribute little to the group.

Because reelection is a prerequisite to influence in the House, the effect of constituency similarities or differences upon delegation cohesion must be considered. Clearly a congressman will not participate in a group that requires him to act in a manner that would reduce his

11. See Lewis A. Froman, Jr., "Organization Theory and the Explanation of Important Characteristics of Congress," *American Political Science Review* 62 (June, 1968):518–26.

probability of reelection. Thus one would expect differences in the constituency demands made upon the members to affect the activities a delegation undertakes. If the members of a delegation perceive their constituents as making clear and different voting demands upon them, they will not vote as a bloc and thus not bargain with votes. If, on some matter, the members of a delegation perceive their districts' interests as conflicting, they will not work together. Mere diversity of district interests seems less likely than a traditional sectional rivalry in the state to result in perceptions of mutually exclusive district interests. Thus joint delegation action is limited to those areas in which the members perceive their constituents' demands as not in conflict. Nevertheless, such differences need not prevent the sharing of information, nor will such differences be relevant to many matters on which members could act as allies for one another. The picture of the congressman as pragmatist, which most studies convey, makes it seem unlikely that congressmen will let conflicts in one area prevent mutually advantageous cooperation in another. The final hypothesis states that *neither ideological nor district homogeneity is a necessary condition for delegation cohesion.*

Clearly many of the data needed to test these hypotheses could only be obtained through interviews with members of state party delegations in the House. It was therefore necessary to select certain delegations for study. The decision to concentrate on the larger delegations[12] was based on the expectation that the larger number of members interviewed from each would provide a check on the accuracy of the data. Both [of the] party delegations from New York, California, Pennsylvania, and Illinois [were studied, as were] the Texas Democratic, Wisconsin Republican, North Carolina Democratic and Massachusetts Democratic delegations.[13]

Cohesion

Given the size of the sample necessary and the consequent impossibility of combining participant-observer and interview tech-

12. In the Ninetieth Congress twenty state party delegations had seven or more members. Of the 435 U.S. Representatives, 58 percent were members of these twenty delegations.

13. The author interviewed 111 congressmen and a number of staff members during the Ninetieth and the first two months of the Ninety-first Congress. The number of congressmen interviewed from each delegation were: N.Y. Dem., 13 of 25; N.Y. Rep., 10 of 15; Calif. Dem., 10 of 21; Calif. Rep., 8 of 17; Pa. Dem., 7 of 14; Pa. Rep., 7 of 13; Ill. Dem., 8 of 12; Ill. Rep., 7 of 12; Tex. Dem., 19 of 21; Mass. Dem., 4 of 7; N.C. Dem., 4 of 8; Wisc. Rep., 6 of 7.

niques, a simple operational definition of cohesion was necessary. The rate of interaction among the members is the major indicator used, but since only politically significant groups are of interest the operational definition of cohesion cannot be based solely on the rate of communication among the members of a delegation; the definition must have political content. Group behavior patterns can be considered as being of two types—interaction, and joint action directed at actors outside the group. Interaction is a necessary but not sufficient condition for joint action. Rate of interaction and the internal consequences of interaction will be used as indicators of cohesion. In terms of the functions discussed above, the internal consequences used as indicators are the extent to which the members of a delegation share information and the extent to which they help socialize their new colleagues.

Rate of Interaction

Within four state party delegations, the rate of interaction is very high. The California Democratic delegation meets weekly for breakfast. Attendance is high. The staff member in charge of delegation matters said that normal attendance is about fifteen, that this tends to drop toward the end of the session, but that the scheduled discussion of an important subject usually brings out the full membership. Her figures agree with the estimates given by the congressmen. Only two said they often do not go, one attributing his low attendance— "about half the time"—to the early hour of the meetings. He added, "I make damn sure to be there when patronage is discussed." Intradelegation contact is not restricted to these weekly meetings. The members sit together on the floor, they often have lunch together.

The level of face-to-face contact among the Texas Democrats is also high. One member expressed it thus:

> It's said around here that the Texans don't associate much. They just have coffee together in the morning, eat lunch together, sit together on the floor and go to the same cocktail parties—but aside from that they don't associate much.

The Texas delegation has met for lunch every Wednesday in the Speaker's dining room for the past twenty-five years. Luncheons to which the congressmen bring constituents and other guests alternate with meetings confined to members. The occasional Texas Republican used to be included, but now the luncheons are restricted to Democrats. The Democratic senator attends, as did Lyndon Johnson when vice-president and, for a time, as president. According to the congressmen interviewed, attendance is high; only one man said he did not often attend, but even he had attended or had heard about the two meetings prior to the interview.

Intradelegation contact is not restricted to the Wednesday luncheons. In the private members' dining room there is a round table in one corner that is informally reserved for the Texans. Here a shifting group of Texans lunch together. Although not everyone comes every day and, in fact, the table can accommodate only ten or twelve at a time, almost everyone seems to attend fairly frequently. One busy senior member said that, because he was holding hearings, he had been able to join the group only once that week, aside from having attended the Wednesday luncheon.

Although the Massachusetts Democratic delegation does not hold regularly scheduled meetings, the rate of interaction among members is very high. The members sit together on the floor, many have breakfast together every morning. The members are personal friends, they see each other socially. The whole state delegation meets approximately once a month.

Within the Illinois Democratic delegation the rate of interaction is highest among eight of the nine Chicago members. While formal delegation meetings are infrequent, these men sit together on the floor and often eat breakfast and lunch together. As one man said, "We see each other every day." Although the three downstate members do associate frequently with the Chicago men, the really high rate of interaction is among the Chicago members who numerically dominate the delegation, and it is for that reason that the delegation is included in the high-interaction category.

These four delegations are further distinguished from the others studied by the way in which the congressmen spoke about their delegations. The members of these delegations more often referred to the delegation as "we." Unlike the members of other delegations, they often described their delegation as "tight-knit" or "cohesive." Many expressed pride in the close, friendly relations that exist within their delegations. Two Californians commented as follows:

> The meetings are nice for the camaraderie, the friendship. We're the most cohesive delegation in the House.

> The California delegation is the best organized political unit I've ever seen. The delegation is the most cooperative in the House.

Many Texas Democrats described their delegation as "tight-knit":

> We have close-knit, personal relationships, more than other delegations. In some, one member will hardly talk to another. [He then mentioned the round table.] No other delegation does that.

We're a close delegation socially—we know each otner's views and children and visit with each other.

The Massachusetts Democrats described their state delegation as well as their party delegation as cohesive:

The Massachusetts delegation is very close, we're friendly. In some they don't even speak to each other.

No one would think of having a cocktail party without inviting all the other Massachusetts members, and not as Democrats or Republicans, but as friends. We're by far the closest delegation in the House. Anyone will tell you that. No other delegation is so friendly.

Two Illinois Democrats commented as follows:

We're close. I don't think there is any other delegation in which you will find the mutual respect we have for each other. It's a fine delegation.

We're close. We work and go as a unit.

Within six delegations the rate of interaction is fairly high, although appreciably lower than that in the four delegations discussed above. The Illinois, Pennsylvania, and Wisconsin Republican delegations meet at irregular intervals but at least once a month. Within each, there is considerable informal contact; the members frequently sit together on the floor and sometimes eat lunch together. The California Republicans, although they meet formally only four or five times a year, keep in close touch with one another by telephone and sit together on the floor. The North Carolina Democratic delegation meets weekly but other interaction among the members is less frequent than that within the first four delegations discussed. The Pennsylvania Democrats seldom hold formal meetings but often have informal caucuses on the floor. The rate of interaction among the five Philadelphia men is very high. They meet almost daily and see each other in their home city as well as in Washington. The rate of interaction among these men is as high as that among the members of the first four delegations discussed. They comprise a minority of the delegation, however, and the rate of interaction of the whole state party delegation was used for classification.

The rate of interaction within two delegations is low. The New York Democratic and the New York Republican delegations meet two or three times a year. Both delegations are split. In the New York Democratic delegation, a number of junior members see themselves as "liberal activists" and their seniors as "old-line," "old-guard," "machine" Democrats:

> I don't see anything of people like Rooney and Delany. The younger men just have nothing in common with them.

This feeling is reciprocated by some senior men. Asked if he worked with the junior members, one said, "Some are too leftist. I don't even talk to them." The New York Republican delegation is also "fragmented." There are two loose groupings in which the members differ in party loyalty and in type of district represented. In both delegations, informal contact among members occurs primarily within these subgroupings. None of these subgroupings, however, can be properly called a group. The members do not meet or even sit together regularly on the floor.

Thus, on the basis of rate of interaction, the twelve delegations can be tentatively classified as follows: the California, Texas, Massachusetts, and Illinois Democratic delegations are highly cohesive; the Pennsylvania and North Carolina Democratic delegations and the Pennsylvania, Illinois, Wisconsin, and California Republican delegations are cohesive; the New York Democratic delegation and the New York Republican delegation are not cohesive.

Information Sharing

The first question asked of the more senior members of each delegation (usually those serving their third or subsequent terms) concerned their sources of information. The question contained no mention of delegations and was asked first to avoid suggesting the delegation as an answer. The great majority of the members of the four highly cohesive delegations replied that their delegation colleagues were a major source of information. The Texas and the California Democrats usually explained about the weekly delegation meetings and said that the sharing of information which takes place is the single most useful aspect of the meetings:

> You get the technicalities explained. It gives us a preview. We know what to look at when we get the report. We don't have to read it all. It saves time.

For the Massachusetts Democrats, the daily breakfasts serve the same function. Senior congressmen and other governmental officials stop by to talk with the Speaker, thus making a wide range of information available:

> You find out what is going on in other committees, the plans of the leadership, about general problems.

The time spent waiting on the floor is also used for information exchange as a Texan explained:

> Texas has good [committee] spread. I'll be in hearings this morning. Poage will be in Agriculture hearings; there are Judiciary hearings. If you go to the House at noon you'll see a lot of people milling around on the floor. But really I go up to Poage and see what's happened in the Ag. hearings, ask Jack Brooks about reapportionment.

The members of these delegations emphasized that, because of the workload, a congressman must rely upon his colleagues: "There's such a large number of bills that you can't keep up any other way." Two Illinois Democrats explained:

> We have good committee spread. The man on the committee takes the lead, keeps the rest of us informed about what's going on. We get pretty good intelligence that way.

> We don't always go along but I'd say we vote together ninety percent of the time. You'll say "That's not right. Where's your independence?" But they've done the work, studied the bill. They know what's good for the city.

In each of these delegations, one of the major purposes of interaction is the sharing of information. A result of the high rate of interaction is that these delegations serve as the primary source of information for their members. No member of any of these delegations, unlike their counterparts in less cohesive delegations, mentioned staff work or other groups as a major source of information.

A smaller number of the members of the six cohesive delegations mentioned their delegation in reply to the first question and some of these men do belong to other informal groups in the House. When asked if they rely upon their delegation colleagues for information most said "yes certainly" and many added that a congressman really has to do so.

> We're so busy we have to find shortcuts. If you talk to someone on the delegation, you can find out the inside things—which parts were controversial and who was on which side. The workload is impossible.

These delegations do hold meetings to discuss legislation of major importance:

> We meet when something important comes up, like the surcharge. I was asked to give a presentation of about ten minutes on it. Another member who was going to vote against it was also asked to speak.

Like the members of the highly cohesive delegations, these men reported that much swapping of information takes place on the floor and during other informal intradelegation encounters:

> I see the California Republicans on the floor. I sometimes check with them about what's going on on the floor. It only takes a few moments, but it's important.

Thus, in each of these delegations, the members are an important source of information for one another. Because the rate of interaction is lower, however, the extent to which these delegations serve as sources of information for their members is somewhat less than was the case in the first four delegations discussed.

Neither the New York Democratic nor the New York Republican delegation is a major source of information for its members. Asked how they keep up with what is going on in other committees, none of the members mentioned the delegation. Staff work, informal groups such as the Acorns and the Democratic Study Group, and informal relations with other members were most frequently mentioned. After some probing, the majority said that they occasionally do use some of their delegation colleagues as sources of information.

> I will ask Conable and McEwen how they're going to vote—they're both in the Eighty-ninth Club. I'll ask Goodell about the party position. We see each other on the floor of the House, but we don't sit together.

> You talk to people you know and trust. Reuss and Udall are people I often talk to. It's not necessarily other New Yorkers.

The sharing of information that does take place occurs within loose subgroupings in both delegations. These is little contact between subgroups:

> The old timers and the young liberals have nothing in common. It's like two different states. I wouldn't call Rooney for anything, anymore than I'd call a conservative southerner.

Why, I'm not sure I know what committees they're [the other New York Republicans] on . . . _____ and I represent adjacent districts but I don't ask him about legislation.

The junior men especially find the information problem onerous:

I don't handle it very well. I read. Occasionally I call people.

I just hired a girl to keep up on the other committees. If a constituent writes asking about a bill that I know nothing about, I'll call the staff people on the committees. I just don't have time to read the record.

Socialization

"The House must be a pretty confusing place to a new man. How did you learn your way around when you first came?" was the first question asked of the more junior members of each delegation. The members of the four highly cohesive delegations usually mentioned their delegation colleagues without prompting from the interviewer and when asked directly all said they had received invaluable aid:

Everyone's been very helpful. They'll give you advice. Even someone as busy as Mr. Mahon. I've often called him about some financial matter. He's taken the time to explain how things work . . . or Wright Patman, well you can go right down the line. They've all been as helpful as they can be.

When Eddie and I first came down here in '52, well, every afternoon McCormack goes to cocktail parties. Well, he'd say, "Why don't you come along? There are people you'll want to meet." That way we met people we'd never have had the chance to meet otherwise. I know he did the same thing for Burke. It opens an awful lot of doors that wouldn't be open otherwise.

The six cohesive delegations also help their junior members learn the job. The rate of interaction in these delegations, however, is lower than within the four highly cohesive delegations, and the assistance the freshman receives is somewhat less:

[I learned my way around] by trial and error. That's not quite accurate but it pretty well describes it . . . And last but not least, there were Laird and Byrnes and Davis, they were very helpful. They told me to come to them with questions and were always willing to help.

Well, to be honest, no. [The other Pennsylvania Republicans were not helpful.] The congressman here is pretty much an entity unto himself.

I don't mean they weren't at all helpful. If you went to them and asked them a question they would answer it, but they didn't come and offer help.

The freshman New York congressman receives very little help from his delegation colleagues. Asked how they had learned their way around, two New York Democrats replied:

. . . by the "bump-your-nose" procedure. It can be pretty agonizing.

. . . by stumbling. . . . In the morning I used to wander around the halls introducing myself to other congressmen.

A New York Republican said:

The interest of the other New York Republicans was uneven. Some did a little something, others seemed totally uninterested in getting a new colleague. I'd say they were *under*-whelmed.

None of the delegations studied make an organized group effort to socialize their freshmen. Members of cohesive delegations do try to help the new men on an individual basis, and freshmen are encouraged to call their seniors for information and advice, but socialization is primarily a by-product of delegation interaction. The new member of a cohesive delegation interacts frequently with his senior colleagues. By asking questions and by observation he learns what is expected of him; he learns which modes of behavior are considered acceptable and which are most likely to result in success.

Clearly the extent to which the members of a delegation rely upon one another for information, and the extent to which they socialize their new members, are closely related to the delegation's rate of interaction. Thus the tentative classification of delegations into cohesion categories will now be considered final.

Membership Stability

The need for socialization is, of course, directly related to the delegation's membership stability. As the accompanying chart shows, three of the delegations have recently experienced major membership changes.

The instability of the New York Republican delegation is the result of a severe reduction in size and the loss of the delegation's leadership. For both the California and the New York Democratic delegations,

Table 6–1. Delegation Stability, 87th–90th Congresses

Delegation	Percentage of Freshmen[a]	Variance[b]	
		Newcomers	Seats
Low Regular Turnover			
Massachusetts Democrats	0	0	.18
Pennsylvania Democrats	8.9	.69	.50
Illinois Democrats	9.8	2.69	1.25
North Carolina Democrats	10.8	.50	1.19
Texas Democrats	11.6	.25	.75
Wisconsin Republicans	12.5	.29	.50
High Regular Turnover			
Illinois Republicans	17.4	1.50	.25
California Republicans	18.3	1.69	1.50
Pennsylvania Republicans	20.3	1.19	1.25
High Sudden Turnover			
New York Republicans	14.1	2.25	10.69
California Democrats	17.8	11.19	15.50
New York Democrats	17.8	10.11	7.25

[a] Total number of newcomers/total number of seats = percentage of total terms served by delegation members that were served by freshmen.
[b] Variance in number of newcomers, and in number of seats held, per Congress for the 87th–90th Congresses.

instability took the form of a sudden large increase in membership. The 1962 election increased the size of the California Democratic delegation from sixteen to twenty-four and brought ten freshmen Democrats to the House. But most of these new members did not arrive in Washington as complete strangers. Seven of the ten had served in the Assembly. It was often mentioned that new members knew each other and some of the more senior delegation members as well from earlier service in the state legislature. These men agreed that their senior colleagues had been helpful:

> Of the course the members of your delegation are the most helpful—to varying degrees. George Miller spent an hour spontaneously one day. He took me over to the Senate side—on the floor. I didn't even know we were allowed to do that. McFall took me to lunch.

The 1964 election increased the size of the New York Democratic delegation from twenty to twenty-seven. Nine new men were elected. The men first elected in 1964, all of whom were reelected in 1966, differed appreciably in background from the senior members. Four of the nine had attended prestige universities rather than the city colleges typically attended by representatives elected previously; a smaller percentage were lawyers. Three had held appointive positions in Washington or with the United Nations. Only two were elected from New York City and both had unseated regular Democratic incumbents in bitter primary fights. Senior delegation colleagues made little attempt to assist the new men. "Only the Democratic Study Group really went out of its way to be helpful," an administrative assistant said. The different responses of these two delegations to a similar problem suggests that the extent to which the newcomers are similar to their senior colleagues is as important for stability as is the number of newcomers.

Goals

To ascertain the congressmen's goals, the men interviewed were asked if their delegation colleagues were interested in making the House their career. If the congressman said that he was interested in another office or if at least two of his colleagues attributed such an interest to him, he was classified as having higher office as his goal. Every congressman who replied that he was interested in another office was mentioned by at least two of his colleagues. The reverse was not true.

The number of delegation members mentioned as actively interested in higher office clearly distinguishes two classes of delegations. A third or more of the members of three delegations are interested in another office. But if the hypothesis is to be tested, some further distinctions must be made. The congressman's satisfaction with the job provides another indicator.

When answering the question about goals, members of some delegations often complained about the job. It seems reasonable to suppose that the congressman who is unhappy with certain aspects of the job is less fully committed to staying in the House, whatever his immediate plans may be.[14]

14. The political necessity of belonging to the Tuesday through Thursday Club was the most frequent cause for complaints. Spending at least every weekend in the district is immediately expensive in terms of time and money. It also reduces the probability that the congressman will attain personal influence in the House because he is considered a part-time congressman by other members and has less opportunity to make friends in the House. The Chicago Democrats are the only congressmen interviewed who do not consider membership in the Tuesday through Thursday Club onerous. The Illinois Democratic delegation is also the only delegation studied that regularly bargains with votes. These men may consider membership in the Tuesday through Thursday Club no problem because they make use of a type of influence that is not dependent upon their fulfillment of House norms.

The two indicators yield the following categorization:

(1) Few interested in other office: Massachusetts Democrats, Texas Democrats, California Democrats, California Republicans, Wisconsin Republicans, Illinois Democrats

(2) Few interested in other office but many unhappy with job; Pennsylvania Democrats, Pennsylvania Republicans, North Carolina Democrats

(3) One third or more interested in other office: Illinois Republicans, New York Republicans, New York Democrats

Conclusions

The delegations have now been placed into three ordinal categories on each of the variables—cohesion, interest in a House career, and stability. The hypothesis states that cohesion varies directly with both independent variables. The sample is small and was not randomly selected. Thus the usual statistical tests are inapplicable. But if the relation is strong, inspection of the data should reveal its existence. First some definite predictions[15] must be made, and the following, I believe, are cautious as well as explicit. A delegation that falls into the first (third) category on both independent variables should be highly cohesive (noncohesive). It seems reasonable to assume that the "distance" between the categories noncohesive and cohesive is greater than the "distance" between the categories cohesive and highly cohesive. Thus a delegation that falls into the first category on one independent variable and into the second on the other, as well as a delegation that falls into the second category on both independent variables, should be cohesive. As the accompanying chart shows, nine of the twelve delegations are consistent with the predictions. There are no extreme deviations. The author does not claim that the hypothesis has been fully verified. The number of cases is too small, and the data are not sufficiently precise. But within these limitations, the fit between hypothesis and data is close. If one were to place twelve delegations into three cohesion categories randomly, the probability of correctly placing at least nine of twelve is less than .004.

15. These predictions state sufficient conditions for various levels of cohesion. Since each of the two independent variables can take three values, there are nine possible combinations. Predictions are made for only five of these nine. Given the imprecision of the data, further predictions would be of dubious validity. Thus for a delegation with any of the other four combinations of values on the independent variables no predictions are made. These are, within limits of consistency, indeterminant cases but, to increase the rigor of the test, they are treated as violations of the theory. Also for rigor, the predictions are treated as if they stated necessary and sufficient conditions for various levels of cohesion.

Table 6-2. Cohesion as a Function of Stability and Interest in a House Career

		Interest in a House Career		
		1	2	3
Highly Cohesive	1	*Massachusetts Democrat* *Texas Democrats* *Illinois Democrats*		
	2			
	3	California Democrats		
Cohesive	1	Wisconsin Republicans	*Pennsylvania Democrats* *North Carolina Democrats*	
	2	*California Republicans*	*Pennsylvania Republicans*	
	3			Illinois Republicans
Noncohesive	1			
	2			
	3			*New York Democrats* *New York Republicans*

Stability (row category axis)

Note: Delegations italicized are consistent with predictions

A subsidiary hypothesis states that neither ideological nor district homogeneity are necessary conditions for cohesion. Limitations of space prohibit a rigorous examination of the relation between delegation cohesion and ideological homogeneity. But, since the hypothesis states that ideological homogeneity is not a necessary condition for delegation cohesion, one counterexample is sufficient to falsify the alternative hypothesis. On the basis of both roll-call[16] and interview data, the highly cohesive Texas Democratic delegation is the least ideologically homogeneous delegation studied. The following comments illustrate the members' awareness of the delegation's heterogeneity and something of the manner in which they cope with it.

> We're a close group, tight-knit, even though we have different views, probably because we don't try to force agreement. There's no friction —there would be if we did. We have everything from liberal to conservative—some would say ultraliberal to ultraconservative. . . . And the spread is getting wider.

> There's never any attempt to get people to vote a certain way. . . . We have a wide range of opinions—a diversity of districts, everyone's independent. We respect each other.

As the above comments suggest, heterogeneous delegations do not attempt to bargain with votes. The Texas Democratic delegation has, in fact, developed norms prohibiting ideological arguments and attempts at pressure. Strict observance of these norms probably is, as the members believe, a necessary condition for the continued existence of the group. All cohesive, ideologically homogeneous delegations seek to "stick together" whenever possible but the intensity of such efforts varies greatly among delegations. Ideological homogeneity is a necessary but not sufficient condition for a delegation's attempts to bargain with votes.

It was hypothesized that district heterogeneity is not directly related to cohesion but that it will limit the range of joint action. The term district heterogeneity is used to refer to the perception on the part of the members of a delegation that the interests of their districts are, in general, different. District heterogeneity is defined in terms of perceptions to provide a more stringent test. Any index constructed from district census data can be criticized on the ground that the

---

16. Using the Rice index of voting cohesion on the *New Republic*'s twelve key votes as an admittedly crude indicator of ideological homogeneity, the Texas Democratic delegation, with an index score of 40.4, ranked lowest of the twelve delegations studied. The scores of the other delegations ranged from 94.4 (Mass. Democrats) to 49.4 (N.Y. Republicans).

characteristics included may not be those important to the congressman. The members of a delegation may see the interests of their districts as different without, however, interpreting these differences as conflicts. It was hypothesized that a regional rivalry in the state is the most likely basis for perceptions of conflicting interests.

A pronounced regional rivalry does exist in three of the states studied. The congressmen from California, Illinois, and New York are quite aware of the cleavages within their home states. But only the New York congressmen consider the regional rivalry sufficiently divisive to prevent joint action. The congressmen from Texas and Pennsylvania emphasized the diversity of their states. These men perceive the interests of their districts as different but not as conflicting. The congressmen from Massachusetts, Wisconsin, and North Carolina mentioned no major or divisive differences among their districts.

The accompanying chart summarizes these findings. If district heterogeneity were used to predict cohesion, the six delegations off the main diagonal would be misclassified. Clearly district heterogeneity is not a necessary condition for cohesion. Both noncohesive delegations are from a state with a regional rivalry, but three of the four highly cohesive delegations are from states with either a regional rivalry or considerable district diversity. Furthermore, district heterogeneity does not appreciably limit joint action on the part of a cohesive delegation. The members of all cohesive delegations act as allies for one another on district projects and problems and in the committee-assignment process.

Of the possible determinants of cohesion that were examined, stability and the proportion of delegation members interested in a House career are most closely related to cohesion. Because of limitations of data, the findings are tentative. Still they seem to justify certain methodological and substantive observations. When one studies professionals in their area of professional competence (in this case professional politicians in a political arena) the assumption that professional goals will dominate behavior seems sufficiently realistic to lead to significant predictive accuracy about behavior. This implies that one can assume that professionals, again in their area of professional competence, will act rationally in the common-sense use of that term. In studies of congressional behavior, it may soon be possible to progress from the use of "bits of theory" to an explicit and integrated theoretical framework based upon these assumptions.

Substantively, this study reconfirms the findings of previous studies concerning the congressman's sources of information. Congressmen do rely heavily upon one another for information. Within cohesive dele-

Table 6-3. Cohesion and District Heterogeneity

Source of Perceived Heterogeneity	Noncohesive	Cohesive	Highly Cohesive
Regional Rivalry	New York Democrats New York Republicans	Illinois Republicans California Republicans	California Democrats Illinois Democrats
Diversity		Pennsylvania Democrats Pennsylvania Republicans	Texas Democrats
None Mentioned		Wisconsin Republicans North Carolina Democrats	Massachusetts Democrats

gations, fellow members are the single most important source of information. The complaints made by members of noncohesive delegations indicate that intradelegation sharing of information may well be the least time-consuming way of handling the problem. Since time is crucial, the member of a fairly large cohesive delegation does have an advantage over other congressmen. The cohesiveness of his delegation probably affects the congressman's performance and may well have some effect on his career goals. Certainly, for the member of a cohesive delegation the job of congressman is less hectic than it is for his less-fortunate colleagues.

Membership in a cohesive delegation is clearly useful to the congressman, but what are the effects of such groups on the political process in the House? Cohesive delegations seem to play an important system-maintenance role. Throughout the interviews it was found that a certain amount of impatience with the decision-making process in the House is typical of most junior members. Those delegations with a vigorous group life temper it through the socialization process and by enabling their junior members to exert a certain amount of indirect influence through their senior delegation colleagues. In return for keeping their expressions of impatience within House limits of tolerance, the junior men receive help from their seniors with committee assignments and district projects. Further, cohesive delegations, especially heterogeneous ones, do reinforce House norms of courtesy and compromise. By giving structure to the mass of party members, they expedite communication and facilitate bargaining. But cohesive delegations also reduce their members' dependence upon the party leadership. The members of such delegations serve as an important source of information for one another and are thus less dependent upon other sources of information; as a group, they have much more bargaining strength than they would have as individuals. Without cohesive delegations and other informal groups, and the structure and coordination they provide, the decision-making process in the House might well break down. At the same time, the existence of such groups, by proliferating centers of influence, increases decentralization and decreases the party leadership's chances of dominating even postcommittee decision-making.

7

The Appropriations Committee
as a Political System

Richard F. Fenno, Jr.

Studies of Congress by political scientists have produced a time-tested concensus on the very considerable power and autonomy of congressional committees. Because of these two related characteristics, it makes empirical and analytical sense to treat the congressional committee as a discrete unit for analysis. This paper conceives of the committee as a political system (or, more accurately, as a political subsystem) faced with a number of basic problems which it must solve in order to achieve its goals and maintain itself. Generally speaking these functional problems pertain to the environmental and the internal relations of the committee. This study is concerned almost exclusively with the internal problems of the committee and particularly with the problem of self-integration.[1] It describes how one congressional com-

Reprinted by permission of the author and publishier from "The House Appropriations Committee as a Political System: The Problem of Integration," *American Political Science Review* 56 (June, 1962):310–24. Copyright © 1962 by the American Political Science Association. Footnotes have been renumbered. The author wishes to acknowledge his indebtedness to the Committee on Political Behavior of the Social Science Research Council for the research grant which made possible this study, and the larger study of legislative behavior in the area of appropriations of which it is a part. This is a revised version of a paper read at the Annual Meeting of the American Political Science Association at St. Louis, September, 1961.
1. On social systems, see: George Homans, *The Human Group* (New York, 1950); Robert K. Merton, *Social Theory and Social Structure* (Glencoe, 1957); Talcott Parsons and Edward Shils, *Toward A General Theory of Action* (Cam-

mittee—The Committee on Appropriations of the House of Representatives—has dealt with this problem in the period 1947–1961. Its purpose is to add to our understanding of appropriations politics in Congress and to suggest the usefulness of this type of analysis for studying the activities of any congressional committee.

The necessity for integration in any social system arises from the differentiation among its various elements. Most importantly there is a differentiation among subgroups and among individual positions, together with the roles that flow therefrom.[2] A committee faces the problem, how shall these diverse elements be made to mesh together or function in support of one another? No political system (or subsystem) is perfectly integrated; yet no political system can survive without some minimum degree of integration among its differentiated parts. Committee integration is defined as the degree to which there is a working together or a meshing together or mutual support among its roles and subgroups. Conversely, it is also defined as the degree to which a committee is able to minimize conflict among its roles and its subgroups by heading off or resolving the conflicts that arise.[3] A concomitant of integration is the existence of a fairly consistent set of norms, widely agreed upon and widely followed by the members. Another concomitant of integration is the existence of control mechanisms (i.e., socialization and sanctioning mechanisms) capable of maintaining reasonable conformity to norms. In other words, the more highly integrated a committee, the smaller will be the gap between expected and actual behavior.

This study is concerned with integration both as a structural characteristic of, and as a functional problem for, the Appropriations Committee. First, certain basic characteristics of the committee need description, to help explain the integration of its parts. Second comes a partial description of the degree to which and the ways in which the committee achieves integration. No attempt is made to state this in quantitative terms, but the object is to examine the meshing together or the minimization of conflict among certain subgroups and among

---

bridge, 1951), pp. 190–234. Most helpful with reference to the political system has been David Easton, "An Approach to the Analysis of Political Systems," *World Politics* (April, 1957):383–400.

2. On the idea of subgroups as used here, see Harry M. Johnson, *Sociology* (New York, 1960), ch. 3. On role, see specifically Theodore M. Newcomb *Social Psychology* (New York, 1951), p. 280; see generally N. Gross, W. Mason, and A. McEachern, *Explorations in Role Analysis: Studies of the School Superintendency Role* (New York, 1958). On differentiation and its relation to integration, see Scott Greer, *Social Organization* (New York, 1955).

3. The usage here follows most closely that of Robert Merton, op. cit., pp. 26–29.

certain key roles. Also, important control mechanisms are described. The study concludes with some comments on the consequences of committee integration for appropriations politics and on the usefulness of further congressional committee analysis in terms of functional problems such as this one.

I

Five important characteristics of the Appropriations Committee which help explain committee integration are (1) the existence of a well-articulated and deeply rooted consensus on committee goals or tasks; (2) the nature of the committee's subject matter; (3) the legislative orientation of its members; (4) the attractiveness of the committee for its members; and (5) the stability of committee membership.

Consensus

The Appropriations Committee sees its tasks as taking form within the broad guidelines set by its parent body, the House of Representatives. For it is the primary condition of the committee's existence that it was created by the House for the purpose of assisting the House in the performance of House legislative tasks dealing with appropriations. Committee members agree that their fundamental duty is to serve the House in the manner and with the substantive results that the House prescribes. Given, however, the imprecision of House expectations and the permissiveness of House surveillance, the committee must elaborate for itself a definition of tasks plus a supporting set of perceptions (of itself and of others) explicit enough to furnish day-to-day guidance.

The committee's view begins with the preeminence of the House— often mistakenly attributed to the Constitution ("all bills for raising revenue," Art. I, sec. 7) but nevertheless firmly sanctioned by custom —in appropriations affairs.

It moves easily to the conviction that, as the efficient part of the House in this matter, the Constitution has endowed it with special obligations and special prerogatives. It ends in the view that the Committee on Appropriations, far from being merely one among many units in a complicated legislative-executive system, is *the* most responsible unit in the whole appropriations process.[4] Hand in hand with

4. This and all other generalizations about member attitudes and perceptions depend heavily on extensive interviews with committee members. Semistructured

the consensus on their primacy goes a consensus that all of their House-prescribed tasks can be fulfilled by superimposing upon them one, single, paramount task—*to guard the federal treasury.* Committee members state their goals in the essentially negative terms of guardianship—screening requests for money, checking against ill-advised expenditures, and protecting the taxpayer's dollar. In the language of the committee's official history, the job of each member is "constantly and courageously to protect the federal treasury against thousands of appeals and imperative demands for unnecessary, unwise, and excessive expenditures."[5]

To buttress its self-image as guardian of public funds, the committee elaborates a set of perceptions about other participants in the appropriations process to which most members hold most of the time. Each executive official, for example, is seen to be interested in the expansion of his own particular program. Each one asks, therefore, for more money than he really needs, in view of the total picture, to run an adequate program. This and other committee perceptions—of the Budget Bureau, of the Senate, and of their fellow Representatives—help to shape and support the committee members in their belief that most budget estimates can, should, and must be reduced and that, since no one else can be relied upon, the House committee must do the job. To the consensus on the main task of protecting the treasury is added, therefore, a consensus on the instrumental task of *cutting whatever budget estimates are submitted.*

As an immediate goal, committee members agree that they must strike a highly critical, aggressive posture toward budget requests, and that they should, on principle, reduce them. In the words of the committee's veterans: "There has never been a budget submitted to the Congress that couldn't be cut." "There isn't a budget that can't be cut 10 percent immediately." "I've been on the committee for seventeen years. No subcommittee of which I have been a member has ever

---

interviews averaging forty-five minutes in length were held with forty-five of the fifty committee members during the Eighty-sixth Congress. Certain key questions, all open-ended, were asked of all respondents. The schedule was kept very flexible, however, in order to permit particular topics to be explored with those individuals best equipped to discuss them. In a few cases, where respondents encouraged it, notes were taken during the interviews. In most cases notes were not taken, but were transcribed immediately after the interview. Where unattributed quotations occur in the text, therefore, they are as nearly verbatim as the author's power of immediate recall could make them. These techniques were all used so as to improve rapport between interviewer and respondent.

5. "History of the Committee on Appropriations," House Doc. 299, 77th Cong., 1st sess., 1941–1942, p. 11.

reported out a bill without a cut in the budget. I'm proud of that record." The aim of budget-cutting is strongly internalized for the committee member. "It's a tradition in the Appropriations Committee to cut." "You're grounded in it. . . . It's ingrained in you from the time you get on the committee." For the purposes of a larger study, the appropriations case histories of thirty-seven executive bureaus have been examined for a twelve-year period, 1947 to 1959.[6] Of 443 separate bureau estimates, the committee reduced 77.2 percent (342) of them.

It is a mark of the intensity and self-consciousness of the committee consensus on budget-cutting that it is couched in a distinctive vocabulary. The workaday lingo of the committee member is replete with negative verbs, undesirable objects of attention, and effective instruments of action. Agency budgets are said to be filled with "fat," "padding," "grease," "pork," "oleaginous substance," "water," "oil," "cushions," "avoirdupois," "waste tissue," and "soft spots." The action verbs most commonly used are "cut," "carve," "slice," "prune," "whittle," "squeeze," "wring," "trim," "lop off," "chop," "slash," "pare," "shave," "fry," and "whack." The tools of the trade are appropriately referred to as "knife," "blade," "meat axe," "scalpel," "meat cleaver," "hatchet," "shears," "wringer," and "fine-tooth comb." Members are hailed by their fellows as being "pretty sharp with the knife." Agencies may "have the meat axe thrown at them." Executives are urged to put their agencies "on a fat boy's diet." Budgets are praised when they are "cut to the bone." And members agree that "You can always get a little more fat out of a piece of pork if you fry it a little longer and a little harder."

To the major task of protecting the treasury and the instrumental task of cutting budget estimates, each committee member adds, usually by way of exception, a third task—*serving the constituency to which he owes his election.* This creates no problem for him when, as is sometimes the case, he can serve his district best by cutting the budget requests of a federal agency whose program is in conflict with the demands of his constituency.[7] Normally, however, members find that their most common role conflict is between a committee-oriented budget-reducing role and a constituency-oriented budget-increasing

6. The bureaus being studied are all concerned with domestic policy and are situated in the Agriculture, Interior, Labor, Commerce, Treasury, Justice, and Health, Education, and Welfare Departments. For a similar pattern of committee decisions in foreign affairs, see Holbert Carroll, *The House of Representatives and Foreign Affairs* (Pittsburgh, 1958), ch. 9.

7. See, for example, Philip A. Foss, "The Grazing Fee Dilemma," Inter-University Case Program, No. 57 (University, Alabama, 1960).

role. Committee ideology resolves the conflict by assigning top, long-run priority to the budget-cutting task and making of the constituency service a permissible, short-run exception. No member is expected to commit electoral suicide; but no member is expected to allow his district's desire for federal funds to dominate his committee behavior.

Subject Matter

Appropriations Committee integration is facilitated by the subject matter with which the group deals. The committee makes decisions on the same controversial issues as do the committees handling substantive legislation. But a money decision—however vitally it affects national policy—is, or at least seems to be, less directly a policy decision. Since they deal immediately with dollars and cents, it is easy for the members to hold to the idea that they are not dealing with programmatic questions, that theirs is a "business" rather than a "policy" committee. The subject matter, furthermore, keeps committee members relatively free agents, which promotes intracommittee maneuvering and, hence, conflict avoidance. Members do not commit themselves to their constituents in terms of precise money amounts, and no dollar sum is sacred—it can always be adjusted without conceding that a principle has been breached. By contrast, members of committees dealing directly with controversial issues are often pressured into taking concrete stands on these issues; consequently, they may come to their committee work with fixed and hardened attitudes. This leads to unavoidable, head-on intracommittee conflict and renders integrative mechanisms relatively ineffective.

The fact of an annual appropriations process means the committee members repeat the same operations with respect to the same subject matters year after year—and frequently more than once in a given year. Substantive and procedural repetition promotes familiarity with key problems and provides ample opportunity to test and confirm the most satisfactory methods of dealing with them. And the absolute necessity that appropriations bills do ultimately pass gives urgency to the search for such methods. Furthermore, the House rule that no member of the committee can serve on another standing committee is a deterrent against a fragmentation of committee member activity which could be a source of difficulty in holding the group together. If a committee has developed (as this one has) a number of norms designed to foster integration, repeated and concentrated exposure to them increases the likelihood that they will be understood, accepted, and followed.

Legislative Orientation

The recruitment of members for the Appropriations Committee produces a group of individuals with an orientation especially conducive to committee integration. Those who make the selection pay special attention to the characteristics which Masters has described as those of the "responsible legislator"—approval of and conformity to the norms of the legislative process and of the House of Representatives.[8]

Key selectors speak of wanting, for the Appropriations Committee, "the kind of man you can deal with" or "a fellow who is well-balanced and won't go off half-cocked on things." A northern liberal Democrat felt that he had been chosen over eight competitors because "I had made a lot of friends and was known as a nice guy"—especially, he noted, among southern Congressmen. Another Democrat explained, "I got the blessing of the Speaker and the leadership. It's personal friendships. I had done a lot of things for them in the past, and when I went to them and asked them, they gave it to me." A Republican chosen for the committee in his first term recalled,

> The chairman [Rep. Taber], I guess, did some checking around in my area. After all, I was new and he didn't know me. People told me that they were called to see if I was—well, unstable or apt to go off on tangents . . . to see whether or not I had any preconceived notions about things and would not be flexible—whether I would oppose things even though it was obvious.

A key criterion in each of the cases mentioned was a demonstrable record of, or an assumed predisposition toward, legislative give-and-take.

The 106 Appropriations Committee members serving between 1947 and 1961 spent an average of 3.6 years on other House committees before coming to the committee. Only 17 of the 106 were selected as first-term congressmen. A House apprenticeship (which Appropriations maintains more successfully than all committees save Ways and Means and Rules[9]) provides the time in which legislative reputations can be

---

8. Nicholas A. Masters, "House Committee Assignments," *American Political Science Review* 55 (June, 1961): 345–57.

9. In the period from 1947 through 1959, (Eightieth to Eighty-sixth Congress) seventy-nine separate appointments were made to the Appropriations Committee, with fourteen going to freshmen. The committee filled, in other words, 17.7 percent of its vacancies with freshmen. The Rules Committee had twenty-six vacancies and selected no freshmen at all. The Ways and Means Committee had thirty-six vacancies and selected two freshmen (5.6 percent). All other committees had a

established by the member and an assessment of that reputation in terms of Appropriations Committee requirements can be made. Moreover, the mere fact that a member survives for a couple of terms is some indication of an electoral situation conducive to his "responsible" legislative behavior. The optimum bet for the committee is a member from a sufficiently safe district to permit him freedom of maneuver inside the House without fear of reprisal at the polls.[10] The degree of responsiveness to House norms which the committee selectors value may be the product of a safe district as well as an individual temperament.

Attractiveness

A fourth factor is the extraordinarily high degree of attractiveness which the committee holds for its members as measured by the low rate of departure from it. Committee members do not leave it for service on other committees. To the contrary, they are attracted to it from nearly every other committee.[11] Of the 106 members in the 1947 to 1961 period, only two men left the committee voluntarily; and neither of them initiated the move.[12] Committee attractiveness is a measure of its capacity to satisfy individual member needs—for power, prestige, recognition, respect, self-esteem, friendship, etc. Such satisfaction in turn increases the likelihood that members will behave in such a way as to hold the group together.

The most frequently mentioned source of committee attractiveness is its power, based on its control of financial resources. "Where the money is, that's where the power is," sums up the feeling of the members. They prize their ability to reward or punish so many other participants in the political process—executive officials, fellow congressmen, constituents, and other clientele groups. In the eyes of its own members, the committee is either the most powerful in the House

---

higher percentage of freshmen appointments. Armed Services ranked fourth, with forty-five vacancies and twelve freshmen appointed, for a percentage of 26.7. Foreign affairs figures were forty-six and fourteen, or 30.4 percent; Un-American Activities figures were twenty-two and seven, or 31.8 percent. cf. Masters, op. cit.

10. In the 1960 elections, forty-one out of the current fifty members received more than 55.1 percent of the vote in their districts. By a common definition, that is, only nine of the fifty came from marginal districts.

11. The 106 members came to Appropriations from every committee except Ways and Means.

12. One was personally requested by the Speaker to move to Ways and Means. The other was chosen by a caucus of regional congressmen to be his party's representative on the Rules Committee. Of the twenty-one members who were forced off the committee for lack of seniority during a change in party control, or who were defeated for reelection and later returned, twenty sought to regain committee membership at the earliest opportunity.

or it is on a par with Ways and Means or, less frequently, on a par with Ways and Means and Rules. The second important ingredient in member satisfaction is the government-wide scope of committee activity. The ordinary congressman may feel that he has too little knowledge of and too little control over his environment. Membership on this committee compensates for this feeling of helplessness by the wider contacts, the greater amount of information, and the sense of being "in the middle of things" which are consequent, if not to subcommittee activity, at least to the full committee's overview of the federal government.

Thirdly, committee attractiveness is heightened by the group's recognizable and distinctive political style—one that is, moreover, highly valued in American political culture. The style is that of *hard work;* and the committee's self-image is that of "the hardest-working committee in Congress." His willingness to work is the committee member's badge of identification, and it is proudly worn. It colors his perceptions of others and their perceptions of him.[13] It is a cherished axiom of all members that "this committee is no place for a man who doesn't work. They have to be hard working. It's a way of life. It isn't just a job; it's a way of life."

The mere existence of some identifiable and valued style or "way of life" is a cohesive force for a group. But the particular style of hard work is one which increases group morale and group identification twice over. Hard work means a long, dull, and tedious application to detail, via the technique of "dig, dig, dig, day after day behind closed doors," in an estimated 460 subcommittee and full committee meetings a year. And virtually all of these meetings are in executive session. By adopting the style of hard work, the committee discourages highly individualized forms of legislative behavior, which could be disruptive within the committee. It rewards its members with power, but it is power based rather on work inside the committee than on the political glamour of activities carried on in the limelight of the mass media. Prolonged daily work together encourages sentiments of mutual regard,

13. A sidelight on this attitude is displayed in a current feud between the House and Senate Appropriations Committees over the meeting place for their conference committees. The House Committee is trying to break the century-old custom that conferences to resolve differences on money bills are always held on the Senate side of the Capitol. House Committee members "complain that they often have to trudge back to the House two or three times to answer roll calls during a conference. They say they go over in a body to work, while Senators flit in and out. . . . The House Appropriations Committee feels that it does all the hard work listening to witnesses for months on each bill, only to have the Senate Committee sit as a court of appeals and, with little more than a cursory glance, restore most of the funds cut." *Washington Post* (April 24, 1962): 1.

sympathy, and solidarity. This esprit is, in turn, functional for integration on the committee. A Republican leader summed up,

> I think it's more closely knit than any other committee. Yet it's the biggest committee, and you'd think it would be the reverse. I know on my subcommittee, you sit together day after day. You get better acquainted. You have sympathy when other fellows go off to play golf. There's a lot of esprit de corps in the committee.

The strong attraction which members have for the committee increases the influence which the committee and its norms exercise on all of them. It increases the susceptibility of the newcomer to committee socialization and of the veteran to committee sanctions applicable against deviant behavior.[14]

Membership Stability

Members of the Appropriations Committee are strongly attracted to it; they also have, which bears out their selection as "responsible legislators," a strong attraction for a career in the House of Representatives. The fifty members on the committee in 1961 had served an average of 13.1 years in the House. These twin attractions produce a noteworthy stability of committee membership. In the period from the Eightieth to the Eighty-seventh Congress, 35.7 percent of the committee's membership remained constant. That is to say, fifteen of the forty-two members on the committee in March, 1947, were still on the committee in March, 1961.[15] The fifty members of the committee in 1961 averaged 9.3 years of prior service on that committee. In no single year during the last fourteen has the committee had to absorb an influx of new members totalling more than one-quarter of its membership. At all times, in other words, at least three-fourths of the members have had previous committee experience. This extraordinary stability of personnel extends into the staff as well. As of June, 1961, its fifteen professionals had served an average of 10.7 years with the committee.[16]

14. This proposition is spelled out at some length in J. Thibaut and H. Kelley, *The Social Psychology of Groups* (New York, 1959), p. 247, and in D. Cartwright and A. Zander, *Group Dynamics: Research and Theory* (Evanston, 1953), p. 420.

15. This figure is 9 percent greater than the next most stable House Committee during this particular period. The top four, in order, were Appropriations (35.7 percent), Agriculture (26.7 percent), Armed Services (25 percent), [and] Foreign Affairs (20.8 percent).

16. The committee's permanent and well-integrated professional staff (as distinguished from its temporary investigating staff) might be considered as part of the subsystem though it will not be treated in this paper.

The opportunity exists, therefore, for the development of a stable leadership group, a set of traditional norms for the regulation of internal committee behavior, and informal techniques of personal accommodation. Time is provided in which new members can learn and internalize committee norms before they attain high seniority rankings. The committee does not suffer from the potentially disruptive consequences of rapid changeovers in its leadership group, nor of sudden impositions of new sets of norms governing internal committee behavior.

II

If one considers the main activity of a political system to be decision-making, the acid test of its internal integration is its capacity to make collective decisions without flying apart in the process. Analysis of committee integration should focus directly, therefore, upon its subgroups and the roles of its members. Two kinds of subgroups are of central importance—subcommittees and majority or minority party groups. The roles which are most relevant derive from: (1) positions which each member holds by virtue of his subgroup attachments, e.g., as subcommittee member, majority (or minority) party member; (2) positions which relate to full committee membership, e.g., committee member, and the seniority rankings of veteran, man of moderate experience, and newcomer;[17] (3) positions which relate to both subgroup and full committee membership, e.g., chairman of the committee, ranking minority member of the committee, subcommittee chairman, ranking subcommittee member. Clusters of norms state the expectations about subgroup and role behavior. The description which follows treats the ways in which these norms and their associated behaviors mesh and clash. It treats, also, the internal control mechanisms by which behavior is brought into reasonable conformity with expectations.

Subgroup Integration

The day-to-day work of the committee is carried on in its subcommittees, each of which is given jurisdiction over a number of related governmental units. The number of subcommittees is determined by the committee chairman, and has varied recently from a low

17. "Newcomers" are defined as men who have served no more than two terms on the committee. "Men of moderate experience" are those with three to five terms of service. "Veterans" are those who have six or more terms of committee service.

of nine in 1949 to a high of fifteen in 1959. The present total of fourteen reflects, as always, a set of strategic and personal judgments by
the chairman balanced against the limitations placed on him by committee tradition and member wishes. The chairman also determines
subcommittee jurisdiction, appoints subcommittee chairmen, and se-
lects the majority party members of each group. The ranking minority
member of the committee exercises similar control over subcommittee
assignments on his side of the aisle.

Each subcommittee holds hearings on the budget estimates of the
agencies assigned to it, meets in executive session to decide what
figures and what language to recommend to the full committee (to
"mark up" the bill), defends its recommendations before the full committee, writes the committee's report to the House, dominates the debate on the floor, and bargains for the House in conference committee.
Within its jurisdiction, each subcommittee functions independently of
the others and guards its autonomy jealously. The chairman and ranking minority member of the full committee have, as we shall see, certain
opportunities to oversee and dip into the operations of all subcommittees. But their intervention is expected to be minimal. Moreover, they
themselves operate importantly within the subcommittee framework
by sitting as chairman or ranking minority member of the subcommittee in which they are most interested. Each subcommittee, under
the guidance of its chairman, transacts its business in considerable
isolation from every other one. One subcommittee chairman exclaimed,

> Why, you'd be branded an impostor if you went into one of these
> other subcommittee meetings. The only time I go is by appointment, by
> arrangement with the chairman at a special time. I'm as much a
> stranger in another subcommittee as I would be in the legislative Com-
> mittee on Post Office and Civil Service. Each one does its work apart
> from all others.

All members of all subcommittees are expected to behave in similar
fashion in the role of subcommittee member. Three main norms define
this role; to the extent that they are observed, they promote harmony
and reduce conflict among subcommittees.[18] Subcommittee autonomy
gives to the House norm of *specialization* an intensified application on
the Appropriations Committee. Each member is expected to play the

18. A statements of expected behavior was taken to be a committee norm when
it was expressed by a substantial number of respondents (a dozen or so) who
represented both parties and [had] varying degrees of experience. In nearly every
case, moreover, no refutation of them was encountered, and ample confirmation of
their existence can be found in the public record. Their articulation came most
frequently from the veterans of the group.

role of specialist in the activities of one subcommittee. He will sit on from one to four subcommittees, but normally will specialize in the work, or a portion of the work, of only one. Except for the chairman, [the] ranking minority member, and their confidants, a committee member's time, energy, contacts, and experience are devoted to his subcommittees. Specialization is, therefore, among the earliest and most compelling of the committee norms to which a newcomer is exposed. Within the committee, respect, deference, and power are earned through subcommittee activity and hence, to a degree, through specialization. Specialization is valued further because it is well-suited to the task of guarding the treasury. Only by specializing, committee members believe, can they unearth the volume of factual information necessary for the intelligent screening of budget requests. Since "the facts" are acquired only through industry, an effective specialist will perforce adopt and promote the committee's style of hard work.

Committeewide acceptance of specialization is an integrative force in decision-making because it helps support a second norm—*reciprocity*. The stage at which a subcommittee makes its recommendations is a potential point of internal friction. Conflict among subcommittees (or between one subcommittee and the rest of the committee) is minimized by the deference traditionally accorded to the recommendation of the subcommittee which has specialized in the area, has worked hard, and has "the facts." "It's a matter of 'you respect my work and I'll respect yours.' " "It's frowned upon if you offer an amendment in the full committee if you aren't on the subcommittee. It's considered presumptuous to pose as an expert if you aren't on the subcommittee." Though records of full committee decisions are not available, members agree that subcommittee recommendations are "very rarely changed," "almost always approved," "changed one time in fifty," "very seldom changed," etc.

No subcommittee is likely to keep the deference of the full committee for long unless its recommendations have widespread support among its own members. To this end, a third norm—*subcommittee unity*—is expected to be observed by subcommittee members. Unity means a willingness to support (or not to oppose) the recommendations of one's own subcommittee. Reciprocity and unity are closely dependent upon one another. Reciprocity is difficult to maintain when subcommittees themselves are badly divided; and unity has little appeal unless reciprocity will subsequently be observed. The norm of reciprocity functions to minimize intersubcommittee conflict. The norm of unity functions to minimize intrasubcommittee conflict. Both are deemed essential to subcommittee influence.

One payoff for the original selection of "responsible legislators" is their special willingness to compromise in pursuit of subcommittee unity. The impulse to this end is registered most strongly at the time when the subcommittee meets in executive session to mark up the bill. Two ranking minority member explained this aspect of markup procedure in their subcommittees:

> If there's agreement, we go right along. If there's a lot of controversy we put the item aside and go on. Then, after a day or two, we may have a list of ten controversial items. We give and take and pound them down till we get agreement.

> We have a unanimous agreement on everything. If a fellow enters an objection and we can't talk him out of it—and sometimes we can get him to go along—that's it. We put it in there.

Once the bargain is struck, the subcommittee is expected to "stick together."

It is, of course, easier to achieve unity among the five, seven, or nine members of a subcommittee than among the fifty members of the full committee. But members are expected, wherever possible, to observe the norm of unity in the full committee as well. That is, they should not only defer to the recommendations of the subcommittee involved, but they should support (or not oppose) that recommendation when it reaches the floor in the form of a committee decision. On the floor, committee members believe, their power and prestige depend largely on the degree to which the norms of reciprocity and unity continue to be observed. Members warn each other that if they go to the floor in disarray they will be "rolled," "jumped," or "run over" by the membership. It is a cardinal maxim among committee members that "you can't turn an appropriations bill loose on the floor." Two senior subcommittee chairmen explain,

> We iron out our differences in committee. We argue it out and usually have a meeting of the minds, a composite view of the committee. . . . If we went on the floor in wide disagreement, they would say, "If you can't agree after listening to the testimony and discussing it, how can we understand it? We'll just vote on the basis of who we like the best."

> I tell them (the full committee) we should have a united front. If there are any objections or changes, we ought to hear it now, and not wash our dirty linen out on the floor. If we don't have a bill that we can all agree on and support, we ought not to report it out. To do that is like throwing a piece of meat to a bunch of hungry animals.

One of the most functional committee practices supporting the norm of unity is the tradition against minority reports in the subcommittee and in the full committee. It is symptomatic of committee integration that custom should proscribe the use of the most formal and irrevocable symbol of congressional committee disunity—the minority report. A few have been written—but only 9 out of a possible 141 during the 11 years 1947 to 1957. That is to say, 95 percent of all original appropriations bills in this period were reported out without dissent. The technique of "reserving" is the committee member's equivalent for the registering of dissent. In subcommittee or committee, when a member reserves, he goes on record informally by informing his colleagues that he reserves the right to disagree on a specified item later on in the proceedings. He may seek a change or support a change in that particular item in full committee or on the floor. But he does not publicize his dissent. The subcommittee or the full committee can then make an unopposed recommendation. The individual retains some freedom of maneuver without firm commitment. Often a member reserves on an appropriations item but takes no further action. A member explained how the procedure operates in subcommittee,

> If there's something I feel too strongly about, and just go along, I'll say "Mr. Chairman, we can have a unanimous report, but I reserve the right to bring this up in full committee. I feel duty bound to make a play for it and see if I can't sell it to the other members." But if I don't say anything, or don't reserve this right, and then I bring it up in full committee, they'll say, "Who are you trying to embarrass? You're a member of the team, aren't you? That's not the way to get along."

Disagreement cannot, of course, be eliminated from the committee. But the committee has accepted a method for ventilating it which produces a minimum of internal disruption. And members believe that the greater their internal unity, the greater the likelihood that their recommendations will pass the House.

The degree to which the role of the subcommittee member can be so played and subcommittee conflict thereby minimized depends upon the minimization of conflict between the majority and minority party subgroups. Nothing would be more disruptive to the committee's work than bitter and extended partisan controversy. It is, therefore, important to Appropriations Committee integration that a fourth norm— *minimal partisanship*—should be observed by members of both party contingents. Nearly every respondent emphasized, with approval, that "very little" or "not much" partisanship prevailed on the committee. One subcommittee chairman stated flatly, "My job is to keep down partisanship." A ranking minority member said, "You might think that we Republicans would defend the administration and the budget, but we don't." Majority and minority party ratios are constant and do not change (i.e., in 1958) to reflect changes in the strength of the controlling party. The committee operates with a completely non-partisan professional staff, which does not change in tune with shifts in party control. Requests for studies by the committee's investigating staff must be made by the chairman and ranking minority member of the full committee and by the chairman and ranking minority member of the subcommittee involved. Subcommittees can produce recommendations without dissent and the full committee can adopt reports without dissent precisely because party conflict is (during the period 1947 to 1961) the exception rather than the rule.

The committee is in no sense immune from the temperature of party conflict, but it does have a relatively high specific heat. Intense party strife or a strongly taken presidential position will get reflected in subcommittee and in committee recommendations. Sharp divisions in party policy were carried, with disruptive impact, into some areas of committee activity during the Eightieth Congress and subsequently, by way of reaction, into the Eighty-first Congress.[19] During the Eisenhower years, extraordinary presidential pleas, especially concerning foreign aid, were given special heed by the Republican members of the committee.[20] Partisanship is normally generated from the environment and not from within the committee's party groups. Partisanship is, therefore, likely to be least evident in subcommittee activity, stronger in the full committee, and most potent at the floor stage. Studies which have focused on roll-call analysis have stressed the influence of party in legislative decision-making.[21] In the appropriations process, at any rate, the floor stage probably represents party influence at its maximum. Our examination, by interview, of decision-making at the subcommittee and full committee level would stress the influence of committee-oriented norms—the strength of which tends to vary inversely with that of party bonds. In the secrecy and intimacy of the subcommittee and full committee hearing rooms, the member finds it easy to compromise on questions of more or less, to take money from one program and give it to another and, in general, to avoid yes-or-no

19. See, for example, the internal conflict on the subcommittee dealing with the Labor Department. *Congressional Record* 93, pp. 2465–2562 passim; *Congressional Record* 94, pp. 7605–7.

20. See, for example, the unusual minority report of committee Republicans on the foreign aid appropriations bill in 1960. Their protest against committee cuts in the budget estimates was the result of strenuous urging by the Eisenhower Administration. House Report No. 1798, *Mutual Security and Related Agency Appropriation Bill,* 1961, Eighty-sixth Congress, 2d sess. 1960.

21. David Truman, *The Congressional Party* (New York, 1959); Julius Turner, *Party and Constituency: Pressures on Congress* (Baltimore, 1951).

type party stands. These decisions, taken in response to the integrative norms of the committee, are the most important ones in the entire appropriations process.

Role Integration

The roles of subcommittee member and party member are common to all.

Other more specific decision-making positions are allocated among the members. Different positions produce different roles, and in an integrated system those too must fit together. Integration, in other words, must be achieved through the complementarity or reciprocity of roles as well as through a similarity of roles. This may mean a pattern in which expectations are so different that there is very little contact between individuals; or it may mean a pattern in which contacts require the working out of an involved system of exchange of obligations and rewards.[22] In either case, the desired result is the minimization of conflict among prominent committee roles. Two crucial instances of role reciprocity on the committee involve the seniority positions of old-timer and newcomer and the leadership positions of chairman and ranking minority member, on both the full committee and on each subcommittee.

The differentiation between senior and junior members is the broadest definition of who shall and who shall not actively participate in committee decisions. Of a junior member, it will be said, "Oh, he doesn't count—what I mean is, he hasn't been on the committee long enough." He is not expected to and ordinarily does not have much influence. His role is that of apprentice. He is expected to learn the business and the norms of the committee by applying himself to its work. He is expected to acquiesce in an arrangement which gives most influence (except in affairs involving him locally) to the veterans of the group. Newcomers will be advised to "follow the chairman until you get your bearings. For the first two years, follow the chairman. He knows." "Work hard, keep quiet, and attend the committee sessions. We don't want to listen to some new person coming in here." And newcomers perceive their role in identical terms: "You have to sit in the back seat and edge up little by little." "You just go to subcommittee

22. The ideas of "reciprocity" and "complementarity," which are used interchangeably here, are discussed in Alvin Gouldner, "The Norm of Reciprocity," *American Sociological Review* (April, 1960). Most helpful in explaining the idea of a role system has been the work of J. Wahlke, H. Eulau, W. Buchanan, and L. Ferguson. See their study, *The Legislative System* (New York, 1962), esp. Intro.

meetings and assimilate the routine. The new members are made to feel welcome, but you have a lot of rope-learning to do before you carry much weight."

At every stage of committee work, this differentiation prevails. There is remarkable agreement on the radically different sets of expectations involved. During the hearings, the view of the elders is that "Newcomers . . . don't know what the score is and they don't have enough information to ask intelligent questions." A newcomer described his behavior in typically similar terms: "I attend all the hearings and studied and collected information that I can use next year. I'm just marking time now." During the crucial subcommittee markup, the newcomer will have little opportunity to speak, save in locally important matters. A subcommittee chairman stated the norm from his viewpoint this way: "When we get a compromise, nobody's going to break that up. If someone tries, we sit on him fast. We don't want young people who throw bricks or slow things down." And a newcomer reciprocated, describing his markup conduct: "I'm not provocative. I'm in there for information. They're the experts in the field. I go along." In full committee, on the floor, and in conference committee, the committee's senior members take the lead and the junior members are expected to follow. The apprentice role is common to all new members of the House. But it is wrong to assume that each committee will give it the same emphasis. Some pay it scant heed.[23] The Appropriations Committee makes it a cornerstone of its internal structure.

Among the committee's veterans, the key roles are those of committee chairman and ranking minority member, and their counterparts in every subcommittee. It is a measure of committee integration and the low degree of partisanship that considerable reciprocity obtains between these roles. Their partisan status nevertheless sets limits to the degree of possible integration. The chairman is given certain authority which he and only he can exercise. But save in times of extreme party controversy, the expectation is that consultation and cooperation between the chairman [and the] ranking minority member shall lubricate the committee's entire work. For example, by committee tradition, its chairman and [its] ranking minority member are both ex officio voting members of each subcommittee and of every conference committee. The two of them thus have joint access at every stage of the internal process. A subcommittee chairman, too, is expected to discuss matters of scheduling and agenda with his opposite minority number. He is expected to work with him during the markup session and to give him (and normally only him) an opportunity to

23. For example, the Committee on Education and Labor, see footnote 28.

read and comment on the subcommittee report.[24] A ranking minority member described his subcommittee markup procedure approvingly:

> Frequently the chairman has a figure which he states. Sometimes he will have no figure, and he'll turn to me and say, "_____, what do you think?" Maybe I'll have a figure. It's very flexible. Everyone has a chance to say what he thinks, and we'll move it around. Sometimes it takes a long time. . . . He's a rabid partisan on the floor, but he is a very fair man in the subcommittee.

Where influence is shared, an important exchange of rewards occurs. The chairman gains support for his leadership and the ranking minority member gains intracommittee power. The committee as a whole insures against the possibility of drastic change in its internal structure by giving to its key minority members a stake in its operation. Chairmen and ranking minority members will, in the course of time, exchange positions; and it is expected that such a switch will produce no form of retribution nor any drastic change in the functioning of the committee. Reciprocity of roles, in this case, promotes continued integration. A ranking minority member testified to one successful arrangement when he took the floor in the Eighty-third Congress to say:

> The gentleman and I have been seesawing back and forth on this committee for some time. He was chairman in the Eightieth Congress. I had the privilege of serving as chairman in the Eighty-first and Eighty-second Congress. Now he is back in the saddle. I can say that he has never failed to give me his utmost cooperation, and I have tried to give him the same cooperation during his service as chairman of this committee. We seldom disagree, but we have found out that we can disagree without being disagreeable. Consequently, we have unusual harmony on this committee.[25]

Reciprocity between chairmen and ranking minority members on the Appropriations Committee is to some incalculable degree a function of the stability of membership which allows a pair of particular individuals to work out the kind of personal accommodation described above. The close working relationship of Clarence Cannon and John Taber, whose service on the committee totals sixty-eight years and who have been changing places as chairman and ranking minority member for nineteen years, highlights and sustains a pattern of majority-minority reciprocity throughout the group.

24. See the exchange in *Congressional Record* 101, pp. 3832, 3844, 3874.
25. *Congressional Record* 99, p. 4933.

Internal Control Mechanisms

The expectations which apply to subcommittee, to party, to veterans and newcomers, to chairmen, and to ranking minority members prescribe highly integrative behaviors. We have concentrated on these expectations and have both illustrated and assumed the close correlation between expected and actual behavior. This does not mean that all the norms of the committee have been canvassed. Nor does it mean that deviation from the integrative norms does not occur. It does. From what can be gathered, however, from piecing together a study of the public record on appropriations from 1947 to 1961 with interview materials, the committee has been markedly successful in maintaining a stable internal structure over time. As might be expected, therefore, changes and threats of change have been generated more from the environment—when outsiders consider the committee as unresponsive—than from inside the subsystem itself. One source of internal stability, and an added reason for assuming a correlation between expected and actual behavior, is the existence of what appear to be reasonably effective internal control mechanisms. Two of these are the socialization processes applied to newcomers and the sanctioning mechanisms applicable to all committee members.

Socialization is in part a training in perception. Before members of a group can be expected to behave in accordance with its norms, they must learn to see and interpret the world around them with reasonable similarity. The socialization of the committee newcomer during his term or two of apprenticeship serves to bring his perceptions and his attitudes sufficiently into line with those of the other members to serve as a basis for committee integration. The committee, as we have seen, is chosen from congressmen whose political flexibility connotes an aptitude for learning new lessons of power. Furthermore, its members' high degree of satisfaction with the group increases their susceptibility to its processes of learning and training.

For example, one-half of the committee's Democrats are Northerners and Westerners from urban constituencies, whose voting records are just as "liberal" on behalf of domestic social welfare programs as non-committee Democrats from like constituencies. They come to the committee favorably disposed toward the high level of federal spending necessary to support such programs, and with no sense of urgency about the committee's tasks of guarding the treasury or reducing budget estimates. Given the criteria governing their selection, however, they come without rigid preconceptions and with a built-in responsiveness to the socialization processes of any legislative group of which they are members. It is crucial to committee integration that they learn to temper their potentially disruptive welfare-state ideology with a conservative's concern for saving money. They must change their perceptions and attitudes sufficiently to view the committee's tasks in nearly the same terms as their more conservative southern Democratic and Republican colleagues. What their elders perceive as reality (i.e., the disposition of executives to ask for more money than is necessary) they, too, must see as reality. A subcommittee chairman explained:

> When you have sat on the committee, you see that these bureaus are always asking for more money—always up, never down. They want to build up their organization. You reach the point—I have—where it sickens you, where you rebel against it. Year after year, they want more money. They say, "Only $50,000 this year," but you know the pattern. Next year they'll be back for $100,000, then $200,000. The younger members haven't been on the committee long enough, haven't had the experience to know this.

The younger men, in this case the younger liberals, do learn from their committee experience. Within one or two terms, they are differentiating between themselves and the "wildeyed spenders" or the "free spenders" in the House. "Some of these guys would spend you through the roof," exclaimed one liberal of moderate seniority. Repeated exposure to committee work and to fellow members has altered their perceptions and their attitudes in money matters. Half a dozen northern Democrats of low or moderate seniority agreed with one of their number who said: "Yes, it's true. I can see it myself. I suppose I came here a flaming liberal; but as the years go by I get more conservative. You just hate like hell to spend all this money. . . . You come to the point where you say, 'By God, this is enough jobs.'" These men will remain more inclined toward spending than their committee colleagues, but their perceptions and hence their attitudes have been brought close enough to the others to support a consensus on tasks. They are responsive to appeals on budget-cutting grounds that would not have registered earlier and which remain meaningless to liberals outside the committee. In cases, therefore, where committee selection does not and cannot initially produce individuals with a predisposition toward protecting the treasury, the same result is achieved by socialization.

Socialization is a training in behavior as well as in perception. For the newcomer, conformity to norms in specific situations is insured through the appropriate application, by the committee veterans, of rewards and punishments. For the committee member who serves his apprenticeship creditably, the passage of time holds the promise that he will inherit a position of influence. He may, as an incentive, be given some small reward early in his committee career. One man, in his second year, had been assigned the task of specializing in one particular program. However narrow the scope of his specialization, it had placed him on the road to influence within the committee. He explained with evident pleasure:

> The first year, you let things go by. You can't participate. But you learn by watching the others operate. The next year, you know what you're interested in and when to step in. . . . For instance, I've become an expert on the _____ program. The chairman said to me, "This is something you ought to get interested in." I did; and now I'm the expert on the committee. Whatever I say on that, the other members listen to me and do what I want.

At some later date, provided he continues to observe committee norms, he will be granted additional influence, perhaps through a prominent floor role. A model committee man of moderate seniority who had just attained to this stage of accomplishment, and who had suffered through several political campaigns back home fending off charges that he was a do-nothing congressman, spoke about the rewards he was beginning to reap.

> When you perform well on the floor when you bring out a bill, and members know that you know the bill, you develop prestige with other members of Congress. They come over and ask you what you think, because they know you've studied it. You begin to get a reputation beyond your subcommittee. And you get inner satisfaction, too. You don't feel that you're down here doing nothing.

The first taste of influence which comes to men on this committee is compensation for the frustrations of apprenticeship. Committee integration in general, and the meshing of roles between elders and newcomers in particular, rests on the fact that conformity to role expectations over time does guarantee to the young positive rewards— the very kind of rewards of power, prestige, and personal satisfaction which led most of them to seek committee membership in the first place.

The important function of apprenticeship is that it provides the necessary time during which socialization can go forward. And teaching proceeds with the aid of punishments as well as rewards. Should a new member inadvertently or deliberately run afoul of committee norms during his apprenticeship, he will find himself confronted with negative sanctions ranging in subtlety from "jaundiced eyes" to a changed subcommittee assignment. Several members, for example, recalled their earliest encounter with the norm of unity and the tradition against minority reports. One remembered his attempt to file a minority report. "The chairman was pretty upset about it. It's just a tradition, I guess, not to have minority reports. I didn't know it was a tradition. When I said I was going to write a minority report, some eyebrows were raised. The chairman said it just wasn't the thing to do. Nothing more was said about it. But it wasn't a very popular thing to do, I guess." He added that he had not filed one since.

Some younger members have congenital difficulty in observing the norms of the apprentice's role. In the Eighty-sixth Congress, these types tended to come from the Republican minority. The minority newcomers (described by one of the men who selected them as "eight young, energetic, fighting conservatives") were a group of economy-minded individuals some of whom chafed against any barrier which kept them from immediate influence on committee policy. Their reaction was quite different from that of the young Democrats, whose difficulty was in learning to become economy-minded, but who did not actively resent their lack of influence. One freshman, who felt that "the appropriations system is lousy, inadequate and old-fashioned," recalled that he had spoken out in full committee against the recommendations of a subcommittee of which he was not a member. Having failed, he continued to oppose the recommendation during floor debate. By speaking up, speaking in relation to the work of another subcommittee and by opposing a committee recommendation, he had violated the particular norms of his apprentice role as well of the generally applicable norms of reciprocity and unity. He explained what he had learned, but remained only partially socialized:

> They want to wash their dirty linen in the committee and they want no opposition afterward. They let me say my piece in committee. . . . But I just couldn't keep quiet. I said some things on the floor, and I found out that's about all they would take. . . . If you don't get along with your committee and have their support, you don't get anyhing accomplished around here. . . . I'm trying to be a loyal, cooperative member of the committee. You hate to be a stinker; but I'm still picking at the little things because I can't work on the big things. There's nothing for the new men to do, so they have to find places to needle in order to take some part in it.

Another freshman, who had deliberately violated apprenticeship norms by trying to ask "as many questions as the chairman" during subcommittee hearings, reported a story of unremitting counteraction against his deviation:

> In the hearings, I have to wait sometimes nine or ten hours for a chance; and he hopes I'll get tired and stay home. I've had to wait till some pretty unreasonable hours. Once I've gotten the floor, though, I've been able to make a good case. Sometimes I've been the only person there. . . . He's all-powerful. He's got all the power. He wouldn't think of taking me on a trip with him when he goes to hold hearings. Last year, he went to _____. He wouldn't give me a nudge there. And in the hearings, when I'm questioning a witness, he'll keep butting in so that my case won't appear to be too rosy.

Carried on over a period of two years, this behavior resulted in considerable personal friction between a committee elder and the newcomer. Other members of his subcommittee pointedly gave him a great lack of support for his nonconformity. "They tried to slow him down and tone him down a little," not because he and his subcommittee chairman disagreed, but on the grounds that the committee has developed accepted ways of disagreeing which minimize, rather than exacerbate, interpersonal friction.

One internal threat to committee integration comes from new members who from untutored perceptions, from ignorance of norms, or from dissatisfaction with the apprentice role may not act in accordance with committee expectations. The seriousness of this threat is minimized, however, by the fact that the deviant newcomer does not possess sufficient resources to affect adversely the operation of the system. Even if he does not respond immediately to the application of sanctions, he can be held in check and subjected to an extended and (given the frequency of interaction among members) intensive period of socialization. The success of committee socialization is indicated by the fact that whereas wholesale criticism of committee operations was frequently voiced among junior members, it had disappeared among the men of moderate experience. And what these middle-seniority members now accept as the facts of committee life, the veterans vigorously assert and defend as the essentials of a smoothly functioning system. Satisfaction with the committee's internal structure increases with length of committee service.

An important reason for changing member attitudes is that those who have attained leadership positions have learned, as newcomers characteristically have not, that their conformity to committee norms is the ultimate source of their influence inside the group. Freshman members do not as readily perceive the degree to which interpersonal influence is rooted in obedience to group norms. They seem to convert their own sense of powerlessness into the view that the committee's leaders possess, by virtue of their positions, arbitrary, absolute, and awesome power. Typically, they say: "If you're a subcommittee chairman, it's your committee." "The chairman runs the show. He gets what he wants. He decides what he wants and gets it through." Older members of the committee, however, view the power of the leaders as a highly contingent and revocable grant, tendered by the committee for so long and only so long as their leaders abide by committee expectations. In commenting on internal influence, their typical reaction is: "Of course, the committee wouldn't follow him if it didn't want to. He has a great deal of respect. He's an able man, a hard-working man." "He knows the bill backwards and forwards. He works hard, awfully hard and the members know it." Committee leaders have an imposing set of formal prerogatives. But they can capitalize on them only if they command the respect, confidence, and deference of their colleagues.

It is basic to committee integration that members who have the greatest power to change the system evidence the least disposition to do so. Despite their institutional conservatism, however, committee elders do occasionally violate the norms applicable to them and hence represent a potential threat to successful integration. Excessive deviation from committee expectations by some leaders will bring countermeasures by other leaders. Thus, for example, the chairman and his subcommittee chairmen exercise reciprocal controls over one another's behavior. The chairman has the authority to appoint the chairman and members of each subcommittee and fix its jurisdiction. "He runs the committee. He has a lot of power," agrees one subcommittee chairman. "But it's all done on the basis of personal friendship. If he tries to get too big, the members can whack him down by majority vote."

In the Eighty-fourth Congress, Chairman Cannon attempted an unusually broad reorganization of subcommittee jurisdictions. The subcommittee chairman most adversely affected rallied his senior colleagues against the chairman's action on the ground that it was an excessive violation of role expectations and threatening to subcommittee autonomy. Faced with the prospect of a negative committee vote, the chairman was forced to act in closer conformity to the expectations of the other leaders. As one participant described the episode,

> Mr. Cannon, for reasons of his own, tried to bust up one of the subcommittees. We didn't like that. . . . He was breaking up the whole committee. A couple of weeks later, a few of the senior members got together and worked out a compromise. By that time, he had seen a few things, so we went to him and talked to him and worked it out.

On the subcommittees, too, it is the veterans of both parties who will levy sanctions against an offending chairman. It is they who speak of "cutting down to size" and "trimming the whiskers" of leaders who become "too cocky," "too stubborn," or who "do things wrong too often." Committee integration is underwritten by the fact that no member, high or low, is permanently immune from the operation of its sanctioning mechanisms.

III

Data concerning internal committee activity can be organized and presented in various ways. One way is to use key functional problems like integration as the focal points for descriptive analysis. On the basis of our analysis (and without, for the time being, having devised any precise measure of integration), we are led to the summary observation that the House Appropriations Committee appears to be a well-integrated, if not an extremely well-integrated, committee. The question arises as to whether anything can be gained from this study other than a description of one property of one political subsystem. If it is reasonable to assume that the internal life of a congressional committee affects all legislative activity involving that committee, and if it is reasonable to assume that the analysis of a committee's internal relationships will produce useful knowledge about legislative behavior, some broader implications for this study are indicated.

In the first place, the success of the House Appropriations Committee in solving the problem of integration probably does have important consequences for the appropriations process. Some of the possible relationships can be stated as hypotheses and tested; others can be suggested as possible guides to understanding. All of them require further research. Of primary interest is the relationship between integration and the power of the committee. There is little doubt about the fact of committee power. Of the 443 separate case histories of bureau appropriations examined, the House accepted committee recommendations in 387, or 87.4 percent of them; and in 159, or 33.6 percent of the cases, the House Committee's original recommendations on money amounts were the exact ones enacted into law. The hypothesis that the greater the degree of committee unity the greater the probability that its recommendations will be accepted is being tested as part of a larger study.[26] House committee integration may be

26. Cf. Dwaine Marvick, "Congressional Appropriations Politics," unpublished manuscript (Columbia, 1952).

a key factor in producing House victories in conference committee. This relationship, too, might be tested. Integration appears to help provide the House conferees with a feeling of confidence and superiority which is one of their important advantages in the mix of psychological factors affecting conference deliberations.

Another suggested consequence of high integration is that party groups have a relatively small influence upon appropriations decisions. It suggests, too, that committee-oriented behavior should be duly emphasized in any analysis of congressional oversight of administrative activity by this committee. Successful integration promotes the achievement of the committee's goals, and doubtless helps account for the fairly consistent production of budget-cutting decisions. Another consequence will be found in the strategies adopted by people seeking favorable committee decisions. For example, the characteristic lines of contact from executive officials to the committee will run to the chairman and the ranking minority member (and to the professional staff man) of the single subcommittee handling their agency's appropriations. The ways in which the committee achieves integration may even affect the success or failure of a bureau in getting its appropriations. Committee members, for instance, will react more favorably toward an administrator who conforms to their self-image of the hard-working master-of-detail than to one who does not—and committee response to individual administrators bulks large in their determinations.

Finally, the internal integration of this committee helps to explain the extraordinary stability, since 1920, of appropriations procedures in the face of repeated proposals to change them through omnibus appropriations, legislative budgets, new budgetary forms, item veto, treasury borrowing, etc. Integration is a stabilizing force, and the stability of the House Appropriations Committee has been a force for stabilization throughout the entire process. It was, for example, the disagreement between Cannon and Taber which led to the indecisiveness reflected in the short-lived experiment with a single appropriations bill.[27] One need only examine the conditions most likely to decrease committee integration to ascertain some of the critical factors for producing changes in the appropriations process. A description of integration is also an excellent baseline from which to analyze changes in internal structure.

All of these are speculative propositions which call for further research. But they suggest, as a second implication, that committee

27. See Dalmas Nelson, "The Omnibus Appropriations Act of 1950," *Journal of Politics* (May, 1953).

integration does have important consequences for legislative activity and, hence, that it is a key variable in the study of legislative politics. It would seem, therefore, to be a fruitful focal point for the study of other congressional committees.[28] Comparative committee analysis could usefully be devoted to (1) the factors which tend to increase or decrease integration; (2) the degree to which integration is achieved; and (3) the consequences of varying degrees of integration for committee behavior and influence. If analyses of committee integration are of any value, they should encourage the analysis and the classification of congressional committees along functional lines. And they should lead to the discussion of interrelated problems of committee survival. Functional classifications of committees (i.e., well- or poorly integrated) derived from a large number of descriptive analyses of several functional problems may prove helpful in constructing more general propositions about the legislative process.

28. This view has been confirmed by the results of interviews conducted by the author with members of the House Committee on Education and Labor, together with an examination of that committee's activity in one policy area. They indicate very significant contrasts between the internal structure of that committee and the Appropriations Committee—contrasts which center around their comparative success in meeting the problem of integration. The House Committee on Education and Labor appears to be a poorly integrated committee. Its internal structure is characterized by a great deal of subgroup conflict, relatively little role reciprocity, and minimally effective internal control mechanisms. External concerns, like those of party, constituency, and clientele groups, are probably more effective in determining its decisions than is likely to be the case in a well-integrated committee. An analysis of the internal life of the Committee on Education and Labor, drawn partly from interviews with nineteen members of that group, will appear in a forthcoming study, *Federal Aid to Education and National Politics,* by Professor Frank Munger and the author, to be published by Syracuse University Press. See also Nicholas R. Masters, op. cit., note 8 above, pp. 354–55 and Seymour Scher, "Congressional Committee Members as Independent Agency Overseers: A Case Study," *American Political Science Review* 54 (December, 1960): 911–20.

8

The Agriculture Committee and the Problem of Representation

Charles O. Jones

Students of American politics are told that our political system is fundamentally a *representative* democracy. Concepts of representation, since Burke, have commonly employed his distinction between action taken in response to instructions from constituents and action based on an independent appraisal of the national interest.[1] A very recent analysis has offered a refinement of this, by distinguishing three

Reprinted by permission of the author and publisher from "Representation in Congress: The Case of the House Agriculture Committee," *American Political Science Review* 55 (June, 1961): 358–67. Copyright © 1961 by the American Political Science Association. The author wishes to acknowledge the generosity of Congressman E. Y. Berry (R., S.D.) in providing office space and other aids, as well as the helpful suggestions and comments of Leon D. Epstein and Ralph K. Huitt, University of Wisconsin; Samuel C. Patterson, State University of Iowa; and Wayne G. Rollins, Wellesley College.

1. Some of the most useful studies of representation are: Charles Beard and J. D. Lewis, "Representative Government in Evolution," *American Political Science Review* 26 (April, 1932): 223–40; Francis M. Carney, "Concepts of Political Representation in the United States Today," unpublished Ph.D. dissertation, University of California, Los Angeles, 1956; Alfred de Grazia, *Public and Republic* (New York, 1951); John A. Fairlie, "The Nature of Political Representation," *American Political Science Review* 34 (April and June, 1940): 236–48, 456–66; H. F. Gosnell, *Democracy: The Threshold of Freedom* (New York, 1948); James Hogan, *Election and Representation* (Oxford, 1945). For an extended bibliography, see Charles O. Jones, "The Relationship of Congressional Committee Action to a Theory of Representation," unpublished Ph.D. dissertation, University of Wisconsin, 1960, pp. 413–28, from which materials for this article were drawn.

types: "delegate," "trustee," and "politico."[2] Theory and history alike tell us, however, that a representative does not invariably act in only one of these roles. There have been a number of empirical studies of representatives, few of which concentrate on specific policy fields;[3] and studies also of the play of interests in the enactment of specific legislation, but without a systematic account of the legislative committee members involved, acting in their representative capacities as they saw them. How then can we tell when to expect a representative to view his role in one way rather than another? The aim of this article is to shed a little light on some aspects of this broad question by means of a case study.

The subjects of the study were the members of the House Agriculture Committee and their action on the omnibus farm legislation (HR 12954 and S 4071) in 1958 (Eighty-fifth Congress, second session).[4] Most of the data were obtained from interviews[5] with thirty of the thirty-four committee members, but, in addition, the specific stands of members in subcommittees, the full committee, and on the House floor were traced, through the printed hearings and the *Congressional Record* of floor debates. Finally, other interested and knowledgeable people were interviewed, newspaper accounts were studied, and the characteristics of constituencies were examined.

For analytical purposes the most useful concept I developed to account for the behavior of a representative was one I shall call his "policy constituency." This may be defined as those interests within his geographical or legal constituency which he perceives to be affected by the policy under consideration. When he regards these interests as actively and homogeneously concerned, they are ordinarily sufficient

2. Heinz Eulau et. al., "The Role of the Representative: Some Empirical Observations on the Theory of Edmund Burke," *American Political Science Review* 53 (September, 1959): 742–56.

3. Two studies which do concentrate on specific policies are: Lewis Dexter, "The Representative and His District," *Human Organization* 16 (Spring, 1957): 2–13 [Reprinted as Chapter I of the present volume]; and L. E. Gleeck, "Ninety-six Congressmen Make up Their Minds," *Public Opinion Quarterly* 4 (March, 1940): 3–24.

4. I selected a committee which is more likely than most to be constituency-oriented. Commonly, representatives from farm areas are anxious to get on this committee to represent their constituency interests, though interviews with Republican members indicate that this generalization would now need modification since recent farm policies have not been notably successful. See Nicholas A. Masters, "House Committee Assignments," *American Political Science Review,* 53 (June, 1961): 345–57.

5. Focused interviews were conducted in March, 1959. An interview guide was followed but it was kept flexible. I wrote as the respondents discussed the questions and typed the responses immediately after the interview. All respondents were guaranteed anonymity.

to determine his public stand. When he sees them as weak, indifferent, or divided, other factors come into play. But he is affected too by the nature of the committee institution within which the policy is being formed.

I. The House Agriculture Committee and Its Work

Organization

In 1958 a Republican President was again faced with a Democratic Congress in a congressional campaign year. The margin of control for Democrats in the House Agriculture Committee was a less-than-comfortable four votes; the split was nineteen to fifteen. The margin in subcommittees was one vote in most cases.

Harold D. Cooley (D., N.C.) was chairman in 1958, as he had been in every Democratic Congress since 1949. Members did not class him among the strong House committee chairmen, but respected him as fair and honest. W. R. Poage (D., Tex.) was vice-chairman. The Agriculture Committee was the only House committee in 1958 to have a vice-chairman, and one member suggested that this was due to the chairman's complete and admitted willingness to share the responsibility of leadership with the very forceful, knowledgeable, and capable "Bob" Poage.

The ranking minority member in 1958 was William S. Hill (R., Colo.). Like Cooley, he was not considered a strong leader and it became apparent that Charles Hoeven (R., Ia.) was recognized as the spokesman of the minority viewpoint. Hoeven has since become the ranking minority member.

The principal work units in the House Agriculture Committee are the subcommittees. In 1958 there were eighteen subcommittees of two kinds—ten commodity subcommittees and eight special-action subcommittees. The former are more important since they consider legislation designed to solve the many crises for specific commodities. Usually a member is assigned to at least one commodity subcommittee of his choice. The chairman consults the ranking minority leader but has the last word on appointments. Actually few decisions have to be made, since most commodity subcommittees are permanent and their membership is continuing; only the new members need assignments. The size of subcommittees varies considerably (from twelve for tobacco to five for rice), giving the chairman some flexibility in case several members are interested in one commodity

Finally, the House Agriculture Committee has been able to rely on a small expert staff consisting of a counsel, research director, majority and minority clerks, and five staff assistants.

Representing Agriculture

As might be expected, congressmen from constituencies with significant interests in farm policy make up the membership of the House Agriculture Committee. In 1958 there was but one exception to this rule—Victor Anfuso, Democrat from Brooklyn. Thirteen of the nineteen Democrats came from areas where tobacco, cotton, peanuts, and rice are the principal commodities. Republican committee members came from areas producing corn, hogs, small grain, wheat, and areas where the farming is diversified. Table 8–1 shows the geographical distribution of members.

Table 8–1. Geographical Representation on the House Agriculture Committee

Land-Use Area	Democrats	Republicans	Totals
Northeast	1	3	4
Appalachian	5	—	5
Southeast	3	—	3
Mississippi Delta	2	—	2
Southern Plains	3	1	4
Corn Belt	2	3	5
Lake States	2	2	4
Northern Plains	—	3	3
Mountain	—	2	2
Pacific	1	1	2
Totals	19	15	34

Note: Based on the areas presented in Bureau of Census and Department of Agriculture, Bureau of Agricultural Economics, *Land Utilization, A Graphic Summary, 1950* (December, 1952), p. 5.

Committee members may be classified by commodities of greatest interest to their constituencies, as in Table 8–2. Commodities receiving price supports are grown in the constituencies of members of all six groups there listed. The *basic* commodities, so labeled by the Agricultural Adjustment Act of 1938, are corn, cotton, tobacco, rice, wheat, and peanuts; price supports have been mandatory for them. An increasing number of *nonbasics* have also received price supports, e.g., milk and wool. The "diversified" (mainly nonbasics) group often find their interests conflicting with those of representatives in the other groups.

**Table 8–2. Committee Members and Their Constituencies'
Commodities**

1. *Corn and Livestock*	4. *Diversified (nonbasics)*
Harrison (R., Neb.)	Anfuso (D., N.Y.)
Harvey (R., Ind.)	Dague (R., Pa.)
Hill (R., Colo.)[a]	Dixon (R., Ut.)
Hoeven (R., Ia.)	Hagen (D., Calif.)
Polk (D., Oh.)	McIntire (R., Me.)
Simpson (R., Ill.)[a]	Teague (R., Calif.)
2. *Cotton and Rice*	5. *Tobacco*
Abernethy (D., Miss.)	Abbitt (D., Va.)
Albert (D., Okla.)	Bass (D., Tenn.)
Gathings (D., Ark.)	Cooley (D., N.C.)
Grant (D., Ala.)	Jennings (D., Va.)
Jones (D., Mo.)	McMillan (D., S.C.)
Poage (D., Tex.)	Matthews (D., Fla.)
Thompson (D., Tex.)	Watts (D., Ky.)
3. *Dairy, Livestock, Small Grains*	6. *Wheat*
Johnson (D., Wisc.)	Belcher (R., Okla.)
Knutson (D., Minn.)	Krueger (R., N.D.)[a]
Quie (R., Minn.)	Smith (R., Kan.)
Tewes (R., Wisc.)	
Williams (R., N.Y.)[a]	

Note: Members were classified on the basis of their constituencies' principal commodities, as listed in the *Census of Agriculture,* Vol. 1, 1956, and interviews with the members.
[a] These members were not interviewed. Simpson, Williams, and Krueger clearly belong to the groups to which they have been assigned. Hill might also have been included in the wheat group.

They complain that their farmers are at a disadvantage since their nonbasics either do not receive price supports or receive less support than the basics; the price supports for the few basics grown do not make up for the deprivation of profits attributable to acreage and marketing controls (the complaint of California cotton farmers); and they must pay higher prices for the basics as well as pay higher taxes.

Almost without exception the six groups show an alignment between commodity interests and party allegiance. The corn and livestock group has five Republicans and one Democrat; the cotton and rice group, seven Democrats; the dairy, livestock, small grains group, two Democrats and three Republicans; the diversified group, four Republicans and two Democrats; the tobacco group, seven Democrats; and the wheat group, three or four Republicans.[6] Consequently, differ-

6. Four, if Hill were also assigned to it. Anfuso is assigned to the diversified (nonbasics) group because he does not fit elsewhere. The overlap between the corn and livestock, and the diary, livestock, small grains group is explained by the fact that livestock production is important to both but corn is more important in one and dairy products in the other.

Table 8–3. Constituency Interests and Commodity Subcommittee Assignments

Member[a]	Major Agricultural Interests In Constituency	Commodity Subcommittees
Democrats		
Poage	Cotton, Livestock, Peanuts	Cotton; Livestock and Feed Grains (C)
Grant	Cotton, Peanuts, Wood Products	Forests (C); Peanuts
Gathings	Cotton, Rice, Soybeans	Cotton (C); Rice; Soybeans-Oilseeds
McMillan	Cotton, Tobacco, Peanuts	Forests; Peanuts (C); Tobacco
Abernethy	Cotton	Cotton; Dairy Products (C); Soybeans-Oilseeds
Albert	Cotton, Livestock	Livestock and Feed Grains; Peanuts; Wheat (C)
Abbitt	Tobacco, Peanuts	Tobacco (C); Peanuts
Polk	Feed Grains, Livestock, Dairy	Dairy Products; Tobacco
Thompson	Rice, Cotton, Peanuts	Rice (C); Poultry-Eggs
Jones	Cotton, Livestock, Soybeans	Rice; Soybeans-Oilseeds (C); Wheat
Watts	Tobacco, Feed Grains, Seeds	Tobacco; Wheat
Hagen	Cotton, Alfalfa Seed, Potatoes, Fruit	Cotton; Soybeans-Oilseeds
Johnson	Dairy, Forests, Livestock	Dairy Products; Forests; Poultry-Eggs
Anfuso	None	Poultry-Eggs
Bass	Tobacco, Cotton	Tobacco; Wheat
Knutson	Wheat, Dairy, Feed Grains	Dairy Products
Jennings	Tobacco, Livestock	Livestock and Feed Grains; Tobacco; Wheat
Matthews	Tobacco, Peanuts, Vegetables	Livestock and Feed Grains; Tobacco
Republicans		
Hoeven	Feed Grains, Livestock	Livestock and Feed Grains; Soybeans-Oilseeds
Simpson	Feed Grains, Livestock	Cotton; Livestock and Feed Grains; Soybeans-Oilseeds; Tobacco
Dague	Tobacco, Truck Farming, Poultry, Dairy	Tobacco; Wheat
Harvey	Feed Grains, Livestock	Livestock and Feed Grains; Soybeans-Oilseeds
Belcher	Wheat	Cotton; Peanuts; Wheat
McIntire	Forests, Poultry, Potatoes	Forests; Poultry-Eggs, Tobacco
Williams	Dairy, Truck Farming	Dairy Products; Rice
Harrison	Feed Grains, Livestock	Peanuts; Poultry-Eggs

Table 8–3. (continued)

Member[a]	Major Agricultural Interests In Constituency	Commodity Subcommittees
Dixon	Wheat, Potatoes, Small Grain, Sugar Beets	Forests; Poultry-Eggs
Smith	Wheat	Peanuts; Wheat
Krueger	Wheat, Small Grains	Rice; Wheat
Teague	Vegetables, Fruit, Small Grains, Cotton	Cotton; Forests
Tewes	Dairy, Tobacco, Livestock	Dairy Products; Tobacco
Quie	Dairy, Feed Grains, Livestock	Dairy Products; Tobacco

Note: The major interests were deduced from the *Census of Agriculture, 1954,* Vol. 1, 1956, and from interviews with members.
[a] Members listed according to committee rank. Chairman Cooley, whose principal interests were tobacco, cotton, and poultry, and William Hill, whose principal interests were wheat, feed grains, and sugar beets, were ex officio members of all subcommittees by virtue of their positions as chairman and ranking minority member, respectively.

ent commodities will ordinarily be favored when different parties are in control. For example, cotton, rice, and tobacco usually receive more attention when the Democrats are a majority in the committee.[7]

Committee organization has been strongly influenced by the commodity problems in agriculture. First, subcommittees are established to deal with currently critical commodity problems. Second, members are assigned to commodity subcommittees on the basis of their constituency interests. Table 8–3 shows the high correlation prevailing. Only one Democrat (Anfuso) was assigned to no commodity subcommittee representing producers in his constituency and he has no agricultural production at all in his Brooklyn district, though the poultry trade is important there.[8] Two Republicans (Harrison and Dixon) found themselves on subcommittees of little or no concern to their constituencies. Significantly, both of these members were identified by other members as being supporters of Secretary Benson's recommendations.

Party considerations dictate that some members must be on subcommittees of no concern to their constituencies: there must be

7. Recent Democratic victories in the Middle West have changed the pattern somewhat. There are more Democrats from corn, livestock, and dairy constituencies than previously.

8. Anfuso almost monopolized the committee hearings on the extension of the Agricultural Trade Development and Assistance Act, since many New York City firms were testifying. His activity in these hearings provided unexpected evidence of constituency-representative relationships.

Republicans on the cotton subcommittee and Democrats on the wheat subcommittee. For the most part, members who have little interest in the proceedings are expected either to remain silent during hearings or not to attend.

The Work of the Committee—1958

In 1958 serious problems existed for cotton, rice, wheat, dairy products, and corn. These crises involved four of the six commodity groups shown in Table 8–2, leaving the tobacco and diversified groups with little direct and positive interest in the legislation. The committee decided to employ the "omnibus" procedure so as to get as much backing for the bill as possible. Apparently the leadership on both sides agreed to this, though some Republicans complained about such obvious "logrolling."

The work of the committee proceeded according to plan with the cotton, dairy products, livestock and feed grains, and wheat subcommittees holding extensive hearings. The result was a sixty-two-page bill (HR 12954) which included eight titles. In addition to titles designed to solve immediate crises, titles to extend certain popular programs were added so as to increase the bill's dubious chances of passage.[9]

The committee voted on June 13 to report HR 12954 favorably, but on June 25, the Rules Committee's motion to debate the bill (H. Res. 609) was lost in the House, thereby defeating the bill.[10] Shortly afterward, on June 27, the Senate passed its farm bill (S 4071) and sent it to the House. The House Agriculture Committee amended S 4071 to bring it into line with their previously defeated bill and reported it on August 4. On August 6, Chairman Cooley moved that the House suspend the rules and pass S 4071 as amended. The motion received a simple majority, but not the two-thirds vote required for such a motion, and so S 4071 was also defeated. The House Agriculture Committee made a final attempt to modify their amendments to S 4071, and on August 14 Chairman Cooley once again moved that the House suspend the rules and pass the bill as amended. This time S 4071 was accepted after a short debate by a voice vote, and on August 28 it was signed into law by the President. (PL 85–835).

In general, HR 12954 solved the cotton, rice, and feed grain prob-

9. The titles were: I—Foreign Trade; II—Rice; III—Cotton; IV—Wool; V—Wheat; VI—Milk; VII—Feed Grains; and VIII—Miscellaneous. Titles I and IV in particular were included because they were popular programs.

10. The reported vote in Committee was 21 to 10. The House vote on H. Res. 609 was 171 to 214.

lems to the satisfaction of committee representatives from those areas and they were apparently willing to trade their support. Their modifications of S 4071 were attempts to bring that bill closer to the provisions of HR 12954 for these commodities. The wheat and dairy titles in HR 12954 had little support outside the groups representing those interests. Though the Secretary of Agriculture and the American Farm Bureau Federation had objections to all titles in HR 12954, their most serious protests were directed against the dairy and wheat titles. Cotton and rice representatives were willing to drop these objectionable titles when the bill reached the House floor in order to save the sections of the bill they wanted most. Neither wheat nor dairy was included in S 4071.[11]

S 4071 was more in line with the Secretary of Agriculture's recommendations for fewer controls and lower supports.[12] Its ultimate passage, even with the modifications to bring it closer to HR 12954, was generally conceded to have been a victory for the Eisenhower administration.

II. Member Discussion and Evaluation

The vote on the rule to debate HR 12954 was split along party lines (Democrats for, Republicans against) with the major exception of urban Democrats. Of the fifty-nine Democrats who indicated opposition (either by voting against, pairing against, or answering the *Congressional Quarterly* poll), forty-seven were from metropolitan or mid-urban districts. Several committee members charged that the opponents of HR 12954 had tried to identify it as a "consumers' tax" bill in order to win the support of the urban representatives. The committee vote, also split along party lines, is indicated in Table 8–4.

Opinion of the Legislation

Members were asked in interviews for their opinions of the legislation, both HR 12954 and S 4071. Two conclusions emerged.

11. The dairy situation illustrates the infighting. Evidently the cotton and rice Democrats were opposed to any dairy legislation. Hearings were held but only after long delays. The Secretary of Agriculture's objections to the "self-help" bill proposed by dairy representatives were given the spotlight of a full committee hearing rather than a less sensational subcommittee hearing. The title which resulted was developed at the last minute and had little support, even among the national dairy groups.

12. See *The Congressional Digest* 37 (March, 1958): 75–77, for details of the administration's recommendations.

Table 8–4. House Agriculture Committee Vote on House Resolution 609

Democrats			Republicans		
Yea	Nay	Not Voting or Paired	Yea	Nay	Not Voting or Paired
Cooley	Hagen	McMillan	Harvey	Hill	McIntire
Poage		(paired for)	Smith	Hoeven	(paired against)
Grant			Quie	Simpson	Williams
Gathings				Dague	
Abernethy				Belcher	
Albert				Harrison	
Abbitt				Dixon	
Polk				Krueger	
Thompson				Teague	
Jones				Tewes	
Watts					
Johnson					
Anfuso					
Bass					
Knutson					
Jennings					
Matthews					

	Totals		
	Yea	Nay	Not Voting or Paired
Democrats	18	1	1
Republicans	3	11	2
Committee	21	12	3

Source: Compiled from data in the *Congressional Quarterly Almanac*, 85th Cong., 2d sess., 1958, pp. 392–93. Members are listed according to committee rank.

First, there was little unqualified opinion in support of either bill. Of the thirty members interviewed in regard to HR 12954, three considered it good, five said that most of it was good, fifteen were equivocal (some sections good, some sections bad); and seven considered it poor. Of the twenty-eight who were interviewed in regard to S 4071, four labeled it good, eight thought it "mostly good," fourteen were equivocal, and only two considered it bad. Table 8–5 distributes the opinions by commodity group.

Several comments are appropriate. The commodity groups can be classified into the principal beneficiaries of HR 12954 (corn and livestock, cotton and rice) who enjoyed broad support; the champions of controversial titles who were also directly and positively affected

Table 8–5. Member Opinion of the Legislation, by Commodity Group

Commodity Interest	HR 12954				S 4071			
	Good	Mostly Good	Equiv- ocal	Bad	Good	Mostly Good	Equiv- ocal	Bad
Corn and Livestock								
Democrats[a]			1					
Republicans		1	1	1	1	2		
Cotton and Rice								
Democrats	3	2	2			1	6	
Dairy, Livestock, Small Grains								
Democrats			2					2
Republicans				2		2		
Diversified								
Democrats[b]			1	1		1		
Republicans		1	2	1	2	1	1	
Tobacco								
Democrats		1	6			1	6	
Wheat								
Republicans				2		1	1	
Totals	3	5	15	7	4	8	14	2

Note: [Opinion given] in answer to the question, "Did you consider HR 12954 (S 4071) a good bill, a bad bill, something in between, or just what?"
[a] Polk not interviewed on S 4071.
[b] Anfuso not interviewed on S 4071.

(dairy, wheat); and the onlookers who were not involved or only indirectly affected (diversified, tobacco). Examined in this way the most favorable opinions were offered by those most affected: six of the eight "good" or "mostly good" responses came from representatives of the main beneficiaries. The middle category, concerned with controversial titles, tended to be suspicious of the bill. Both dairy and wheat members suggested that their titles would be sacrificed once the bill got to the floor.

Though it might be expected that Democratic tobacco representatives would actively support a bill from a Democratic committee, they were equivocal about HR 12954. On the basis of such comments as, "Frankly, I didn't think it would help very much," indications were that the tobacco representatives did little more than vote for the rule to debate. Nothing in either bill was of primary concern to their constituencies.

The diversified group offered very little favorable comment on HR

12954 and only one of them, a Democrat, voted for the bill on the floor. Once again, the bill gave very little direct, positive benefit to the group's constituencies though, as will appear, it soon became evident that they did have a constituency interest in the bill.

Opinion on the second bill shows a party split. Though the Republicans had less direct constituency interest in the bill (except for the corn and livestock group which considered it "good" or "mostly good"), nine of eleven committee Republicans considered the bill "good" or "mostly good." The Democrats were more qualified, with many of the cotton and rice group stating, "It was the best we could get." The tobacco group was no more enthusiastic about S 4071 than they had been about HR 12954. Republicans obviously considered this a better bill because it was not a clearcut victory for Democratic commodities. Though Republican commodities had not fared too well, the Democrats were not able to write the legislation with a free hand. Republicans from diversified farming areas were much more satisfied with S 4071 since it reduced controls and price supports.

Second, the members' opinions, not only of the bill as a whole but also of specific titles, were influenced by their constituencies' interests. When asked what they liked most and least about the bills, members whose constituencies were directly affected replied that they liked best those sections which were designed to solve commodity problems in their own constituencies. On HR 12954, four from the cotton and rice group mentioned those titles, one from corn and livestock, both members from wheat, and two from dairy. The same held true for S 4071.

Members were reluctant to say what sections they liked least. Some spoke in general terms, mentioning the overall cost, the politics involved, the issues not faced, etc. Only the dairy title drew much critical comment. Ten members (six Democrats and four Republicans) suggested that the dairy title was not good legislation and was harmful to the bill. The most numerous response for S 4071 was that no sections were "least liked."

As a followup question, members were asked which sections had beneficial or adverse effects on their constituencies. Once again, the replies supported the conclusion. In discussing HR 12954 all groups directly affected by the bill mentioned most often, as being beneficial, those titles of greatest interest to their respective constituencies. The most frequent response from the two least affected groups (diversified, tobacco) was that no section was beneficial. For S 4071, those most affected were the cotton and rice and corn and livestock members. They all mentioned the titles of interest to their constituencies as most beneficial. Other groups either chose some section which was of tangential importance or stated that none was beneficial. Hardly any member admitted that any sections adversely affected his constituency.

Concepts of Representation

Members were also asked to discuss what they relied on in their action on the first bill (HR 12954)—independent judgment, constituency wishes, a combination of factors, or something else. The results are summarized in the following conclusions.

First, a majority of members stated that in making up their minds they relied on independent judgment or a combination of factors (twenty-two of twenty-seven interviewed on this question). There was no important difference between Republicans and Democrats on this question. (See Table 8–6.)

Second, analysis by commodity groups reveals that those groups least positively affected by the legislation most often responded that they relied on "independent judgment." But the record shows that the diversified group did act to benefit constituency interests.

The members' replies must be weighed after taking into considera-

Table 8–6. Bases Asserted for Action on HR 12954

Commodity Groups	Independent Judgment	Constituency Wishes	Combination	Other (Party)
Corn and Livestock[a]				
Republicans	1		2	
Cotton and Rice				
Democrats	1	2	3	1
Dairy, Livestock, Small Grains				
Democrats			2	
Republicans	1		1	
Diversified[b]				
Democrats	1			
Republicans	2		1	1[c]
Tobacco[d]				
Democrats	4		2	
Wheat				
Republicans	—	1	1	—
Totals	10	3	12	2

Note: [Asserted] in answer to the question, "What did you rely on in your action on HR 12954—(1) independent judgement, (2) the wishes of your constituency, (3) perhaps a combination of these, or (4) something else?"
[a] Polk not included.
[b] Anfuso not included.
[c] Usually relied on independent judgment.
[d] Cooley not included.

tion both the importance of the legislation to their constituencies and the effect of their action for their constituencies. Of the ten who said that they followed independent judgment, four were from the tobacco group and three from the diversified. One other member from the diversified group said he supported his party in this instance but usually relied on independent judgment.

Despite these replies, two observations are pertinent: (*a*) all tobacco representatives who relied on independent judgment nevertheless voted in support of their party[13] and (*b*) the voting action (against the bill) of the diversified group tended to favor the best interests of their farmers as they themselves described these interests. As one member put it: "Benson is an asset to me. I agree with him and there is nothing political involved because his philosophy is good for my farmers." All of the diversified group who responded "independent judgment" indicated that a continued program of high supports and controls for *basic* commodities was bad for their farmers, who grow principally nonbasics.

The other three members who mentioned independent judgment were from the corn and livestock group (an admitted administration and American Farm Bureau Federation supporter—he thought their programs would be best for his constituency in the long run); the cotton and rice group (a generally inactive member who "didn't have too much information from my constituency"); and a dairy Republican who said, "I only had this chance to vote against the cotton deal."

Third, those groups most directly and positively affected by the legislation relied on a "combination" or on "constituency wishes." Replies of these members indicated they were well aware of the problems involved in representing *all* interests in their legal constituency on such a piece of legislation.

Nine of the twelve responses indicating a reliance on a combination of factors came from members whose constituency interests were directly affected by the legislation. Some of the most detailed analyses of the process of representation were offered by senior members who replied that representation on policy was not a simple choice between independent judgment on the one hand and constituency wishes on the other. Typical of the extended remarks are the following:

> I understand the problems of that area [his district]. I know what is best for the farm section. And I think that the majority in my area reflect my views.

13. Some tobacco representatives noted the importance of the wheat and feed grain titles for their constituencies. They thought these might eventually affect their livestock farmers (using the slogan, "cheap feed means cheap livestock"). Many of their farmers relied on wheat as an alternative crop.

I am in close contact with them at all times. I meet with them, ask their opinions on all matters. I don't use polls. I know the people. I vote my convictions and hope that they [constituents] will follow these. They expect this unless a real organized group is excited about something. They generally expect that you have more information than they do.

I am sent here as a representative of 600,000 people. They are supposed to be voting on all the legislation. I try to follow my constituents—to ignore them would be a breach of trust—but I use my judgment often because they are misinformed. I know that they would vote as I do if they had the facts that I have. A lot of people expect you to use your judgment.

Under our form of government you have to rely on a combination. If I know the views of the constituents I will vote these views—as a representative, I must—but when I don't know I substitute my best judgment. There is not one case in a hundred where I do know their views fully. I figure if they knew what I know . . . they would understand my vote. Most of us vote what we believe is sound, based on the information and our judgment. This can be changed if the people express themselves clearly enough. This, however, is improbable and doesn't happen very often.

Even the junior members in these groups had definite ideas about how their constituencies were affected:

I thought that it was a good bill and then I thought that I could go ahead in view of the referendum and support the bill. If there weren't a referendum [included in the bill], I would have checked [with the constituency] but I felt I could go ahead. On some legislation I hear from the people and rely on their judgment . . . [after probing for specifics]. On labor legislation I rely on groups in my area since I don't know too much about it.

I depend on a combination. I should educate them; they don't really care how you vote. I make up my mind and then temper it with what the people want. After all, I think as they do.

One member who relied on constituency wishes was frank in explaining his position:

I vote for what I think will be the best economic interests of my people. Throughout the years I have gained an idea of what those best interests are. This is the way representative government should work.

Fourth, an analysis of members' extended discussions coupled with an examination of their interest and activity on the legislation reveals the importance of a concept of "constituency" in the action of members.

Those who purported to rely on independent judgment were of three types: members who had no commodities to represent on the legislation but opposed the bill—an action evidently in the best interests of their constituencies; members in the tobacco group who supported their party but had no direct interest in the legislation (though some expressed indirect interest); and members who had a constituency interest in the bill but said they relied on independent judgment in their actions, though this did not seem the case in fact.

Those relying on a combination of factors argued that defining constituency interests was no simple, straightforward interpretation. In their subcommittee work on the bill, however, these members—the most active of all who worked on the bill—evinced a shrewd conception of their constituencies' commodity interests.

Clearly, more evidence than the self-explained motivation for voting is relevant in appraising a representative's action and in interpreting his conception of representation: his work in subcommittee on acceptable compromises, [for example], or his interrogation of witnesses in hearings, or his part in the committee's executive sessions. The data gathered here from such successive stages of action as these tend to confirm Eulau's typology of "delegates," "trustees," and "politicos," and his suggestion that a representative might act in more than one of these roles.[14]

Knowing the Constituency

In order to discover some of the relationships and means of communication between the representative and his constituency, members were asked how they knew their constituency wishes on HD 12954. Table 8–7 summarizes the responses. The most important method, members said, was a type of individual "sounding-board" procedure. Some of those mentioning "intuition" or "sixth sense" observed that their own identity with the culture or mood of the district made it natural that they would know their neighbors' wishes. Responses which typified the members' analyses were:

> You are in a position to know, of course, on a lot of things. I live there —there are many things I just know. I don't have to ask anybody. There are very few bills where I have to guess. If I did, I wouldn't be here as the representative.

14. Above, note 2.

Table 8–7. Methods for Determining Constituency Wishes

Method	Democrats[a] Mentioning	Republicans Mentioning	Totals
Just know it (live there, sense it)	8	5	13
Meetings	6	3	9
Correspondence	4	3	7
Questionnaire	1	2	3
Newspaper	–	2	2
Testimony	1	1	2
Advisory Committee (to advise on agricultural policy)	–	1	1
Telephone calls	–	1	1
Visitors	1	–	1

Note: [Responses given] in answer to the questions, "How did you find out what your constituency wishes were on this bill?" and "Are there other ways you use to tap opinion and get information about your constituency's agricultural interests? What are these?"
[a] Does not include Cooley, Polk, or Anfuso.

I am a native of _____. I get letters, though I don't get very much mail. I have sent out questionnaires but I don't now. It is just the fact that I know and I can judge their needs.

Some of the members pointed out that they were farmers and reasoned that this gave them a special ability to know the needs of fellow farmers. Others indicated that their familiarity with the district through campaigns or frequent visits made it possible for them to know. Either way, they were identifying a "policy constituency."

Though such responses suggest that the representative has a concept of his constituency interests on legislation, there is still no reliable evidence as to how he develops it. But whether he gets it by divination, intuition, or instruction, it appears to dominate his behavior as a representative where its outline is sharp.

III. Conclusions

The conclusions suggested by this case study can be set forth somewhat more systematically as follows:

1. If a policy measure is seen to affect substantial interests in a representative's legal constituency, then he will rely on his perception of the interests affected (his "policy constituency") when he acts

at the working level (usually the subcommittee) in regard to this measure.

A. Institutional arrangements affect his ability to represent his policy constituency. The House Agriculture Committee is organized to allow a maximum of constituency-oriented representation.

B. The representative has a "sense" of constituency interests drawn from first-hand experience in the "legal" constituency and this "sense" influences his perception of a policy constituency.

C. Party allegiance is an important modifying factor.

   (1) The legislative majority party may demand a vote in support of its policies. The legislative minority party may demand a vote in opposition to the majority's policies. The administration may press for support for its stands.

   (2) Representatives, whether or not affected by the legislation, tend to support their party's position more as the action moves beyond the basic working level, and most at the final vote.

2. If a measure is seen to have little or no direct effect on interests in a representative's legal constituency, then he will tend more readily to look to his political party for a cue when he acts in regard to this measure.

A. The representative will tend the more to suggest that he relies on "independent judgment," the less his constituency's interests are seen to be directly or positively affected by a policy.

B. He will vote in support of his political party but will not actively support the policy in other ways if his constituency interests are not perceived to be affected.

A final comment suggests a further and more tentative generalization. In this case study it became necessary to reconcile actions of certain members who seemed motivated by different forces at different action points. Table 8–4 shows that eleven Republicans voted or paired against the rule to debate HR 12954. Of these, seven were from constituencies which had a direct, positive interest in the legislation. Four of the seven were particularly active in effecting compromises in titles of major concern to their constituencies. They were apparently satisfied with the respective titles, yet had no difficulty in rationalizing opposition to the entire bill on the House floor. Further, while members of the diversified group apparently did little to obstruct the work on HR 12954 at the subcommittee level (thereby following an apparent norm for Agriculture Committee members), it nevertheless became obvious that some of them worked actively to defeat the bill on the House floor.[15]

An adequate concept of representation should account for a total action pattern, not merely a final vote. The representative on the House Agriculture Committee can view his composite role retrospectively as one in which he has taken several separate actions to make up a total pattern in regard to the omnibus farm legislation. He also can recognize that on different occasions he felt differing demands upon him in his several capacities, as a member of a party, a representative of a constituency, a member of a committtee, of a Congress, of interest groups, etc. He was able to reconcile, compromise or avoid some of the inherent conflicts in these demands, at least in part, because of the multiple action points. Examples of such reconciliations in this case study justify a final hypothesis which merits separate study:

3. If a representative has a multiplicity of conflicting demands upon him in any series of actions on policy, he can satisfy many of them, over a period of time, because of the multiplicity of action points at successive stages in the legislative process.

15. Minority party members are more likely to feel conflicting demands since the majority party's commodities will probably be favored. Some majority party members will find, however, that they are not as directly concerned with the legislation and so will be less actively involved at all stages of action.

9

Shifting Forces, Changing Rules, and Political Outcomes: The Impact of Congressional Change on Four House Committees

Norman J. Ornstein and David W. Rohde

The U.S. House of Representatives has undergone vast changes in the early 1970's. As a result of the elections of 1970, 1972, and 1974, the membership of the House in the Ninety-fourth Congress is substantially different from what it was in the Ninety-first Congress; 200

Reprinted by permission of the authors. Copyright © 1977 by Norman J. Ornstein and David W. Rohde. This article was originally presented as a paper at a Symposium on Legislative Reform and Public Policy, in Lincoln, Nebraska, sponsored by the Department of Political Science, The University of Nebraska. A summary version of the paper, narrower in scope, will appear in a forthcoming conference volume, edited by John Peters and Susan Welch.

A substantial portion of the data employed in this paper is derived from a series of semistructured interviews with members of the four committees on which we focus, with members of their personal staff and of committee staffs, and with a few observers of these committees from outside the Congress. Most of the interviews were tape recorded and later transcribed; in a few cases recording was not possible and notes were taken. All interviewees were offered anonymity; however, a few permitted us to quote them. In selecting potential interviewees, we attempted to guarantee that we would secure a variety of perspectives. However, we did not attempt to secure (and did not secure) a random sample. In all, twenty-three interviews were conducted.

Unless otherwise identified, all quotations in this paper were taken from these interviews. Of course, we are very grateful to our interviewees for taking the time to talk to us; without their help, there would have no paper.

members (46.0 percent of the House) have been elected since then. Reforms by the House and its majority Democratic caucus have altered floor procedures, selection processes for committee and sub-committee chairmen, the powers of committee chairmen and of sub-committees, and the jurisdictions of many House committees.[1] The interaction of these shifts in membership and in procedures have led to significant alterations in the power structure of the House of Representatives. Formal power has been given to the Speaker and the majority party leadership, to the House Democratic caucus, to individual Democratic committee caucuses, and to subcommittees and their chairmen. Power has been taken from committee chairmen and the old Democratic Committee on Committees, and checks have been placed on the "prestige" committees. Simultaneously, the turnover in House membership has debilitated the strength of the senior, southern-dominated group which had been most powerful in earlier Congresses, reducing the southern share of the majority party delegation and boosting the ranks of Democratic liberals, North *and* South.

Membership, rules, and power alignments have shifted; each of these areas of change has been reflected by the standing committees of the House. Some committees have had virtually their entire membership rosters replaced in the past three Congresses. Other panels have completely altered their committee rules. Still others have had their chairmen replaced, either by retirement or by removal by the majority party caucus. In addition, some committees have restructured their subcommittees and/or replaced subcommittee chairmen. All in all, few of the twenty-two House standing committees have been even partially insulated from the vast alterations in the Congressional landscape in the 1970s.

The task of this paper will be to try to sort out the relative impact of these various changes in the House on its committees and their outputs. How important have reforms been, vis-à-vis House turnover,

1. A good deal has been written about these reforms. See, for example, Ornstein, "Causes and Consequences of Congressional Change: Subcommittee Reforms in the House of Representatives," in Ornstein (ed.), *Congress in Change: Evolution and Reform* (New York: Praeger, 1975), pp. 88–114; Ornstein and Rohde, "Seniority and Future Power in Congress," in ibid., pp. 72–87; Rohde, "Committee Reform in the House of Representatives and the Subcommittee Bill of Rights," *The Annals*, 411 (January, 1974): 39–47; and Ornstein and Rohde, "The Strategy of Reform: Recorded Teller Voting in the U.S. House of Representatives," a paper delivered at the 1974 Annual Meeting of the Midwest Political Science Association. An overview and summary of all of the reforms can be found in Ornstein and Rohde, "Congressional Reform and Political Parties in the U.S. House of Representatives," in Jeff Fishel and David Broder (eds.), *Parties and Elections in an Anti-Party Age* (Bloomington: Indiana University Press, forthcoming 1976).

in realigning power on House committees? To what extent are changes the product of outside factors, such as Watergate and the Vietnam War? And most importantly, do these changes in House membership, in internal House procedures, and in power relationships mean changes in Congress' role in the American political system, or in the policies legislated and overseen by Congress? To begin to unravel the complexities contained in these questions, we will examine changes in four House committees, which provide a rough cross-section of Congressional policy-making: Agriculture, Government Operations, Interstate and Foreign Commerce, and International Relations.

We should note at the outset, however, that many of the important shifts in congressional structure and power occurred with the 1974 elections and the onset of the Ninety-fourth Congress. Thus, the fact that this paper is written in the early part of the Ninety-fourth Congress limits the analysis of change in committee behavior and policies and makes our conclusions very tentative.

I. Changes in the House: 1970-1975

Simply cataloguing the various reforms enacted in the House in the past five years would take many pages. What we will try to do here is simply to give an overview of the patterns of change in the 1970s.

Turnover

The 1970, 1972, and 1974 elections produced substantial changes in the membership of the House. Overall, 46 percent of the members of the Ninety-first Congress (1969–1970) were not still members of the House by December, 1975[2] The impact of this turnover was disproportionately felt by Republicans and by senior members. (See Table 9–1.) Among Republican members of the Ninety-first Congress, the turnover was 59.3 percent, as opposed to only 35.8 percent among Democrats. For members elected before 1952, the turnover rate was 62.5 percent, while the rate for most other seniority categories was near the House average. Indeed, where these two groups overlapped, the turnover was total; all eighteen Republican

2. All data on membership and turnover employed in this paper were taken from various issues of *Congressional Quarterly Weekly Report* and from volumes of *Congressional Quarterly Almanac*. With regard to the Ninety-first Congress, the last occupant of a seat before the November, 1970, election was counted as the member for purposes of analysis.

Table 9–1. House Turnover, 1970 to 1975
(Percent, by Party and Seniority)

Date of Election	Democrats	Republicans	All Members
Before Nov. 1952	50.0	100.0	62.5
	(N = 54)	(18)	(72)
Nov. 1952–Oct. 1958	28.9	73.9	45.9
	(38)	(23)	(61)
Nov. 1958–Oct. 1962	33.3	58.1	43.0
	(48)	(31)	(79)
Nov. 1962–Oct. 1966	33.3	33.3	33.3
	(63)	(36)	(99)
Nov. 1966 and After	30.2	58.0	48.4
	(43)	(81)	(124)
Total	35.8	59.3	46.0
	(246)	(189)	(435)

Note: Each cell gives the percent of the members in that category (the number in the category is in parentheses) who were no longer members of the House in December, 1975.

members of the Ninety-first who were elected before 1952 were gone by 1975.

The turnover between 1970 and 1975 was not only great, but also politically significant. The most obvious change was the increase in Democratic membership, mainly as a consequence of the 1974 election, from 246 to 290. The character of the turnover altered the composition of both parties and of the House. The dominance of the South[3] within the Democratic party continued to decline; while the proportion of House Democrats coming from the South averaged 42 percent in the 1950s and 35 percent in the 1960s,[4] it had dropped to 28 percent by 1975. The turnover has also produced some ideological shifts.[5] Table 9–2 shows that, within party and regional categories, the members who entered the House since 1970 are similar ideologically to those who departed since then with one salient exception: The difference

3. The South is defined as the eleven states of the Confederacy.
4. See Ornstein and Rohde, "Seniority and Future Power in Congress, op. cit., pp. 73–74.
5. Throughout this paper, we use the mean conservative-coalition support ratio to describe the ideological makeup of groups of members. The support ratio is computed from the conservative-coalition support and opposition scores calculated annually by *Congressional Quarterly,* and is simply the support score divided by the sum of the support and opposition scores. This removes the impact of differential rates of absenteeism on the support scores. The Ninety-first Congress scores are taken from *Congressional Quarterly Almanac, 1970,* pp. 40–41, and the Ninety-fourth Congress scores (which cover only the first session) are taken from *Congressional Quarterly Weekly Report* (January 24, 1976): 172–73.

Table 9–2. Mean Conservative Coalition Support Ratios, 91st and 94th Congresses (By Region, Party and Turnover)

	Democrats			Republicans			All Members
	North	South	All	North	South	All	
91st Cong.							
Departing Members	23.1 (N = 59)	84.6 (28)	42.9 (87)	76.2 (98)	94.6 (14)	78.5 (112)	62.9 (199)
Holdovers	20.9 (105)	77.4 (52)	39.6 (157)	70.7 (65)	93.4 (12)	74.2 (77)	51.0 (234)
All 91st	21.7 (164)	79.9 (80)	40.8 (244)	74.0 (163)	94.1 (26)	76.7 (189)	56.5 (433)
94th Cong.							
Holdovers	25.4 (105)	76.3 (52)	42.2 (157)	76.8 (65)	91.8 (12)	79.2 (77)	54.4 (234)
New Members	22.5 (103)	57.8 (29)	30.3 (132)	77.0 (53)	94.3 (15)	80.8 (68)	47.5 (200)
All 94th	24.0 (208)	70.0 (81)	36.8 (289)	76.9 (118)	93.2 (27)	80.0 (145)	51.2 (434)

Note: "Holdovers" are Representatives who were in the House in the 91st Congress and remained in the House as of December, 1975. Speakers John McCormack and Carl Albert are excluded from this table because of the lack of data.

between the mean conservative-coalition support ratios of departing southern Democrats and new Democrats from the region is almost 27 points. This decrease in conservatism among southern Democrats, coupled with the substantial increase in the *number* of northern Democrats, has had two important effects on the Democratic party in the House: the ideological character of the party has been shifted somewhat to the left, and a significant gap now exists between Democrats who were members of the Ninety-first Congress and members who entered since then. Moreover, at the same time that the Democrats have shifted somewhat to the left, the average conservative-coalition score of Republicans has increased,[6] so that the ideological gap between the parties has also increased, from 36 points in the Ninety-first Congress to 43 points in the Ninety-fourth.

Rules Changes and Reforms

While the membership of the House was undergoing extensive change, the rules of the House and of the Democratic caucus were also being greatly altered. The changes in character of membership served to facilitate the reform process, as did political issues like the Vietnam War and Watergate, and the growth of interest groups like Common Cause. Reforms were mainly of two types: those that opened up the process to public scrutiny, and those that altered the distribution of power and resources. In the former category, the House implemented recorded teller-voting in the Legislative Reorganization Act of 1970, which allowed many votes on amendments to be recorded for the first time, and greatly opened up its committee proceedings to public view.

In the latter category, the House Democratic caucus passed reforms in January of 1971 which allowed for separate, secret-ballot votes on nominees for committee chairmanships upon the demand of ten members; limited subcommittee chairmanships to one per member; and allowed each subcommittee chairman to hire one professional staff member, subject to ratification by committee Democrats.

In January of 1973, the House Democratic caucus built on the earlier changes, making separate votes on committee chairmen automatic, and specifying a range of powers and privileges to subcommittees which came to be called the "Subcommittee Bill of Rights." In addition, Democrats reactivated a twenty-four member Steering and Policy Committee, chaired by the Speaker, and added the three elected

6. As Table 9–2 shows, the increased score for Republicans is primarily due to increased scores among Republican holdovers. We will discuss this point further below.

party leaders—Speaker, majority leader, caucus chairman—to the Democratic Committee on Committees.

In 1974 the House considered a committee reorganization proposal which grew out of the deliberations of a Select Committee on Committees, appointed by the Speaker in 1973 and chaired by Richard Bolling (D., Mo.). However, the Bolling committee proposal (which would have limited members to one major committee assignment, abolished two committees, and substantially restructured a dozen others) went too far for most members, and the House instead adopted an alternative plan proposed by a committee of the Democratic caucus, chaired by Julia B. Hansen (Wash.) Among the provisions of the "Bolling-Hansen" proposal were: some rejurisdiction; substantial enlargement of committee staff allowances, with the minority party receiving one-third of each committee's allowance; a requirement that each committee with more than fifteen members (later changed to twenty) set up at least four subcommittees; a grant to the Speaker of broad power over bill referral; and a provision that required party caucuses to organize in advance of the next Congress in December of election years.

In December, 1974, and January, 1975, a series of additional changes took place through the Democratic caucus. The Democratic committee assignment authority, which had rested for better than sixty years with the Democratic members of the Ways and Means Committee, was taken from them and given to the two-year-old Steering and Policy Committee (except for recommendations for Rules Committee slots, which are now handled by the Speaker alone). Ways and Means, the revenue committee with broad jurisdiction, was enlarged by twelve to thirty-seven members and forced to set up subcommittees. The other money committee, Appropriations, was forced to have its subcommittee chairmanships ratified by the House Democratic caucus in the same manner as full committee chairmanships. In its most highly publicized action, the caucus in January, 1975, used its recently reformed procedures to reject three committee chairmen, W. R. Poage (Tex.) of Agriculture; F. Edward Hebert (La.) of Armed Services; and Wright Patman (Tex.) of Banking, Currency, and Housing. They were respectively replaced by second-ranking Tom Foley (Wash.) and Melvin Price (Ill.), and fourth-ranking Henry Reuss (Wisc.). When the individual committees met to organize at the beginning of the Ninety-fourth Congress, additional changes occurred, some mandated by new caucus and House rules, others the product of committee activists. We will discuss the structural realignments which took place within the four committees at a later point in this paper.

Taken as a whole, what did these reforms do? They took power from the chairmen of the standing committees and spread it out in several directions. The right to approve individual chairmen was given to the House Democratic caucus. The Speaker was given a major role in the committee assignment process, and new power in bill referrals. The major share of power and resources, though, went to the subcommittees. Control over subcommittees was taken in large part from the committee chairmen. Their selection was also taken from the chairmen, and is now handled, through a seniority process, by the committees' Democratic caucuses. The major thrust of the changes, then, was to shift the initiative from the full committees and their chairmen to the subcommittees and their leaders.

II. House Turnover in the 1970s: The Committee Impact

As we have noted, the House (especially its majority party) became more liberal and less southern-dominated through the 1970, 1972, and 1974 elections. Committees have been called "little legislatures," but they do not each wholly reflect changes which occur in the larger body. In a period of heavy turnover, a committee might remain perfectly stable. Conversely, an election with few personnel changes might actually decimate the ranks of a particular committee. In the landslide 1974 election, for example, the House Rules Committee lost only one of ten Democrats and one of five Republicans. In the comparatively placid 1970 election, the House District of Columbia Committee lost seven of fourteen Democrats and four of eleven Republicans.

Change in membership on a committee can come about through an influx of freshmen, of more senior members, or of some combination. The "mix" depends on the prestige and attractiveness of a committee to the legislators, the number of vacancies, and the number of incoming freshmen. Some committees, like Rules, Ways and Means, and Appropriations remain consistently alluring to senior and junior members alike. Other committees can change in their attractiveness quite markedly over time, with issues, events, or political pressures. As we will see, the attractiveness of each of our four committees has changed considerably, sometimes in surprising directions, with significant implications for their makeups and roles.

Agriculture

Over these three elections, no committee in the House was more transformed in its membership than the Agriculture Committee. Between the Ninety-first and Ninety-second Congresses, the Agriculture Committee lost three Democrats and five Republicans (and gained six new Democrats and three new Republicans as committee ratios changed); between the Ninety-second and Ninety-third Congresses, Agriculture lost seven Democrats and five Republicans, gaining five and six respectively. And in the Ninety-fourth Congress, the committee lost seven Democrats and nine Republicans, gaining fourteen new Democratic and seven new Republican committee members. By 1975, through the ebbs and flows of elections and new committee ratios, the committee had only six Democrats remaining from the nineteen who were there for the Ninety-first Congress in 1970. Even more remarkable, thirteen of the fifteen Ninety-first Congress Republicans are gone from the 1975 Agriculture Committee roster. Looking at the other side, twenty-one of twenty-seven Agriculture Democrats and twelve of fourteen Republicans in the Ninety-fourth Congress are new since 1970. What was the character of this massive turnover? On the Democratic side, the regional shift has been marked. In 1970, southern members had eight of the nine most senior slots, and were fourteen of the total of nineteen Democrats (74 percent). In 1975, southern Democratic members controlled only five of ten senior positions, and comprised only 37 percent of the Democratic membership.

The ideological change is displayed in Table 9–3. Though the measures and comparisons are somewhat crude, Table 9–3 makes clear that the committee membership has shifted in a more liberal direction, thanks to the nature of turnover; the movement leftward has been true for both Democrats and Republicans. For Democrats the members

Table 9–3. Agriculture Committee Conservative Coalition Mean Support Ratios, 91st and 94th Congresses

	Democrats		Republicans	
	91st Cong.	94th Cong.	91st Cong.	94th Cong.
Committee Members	70 ($N = 19$)	45 (27)	88 (15)	77 (14)
Departing Members (91st Cong.)	73 (13)	—	87 (13)	—
Remaining Members (91st Cong.)	63 (6)	64 (6)	96 (2)	96 (2)
New Members (92nd–93rd Cong.)	—	51 (7)	—	82 (5)
New Members (94th Cong.)	—	34 (14)	—	68 (7)
Full Committee	91st Cong., 78 (34)		94th Cong., 56 (41)	

who have departed since the Ninety-first Congress were more conservative than those remaining, while the newer members are significantly more liberal, particularly the most recent additions. Overall, Agriculture Democrats have moved from an average 70 conservative-coalition support ratio to a 45 support ratio; new committee Democrats in the Ninety-fourth Congress average 34 in conservative-coalition support. Republican changes have been less dramatic, though in parallel directions.

Interviews with committee members and staff indicate other, similar changes that aren't easily reflected in floor voting patterns. The new southern members are clearly different from their predecessors. As one northern liberal Democat commented:

> We have had a real change in the cotton South—you have David Bowen as chairman of the Cotton Subcommittee, Harvard, a Rhodes scholar—compare him with Abernethy, the guy he replaced! It's like night and day.

A staff member described other newer southern colleagues:

> Charlie Rose [D., N.C.] is politically astute, savvy, quick, surprisingly liberal. Dawson Mathis [D., Ga.] isn't as liberal, but is extremely fast and competent—and Mathis and Bergland [D., Minn.] can work together.

The recent influx of midwestern Democrats has also given *them* a key position on the committee, as the following comments show.

> Bergland is the fulcrum now. He supports liberal legislation of interest to rural areas, but without a lot of ballyhoo.

> Bob [Bergland] is a key man; his influence goes beyond the subcommittee he chairs.

> We have a new coalition now, with three groups—the new Southerners, the Bowens and Roses; the new northern members from rural districts in the heartland, the Bedalls, Fithians, Harkins; and the urban members.

The increasing importance of food and food prices as a political issue, and the inroads made by Democrats in the traditionally Republican midwestern farm belt, have resulted in an increased demand among Democrats for assignment to the Agriculture Committee.[7]

7. These data are taken from the actual preferences submitted by members to the Democratic Committee on Committees. A further description of the source and character of these data, and an analysis of some of them, may be found in David Rohde and Kenneth Shepsle, "Democratic Committee Assignments in the House of Representatives: Strategic Aspects of a Social Choice Process," *American*

Figure 9–1. Freshman Requests for Assignment to Agriculture Committee, 86th–94th Congresses

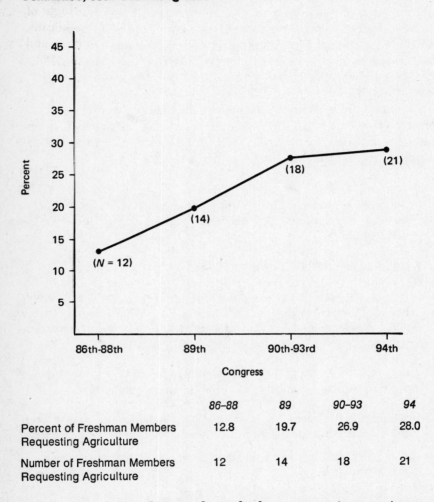

	86–88	*89*	*90–93*	*94*
Percent of Freshman Members Requesting Agriculture	12.8	19.7	26.9	28.0
Number of Freshman Members Requesting Agriculture	12	14	18	21

Figure 9–1 shows the trend in freshman committee assignment requests.

However, this has not resulted in a great influx of urban or big-city members. The committee has always been rural-oriented and rural-dominated. The major regional and ideological shifts in recent years have included the beginnings of an urban-oriented membership, but

Political Science Review 67 (September, 1973: 889–905 [reprinted as Chapter IX of the present volume]. Unfortunately, parallel data are not available on Republicans.

All analyses of these data exclude the Ninety-first Congress, for which data were not available.

in a very limited way. Among newer committee Democrats, only Fred Richmond of Brooklyn has a wholly urban district. A few others, like Norman D'Amours of New Hampshire and Matthew McHugh of New York, have some urban and suburban areas. Among Republicans, Margaret Heckler of Massachusetts (Boston's northern suburbs) and Peter Peyser of New York's Westchester County and the north Bronx are urban-oriented. The major influx of new people on the committee, though, is from midwestern or western farm-belt areas.

Government Operations

Government Operations has changed its membership as well, but as much from an enlargement of the committee as from electoral forces. Nine of the twenty Democrats on the Government Operations Committee in the Ninety-first Congress are gone; eleven remain, with an additional eighteen Democrats added since then. Of these, eleven are newcomers in the Ninety-fourth Congress (with one, John Burton (D. Calif.) added near the end of the Ninety-third Congress). Among Republicans, seven of the fifteen committee members present in the Ninety-first Congress remain, with half of the fourteen Republicans in the Ninety-fourth Congress new since 1970. Of these, three are new to the committee in 1975. Few regional patterns are apparent. Ideologically, as Table 9–4 shows, the Democratic membership on the committee has not become more liberal, while committee Republican membership has become measurably more conservative. Membership

Table 9–4. Government Operations Committee Conservative Coalition Mean Support Ratios, 91st and 94th Congresses

	Democrats		Republicans	
	91st Cong.	94th Cong.	91st Cong.	94th Cong.
Committee Members	27 ($N = 20$)	29 (29)	58 (15)	72 (14)
Departing Members (91st Cong.)	21 (9)	—	60 (8)	—
Remaining Members (91st Cong.)	31 (11)	37 (11)	55 (7)	65 (7)
New Members (92nd–93rd Cong.)	—	22 (6)	—	80 (4)
New Members (94th Cong.)	—	27 (12)	—	80 (3)
Full Committee	91st Cong., 40 (35)		94th Cong., 43 (43)	

losses among Democrats were disproportionately liberal, and the new members in the past three Congresses are somewhat more liberal than their veteran colleagues. So, on balance, the committee Democrats remain pretty much the same in floor voting patterns—quite liberal. Republicans, on the other hand, have added mainly conservative members to Government Operations in the 1970s. In addition, the average score of Republicans who remained on the committee has increased by 10 points. These factors combined to increase the average score of Republican members from 58 to 72.

Voting patterns, however, disguise somewhat the character of membership change on Government Operations. The new members—those added in the Ninety-second-to-Ninety-fourth Congresses—are among the most activist liberals in the House, many with reputations as mavericks. One member exclaimed,

> Look who we've got on this committee—Bella [Abzug], Drinan, Aspin, Moffett, Harrington, Conyers, John Burton, Andy Maguire. You couldn't pick another group of agitators like that!

Much of the change on Government Operations has come from an influx of members who were not freshmen when appointed. One staff member noted,

> In 1975, we got ten new members, later eleven when Reuss resigned. The second, third, and fourth termers who requested to get on the committee demonstrated their recognition of a new, enhanced role of Government Operations—this was partly the role of Brooks in investigating the Nixon administration. That role becomes clear when we see that three of five new nonfreshmen Democrats came from Judiciary [where Brooks also serves]—Jordan, Drinan and Mezvinsky—plus Harrington, Preyer, and later, Aspin.

Partly because of Watergate and other abuses in the recent Republican administrations, and partly because of increased payoffs seen by legislators in aggressive oversight, Government Operations is clearly more attractive to members now than it was in earlier Congresses. Figure 9–2, which shows freshman requests for assignment to Government Operations, demonstrates the upsurge in interest.

Commerce

Interstate and Foreign Commerce is a committee which has faced heavy losses of veteran Republicans in the past three Congresses, while senior Democrats have basically continued on the committee. Nevertheless, the tide of new members has been much more heavily Democratic, due largely to an expansion of the committee's size (a

Figure 9–2. Freshman Requests for Assignment to Government Operations Committee, 86th–94th Congresses

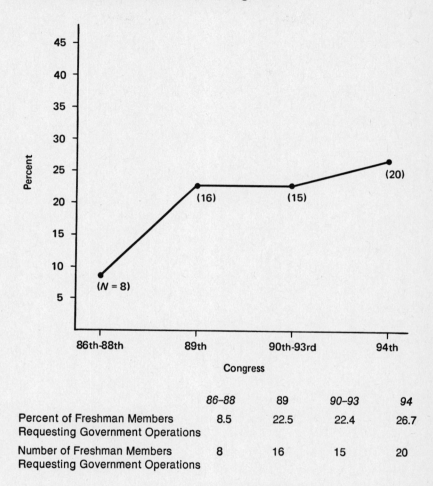

	86–88	89	90–93	94
Percent of Freshman Members Requesting Government Operations	8.5	22.5	22.4	26.7
Number of Freshman Members Requesting Government Operations	8	16	15	20

common occurrence in the Ninety-fourth Congress), and the two-to-one party ratios induced by the 1974 election. Eight of twenty-one Democrats present on the committee in 1970 were gone by 1975,[8] but only two were in the most senior eight—and one of these (John Jarman of Oklahoma) remained in the House but switched parties. Since 1970, sixteen new Democrats have joined the committee, a dozen coming on in 1975.

Among Republicans, ten of sixteen Ninety-first Congress Republicans are gone, including six of the most senior eight. The number of

8. One of these, Richard Ottinger (N.Y.), left to run for the Senate in 1970, then returned to the House and the committee in 1975.

committee Republicans has shrunk from sixteen to fourteen as Democrats have increased from twenty-one to twenty-nine. Thus there are eight new Republicans since 1970; three of these are 1975 additions. On both sides of the aisle, the committee has become slightly more liberal. However, the new members are a good deal more liberal than their senior colleagues, as Table 9–5 shows. As we shall see, this fact had much to do with the reforms which shook Commerce in the Ninety-fourth Congress.

Table 9–5. Commerce Committee Conservative Coalition Mean Support Ratios, 91st and 94th Congresses

	Democrats		Republicans	
	91st Cong.	94th Cong.	91st Cong.	94th Cong.
Committee Members	38 (N = 21)	34 (29)	85 (16)	81 (14)
Departing Members (91st Cong.)	35 (8)	—	84 (10)	—
Remaining Members (91st Cong.)	39 (13)	40 (13)	88 (6)	87 (6)
New Members (92nd–93rd Cong.)	—	36 (4)	—	80 (5)
New Members (94th Cong.)	—	26 (12)	—	71 (3)
Full Committee	91st Cong., 58 (37)		94th Cong., 49 (43)	

Of the twelve new Democrats coming on in 1975, ten were new to the House, and had diverse geographical bases (three West, two South, two Midwest, three Northeast); the other two, James Scheuer and Richard Ottinger, both from New York, are veteran liberals returning to the House after respective two and four year absences. The three new Republicans—Edward Madigan of Illinois, Carlos Moorhead of California, Matthew Rinaldo of New Jersey—are all one-term members.

Commerce, with jurisdiction that includes health, transportation, energy, and finance, has always been a desirable assignment. It has become even more coveted in recent Congresses, as the trend in freshmen requests in Figure 9–3 demonstrates. This probably accounts in part for the expansion of the committee size.[9]

9. For a discussion of the relationship between demand for assignments and committee size, see Louis P. Westerfield, "Majority Party Leadership and the

Figure 9–3. Freshman Requests for Assignment to Commerce Committee, 86th–94th Congresses

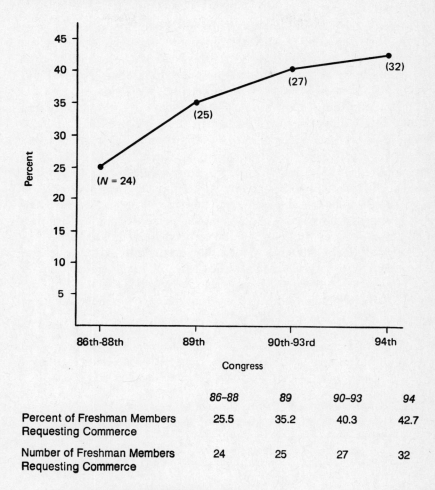

	86–88	*89*	*90–93*	*94*
Percent of Freshman Members Requesting Commerce	25.5	35.2	40.3	42.7
Number of Freshman Members Requesting Commerce	24	25	27	32

International Relations

Of the four committees under study, International Relations (formerly Foreign Affairs) faced the fewest changes on the Democratic side, with a greater turnover among minority party members. Of the twenty-one Ninety-first Congress Democrats, eight, mainly junior, members departed, while nine new members joined the committee in the 1971-to-1975 period. With four 1975 additions, the

Committee System in the U.S. House of Representatives," *American Political Science Review* 68 (December, 1974): 1593–1604 [reprinted as Chapter X of the present volume].

Democratic side still had three vacancies. Twelve of seventeen committee Republicans departed after 1970; there were eight new members since that time.

There are no perceptible regional trends. This committee has been a liberal one in recent years, and unlike our other committees, it has become slightly more conservative on the Democratic side in the past three Congresses. Republican members, in contrast, are more liberal than their Ninety-first Congress predecessors (see Table 9–6).

One striking thing about the membership data on International Relations is that three vacancies remain in the Ninety-fourth Congress. Some observers believe that this reflects a general decline of interest in the country in foreign affairs as a policy area, and that this is in turn reflected in a decline of interest among members in the committees which deal with these matters. Indeed, as Figures 9–4 and 9–5 show, there has been a decrease over time in the proportion of freshman members who request assignment to both Internationl Relations *and* Armed Services (although the latter decrease is only evidenced in the Ninety-fourth Congress). Others, however, think that this decline is a passing thing, reflecting only the desire of members brought in by a landslide to build up electoral security by service on a committee more closely related to constituency interests. One senior Democrat on International Relations told us:

> This is a temporary phenomenon. I've talked to at least twenty-five freshmen; they've said, "I'd like to come on your committee, but I need a base in my district first. Once I'm established . . ."

Table 9–6. International Relations Committee Conservative Coalition Mean Support Ratios, 91st and 94th Congresses

	Democrats		Republicans	
	91st Cong.	94th Cong.	91st Cong.	94th Cong.
Committee Members	20 (N = 21)	28 (22)	70 (17)	68 (12)
Departing Members (91st Cong.)	16 (8)	–	68 (12)	–
Remaining Members (91st Cong.)	22 (13)	30 (13)	76 (5)	78 (5)
New Members (92nd–93rd Cong.)	–	31 (6)	–	56 (6)
New Members (94th Cong.)	–	13 (3)	–	92 (1)
Full Committee	91st Cong., 42 (38)		94th Cong., 42 (34)	

III. Rules Changes, Rule Implementation, and Reorganization in the Four Committees

    In the first section of this paper, we briefly outlined the committee-related reforms which the House and its majority party caucus passed in the 1970-to-1975 period. Because many of the reforms required action to be taken by the individual committees and their Democratic caucuses, the impact of the reforms varied from committee to committee across the three Congresses. As we shall see, it often takes a particular combination of circumstances, each with its own

Figure 9–4. Freshman Democrats' Requests for Assignment to International Relations Committee, 86th–94th Congresses

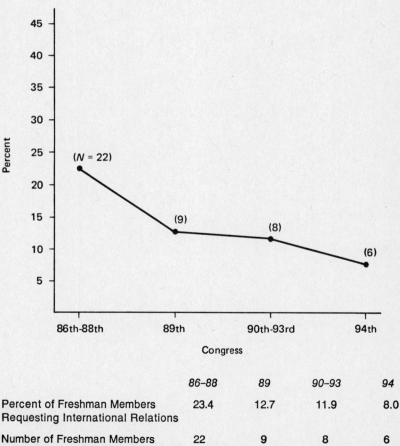

	86–88	89	90–93	94
Percent of Freshman Members Requesting International Relations	23.4	12.7	11.9	8.0
Number of Freshman Members Requesting International Relations	22	9	8	6

Figure 9–5. Freshman Democrats' Requests for Assignment to the Armed Services Committee, 86th–94th Congresses

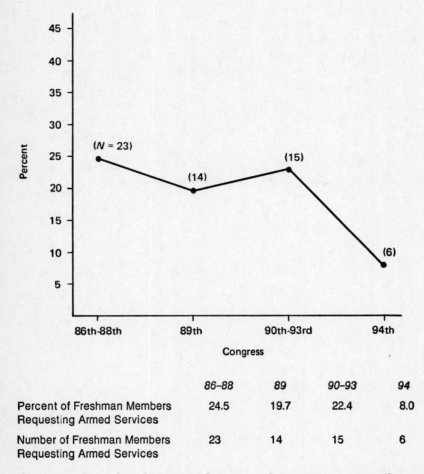

	86–88	89	90–93	94
Percent of Freshman Members Requesting Armed Services	24.5	19.7	22.4	8.0
Number of Freshman Members Requesting Armed Services	23	14	15	6

dynamics, for rules changes to have a real impact on a specific committee. In 1973, for example, John Moss's attempt to get the Commerce Committee to enforce the provisions of the new "Subcommittee Bill of Rights" was overwhelmingly rejected by the committee's Democratic caucus; Moss's proposal got only two favorable votes from the twenty-four Democrats.[10] In the Ninety-fourth Congress, two years later, a new set of circumstances that we will relate more fully in the following pages allowed Moss to capture enough votes to dramatically transform Interstate and Foreign Commerce. International Relations (née Foreign Affairs), on the other hand, changed a great deal in

10. See Ornstein, "Causes and Consequences" op. cit., p. 108.

1971 after the initial set of reforms and changed substantially again with a major reorganization of subcommittees in 1975. In this section we will explore the structural changes which took place in the four committees and the reasons behind them.

Agriculture

With the exception of the membership changes we have already discussed, which altered the rankings of particular members and cut into the strength of southern Democrats, the Agriculture Committee itself was largely untouched by the House Democratic caucus rules changes of the Ninety-second and Ninety-third Congresses. The Ninety-third Congress changes allowed for a separate secret ballot vote on party nominees for committee chairmanships; incumbent chairman W. R. Poage of Texas was voted on, but was retained by a wide margin.[11] In addition, the Ninety-second Congress reforms limited subcommittee chairmanships to one per member and provided for a professional staff member for each subcommittee, if approved by the committee's Democratic membership. No subcommittee chairmen on Agriculture were forced to give up their positions under the new rules, and staff continued to be hired by the committee chairman. Similarly, the Agriculture Committee's structure and behavior did not change much following the caucus' passage of the Subcommittee Bill of Rights in 1973. The committee's rules still vested in the chairman control over subcommittees (including their jurisdiction and membership) and over all staff employed by the committee.[12]

Agriculture Democrats didn't vocally protest the failure of the new reforms to transform their committee. Partly this was due to the political makeup of the committee; while it has often had vocal battles and personality conflicts, it has not been dominated by House activists, and the possibility of revolt in the committee was never seriously entertained. In part it was also due to the relatively loose rein held on the committee by Chairman Poage—a change from the style of his predecessor, Harold Cooley (D., N.C.). Poage did streamline the number of subcommittees from fifteen to ten in the Ninety-first Con-

11. Although—perhaps as a portent of the future—there were more negative votes (forty-eight) cast against Poage than against any other chairman. See *Congressional Quarterly Weekly Report* (January 27, 1973): 136.

12. The sources for committee rules are as follows: For the Ninety-second Congress, *Rules Adopted by the Committees of Congress, Ninety-second Congress* (Washington: U.S. Government Printing Office, 1971); for the Ninety-third Congress, copies of rules obtained directly from individual committees; for the Ninety-fourth Congress, *Rules Adopted by the Committees of Congress, Ninety-fourth Congress* (Washington: U.S. Government Printing Office, 1975). The books cited for the Ninety-second and Ninety-fourth Congresses were compiled by the Joint Committee on Congressional Operations.

gress without affecting the commodity panels, but he harmed no sitting chairman and he did not drastically restrict subcommittee activities. He was ideologically very conservative, and, as one southern member described him:

> Poage is fiery, especially on the floor—he was once described as "the only man in the House who could get mad at the sound of his own voice."

But he has also been described by a variety of committee members as "a very fair chairman."

The onset of the Ninety-fourth Congress was a very different story, however. Agriculture provided the first concrete demonstration of the seniority reforms enacted by the Democratic caucus in 1971 and 1973. On Wednesday, January 15, 1975, the Democratic Steering and Policy Committee (the new Committee on Committees) met for the first time to recommend nominees for committee chairmanships. W. R. Poage was renominated by the narrow margin of fourteen to ten. The next day, the full caucus rejected Poage's renomination by a vote of 141 to 144.

Seventy-five new members in the caucus, the result of the 1974 elections, definitely led to Poage's demise as chairman. His appearance before the freshmen on Monday, January 13 (along with other sitting chairmen), had been very poorly received, and by most accounts Poage captured precious few of their votes. On the other hand, Poage was *not* opposed in the caucus by the other Democratic members of the committee. As one liberal commented,

> I supported Poage—he had always been very fair to me and a very fair chairman overall. He knows he wasn't stabbed in the back by liberals on the committee; I think all of us except the new members supported him.

Indeed, Poage would probably have retained his chair if he had not miscalculated politically. A committee insider said,

> Foley [the ranking Democrat on the committee, and a liberal] went to Poage and offered to speak on his behalf in the caucus. Poage declined; he said he thought he had enough votes. No question that if he had let Tom speak up it would have given him [Poage] enough votes to win.

Poage was conciliatory and gracious after his ouster, unlike his fellow deposed chairman F. Edward Hebert, and he was subsequently named vice-chairman of the committee. Thomas Foley of Spokane, Washington, was accepted without controversy as the new chairman. Foley had been the number two-ranking member on Agriculture, which in itself was quite remarkable—he had served on the committee only since 1965, and he moved up seven slots in seniority, from the number eight position, in the five years since the Ninety-first Congress.

The Agriculture Committee rules, adopted on January 29, 1975, contained a large number of changes from those adopted in the Ninety-third Congress. In brief, the new rules incorporated the major elements of the Subcommittee Bill of Rights. They gave subcommittee chairmen the right to floor-manage legislation, to call hearings and meetings, and (for six subcommittees) to hire a professional staff aide.[13] The subcommittees are named and their jurisdiction are described. Rule 27 states: "The Chairman shall insure that each Subcommittee is adequately funded and staffed." As a rough index to the increase in range and specificity of the rules, it is interesting to note that they ran three-and-a-half pages in the Ninety-second Congress and nine pages in the Ninety-fourth.

The ten subcommittees remained basically the same in organization and jurisdiction, though part of the Food for Peace program (PL 480) had been transferred to the International Relations Committee by the 1974 reorganization. Subcommittee chairmen were selected by the method specified under the Subcommittee Bill of Rights—Democratic members of the committee bid for subcommittee chairs by seniority, and were voted up or down, in order, by the committee Democratic caucus. No reversals occurred; Foley declined to bid for a subcommittee chairmanship, while Poage asked for, and was given, the chair of the Livestock and Grains subcommittee, which Foley had headed in the Ninety-third Congress.[14] Poage's ability to secure the chairmanship of a major subcommittee demonstrates his continued esteem on the Agriculture Committee—a point to which we shall return.

Table 9–7 shows the various changes in subcommittee chairmanships over four Congresses. Continuity basically prevailed between the Ninety-first and Ninety-second Congresses. The South Carolina pri-

13. In accord with the committee reorganization plan adopted in 1974, ranking minority members of these subcommittees are also permitted to hire a staff member.

14. Livestock and Grains appears to be more important to committee members than other subcommittees; the others have eleven members while Livestock and Grains has twenty. For a detailed discussion of Agriculture subcommittees in an earlier period, see Charles O. Jones, "Representation in Congress: The Case of the House Agriculture Committee," *American Political Science Review* 55 (June, 1961):358–67 [reprinted as Chapter VIII of the present volume].

Table 9–7. Subcommittee Chairmen of the House Agriculture Committee, 91st–94th Congresses

Subcommittees	Chairmen			
	91st	92nd	93rd	94th
Commodity				
Cotton	Abernethy (Miss.)	Abernethy (Miss.)	Sisk (Calif.)	Bowen (Miss.)
Dairy and Poultry	Stubblefield (Ky.)	Stubblefield (Ky.)	Jones (Tenn.)	Jones (Tenn.)
Forests	McMillan (S.C.)	McMillan (S.C.)	Rarick (La.)	Litton (Mo.)
Livestock and Grains	Purcell (Tex.)	Purcell (Tex.)	Foley (Wash.)	Poage (Tex.)
Oilseeds and Rice	O'Neal (Ga.)	Jones (N.C.)	Jones (N.C.)	Mathis (Ga.)
Tobacco	Abbitt (Va.)	Abbitt (Va.)	Stubblefield (Ky.)	Jones (N.C.)
Operational				
Conservation and Credit	Poage (Tex.)	Poage (Tex.)	Poage (Tex.)	Bergland (Minn.)
Domestic Marketing and Consumer Relations	Foley (Wash.)	Foley (Wash.)	Vigorito (Pa.)	Vigorito (Pa.)
Departmental Operations	de la Garza (Tex.)	de la Garza (Tex.)	de la Garza (Tex.)	de la Garza (Tex.)
Family Farms and Rural Development	Vigorito (Pa.)	Vigorito (Pa.)	Alexander (Ark.)	Rose (N.C.)

mary defeat of John McMillan, the retirement of Watkins Abbitt (Va.) and Tom Abernethy (Miss.), and the defeat of Texas' Graham Purcell in the 1972 election created a considerable shuffling of subcommittee chairs in the Ninety-third Congress, with B. F. Sisk (Calif.), John Rarick (La.), Ed Jones (Tenn.), and Bill Alexander (Ariz.) taking on subcommittee chairmanships for the first time. At that time, Chairman Poage picked subcommittee heads, but he did so unarbitrarily, on the basis of seniority. The 1974 departure of Rarick and Stubblefield from Congress (both through primary defeats), the loss of Sisk and Alexander from the committee,[15] and Foley's move to committee chairman created another major reshuffling of subcommittee leaders in the Ninety-fourth Congress, this time with new selection procedures. New subcommittee chairmen included David Bowen (Miss.), Jerry Litton (Mo.), Dawson Mathis (Ga.), Bob Bergland (Minn.), and Charles Rose (N.C.). Bowen, Rose, and Litton were all elected for the first time in 1972. What is most interesting about Table 9–7, particularly for our forthcoming discussion of policy impact, is the extent to which the commodity subcommittees have been and continue to be dominated by southern members, even at a time when their overall influence on the committee has rapidly declined. Only the Ninety-third Congress (when B. F. Sisk of California chaired Cotton, and Foley of Washington chaired Livestock and Grains) was a partial exception, but both Sisk and Foley were gone by the next Congress to be replaced by Mississippi's Bowen and Texas' Poage. The dramatic regional change in committee membership did not result in a corresponding shift in the heads of the commodity subcommittees, and since most of the current subcommittee chairmen are quite junior (Poage is the exception), and the next ranking member due to get a subcommittee when a vacancy occurs is John Breckinridge of Kentucky, the lag is likely to endure for some time to come.

Government Operations

Government Operations underwent substantial change in the 1970-to-1971 period. Its longtime chairman, William Dawson of Illinois, died in 1970 and Chet Holifield of California succeeded him. When the Ninety-second Congress began, Holifield, in his first full term as chairman, effected some reorganization of his own and was then forced to deal with a major shift in subcommittee chairmanships brought about through the new caucus reforms. Holifield's own change

---

15. Alexander transferred to Appropriations, and Sisk was forced (by a new caucus rule) to give up his seat on Agriculture because he was a member of the Rules Committee.

was to merge two subcommittees (Executive and Legislative Reorganization and Military Operations) into a new Legislation and Military Operations Subcommittee. Executive and Legislative Reorganization handled all plans for new agencies and virtually all legislation going to the committee. Military Operations had been chaired by Holifield and dealt, among other things, with oversight of the defense and intelligence establishments. Holifield's merger attempt was seen by some members, notably Benjamin Rosenthal (D., N.Y.), as an unwarranted power grab by the new chairman. As a staff member noted,

> Rosenthal led a fight to split the two subcommittees, and lost on a procedural fight—the question was whether to vote on subcommittee reorganization in toto, or on each one separately. The vote was taken on reorganization in toto, and Holifield won.

Conflict on other matters between Holifield and Rosenthal had preceded this particular battle. Rosenthal had chaired a "task force" (an informal subcommittee appointed by Dawson) on consumer action. When Holifield took over the committee, he abolished the task force, much to Rosenthal's dismay.

After winning the subcommittee merger battle, Holifield tried to circumvent the new Democratic caucus rule limiting subcommittee chairmanships to one per member—a reform he had vocally opposed on the caucus floor. He claimed that Government Operations subcommittees were "investigative," not "legislative," and thus did not come under the reform's restrictions. The Democratic party leadership and caucus reformers soon pressured him into abiding by the new rules, and a substantial reshuffling took place. John Blatnik (Minn.), Dante Fascell (Fla.), and John Moss (Calif.), gave up Government Operations subcommittees for others on Public Works, Foreign Affairs, and Interstate and Foreign Commerce respectively. Two new subcommittee chairmen, William Moorhead (Pa.) and William Randall (Mo.), were added. (Table 9–8 gives details on subcommittees and chairmen for the Ninety-first-to-Ninety-fourth Congresses.)

Few other changes took place in Government Operations' structures or procedures in the Ninety-second Congress. To liberal Democrats on the committee, the period was characterized by continued attempts by Holifield—a one-time founder of, and leader in, the liberal Democratic Study Group—to combine all the committee's powers in the hands of the chairman. As a veteran staff member commented,

> Let me tell you what Holifield said to [a committee member] when he complained about some of what he regarded as dictatorial tactics.

Table 9–8. Government Operations Subcommittee and Chairmen, 91st–94th Congresses

Subcommittees, 91st–93rd Cong.	91st Cong.	Chairmen 92nd Cong.	93rd Cong.
Conservation and Natural Resources	Reuss (Wisc.)	Reuss (Wisc.)	Reuss (Wisc.)
Executive and Legislative Reorganization[a]	Blatnik (Minn.)	Holifield (Calif.)	Holifield (Calif.)
Military Operations[a]	Holifield (Calif.)		
Foreign Operations and Government Information	Moss (Calif.)	Moorhead (Pa.)	Moorhead (Pa.)
Government Activities	Brooks (Tex.)	Brooks (Tex.)	Brooks (Tex.)
Intergovernmental Relations	Fountain (N.C.)	Fountain (N.C.)	Fountain (N.C.)
Legal and Monetary Affairs	Fascell (Fla.)	Monagan (Conn.)	Randall (Mo.)
Special Studies	Monagan (Conn.)	Randall (Mo.)	Hicks (Wash.)

Subcommittees, 94th Cong.	Chairpersons, 94th Cong.
Conservation, *Energy* and Natural Resources	Moorhead (Pa.)
Legislation and *National Security*	Brooks (Tex.)
Government Information and *Individual Rights*	Abzug (N.Y.)
Government Activity and *Transportation*	Randall (Mo.)
Intergovernmental Relations and *Human Resources*	Fountain (N.C.)
Commerce, Consumer, and Monetary Affairs	Rosenthal (N.Y.)
Manpower and Housing	Hicks (Wash.)

Note: Italicized names in 94th Congress subcommittees are those referring to new political issues.
[a] Merged into Legislation and Military Operations Subcommittee.

Holifield said to him, he said "I've waited twenty-seven years to be chairman of a committee, and now that I am chairman I am going to run the committee the way I want to run it."

This staffer continued,

Holifield ran the committee in that same spirit of trying to consolidate all the power as the chairman. In other words, all staff people, even subcommittee people, had to be hired through Holifield. All subcommittee reports, before they were even submitted in draft form to the subcommittee members, had to go through a review process by Holifield's staff people. Holifield refused to allow the committee to travel overseas. Moorhead, for example, had a running battle with Holifield. Moorhead was chairman of the Foreign Operations Subcommittee and he tried to take a number of overseas trips. Holifield wouldn't let him. We are not talking about denying staff people overseas travel. We are talking about the members themselves.

The outrage voiced by a handful of the most activist liberals on the committee was not translated into any committee action against Holifield. To be sure Holifield's tactics did cause some discomfort among a wider group of members. One southern Democrat commented delicately,

I think there were several members of the committee who felt a little upset that they had not been given sufficient opportunity to participate in the making of major decisions.

Nevertheless any committee votes on questions of curbing the chairman showed substantial support for Holifield. This was partly because of the low interest expressed in Government Operations by many of its members (it was a low priority, second committee for most), partly because Holifield received substantial Republican support and partly because the activists were few in number (a situation which changed markedly in the Ninety-third and Ninety-fourth Congresses). Moreover, Benjamin Rosenthal, due to the new reforms, took a subcommittee chair on Foreign Affairs at the start of the Ninety-second Congress, and devoted somewhat less energy in Government Operations to implementing the new rules. The tension was not reduced, but Rosenthal's immediate stake in Government Operations' rules was lessened. In the meantime, Holifield defused any role by the committee's Democratic caucus by ignoring it. He never called meetings of either the caucus or of subcommittee chairmen, and so that forum was not readily available. At the beginning of the Ninety-third Congress, the conflict between Holifield and Rosenthal reached its peak, when Rosenthal formally challenged Holifield's renomination for chairman in the House Democratic caucus, supporting his challenge with a ten-page documented bill of particulars which was distributed to every House Democrat. The effort was resoundingly unsuccessful, but (as one member commented in 1975) "it was the first organized effort to depose a sitting committee chairman. Perhaps it laid the basis for more active efforts that came to fruition this year."

The challenge had little effect on Holifield's dominant rule on the committee in the Ninety-third Congress; about the only effect of the newly passed Subcommittee Bill of Rights, said a staff member, was "it allowed Moorhead to hire one staff person and Holifield didn't like that staff person."

Reaching an advanced age, frustrated by the sudden changes in the congressional process and the resulting tensions on this committee, and damaged politically by a court-imposed redistricting, Holifield retired in 1974. The new chairman in 1975, Jack Brooks of Texas, brought with him a different set of ideas about the committee chairmanship, conditioned at least in part by the events of January and by the enlarged group of activists on the Democratic side of the committee.

The major structural change brought about by Brooks was a large-scale reorganization of subcommittees in the Ninety-fourth Congress. Brooks set about redesigning the subcommittees by getting together with his staff director and other committee staff members. One of these staffers outlined the rationale for the new jurisdictions:

> Special Studies had been our "orphan"—the catchall. We set up a new Manpower and Housing Subcommittee essentially as a replacement for Special Studies—we gave it Labor, Civil Service Commission, Veterans Affairs, taking some jurisdiction from Fountain's subcommittee (which got revenue sharing) . . . With Foreign Operations and Government Information, we spread around foreign operations to other subcommittees. [Moorhead made no objection, though he ultimately took another subcommittee.] To balance that subcommittee, we took the legal side of the old Legal and Monetary Affairs subcommittee and gave it to Government Information, plus archives and postal service. Now we needed to balance Legal and Monetary Affairs, so we gave it a commercial side—the word "consumer" was added to the title to balance the commerce end.

This description of a rational process is somewhat incomplete. It is clear from a series of interviews that the subcommittee rejurisdiction was accompanied by a lot of fierce politicking between Brooks and prospective subcommittee chairmen, with many compromises and bargains. Committee activists Rosenthal, Abzug, and Moorhead received subcommittees with broad (and, to them, politically attractive) jurisdictions. Brooks kept Legislation and (now) National Security intact. With Rosenthal receiving a new Commerce, Consumer, and Monetary Affairs Subcommittee, there was a noticeable lack of protest over Brooks's retention of the important Consumer Protection Agency bill in his own subcommittee.

A look at the names of the new subcommittees shows a clear concern for covering current political issues. In Table 9–8, we have italicized the new areas mentioned in subcommittee names. Energy, Individual Rights, Transportation, Human Resources, Commerce, Consumer, National Security, Manpower, Housing—the titles alone show an activist intent and the building of a new agenda on Government Operations. We should note that words like "energy" and "consumer" have cropped up in the titles of subcommittees on a large number of House panels.

Commerce

The reforms of the Ninety-second and Ninety-third Congresses had little impact on the Interstate and Foreign Commerce Committee, despite the efforts of committee activist John Moss. Moss had been a victim of the 1971 Hansen Committee reform which limited subcommittee chairmen to one per member; he gave up his Government Operations subcommittee on Foreign Operation and Government Information in order to retain his Commerce and Finance Subcommittee. Moss, an extraordinarily active and issue-oriented liberal, had bitterly fought the subcommittee chairmanship limitation, along with fellow committee member John Dingell (D., Mich.). By the beginning of the Ninety-third Congress, he was restless and frustrated by his inability to overcome the obstacles placed in his way by Committee Chairman Harley Staggers (W.Va.), especially over the right of a subcommittee chairman to hold hearings. The 1971 Hansen reforms, as implemented by the Commerce Democrats, allowed the subcommittee chairmen one counsel each, but this did not add to Moss's ability to move legislation. He was frequently frustrated by his subcommittee ratio of five Democrats to four Republicans. As a subcommittee member commented,

> We got some good legislation out of that Subcommittee—the Consumer Product Safety Commission. Truth in Packaging, securities—but it took very careful handling. We had Stuckey, you know, and he would most often vote with the Republicans, giving them a functional majority.

Moss supported the January, 1973, subcommittee reforms of the caucus, and made a strenuous effort to strictly implement them in the Commerce Committee. In particular, Moss pressed for application of the requirement that party ratios on subcommittees be at least as favorable to the Democrats as was the ratio on the full committee. Moss wanted the ratio of the Commerce and Finance Subcommittee increased from five to four (or 55.56 percent Democratic, which was slightly less favorable than the Committee's 24 to 19, or 55.81 percent, ratio) to six to four (60 percent). As Moss commented in retrospect,

> I failed overwhelmingly. I entered the issue with committed votes adequate to make the moves that had been started along this path a few years earlier, and when it was done I had myself and Mr. Dingell. All of the troops had left. There were implied threats of reprisal from the chairman.

A committee insider close to Moss offered a slightly different perspective:

> Not many members like John Moss—he has put down a lot of members. He is brilliant and most are uncomfortable with him. When he made his move two years ago, he would have been the committee leader, and the other committee Democrats didn't really want that.

Moss's overwhelming defeat when he attempted to change the rules in 1973 turned to success one Congress later. Several developments combined to bring about a massive reorganization on Interstate and Foreign Commerce in the Ninety-fourth Congress. The first was the 1974 committee reorganization, which contained some limited rejurisdiction and several changes in House rules. The Bolling-Hansen reforms took several areas of jurisdiction away from Commerce and gave them to other committees (Commerce lost the transportation areas of aviation and trucks), but it was in turn given new health jurisdiction, including Medicaid, along with some additional jurisdiction in the energy field. These changes in the committee's areas forced a redefinition of subcommittee boundaries. In addition, Caucus rules now institutionalized the Subcommittee Bill of Rights; all committees had to implement reforms for selection of subcommittee chairmen. A staff member recounted the rationale for subcommittee reorganization:

> With the committee rejurisdiction we lost a major chunk, and it created a tremendous imbalance in the four legislative subcommittees. That forced the hand. We had two diverse areas, communications and power, compressed into one subcommittee, but subcommittee chairmen

felt divided—an increase in the number of subcommittees would diminish the power of each subcommittee, especially under the committee's old rules.

Discussions about possible realignment continued through December, 1974, and into January, 1975. Concern soon developed among senior Democrats on the committee over possible changes in the subcommittee chairmen themselves precipitated by the new jurisdictions and by the caucus-mandated methods for selection of subcommittee chairmen. John Moss, frustrated by his old subcommittee and bored with its limited and somewhat esoteric jurisdiction, decided to switch subcommittee chairs and to bid for the newly enhanced health area. Democratic members bid for subcommittee chairs in order of full committee seniority, and Moss outranked Health Subcommittee Chairman Paul Rogers of Florida. To quote a knowledgeable committee Democrat:

> The Bolling-Hansen reforms had given us some new health jurisdiction, and Moss wanted to take it; he was bored with his old subject matter, which got quite legalistic. He had seniority over Rogers, and Rogers had had Health for so long, he'd become identified with it, he hated to give it up. So Moss and Rogers worked an arrangement. . . .

The "arrangement" which Moss and Rogers effected was put together with the approval of the other legislative subcommittee chairmen; it involved an expansion of the legislative subcommittees to five, plus Investigations (a plan first proposed by Chairman Staggers, incidentally) with a rejurisdiction and renaming of most of them. Instead of supplanting Rogers in Health, Moss would concentrate on removing Staggers from his chairmanship of the broad and powerful Investigations subcommittee. As the member quoted above commented, the other potential subcommittee chairmen went along:

> Dingell had the chance to get a powerful new subcommittee on energy, and while he loved his Merchant Marine and Fisheries Subcommittee, this was a great opportunity. Torby Macdonald hasn't been to active—he's not in good health[16]—and he wasn't too concerned about giving up power and just keeping communications, and (Fred) Rooney was going to be able to get railroads. So they joined forces. And Staggers *had* badly abused and misused the Investigations Subcommittee. . . . What we had was another Runnymede. A revolt of the barons against the king.

16. Torbert Macdonald died in 1976.

Conservative Democrat John Jarman of Oklahoma, chairman of the old Transportation and Aeronautics Subcommittee, would also have been jettisoned by the other subcommittee chairmen. However, being aware of the changes on the committee, Jarman switched to the Republican party and went off the committee before the Ninety-fourth Congress convened. This opened the transportation area to Fred Rooney of Pennsylvania. With the expansion in the number of subcommittees, an additional member, California's Lionel Van Deerlin, became eligible to bid for a subcommittee chair.

This "plan" by subcommittee chairmen was workable because of the influx of twelve new Democratic committee members, most of whom favored committee reform. Courted by the subcommittee chairmen with promises of new committee rules to maximize freshmen participation, many of the freshmen supported Moss and the reorganization plan. When the committee's Democratic caucus met on Tuesday, January 28, 1975, to select subcommittee chairmen, Harley Staggers lost his Investigations Subcommittee to John Moss, though not by any wide margin. Six ballots on Staggers resulted in fourteen-to-fourteen tie votes; on the seventh ballot, Staggers was deposed by a fifteen-to-thirteen vote. In Moss's account of the votes,

> Actually the true story of the vote on the issue of my chairmanship or Mr. Staggers has not really been properly told. The rules are that each person bids for a chairmanship. The vote is then handled and if that vote is not carried then the next person in rank bids on the chairmanship. Mr. Staggers ignored the rule and kept calling for votes; the initial vote was a tie, which meant that the motion to name him chairman of Investigations failed. The only way it could have been brought back before the committee caucus was by a motion to reconsider, which would have taken a vote of two-thirds. This was not requested. He merely ordered another roll call. The roll call should have occurred then with Mr. Macdonald's bid for communications and I would have bid for Investigations. And at that point I would have had twenty-one votes and not sixteen.

Moss did not object to the irregular procedure, because

> I was running about a 104 fever at that point, and I wasn't quite up to par. I knew that my votes were solid so I let Mr. Staggers go through five votes. Then I told him if you don't prevail on the next one I'm going to insist on the regular order. You cannot continue this business of calling for roll calls. You lost on the first call and I've just been inclined to be tolerant. At which time he continued his charade. Then of course the tie was broken.

The closeness of the vote was probably a reflection both of Staggers's pleasant personality and of Moss's relative lack of popularity among veteran committee Democrats, the latter a quality we referred to earlier. To one committee veteran, the close votes took place because Moss "was not just seeking change, he was going to take leadership."

The other subcommittee chairmanship votes followed the regular lines of seniority; Table 9–9 shows the subcommittee jurisdictions and chairmen for the Ninety-first through Ninety-fourth Congresses.

As with Government Operations, one can see the movement toward incorporating contemporary political issues into the new subcommittee names. Commerce and Finance was changed to Consumer Protection and Finance. In addition, the titles "environment" and "energy" appeared for the first time.

Flushed with their success, the Moss-led subcommittee chairmen drew up a set of new committee rules. As adopted on February 26, 1975, the committee's rules numbered twenty, up from a mere five for the Ninety-third Congress. The new rules included such provisions as:

1. Subcommittees were to be set up by the committee Democratic caucus (Rule 10).
2. Subcommittees were authorized to hold hearings and mark up legislation, a right which had previously been controlled by the committee chairman (Rule 11).
3. Legislation would be referred to the appropriate subcommittee within five days (Rule 12).
4. The ratio of subcommittee Democrats to Republicans would be set by the majority caucus, provided that each subcommittee ratio would be at least as favorable as the full-committee ratio, and no ratio would provide for a majority of less than two majority members (Rule 13).
5. The ratio of Democratic to Republican conferees would be identical to those of the subcommittees (Rule 14).
6. Majority members of the committee would bid in order of full-committee seniority for subcommittee chairmanships, subject to approval, by secret ballot vote, by a majority of the committee Democratic Caucus (Rule 16).
7. Subcommittee budgets would be set by subcommittee chairmen, subject to approval by the majority caucus and the full committee.

Rule 15 of the new Ninety-fourth Congress Interstate and Foreign Commerce Committee rules regulated subcommittee membership. Part (*a*) of that rule reads as follows:

Table 9-9. Subcommittee Chairmen on House Interstate and Foreign Commerce Committee, 91st–94th Congresses

Subcommittees, 91st–93rd Cong.

		Chairmen	
	91st Cong.	*92nd Cong.*	*93rd Cong.*
Investigations	Staggers (W. Va.)	Staggers (W. Va.)	Staggers (W. Va.)
Commerce and Finance	Moss (Calif.)	Moss (Calif.)	Moss (Calif.)
Communications and Power	Macdonald (Mass.)	Macdonald (Mass.)	Macdonald (Mass.)
Public Health and Welfare	Jarman (Okla.)	Rogers (Fla.)	Rogers (Fla.)
Transportation and Aeronautics	Friedel (Md.)	Jarman (Okla.)	Jarman (Okla.)

Subcommittees, 94th Cong.

	Chairmen
Oversight and Investigations	Moss (Calif.)
Consumer Protection and Finance	Van Deerlin (Calif.)
Communications	Macdonald (Mass.)
Health and Environment	Rogers (Fla.)
Transportation and Commerce	Rooney (Pa.)
Energy and Power	Dingell (Mich.)

Subcommittee Membership. (*a*) Each majority member other than the chairman of the full committee or the chairman of a subcommittee shall in order of committee seniority be entitled to membership on two subcommittees of said member's choice. Proceeding in order of seniority on the committee, each majority member, other than the chairman of the full committee and the chairmen of several subcommittees, shall be entitled to select one subcommittee position each. The subcommittee selection process shall then continue in sequence of committee seniority, including the chairmen of the several subcommittees, for succeeding rounds of selection until all subcommittee positions are filled. The subcommittee selection process shall be conducted at a meeting of the majority party caucus of the committee held prior to any organizational meeting of the full committee. Subcommittee selections of each member shall be recorded by the clerk as made and shall be available for examination by the members.[17]

This rule greatly benefited the new members, especially with respect to the Energy and Power Subcommittee, the only wholly new subcommittee. Most senior Democrats first opted for a subcommittee on which they already served.

As one veteran noted,

> Everyone was so anxious to get the freshmen in their camp that the members in the middle got squeezed. The result was that Wirth, Sharp, and Brodhead ended up second-, third-, and fourth-ranking on the Dingell subcommittee.

The Energy and Power Subcommittee ended up with seven of its ten Democrats being new members; Oversight and Investigations, curiously, also ended up with a large number of new Democrats, eight out of ten.

Thus Commerce went from a decisive rejection of reform in the Ninety-third Congress to a sweeping set of changes in the Ninety-fourth that drastically cut the powers of the chairman of the full committee, ousted him from his subcommittee chair, and gave virtual autonomy to its six subcommittees.

International Relations

No committee changed more as a result of the 1971 Democratic caucus reforms than Foreign Affairs (renamed International Relations in 1975). The limitation of subcommittee chairmanships to

17. *Rules Adopted by the Committees of Congress, Ninety-fourth Congress,* op. cit., p. 123.

one per member opened up three subcommittees, as Robert N.C. Nix (Pa.) opted for a Post Office and Civil Service subcommittee, and L. H. Fountain (N.C.) and John Monagan (Conn.) took Government Operations chairs after Holifield's attempt to circumvent the reforms had failed. The three new chairmen brought in by the reforms on Foreign Affairs (and their subcommittees) were Benjamin Rosenthal of New York (Europe), Lee Hamilton of Indiana (Near East), and John Culver of Iowa (Foreign Economic Policy). In addition, in the Ninety-second Congress a fourth new subcommittee chairman—Minnesota's Don Fraser (International Organizations and Movement)—was installed as a result of Leonard Farbstein's primary defeat in New York City in 1970.

The chairman of Foreign Affairs, Thomas E. "Doc" Morgan (Pa), is not an activist, but he has not been an aggressive or vigorous opponent of change either. He placidly allowed committee Democrats to effect rules changes which permitted each subcommittee chairman to hire a professional staff member, and he gave his subcommittee chairmen a relatively free rein on travel, holding hearings, and considering appropiate legislation. The four new chairmen—all liberal, issue-oriented activists—exploited the new rules by markedly increasing subcommittee activity on Foreign Affairs.

Foreign Affairs had mostly concentrated on the structure of the foreign-aid bill prior to the Ninety-second Congress, while relatively ignoring other policy questions in the international arena. Following the rules changes, the activist subcommittees changed the committee's focus considerably. Passage of the Subcommittee Bill of Rights in the Ninety-third Congress accelerated the pace of change on Foreign Affairs, with a further decentralization of committee activity into the subcommittees. Only one subcommittee chair changed hands (or seats) in the Ninety-third Congress, as Cornelius Gallagher (N.J.) left the House and Robert N.C. Nix (Pa.) moved back from a Post Office subcommittee chairmanship to head the Asian and Pacific Affairs Subcommittee of Foreign Affairs. This was a step backward in terms of subcommittee activity, and helped precipitate the major reorganization of the subcommittees in the Ninety-fourth Congress.

The Ninety-fourth Congress resulted in a new name for the committee, two new subcommittee chairmen, and a major shuffling of subcommittee jurisdictions. The new name was the idea of Donald M. Fraser (Minn.), chairman of the International Organizations and Movements Subcommittee since 1971, and a moving force in the committee's newly aggressive role in the international arena. At organizational meetings when the Ninety-fourth Congress convened, Fraser proposed the name change; it was accepted without prolonged discussion or major dissent. Two reasons were probably most important. The longtime association of foreign-policy influence with the Senate's Foreign Relations Committee had hurt the credibility of the House Committee. (A senior member commented, "We were sick of that Old Alben Barkley joke, the House committee only had affairs, not relations. Basically, we were considered a throwaway committee—our only bill was foreign aid. So we changed our name to change our image.") Secondly, the name change was a result of Fraser's view that, with an increasingly interdependent world, International Relations was a more accurate reflection of the committee's work.

For the most part, members were willing to go along when one of the colleagues felt strongly about the need for a new name. As a staff member noted, "These weren't matters that vitally affect many members."

Two subcommittee chairmanships opened up with the lost of two chairmen who had been favored by the 1971 reforms. John Culver of Iowa was elected to the Senate, and Benjamin Rosenthal of New York opted for a new subcommittee chairmanship on Goveriment Operations. The next two Democrats eligible for subcommittees, by seniority, were Lester Wolff and Johnathan Bingham, both liberals from New York.

The shifts in subcommittee chairs caused by the departure of two chairmen, combined with the committee's gain in jurisdiction (through the 1974 Bolling-Hansen reforms) of PL 480 (food aid) and of an additional role in foreign trade, precipitated the need for some redefinition of subcommittee alignments. The move for a rejurisdiction on functional grounds, away from the old regional alignments, came from two disparate sources. Marian Czarnecki, the committee's staff director, proposed a subcommittee change to Chairman Morgan for practical and theoretical reasons. In a long memorandum to the chairman on December 2, 1974, Czarnecki commented,

> Our subcommittee structure may not be relevant to our members' concerns and effective study of major foreign-policy problems of the 1970s. . . . The major problems with which the committee will be dealing in the future—i.e., food and resource shortages, energy, trade policy, export controls, development, security, arms transfers, human rights issues, etc.—cut across regional lines.

Czarnecki offered the following advantages to a functional reorganization:

1. Foreign policy problems could be considered on the basis of their functional components, without regard to geographic limitations;

2. Each subcommittee could concern itself with all of the economic or political—or strategic—or other—ramifications of a given problem;
3. Two or three subcommittees could approach a major problem from different directions—thereby reviewing it in depth;
4. When the subcommittees' recommendations are submitted to the full committee, all of the relevant political, economic, strategic, and other considerations could be considered at the same time;
5. When the committee speaks on the floor, it would speak with more knowledge and more authority.

Czarnecki left unstated another reason for his desire to create functional subcommittees, one proposed to us in several interviews with members and staff. Since the 1974 reforms, tensions had built between the core full-committee staff and many of the new, activist subcommittee aides who were hired directly by the subcommittee chairmen. At times, the animosities were displayed in petty ways; for example, a State Department invitation to the committee's staff to attend a reception was not circulated to the subcommittee staffers. While it may not have been the moving force behind a decision to realign subcommittees, the fact that this change would likely force some subcommittee aides out of their jobs was certainly known to the full committee staff.

At the same time, movement toward a functional realignment was coming from a very different direction—from Fraser and some of the other activist subcommittee chairmen. Fraser's reasons were partly theoretical, but were also fueled by frustration in the Ninety-third Congress stemming from his inability to hold detailed hearings on the question of political prisoners in Asia, especially Vietnam and Korea. Fraser had followed protocol, going to Asian and Pacific Affairs Subcommittee Chairman Robert Nix for clearance; Nix had refused, saying that his subcommittee would handle the problem. The Nix subcommittee later held one day of hearings on political prisoners. A realignment on functional lines, by eliminating the need for any subcommittee chairman to step on a regional chairman's toes, would free chairmen to pursue their interests more freely.

Fraser was aided in his move to realign the subcommittees by two other chairmen, both of regional subcommittees, Dante Fascell (Fla.) and Lee Hamilton (Ind.). One committee insider offered this interpretation:

Fascell, of course, has all those Cuban-Americans in his district. He felt confined by the Latin America Subcommittee, but he couldn't give it up—as long as there was a Latin America Subcommittee, Dante would have to chair it. Hamilton is a very decent guy, very conscientious, but he must have felt boredom with the Middle East. He had a great staff guy, Mike Van Dusen, but he *never* traveled there in four years as chairman.

One other set of actors figured in the realignment process—the State Department, which worked closely with the full committee staff. To a close follower of the committee,

> The State Department was afraid of Lester Wolff taking over Middle East—he's a New York Jew and, frankly, very unpredictable. The first version of the reorganization plan had only eight subcommittees— Wolff would have been excluded entirely. They [State] worked with the committee staff, many of whom felt Wolff would be a catastrophe, to keep Wolff out.

The plan which ultimately was accepted by the International Relations Committee on February 3, 1975, kept the number of subcommittees at its previous level (ten) but removed all geographic and regional distinctions. (The new subcommittees and their chairmen are presented in Table 9–10.) A participant observed:

> The announcement of the change on February 3 came after two meetings of the full committee in the week preceding. This followed a week of intensive lobbying by Fraser, Fascell, and Hamilton. The others didn't much care, so it passed by acclamation. That's the way the House works—if you are pretty much indifferent, and someone else cares strongly, you'll go along. Most people in Congress don't care much about reorganization principles—they ask, "What will this do to me?" If you aren't a subcommittee chairman, you can't say that these changes would hurt you. As for the chairmen, two of the regional subcommittee chairmen were for it; one, Ben Rosenthal, was giving up his subcommittee; and one of the others [Charles Diggs] was in Africa—disabled, as it were. The two new chairmen—Wolff was opposed to it at first meeting, while Bingham was in favor, though he saw some problems.

A look at Table 9–10 shows the new alignments and chairmen. The previous nonregional subcommittees underwent some changes, but their jurisdictions were basically unchanged, except that Clement Zablocki's former National Security Policy Subcommittee was given scientific affairs. The regional subcommittees were erased. Africa was replaced by International Resources, Food, and Energy, taking the major new jurisdiction of the committee (notice the ubiquitous "energy" in yet another subcommittee title) with Charles Diggs retaining the chair. Asian and Pacific Affairs was replaced by International Trade and Commerce, with new chairman Jonathan Bingham; former Asian and Pacific Affairs head Robert Nix took over Interna-

Table 9–10. International Relations Subcommittee and Chairmen, 91st–94th Congresses

Subcommittees, 91st–93rd Cong.	Chairmen		
	91st Cong.	92nd Cong.	93rd Cong.
Africa	Diggs (Mich.)	Diggs (Mich.)	Diggs (Mich.)
Asian and Pacific Affairs	Murphy (Ill.)	Gallagher (N.J.)	Nix (Pa.)
Europe	Farbstein (N.Y.)	Rosenthal (N.Y.)	Rosenthal (N.Y.)
Inter-American Affairs	Fascell (Fla.)	Fascell (Fla.)	Fascell (Fla.)
Near East	Fountain (N.C.)	Hamilton (Ind.)	Hamilton (Ind.)
International Organizations and Movements	Gallagher (N.J.)	Fraser (Minn.)	Fraser (Minn.)
National Security Policy	Zablocki (Wisc.)	Zablocki (Wisc.)	Zablocki (Wisc.)
Foreign Economic Policy	Nix (Pa.)	Culver (Ia.)	Culver (Ia.)
State Department Organization	Hays (Oh.)	Hays (Oh.)	Hays (Oh.)
Foreign Aid	Morgan (Pa.)	Morgan (Pa.)	Morgan (Pa.)

Subcommittees, 94th Cong.	Chairmen
International Resources, Food, Energy	Diggs (Mich.)
International Trade and Commerce	Bingham (N.Y.)
Future Foreign Policy Research and Development	Wolff (N.Y.)
International Economic Policy	Nix (Pa.)
International Political and Military Affairs	Fascell (Fla.)
International Organizations	Fraser (Minn.)
International Security and Scientific Affairs	Zablocki (Wisc.)
Investigations	Hamilton (Ind.)
International Operations	Hays (Oh.)
Oversight	Morgan (Pa.)

tional Economic Policy, vacated by John Culver's move to the Senate. Europe, formerly chaired by Benjamin Rosenthal, was replaced by Future Foreign Policy Research and Development with a new chairman, Lester Wolff. Inter-American Affairs was replaced by International Political and Military Affairs with Dante Fascell remaining as chairman. Finally, Near East was replaced by a new Investigations Subcommittee, still headed by Lee Hamilton. The new jurisdictions are vaguer and much more overlapping than the earlier alignments, with consequences that we will discuss shortly.

IV. The Consequences of Congressional Change

To this point we have been describing certain changes which have occurred in the House of Representatives during the early 1970's. This paper began with a description of change at the institutional level: the nature of turnover in the 1970, 1972, and 1974 elections, and the character of reforms passed by the House and its Democratic caucus during the period. We then outlined how these institution-level changes impacted on the four committees which are the focus of our analysis. Two general patterns seem apparent: (1) These committees have undergone major personnel changes (including, in some cases, changes in the *kinds* of members represented on the committee); and (2) the reform process has shifted control over resources and policy-making emphasis from the full committee to subcommittees.

We now must turn to address the question of whether all this has made any difference: Have the changes we have described been consequential or merely cosmetic? We shall attempt to ascertain for each committee whether these changes have had an effect on certain key aspects of member behavior and committee operation. In particular, we will be interested in the following questions:

1. Have reforms and turnover, in interaction or separately, altered behavior or policy outputs in the committees?
2. Has the impact of these changes been affected by the chairmen of the various committees; have the changes affected the chairman's role?
3. Has the impact of the changes been limited or shaped by the committee environments, especially the goals of the members?[18]

18. Richard Fenno has argued that three goals are basic among members of the House: reelection, influence within the House, and good public policy. It is this framework that we will employ here. See Richard F. Fenno, *Congressmen in Committees* (Boston: Little, Brown, 1973), esp. pp. 1–14.

Finally, we will return to the institutional level and consider whether the changes have had an effect on behavior and policy outcomes in the House within the areas of jurisdiction of these four committees.

Agriculture

The Agriculture Committee, as we have seen, has changed its members and its chairman, going from a conservative southern-dominated majority-party contingent to one with more regional balance and a more moderate ideological tone, and from a highly conservative southern chairman to a leader of the liberal Democratic Study Group. In addition, the committee has implemented the full array of subcommittee-strengthening reforms. What have been the consequences for policy of these structural and personnel changes?

Unfortunately, Agriculture Committee calendars and activity reports do not contain breakdowns of committee hearings by subcommittee for the Ninety-first or Ninety-second Congresses. The information does exist for the Ninety-third Congress as a whole, and we have data for the first seven months of the Ninety-fourth, but comparisons are obviously very limited. The data we have to this point are displayed in Table 9–11.[19]

We do not have hearing or meeting breakdowns for the Ninety-second Congress, but the total number of meetings *and* hearings, for full committee and subcommittees for the first seven months, was seventy-three, somewhat less than the two Congresses which followed. Though we must be careful about making comparisons between Congresses, the figures in Table 9–11 for the Ninety-third and Ninety-fourth Congresses show some interesting patterns. First and foremost, it is clear that overall activity on the Agriculture Committee has remained quite stable, changing very little for both full committee and subcommittees. When we take a closer look, however, we see that some significant changes are apparent. At the full committee level, there has been a major shift in emphasis, from hearings to meetings. We will discuss this change below. Secondly, activity on commodity subcommittees has dropped for the Ninety-fourth Congress. Thirdly, the only subcommittee which has experienced a marked increase in activity is Conservation and Credit, which went from four meetings and hearings in the first part of the Ninety-third Congress to fifteen in the first part of the Ninety-fourth. The replacement of Robert Poage as subcommittee chairman by Robert Bergland, whose role on the

19. These data, and the activity data on other committees which will be presented below, have been obtained from committee calendars or directly from committee staff.

Table 9–11. Agriculture Committee and Subcommittee Meetings and Hearings Held, 93rd–94th Congresses

	93rd Cong.			94th Cong.		
	Meet-ings	Hear-ings	Total	Meet-ings	Hear-ings	Total
Full Committee	14	22	36	27	13	40
Commodity Subcommittees						
Livestock and Grains	3	9	12	8	10	18
Cotton	3	4	7	1	3	4
Dairy and Poultry	3	4	7	2	0	2
Forests	3	6	9	1	2	3
Oilseeds and Rice	2	4	6	3	3	6
Tobacco	2	3	5	0	5	5
Commodity Subcommittees, Total	16	30	46	15	23	38
Operational Subcommittees						
Conservation and Credit	2	2	4	8	7	15
Departmental Operations	1	8	9	3	3	6
Domestic Marketing	1	7	8	1	6	7
Family Farms	1	5	6	2	6	8
Operational Subcommittees, Total	5	22	27	14	22	36
Subcommittes, Total	21	52	73	29	45	74

Note: Totals are as of August 1 of first session, 94th Congress.

committee was outlined in earlier sections, is the apparent cause of this upsurge in activity. The Conservation and Credit meetings and hearings in this Congress have been on a wide range of subjects, including the Consolidated Farm and Rural Development Act, the Commodity Futures Trading Commission, and livestock credit. Conversely, meetings and hearings for the Forests Subcommittee have dropped from nine to three; the new chairman, Jerry Litton (he replaced John Rarick, who was defeated in a 1974 Louisiana Democratic primary), has been actively seeking the Missouri Senate seat of Stuart Symington, who is retiring in 1976.

Nor do we find surprising increases in quantity when we examine legislation reported out of the committee. In both the Ninety-first and Ninety-second Congresses, the Agriculture Committee reported forty-eight bills to the House floor; in the Ninety-third Congress, the committee sent forty-five bills to the floor. To the August recess in the

Ninety-fourth Congress, fourteen bills were reported to the House floor, which is a rate roughly comparable to the previous Congresses. In the first part of the Ninety-fourth Congress, there was little major legislation enacted by the House Agriculture Committee, with the exception of HR 4296, the farm bill (which we discuss below), and amendments to the Food Stamp Act (which suspended increases in costs to recipients). The other legislation reported by the committee was basically routine; no significant innovations in outlook or policy have thus far emerged from the House Agriculture Committee in the Ninety-fourth Congress.

One major area of controversy presented itself in the committee in the Ninety-fourth Congress, and it was not resolved until October, 1975. This concerned pesticide regulation, through the old Federal Insecticide, Fungicide, and Rodenticide Act (FIFRA). Under the act, pesticide regulation has been handled by the Environmental Protection Agency, under great criticism from farm groups. Originally scheduled to expire June 30, the Act was extended twice by the Committee and the House while it wrangled over attempts to shift the regulatory power from EPA to the U.S. Department of Agriculture. Spearheading the effort were former Chairman Poage and ranking Republican William Wampler (Va.), while EPA and environmental interest groups vigorously opposed it. On September 4, the Committee accepted a compromise offered by Joseph Vigorito (D., Pa.) and Chairman Foley, which extended the program for one year and set up formal channels for the Department of Agriculture to comment in advance on the EPA's pesticide actions. The committee vote was 23 to 18 with Poage backing the compromise (reasoning that the original proposal had no chance on the floor) and Wampler voting against it. Twenty Democrats and three liberal Republicans voted for the compromise; six Democrats (all southerners) and twelve Republicans voted against it. By some accounts, the committee vote actually appears closer than the "real" division; at least two of the Democrats who rejected the compromise would have supported it if their votes had been necessary. The compromise was approved on the House floor, on October 9, 329 to 80, after two attempts to add the original Poage-Wampler provision through amendment were defeated more narrowly.[20]

Thus it appears that despite the fact that the Agriculture Committee has undergone enormous membership change and has been substantially affected by the reform process, little overt change in behavior or policy outputs has occurred.

There appear to be several reasons why the impact of change has

20. See *Congressional Quarterly Weekly Report* (October 11, 1975):2206–7.

been limited within the committee, some of them closely related to individual member goals. While there has been substantial change among the membership, what must be emphasized is that most of the new people (whatever their region or ideology) are from *rural* districts with *farm* interests. The increase in attractiveness of Agriculture as a committee assignment among Democrats, which we documented earlier, is directly related to the increase in the number of Democratic victories in midwestern and western farm districts. The Agriculture Committee serves a very limited and specific set of interests, and these new members—liberal though many of them may be on other issues— see as their major role protecting their constituents' agricultural interests (and thus helping to ensure their own reelection). The fact that their outlook and interests are broader than those of most of their predecessors may well result in an eventual broadening of the scope of agricultural policy, nationally and internationally; however, through the first session of the Ninety-fourth Congress the focus of the committee remains directly on farmers' interests.

The lack of a major urban or consumer focus in agricultural policy is also related to the nature of subcommittee assignments on Agriculture. Through a process of self-selection, the few urban-oriented members (e.g., Brown, D., Calif.; Richmond, D., N.Y.; Heckler, R., Mass.; Peyser, R., N.Y.) have avoided the commodity subcommittees, and have chosen operational subcommittees like Domestic Marketing and Consumer Relations for their first assignment option and their major time commitment.[21] Thus the agricultural legislation which goes through the commodity subcommittees remains dominated by legislators who represent particular commodity interests. In addition, as we demonstrated earlier, the chairmen of the commodity subcommittees are still southern and border Democrats; the overall turnover has not yet been reflected among the chairmen of these subcommittees. While David Bowen of Mississippi (who chairs the Cotton Subcommittee) may not have a great deal in common with Thomas Abernethy, his congressional district predecessor (who also headed that subcommittee), their differences do not extend to legislation affecting cotton.

As we have seen, the subcommittees as a group—with the single exception of Conservation and Credit—have not greatly increased their activity with the advent of the reforms and the concomitant changes in the committee rules. Reforms strengthening subcommittees assume subcommittee chairmen who are active and policy-oriented. Agricul-

21. Or they have chosen to concentrate on another committee. For example, George Brown of California passed up a subcommittee chair on Agriculture to take one on Science and Technology.

ture subcommittee chairmen are not active or policy-oriented, except for Bergland of Minnesota, who has transformed the Conservation and Credit Subcommittee into an active and broad-ranging instrument (though his subcommittee has not reported out much legislation). Bergland has done this even though he has not been able to hire any subcommittee staff; he is seventh in seniority among subcommittee chairmen, and only the top six have been authorized to hire a professional staffer.

Thus the new rules relating to subcommittees appear to have had a limited impact on Agriculture; what about the seniority reforms which removed the old chairman and gave the committee a new leader?

Thomas Foley, the new chairman, is different from his predecessor Robert Poage in almost every respect, and these differences, intermixed with the effects of the reform process, are reflected in their styles as chairman. As one staff member described Foley,

> He is normally inclined toward an open process and he has a background as a professor in constitutional law. He is thoughtfully inclined and he naturally leans toward a more democratic way of handling matters and the committee. He doesn't—and I think this probably is connected to his basic personality—the fact is he doesn't make quick decisions. He slowly drifts into decisions . . . he finds himself reacting to things to a large extent. If there is another thing to be handled, rather than risking any personal relationship he is going to keep the process open and let them have their say. It is partly a question of perceiving [that] you might accomplish something in the short run by closing off debate but this will come back to haunt you when you get out onto the floor.

Foley has thus bent over backwards to accommodate all the members of the committee in debate, and to democratize the process. Poage, in the meantime, has retained a highly important role in the committee, because of his conciliatory attitude after his ouster, his expertise (one member said, "He is canny, he is knowledgeable and he is astute. And he is trustworthy."), and his friendship with Foley. A veteran Republican committee member commented: "Poage as vice-chairman is exerting more influence now than he did as chairman." Another committee insider described the Poage-Foley interaction:

> On the one hand, Poage has been a challenge to the chairman. At the same time he has very shrewdly used his unique position as a former chairman, who understands and can speak with authority of the problems of the committee chairmen, to support Foley on some of the key things. So he sits beside Foley as vice-chairman and supports him in some of these jurisdictional things as ways of controlling the committee . . . that is a positive force in terms of integration of authority

within the committee. Poage has played a suppuring role to Foley and that is one of the reasons that he uses that power base as he wants. . . .

In a very real sense Foley is new at the game and, comparatively speaking, not very senior around this place. So that is part of it. There is a very complex and interesting relationship going on between the chairman and the vice-chairman, and it is significant that all of sudden the position of vice-chairman is a much more powerful one than it has been in the past. He is vice-chairman in fact. No one before ever knew that there was a vice-chairman.

Thus Foley, through the first session of the Ninety-fourth Congress, has leaned heavily on Poage, and has tried to accommodate the junior members. Poage's continued influence on the committee has limited the amount of policy change which has occurred in the committee, while the accommodation of the new members has meant that much of the activity of the full committee is spent allowing everybody to have a full say on all issues. As one member commented, "This doesn't change any outcomes, it just takes a hell of a lot of additional time. Some of these young guys have to say something about everything." So this additional activity has not led the committee in any new policy directions, though it has certainly contributed to the socialization of junior committee members. As time passes, we might expect Foley to gain in confidence as chairman and to rely somewhat less on his predecessor. We might also expect the junior members, as *they* gain expertise and political savvy, to direct their committee activities in more focused and fruitful directions.

Finally, there is some reason to believe that the Agriculture Committee may expand its policy role in the future. The policy activity of the committee is likely to increase when the next group of members eligible for subcommittee chairs receive them. These include Fredrick Richmond (N.Y.), Richard Nolan (Minn.), James Weaver (Ore.), Alvin Baldus (Wisc.), and John Krebs (Calif.). Following the lead of Bergland, these people will probably make their subcommittees more activist than they are now. There is also some evidence that the younger Democrats on the committee are forging a new informal coalition of their own, with Northerners Bergland and Fithian and Southerners Bowen and Rose as major components. To one committee Democrat,

This coalition is somewhat tenuous, but we are trying to solidify it with a new esprit-de-corps, and it's working. These new members are terrific. They're bright and hardworking and I'm convinced that we have a new situation in the House and on the committee.

When asked about the focus of the coalition, this legislator replied:

> We have more internationalism: we're moving toward a reserve system
> —no more boom and bust years. We see the need for stability. We are
> having a new dialogue, which looks at a long-term policy of food as a
> developmental tool . . . We would like to change PL 480 from surplus
> dumping to relate to our commitments. We will need cooperation
> from International Relations, of course, but we're talking to them, too.
> This is all informal now; a couple of us will talk about it on the floor,
> alert each other to new articles, and so forth. But we're moving
> towards formalizing it in terms of hearings and dialogues within the
> committee.

Although traditional farm issues will almost certainly remain dominant within the Committee in coming years, other policy foci within
Agriculture could be slowly but significantly altered. Some of this depends, of course, on the ability of junior Democratic members from
competitive districts—people like Fithian (Ind.), Nolan (Minn.),
Harkin (Ind.), and Bedall (Ia.)—to retain their seats.

We should also comment on the Agriculture Committee's role in
oversight. The subcommittee on Departmental Operations, Investigation, and Oversight is headed by "Kika" de la Garza of Texas, the
third-ranking Democrat on the committee. De la Garza has been
described by committee members and staff as "a feisty guy," and one
who "is interested in power . . . he is kind of on the outside trying to
grab something every chance he gets. He also has a desire to build the
full committee because he thinks Foley may go to the Senate."

One manifestation of de la Garza's ambitions has been his aggressive
move to have an annual authorization of the United States Department of Agriculture, which has been strongly opposed by the department and the administration. A committee insider says that de la Garza

> sees himself becoming committee chairman one of these days, and he
> wants a little power lying around when he becomes committee chair-
> man. And so one way to do that is to try and secure an annual
> authorization. Then, at least, you have some bureaucrats coming up
> and you are holding their money. This is a bargaining, power-base
> affair.

Faced with a hostile Secretary of Agriculture like Earl Butz, many
committee Democrats are leaning toward more aggressive oversight
of the department, though this may not include the time-consuming
step of annual authorization. Should the 1976 elections produce a
Democratic Secretary of Agriculture—conceivably, one of the members

of this committee—the new aggressiveness of the Departmental Operations Subcommittee might fade.

We have seen that congressional change has had little impact on the Agriculture Committee. The jurisdiction of the committee was confined to a narrow range of matters, and the committee attracted members who had constituencies which could be served within this range. The structure of the committee and its leadership (especially after Poage became chairman) before the 1970s had permitted its members to satisfy the interests of their constituents and thus help the members' chances for reelection. Even though the committee's structure and leadership changed in the Ninety-fourth Congress, the nature of the membership and their goals did not, and thus the character of activity and policy outcomes did not change.

However, the narrowness of the committee's jurisdiction and of the interests represented in the constituencies of the members, while they had permitted member satisfaction, had caused the committee difficulty in the past when its bills reached the House floor. Most House members who do not serve on the committee also do not represent districts with narrow agricultural interests. Indeed, with the population shifts and court-imposed redistricting requirements of the late 1960s and early 1970s, the strength of rural areas on the House floor declined precipitously; between 1966 and 1973, the number of districts in which 50 percent or more of the population resided outside of a Standard Metropolitan Statistical Area declined from 181 to 130.[22] Thus, because the committee lacked a natural majority on the floor, it was forced to "logroll"—to trade rural support on nonagricultural matters for nonrural support of farm bills.[23] Moreover, even when the vote trading took place, the size of the majority supporting the bill was far from comfortable; many urban Democrats (especially members from the northeast) were simply antagonistic to farm bills because Southerners dominated the committee. For example, as Table 9–12 shows,[24] only 40 percent of the northern Democrats supported the

22. See Weldon V. Barton, "Coalition-Building in the U.S. House of Representatives: Agricultural Legislation in 1973," a paper prepared for delivery at the 1974 Annual Meeting of the American Political Science Association, Chicago, Illinois, August 29 to September 2, 1974, p. 3.

23. In addition to Barton, op. cit., see Randall B. Ripley, "Legislative Bargaining and the Food Stamp Act, 1964," in Frederick C. Cleveland (ed.), *Congress and Urban Problems* (Washington, D.C.: The Brookings Institution, 1969), pp. 279–310; and Arthur G. Stevens, "Coalitions and Committee Representativeness," a paper prepared for delivery at the Seminar on Mathematical Models of Congress, Aspen, Colorado, June 16–23, 1974.

24. For convenience, in this table we follow *Congressional Quarterly*'s practice of including Kentucky and Oklahoma in the South.

Table 9–12. Support for Major Farm Bills in the House, 1970, 1973, and 1975

Vote	All Members	Repub-licans	Democrats	Northern Democrats	Southern Democrats
	Percent of Members Voting Aye				
House bill, Agriculture Act of 1970	55	49	60	40	91
Conference Report, Agriculture Act of 1970	57	52	60	43	91
House bill, Farm Program Extension (1973)	55	48	61	49	86
House bill, Agriculture Act Amendments (1975)	62	34	75	71	85
Conference Report, Agriculture Act Amendments (1975)	60	30	75	69	87
Agriculture Act Amendments (1975)[a]	57	23	75	71	83

[a] Attempted veto override.

1970 farm bill on final passage—less than the level of Republican support—and only 49 percent supported the extension in 1973.

It is here on the House floor that the membership changes in the House and in the Agriculture Committee appear to have had an impact. Almost three-fourths of the northern Democrats supported the 1975 farm bill. This support was secured by the passage of two floor amendments (backed by the AFL-CIO, the Consumer Federation of America, and Common Cause) which reduced the levels of payments in the bill for dairy products and cotton.[25] And the floor fight for the amendments was led by three freshmen Democratic members of the Agriculture Committee—Frederick Richmond (N.Y.), Norman D'Amours (N.H.), and John Krebs (Calif.). Richmond (who represents a portion of Brooklyn and is the most liberal member of the committee) said "I feel I am trying to represent the consumers and work out a fair consumer-farmer coalition bill."[26]

It appears that he was successful. As Table 9–12 shows, the gap in support for the bill between northern and southern Democrats was

25. See *Congressional Quarterly Weekly Report* (March 22, 1975):624–26.
26. Ibid., p. 624.

remarkably small. Indeed, the basic division over the bill was partisan (President Ford opposed the bill and vetoed it when it came to his desk).

This one bill does not mean that there is now a complete coincidence of interests among rural and urban Democrats, nor does it *guarantee* that the same kind of coalition can be produced on farm bills in the future. As Table 9–13 shows, there was still a substantial amount of

Table 9–13. Support Among Northern Democrats for the Conference Report, Agriculture Act Amendments, 1975, by Seniority (percent)

Congress in Which Service Began	Northeastern Democrats	Democrats From Other Northern States	All Northern Democrats
Before 92nd	52 (40)	78 (63)	68 (103)
92nd or 93rd	25 (12)	86 (28)	67 (40)
94th	70 (23)	77 (39)	74 (62)
Total	53 (75)	79 (130)	70 (205)

Note: Cells give percent of the members in that category (number in parentheses) who voted Aye on the conference report.

opposition to the bill among northeastern Democrats.[27] It does appear, however, that the chances for cooperation among rural and nonrural Democrats have improved, and that this improvement is the consequence of a number of the changes we have been discussing.

First, the election of many new Democrats from northern rural areas helped to break southern domination of the Agriculture committee. Second, the views of most of these new rural Democrats were similar to those of their urban and suburban colleagues. This has made coalition formation easier between the two groups. This has been especially true among freshmen in the Ninety-fourth Congress, because of the close working relationship among the new members which was estab-

27. "Northeast" is defined to include the following states: Maine, New Hampshire, Vermont, Massachusetts, Rhode Island, Connecticut, New York, Pennsylvania, Maryland, Delaware, and New Jersey. "Other northern states" includes all other states save the eleven southern states. Table 9–13 (unlike table 9–12) includes pairs as well as votes actually cast in the calculations.

lished at the beginning of the Congress and continues to the present.[28] As Table 9–13 shows, northeastern freshman Democrats were almost as likely to support the farm bill as were their colleagues from other northern states.

Third, the substantial membership turnover and the character of the reforms passed by the House and the Democratic caucus have reduced the centralization of power in the hands of the senior members. This has permitted junior members to play a larger role in policy making. Thus freshmen committee members like Richmond, Krebs, and D'Amours were able to take the leading role in the coalition-building process on a major bill, and they were even able to overturn the decisions of their committee twice on the floor. In our view this would have been virtually impossible a few years ago. And, as we shall see below, this was not an isolated event confined to a single committee.

Thus, while the changes we have considered do not appear to have altered in any major way the patterns of behavior or policy-making within the Agriculture Committee, they do seem to have led to changes in the relationship between the committee and House Democrats, and thus they have had (and may have in the future) an important impact on the making of Agriculture policy.

Interstate and Foreign Commerce

Commerce is a committee which did not change its procedures or structures significantly in either the Ninety-second or Ninety-third Congresses, but which—prodded by an influx of new members—completely rewrote its rules in 1975. These changes brought a striking decentralization of power and resources to the subcommittees. Yet, as Table 9–14 shows, there was virtually no change in the number of committee hearings between the Ninety-third and Ninety-fourth Congresses. On the other hand, the data show that there was a substantial upsurge of activity between the Ninety-first and Ninety-third Congresses.[29]

Thus the committee changes in the Ninety-fourth Congress appear to have had no direct impact on committee-hearing activity. Now it may be the case that the committee's previous increase in activity was entirely unrelated to the reforms which came before and after. A more plausible argument, however, is that the increase in subcommittee

28. See *Congressional Quarterly Weekly Report* (August 2, 1975):1674–77.
29. The Ninety-second Congress data were unavailable when Table 9–14 was created, hence the timing of the charge in activity cannot be pinpointed.

Table 9–14. Days of Hearings, House Interstate and Foreign Commerce Committee, 91st, 93rd, and 94th Congresses

	91st Cong.	93rd Cong.
Full Committee	34	10
Transportation and Aeronautics	7	25
Communications and Power	15	27
Public Health and Welfare	15	31
Commerce and Finance	15	42
Investigations	5	9
Total	91	144

	94th Cong.
Full Committee	2
Transportation and Commerce	39
Communications	17
Public Health and Environment	26
Consumer Protection and Finance	28
Oversight and Investigations	16
Energy and Power	17
Total	145

Note: Totals are as of September 1 of first session, 94th Congress.

hearing activity was a response to the subcommittee reforms of the Ninety-second and Ninety-third Congress (even though they did not lead at that time to changes in the committee's *rules*), and that the revolt which occurred in 1975 was in part a response to this increase in activity and an attempt to further expand and to protect the power and influence of the subcommittees. Certainly a subcommittee's influence and activity is a matter of much more than just days of hearings, and it is clear that the revolt and the rules changes it produced had an important substantive impact on the committee.[30]

For example, the subcommittees have a greater impact on the formulation of legislation. The most salient instance was the energy bill, produced by the new Energy and Power Subcommittee and the most important bill reported by the committee in the first session of the Ninety-fourth Congress.

> [John] Dingell [D., Mich.], who chairs the energy subcommittee, has played the dominant role in developing the panel's energy bill (HR 7014), managed it on the House floor and is actively serving on the House-Senate conference. . . .
>
> Dingell has been able to take the lead on energy, in large part, because of the expanded staff of ten approved for his subcommittee by the committee's caucus. . . .
>
> The committee's broad jurisdiction over energy also helped Dingell. The committee's responsibility in effect became Dingell's responsibility because of the increased autonomy of subcommittees.[31]

The Communications Subcommittee, still chaired in the Ninety-fourth Congress by Torbert Macdonald, reported a bill giving long-term, five-year financing to the Corporation for Public Broadcasting. The bill, which specifies $634 million for the five-year period, was passed by the House overwhelmingly (336 to 26) on November 10, 1975, over the objections of the House Appropriations Committee, which wanted to limit the financing to a single year.[32]

Another major change in the committee's role in the policy arena has come in the Oversight and Investigations Subcommittee, the center of the 1975 revolt, now chaired by John Moss. This subcommittee does not report out legislation, but it has conducted a number of vigorous investigations into a wide range of federal agencies, including the Federal Energy Administration, the Department of Com-

---

30. See *Congressional Quarterly Weekly Report* (November 8, 1975):2409–10.
31. Ibid., p. 2409. However, as we shall see below, initial dominance by the subcommittee did not guarantee eventual victory for all of its positions.
32. See *Congressional Quarterly Weekly Report* (November 15, 1975):2470.

merce, and the Department of Health, Education, and Welfare. Chairman Moss and his subcommittee colleagues have repeatedly wrangled with officials of the Ford administration, voting a contempt citation to Secretary of Commerce Rogers Morton for his failure to provide the subcommittee with subpoenaed reports that would identify U.S. firms participating in the Arab boycott against companies doing business with Israel, and threatening HEW Secretary David Mathews with a similar contempt citation over administration documents on hospital accreditation.

Other subcommittees, however, have not shown substantial evidence of more or better output. The transportation subcommittee has a new chairman (Fred Rooney of Pennsylvania), and he has moved slowly. One committee Republican commented:

> Brock Adams is the transportation expert in Congress and of course he left the chairmanship to take on the Budget Committee. Fred [Rooney], who took over, is all right, but he really doesn't have Brock's expertise. So the interest group[s] and the members still turn to Brock, though of course he doesn't devote the time to the issue that he used to.

Paul Rodgers has reported out significant legislation in the health area in 1975; however, it has not been new legislation, but largely bills which passed the House in the Ninety-third Congress and were vetoed by President Ford.

Lionel Van Deerlin's Consumer Protection and Finance Subcommittee has acted, after much internal controversy, on no-fault insurance (its fate in the House remains in doubt), but has moved very slowly in other fronts, mostly because he has not yet assimilated the complex materials of this subcommittee; his situation is similar to that of Rooney.

While we have seen that the subcommittees have almost unlimited ability to take initiatives, the full committee is certainly not powerless, nor is Chairman Staggers. The full committee can still play a significant role in markup of legislation and in conference committee negotiations. This was especially apparent on the energy bill, in part because the subcommittee chairman, John Dingell, was out of step with his committee Democratic colleagues on a number of issues, while Staggers was in harmony with them. The full committee spent seventeen days marking up the bill, and made some very significant changes in the subcommittee bill, the most important of which involved oil pricing.

The subcommittee had agreed to a provision which would have permitted gradual decontrol, through 1980, of the price of "old oil" (i.e., oil produced in a domestic well or field up to the quantity that was produced in it in 1972), contingent on the passage by Congress of a windfall profits tax on the increase in oil company revenue which would result.[33] This provision, which was sponsored by Robert Krueger (a freshman subcommittee member from Texas), was supported by Krueger, Dingell, John Murphy of New York (by proxy), and the five Republican subcommittee members. It was opposed by the other seven subcommittee Democrats, all save one of whom (Bob Eckhardt of Texas) were freshmen. When, however, the full committee took up the bill, it rejected the subcommittee's plan by a 22 to 21 vote, substituting instead a proposal sponsored by Eckhardt which provided for a rollback in the price of uncontrolled oil to $7.50 per barrel, and a gradual increase in the price of controlled oil (old oil) to this level.[34] The committee then voted to report the bill by a 26 to 17 vote.[35] One should note that, although the subcommittee was defeated on pricing, most of the other major provisions it had adopted were retained in the bill as reported by the full committee.

The House debate on the bill began on July 15 and lasted, intermittently, until September 23. The importance of the bill, and the difficulty of reaching a resolution to the oil pricing conflict, are indicated by the fact that the House devoted nine days to the debate—an unusually large number for that body. The leading role on the floor on behalf of the committee's position on pricing was taken by Eckhardt and Staggers, because Dingell (the bill's floor manager) admitted on the floor that he had reservations about the bill. At the opening of House consideration, Staggers said:

This debate will show whether we are going to let the OPEC nations dictate to this land what we are going to have in the way of oil and energy and what price we are going to pay for it.[36]

33. See *Congressional Quarterly Weekly Report* (May 17, 1975):1020.
34. See *Congressional Quarterly Weekly Report* (July 19, 1975):1521–23.
35. The minority included all fourteen Republicans, plus Krueger, David Satterfield (D., Va.), and Goodloe Byron (D, Md.).
36. *Congressional Quarterly Weekly Report* (July 19, 1975):1521. Staggers's role in the consideration of this bill not only shows his continuing influence as committee chairman, but also that the revolt against him in committee did not irreparably damage the possibility of alliances between him and committee liberals when their interests coincide. John Moss, who took Staggers's subcommittee chair, commented in late September, 1975:

When he wants to dig in, as he is in energy right now, he is respected. He can be quite helpful. And now I'm going to be on the conference on the energy bill and I expect on that to work very closely with Mr. Staggers. This is one area where we have fought side by side since 1958 under the Eisenhower administration.

Table 9–15. Selected House Floor Votes on the 1975 Energy Bill

| | Percent of Members Voting Aye | | | | |
Vote	All Members	Repub-licans	Democrats	Northern Democrats	Southern Democrats
First Krueger Amendment (#313)	48	87	28	12	67
Wilson Amendment (#315)	52	89	33	18	67
Staggers-Eckhardt Substitute for 2nd Krueger Amendment (#347)	51	10	72	87	37
Second Krueger Amendment, as amended (#348)	54	12	76	91	41
Brown motion to delete pricing provisions (#388)	38	82	20	4	46
Passage of the bill (#405)	63	22	85	97	57
Passage of the conference Report (#584)	60	25	77	91	49

Note: The numbers in parentheses refer to *Congressional Quarterly* roll call vote numbers. The nature of the votes is described in the text.

The division in the House on the oil pricing issue was close, and along conservative coalition lines, as the votes in Table 9–15 indicate. On July 23, the House rejected (by 202 to 220) an amendment offered by Robert Krueger which embodied the language originally adopted by the Energy and Power Subcommittee. Then, however, it adopted (215 to 199) an amendment proposed by Charles Wilson (D., Tex.), which struck the committee's pricing provisions. This left no pricing provisions in the bill, and the House suspended debate on the matter.[37]

The House returned to the bill on July 30. Krueger proposed a second amendment which was similar to the first. Staggers and Eckhardt, however, had another substitute, which embodied a multitiered approach to pricing, but which continued controls and included a price-rollback provision. (Both of these aspects were opposed by producers, the president, and House Republicans.) The substitute was

37. See *Congressional Quarterly Weekly Report* (July 26, 1975):1648–50.

accepted 218 to 207, and then the House adopted the Krueger amendment (as amended) 231 to 193. Obviously unwilling to "go around again" on the issue, the House (on September 17, by a 151 to 242 vote) defeated an amendment proposed by Clarence Brown (R., Oh., the ranking Republican on the energy subcommittee) which would have struck the pricing provisions. The bill then passed 255 to 148.

The energy provision which emerged from conference with the Senate was not identical to the House-passed version, but it included the main features of continued controls and a price rollback on uncontrolled oil. The conference report passed the House on December 15 by a vote of 236 to 160, and to the surprise of many observers, the president signed it.

The saga of the energy bill illustrates a number of the effects of congressional change on the Commerce Committee and the House. First, the promulgation of the Subcommittee Bill of Rights within the committee in 1975 made possible the autonomy the Energy and Power Subcommittee exercised in the initial drafting of the bill. Furthermore, the subsequent consideration by the full committee shows that subcommittee autonomy need not be subcommittee dictatorship; if the subcommittee gets too far out of line, it can be reversed.

Second, the dominant role played by Robert Krueger throughout the debate again illustrates how much the policy-making process in the House has been opened up to junior members.[38] It also, however, illustrates another point. The reason that Krueger had to assume the leading role was that his senior Texas colleague on the energy subcommittee. Eckhardt, was actually the major opponent of decontrol in the House. In the "old days" such a situation would not have occurred, and the more senior member would have been the leader on the issue. We are no longer, however, in the old days, and Eckhardt (who was first elected in 1966) is almost the protoype of the new southern Democrat who has as liberal a record as any of his northern urban colleagues. (He is, for example, the new chairman of the Democratic Study Group.) Indeed, the floor voting on this bill demonstrates very well the change in the kind of southern Democrats who have entered the House in recent years. As Table 9–15 shows,[39] Republicans were overwhelmingly for Krueger's position and against that of Eck-

38. Nor was this the only time during this Congress that Krueger was to play a central role in a debate. In early February, 1976, he was the major floor advocate for another Commerce Committee bill which provided for complete deregulation of the price of natural gas. Again he was opposed by Eckhardt and Staggers, and again he was beaten by a narrow vote: 205 to 201. See *Congressional Quarterly Weekly Report* (February 7, 1976):259–61.

39. Again, in this table, we include Kentucky and Oklahoma in the South.

Table 9-16. Votes of House Southern Democrats on Oil Pricing in the 1975 Energy Bill, by Seniority (percent)

Congress in Which Service Began	Voting Pattern[a]		
	Substitution Nay, Adoption Nay	Substitution Nay, Adoption Aye	Substitution Aye, Adoption Aye
Before 92nd (N=50)	72	6	22
92nd or 93rd (15)	53	7	40
94th (13)	23	–	77
All Seniority Levels (78)	60	5	35

[a] "Substitution" refers to the vote to substitute the Staggers-Eckhardt proposal for the second Krueger amendment. "Adoption" refers to the vote to include the Krueger amendment (as amended by the substitution) in the bill. (See Table 9-15 and the text for more details.) No member voted Aye on the Substitution and Nay on Adoption.

hardt and Staggers. Among northern Democrats, the pattern of support was just the reverse. Only southern Democrats were closely divided on the pricing issue, and Table 9-16 shows that this division was clearly along seniority lines.[40] (The votes chosen for analysis involve the decision to substitute the Staggers-Eckhardt proposal for the second Krueger amendment, and the subsequent vote to include the Staggers-Eckhardt position in the bill.) Among the more senior group of southern Democrats (those elected before November, 1970), 72 percent voted against the position taken by their northern colleagues on the two votes; among freshmen, however, 77 percent voted *with* northern Democrats. Indeed, only three southern freshmen voted nay on the two votes: Robert Krueger, Jack Hightower (also from Texas), and Lawrence McDonald (Ga.), who is a member of the National Board of Directors of the John Birch Society.

Before concluding our discussion of the Commerce Committee, we should note that while there has been an increase in the autonomy of subcommittees and an increase in the activity of some of them, not all observers agree that these changes have moved the committee in productive legislative directions. Many committee members, especially Republicans, are frustrated with the committee's behavior in the Ninety-fourth Congress. To one thoughtful senior minority member,

40. Table 9-16 only includes the votes of Democrats from the eleven former Confederate states. Three members who were not recorded on both votes are excluded. Pairs are counted along with recorded votes.

"above all, reform has served to slow down the process." This member continued,

> The proliferation of power to the subcommittee level in Commerce has created a tendency to set up six separate power structures, each equivalent to a committee chairman. There is much more concern by the subcommittee chairmen with jurisdiction, to broaden their bases. In the health area, with national health insurance, we're headed for a collision with Ways and Means, and their new subcommittee, headed by [Daniel] Rostenkowski [D., Ill.] . . . The subcommittee chairman [on Commerce] feel they have a special responsibility to go over the subject matter with the freshmen and to let them participate fully, with no controls. It takes an enormous amount of time. Because of this coalition [between subcommittee chairman and freshmen] we can't move ahead on legislation. Take clean air—we've been marking it up for two-and-one-half months and we're on page fourteen of an eighty-five page bill! Waxman and Maguire offer *every* amendment that Nader and the Clean Air coalition want, for prolonged discussion; they won't filter them out first. This means more and more work—we've had three two-hour sessions a day, including evenings. We should have been done a long time ago. The chairmen don't exercise any control. It's a helluva way to mark up a bill.

Thus, to some members, the reforms have increased activity on Commerce, but with little benefit. A typical complaint from a committee member, made as he rushed to the floor for a vote, was:

> Boy, I'm just spread too thin, and it's getting worse. We had both transportation and health subcommittees meeting all day yesterday, and they will again tomorrow, and with _____ Committee and the floor. I'm way overcommitted. This is one of the biggest problems we have and it was made much worse by the so-called reforms.

As we look to the future, all the subcommittees on Interstate and Foreign Commerce will probably increase policy and oversight activity, each encouraging the others. The aggressive attitude toward the executive branch exhibited by Moss and his subcommittee would likely be tempered with a Democratic administration, but would not necessarily disappear. With increasing policy initiation and activity, Commerce subcommittees will face increasing jurisdictional disputes with subcommittees on other committees.[41] In health and energy

41. For example, on the energy bill, Ways and Means Committee chairman Al Ullman (D., Ore.) objected to Robert Krueger's first amendment because it made decontrol contingent on the passage of a windfall profits tax. Ullman considered this to be an invasion of the tax jurisdiction of his committee. See *Congressional Quarterly Weekly Report* (July 26, 1975):1648–50.

matters, Commerce and Ways and Means face several areas of contention; in transportation, consumer, environment, banking, and other policy areas, Commerce cross-cuts a variety of committee jurisdictions.

Government Operations

Government Operations was shaken up by the limitation of subcommittee chairmanships to one per member in 1971, and it was changed again in 1975 when it acquired a new chairman and a new set of rules which strengthened subcommittees and staff. As can be seen from Table 9–17, the first change appears to have had a substantial impact on the hearing activity of the committee, with days of investigative hearings almost doubling between the Ninety-first and Ninety-second Congresses. The Ninety-second Congress limitation on subcommittee chairmanships meant less divided attention by dual chairmen, and thus more time to spend on Government Operations activity. Since our comparisons across time are only for the first seven months of each Congress, we must be cautious in our interpretations —the between-Congress differences might well disappear if we had information for each full two-year period—but it appears that several subcommittees underwent significant jumps in activity between the Ninety-first and Ninety-second Congresses. And they are precisely the subcommittees—Foreign Operations and Government Information, Legal and Monetary Affairs, Conservation and Natural Resources— whose chairmen in the Ninety-first Congress had had dual responsibilities.

The changes of the Ninety-fourth Congress have not produced another sharp increase in hearing activity, although a steady increase has apparently continued. There does, however, appear to have been some change in the character of the investigations. Some of the subcommittees, particularly those chaired by Abzug and Rosenthal, have delved into a number of new and controversial areas. Abzug has investigated the role of the CIA and FBI in investigating domestic activities of American citizens, the extent of government agencies' compliance with the Privacy Act, and the role of the FBI in the investigation of the assassination of John F. Kennedy. Rosenthal has looked into, among other things, the political and investigative activities of the Internal Revenue Service, the behavior and operations of the Federal Reserve Board, the impact of the New York City situation on banks, the Federal Trade Commission's activities in the condominium area, and government quality control of alcoholic beverages.

Table 9–17. Days of Investigative Hearings, House Government Operations Committee, 91st–94th Congresses

	91st Cong.	92nd Cong.	93rd Cong.		94th Cong.
Executive and Legislative Reorganization[a]	1	1	1	Legislation and National Security	3
Military Operations[a]	0	–	–		–
Conservation and Natural Resources	5	9	11	Conservation, Energy and Natural Resources	10
Foreign Operations and Govt. Information	2	20	10	Govt. Information and Individual Rights	12
Government Activities	2	2	5	Govt. Activity and Transportation	4
Intergovernmental Relations	9	11	9	Intergovt. Relations and Human Resources	15
Legal and Monetary Affairs	1	7	10	Commerce, Consumer and Monetary Affairs	13
Special Studies	9	6	21	Manpower and Housing	15
Total	29	56	67		72

Note: Totals are as of August 1 of first session, 94th Congress.
[a] The Subcommittee on Executive and Legislative Reorganization and the Subcommittee on Military Operations were merged at the beginning of the 92nd Congress to form the Subcommittee on Legislation and Military Operations.

At least a part of the new aggressiveness on the part of the committee appears to be due to Jack Brooks, the new chairman, and his
relative willingness to accept the spirit, as well as the letter, of the
committee reforms of the past few years. One liberal activist on the
committee commented on Brooks's accession to the chairmanship.

> Brooks saw what was happening to Staggers on Commerce—the total
> devastation. He saw what had happened to Hebert and to those two
> other people. He saw the challenge against Holifield. Notwithstanding
> Brook's relative youth and his relative drive—he has an earnest desire
> to make this committee perform—but what comes out of this is that
> Brooks has been here, I don't know, twenty years or more, and during
> the course of those twenty-five years he developed a perception of the
> prerogatives of a chairman and that perception has hardened over
> those twenty-five years. He has had to amend it in the last five years, or
> scale it down, and strangely enough he scales it down just at the time
> he becomes chairman.

A Democratic subcommittee staff member candidly described the
new chairman:

> Brooks is a Texan and he is a tough Texan. I think he is a Texan in
> the mold of Lyndon Johnson. But when he became chairman of the
> committee, (*a*) he was twenty years younger than Holifield, and (*b*) he
> was aware of the new politics, especially after Watergate, in terms of
> the House and the rest of the country.

Brooks, in his first year as chairman, has been much more open,
loose, and democratic in handling Government Operations subcommittee chairmen and the committee's Democrats. The staffer quoted
above also said,

> It is very different to fault Brooks in the way in which he has been
> running the committee. . . . He has given us almost as much money as
> we need for staffing, he is letting us get into every controversial issue,
> . . . we don't have to clear our investigations through him.

On the other hand, committee Republicans are not happy at all with
Brooks as chairmen. One high ranking minority member said,

> Mr. Holifield . . . came out looking much more like a Republican than
> like a Democrat. I think not in all matters but in many matters . . . he
> was a very fair chairman and very nonpartisan. Brooks is extremely
> partisan and he also tries to do things himself, and he won't, pardon
> the expression, brook any interference. He doesn't have the tact and
> the finesse that Holifield had.

With Brooks's openness to his subcommittees' efforts, oversight on Government Operations has, as we noted, been more aggressive and wider in scope than previously. Some of this, of course, is due to the fact of Republican control of the White House and Brooks's partisanship. However, subcommittee leaders like Benjamin Rosenthal, Bella Abzug, and William Moorhead are naturally activist. They have been given freedom to operate by new rules and expanded resources, and are being abetted by Brooks. A staff assistant to a Democrat on the committee commented,

> Jack is actually helping the subcommittee chairmen. He walked into Bella's subcommittee when she was trying to get information out of [William] Colby, and he said that he applauded her efforts and was sure that the CIA director would cooperate. You could see Colby change his attitude.

Legislatively, the Government Operations Committee has had limited activity in the past, and this is not likely to change. This is, of course, due primarily to the limited legislative jurisdiction of the committee. Indeed, it is probable that legislative activity will *decrease* in the future, especially after the Consumer Protection Agency bill (which had passed the Ninety-third Congress by a wide margin) squeaked by with only a nine-vote margin in November, 1975, even though a series of amendments watered down its powers. Benjamin Rosenthal, the bill's main advocate, said:

> The timing was bad for us. . . . There has grown up, especially in the last six months, a strong anti-government, anti-bureaucracy, anti-new-agency phenomenon in this country. The bill is a victim of this tide.[42]

Table 9–18. Aye Votes on Passage of Consumer Protection Agency Bills, 1974 and 1975 (percent)

Bill	All Members	Repub- licans	Democrats	Northern Democrats	Southern Democrats
1974	76	60	87	99	73
1975	51	14	70	86	34

As Table 9–18 shows, support for the Consumer Agency declined by 25 percent in the nineteen months that intervened between the two

42. *Congressional Quarterly Weekly Report* (November 15, 1975):2451.

votes.[43] The decline in support was greatest among Republicans, primarily because President Ford vigorously spoke out against the proposal, while President Nixon (who was occupied with other matters in April, 1974) did not formally oppose the bill. There was, however, also a substantial erosion of support among Democrats, particularly Southerners, and when we control for seniority among the Democrats, some interesting patterns are apparent (See Table 9–19.)[44]

Table 9–19. Votes of Northern and Southern Democrats, by Seniority, on Passage of 1975 Consumer Protection Agency Bill (percent)

Congress in Which Service Began	Northern Democrats	Southern Democrats	Total
Before 92nd	90 (N=100)	29 (52)	69 (152)
92nd or 93rd	79 (38)	40 (15)	68 (53)
94th	78 (60)	42 (12)	72 (72)
Total	84 (198)	33 (79)	70 (277)

Note: Cells give the percent of members in that category (number in parentheses) who voted Aye on passage of the bill.

It is not surprising that, among Southerners, support for the Consumer Agency is greater among the junior members than among the more senior. Most of the junior moderate Southerners who entered since 1970 supported the agency, while their more conservative colleagues opposed it. Among northern Democrats, however, support for the Consumer Agency proposal is greater among the more senior members. This is primarily due, as might be expected, to ideological variation—most of the more conservative northerners opposed the bill—but that is not the entire story. A few of the more junior opponents of the bill are quite liberal (e.g., Christopher Dodd of Connecticut, Martha Keys of Kansas, Berkley Bedell of Iowa, Don Bonker of Washington, Richard Vander Veen of Michigan).[45] While a cynic might expect

43. The first vote was taken on April 3, 1974, the second on November 6, 1975. In Table 9–18, Kentucky and Oklahoma are again included with the South.
44. In Table 9–19, the South includes only the eleven former Confederate states, and pairs are counted along with roll-call votes.
45. Their respective conservative coalition ratios are: 12, 12, 18, 16, and 13.

that these are merely marginal Democrats worried about Republican opposition in the next election, it is not clear that this is the case. None of these members received less than 55 percent of the vote, and most of their more marginal colleagues thought it safe to support the bill.

Instead, this appears to be a matter of personal commitment on the part of the members. Consider Bonker of Washington, for example. He was first elected in 1974 by 62 percent of the vote in a previously Democratic district. When the Consumer Agency bill came up, he not only voted against the bill, but also subsequently wrote a column for the *Washington Post* (entitled "The Consumer Advocacy Charade"[46]) in which he detailed the reasons for his opposition. Bonker agreed that the "consumer is poorly represented before the regulatory agencies," but he said:

> The Consumer Protection Act is an inadequate response to an understated problem. It embodies yesterday's thinking nostalgically applied to today's changed world. It promises what it cannot deliver.

He predicted that the agency would simply grow into another giant bureaucracy, a "vast data-collecting machine which avidly avoids the fundamental structural problems in our economy," and he went on:

> We need to reintroduce competition into the marketplace. Yet regulation stifles competition and helps protect the largest firms. It restricts entry to market and maintains artificial oligopolies.

> Real consumer reform should follow two parallel roads. First, we can get rid of many existing regulatory agencies and reassign limited regulatory functions to the three branches and states. Secondly, we can and must restructure our economy through a new commitment to vigorous anti-trust action and creation of a national policy on size and market influence of economic organizations, both business firms and unions.

These views sound very much like those of another young Democratic politician: Governor Jerry Brown of California. Certainly we do not want to make too much of the votes of a few members on a single bill, nor of a single column in a newspaper. There is, however, substantial evidence of a growing *liberal* critique of big government and massive new programs within the Democratic party. If there should grow up within the House a group of members organized around these ideas, it could be the most important development of its kind since the

46. February 2, 1976, p. A17.

formation of the Democratic Study Group. Of course, only time will tell, but the possibility should be recognized. In any event, it seems fairly clear that the chances for the Consumer Protection Agency or any other large new agency coming into being in the near future are limited indeed.[47]

International Relations

We have not been able to this point pull together systematic data to make quantitative comparisons including the Ninety-fourth Congress for the International Relations Committee. However, we do have information examining earlier Congresses, and Table 9–20 (the

Table 9–20. Days of Hearings for Subcommittees of the House Foreign Affairs Committee, 91st and 92nd Congresses

	Days of Hearings		
Subcommittees	91st Cong.	92nd Cong.	Change
Foreign Economic Policy[a]	13	21	+ 8
Europe[a]	13	38	+25
Near East[a]	6	34	+28
International Organizations[b]	21	37	+16
All Others (N=6)	104	92	−12
Total	157	222	+65

[a] New chairman in 92nd Congress, who received chairmanship directly as a result of the 1971 reform.
[b] New Chairman in 92nd Congress, who would have chairmanship without the 1971 reform.

data for which was taken from an earlier article[48]) shows that the 1971 reforms limiting subcommittee chairmanships to one per member, which put three Foreign Affairs subcommittees in the hands of activist liberals and which combined with the spreading out of staff resources to the subcommittees, resulted in a major increase in subcommittee activity between the Ninety-first and Ninety-second Congresses.

To one committee Republican, the initial reform process not only transformed the committee, but also altered the outlook of the chairman, Thomas "Doc" Morgan (Pa.).

47. As of the end of February, 1976, the Consumer Protection Agency's supporters had not even bothered to seek a conference to reconcile the House bill with the Senate version.
48. Ornstein, "Causes and Consequences," op. cit., p. 104.

Someone once described him [Morgan] as a GS-15 servant of the Secretary of State. He didn't really view the House as a force in foreign policy. And beginning with that period [1971–1972] he showed some initiative on his own, and I always related that to the ascendancy of the junior members.

Morgan certainly gave his subcommittee chairmen freedom to initiate, with professional staff to assist. And with an influx of liberal activists into subcommittee leadership positions, the challenge to executive-branch supremacy in foreign-policy making increased greatly in the 1970s. The institutional changes and the growth of the liberal activist wing in the committee and in the House both contributed to the substantial change in the committee's role in foreign policy. As a subcommittee chairman commented,

> The outlook of the whole committee has shifted. We're more activist and more liberal. This has changed the role of the committee and was necessary for the subcommittee reforms to be really effective.

The 1975 reorganization of the subcommittees has also had at least some impact: Jonathan Bingham's new subcommittee on International Trade and Commerce has held a series of hearings, still ongoing, on the subject of the U.S. economic embargo of Cuba, a topic which the Inter-American Affairs Subcommittee studiously avoided in past Congresses. In the same area, several committee members have discussed U.S.-Cuban policy with Assistant Secretary of State William Rogers, and at least one member—Representative Charles Whalen (R., Oh.)—has traveled to Cuba.

Another highly important factor in altering the perceptions and behavior of some committee members was the Vietnam War, which was the cutting issue in the House in the 1970s. Another committee member stated,

> Of course, the Vietnam experience contributed to all of this. Like the full membership of the House, this committee was almost in favor of World War III and this experience has made it more sensitive to actions by the executive and recommendations by the executive involving foreign policy.

One result of these events has been a growing involvement of a number of members of the International Relations Committee in a variety of foreign policy areas, as these comments from committee members and staff make clear:

We have an ad hoc group redrafting the [Agency for International Development] program, and on the human rights issue we have had a great impact organizationally on the State Department.

We virtually rewrote the Foreign Aid Act this year. That is not an administration product. It was initiated in almost every respect within the House. One of the turning points may well have been the War Powers Act, which came from the Zablocki subcommittee. His decision in taking that subcommittee at the time of its reorganization was crucial, and the success we had in putting over the War Powers Resolution, and making it stick, I think elevated the prestige of the committee and made it more effective throughout the Congress and throughout the executive branch.

Kissinger and State officials spent two and a half hours with Sarbanes, Brademas, Rosenthal,[49] and three others this past week on the issue of Turkish aid—none of the six are committee chairmen. What a change from the past, to consult for two and one-half hours with members of this committee, and to consult with people who are neither leadership nor chairmen!

We have an informal group on human rights questions which has started to meet regularly with Henry Kissinger; there are roughly twelve to fifteen people, led by Fraser and Alan Cranston in the Senate.

While these changes are important, however, the most significant effects of membership turnover and new rules as they relate to International Relations and the policies produced within that committee's jurisdiction have been felt outside the committee. First, consider the following description by Richard Fenno of the Foreign Affairs Committee and its relationship with its environment in the 1950s and 1960s:

Policy coalitions in the realm of the *Foreign Affairs Committee* are *executive-led.* . . .

The chief executive's only serious rival for policy leadership has been the Congress itself, which raises for us the question of the impact of the parent House on the environment of the Foreign Affairs Committee. A general answer would be simply that Congress on the whole has not mounted a very potent challenge. . . . A specific answer would be that the congressional challenge, such as it is, has come from the Senate, which has its own constitutional prerogatives in this field, and not from

49. Paul Sarbanes (D., Md.), John Brademas (D., Ind.), and Benjamin Rosenthal (D., N.Y.), the three main leaders in the House of the anti-Turkish aid faction. Of the three, only Rosenthal is a committee member, a point which we will consider below.

the House, which has none. . . . House members have no institutional concern in the field of Foreign Affairs, and make no special effort to influence the behavior of its members.

All key prescriptions come, instead, from the president and his executive-branch subordinates. Their prescriptions for behavior emphasize *legitimation* as the basic task of the Foreign Affairs. That is, they want the committee to place a legislative stamp of approval on recommendations that they believe have been thoroughly and expertly worked out in the executive branch.[50]

To make Fenno's description of the committee applicable to the mid-1970s, we do not have to alter the references to the executive branch's desire for legitimation, for this certainly has not changed. Nor do we have to revise to a great extent the subsequent description[51] of the committee majority's willingness to respond to the executive branch's desires. What do have to change are the references to the lack of congressional challenge from the House and the lack of attempts by the House to influence the committee, as an analysis of a number of the issues mentioned in the quotations from members above will make clear.

Perhaps the best issue with which to begin is that of military aid to Turkey, the most extended foreign policy dispute in the Ninety-fourth Congress.[52] The dispute began after Turkey had militarily intervened on Cyprus in July, 1975, and had used American-furnished arms to do so. On September 19, the Senate adopted an amendment (to the Export-Import Bank bill), sponsored by Senator Thomas Eagleton (D., Mo.), expressing the "sense of the Senate" that the president should cut off aid to Turkey. The next week, the House passed, by 307 to 90, an amendment (to a continuing appropriations resolution) sponsored by Benjamin Rosenthal (D., N.Y.) and Pierre DuPont (R., Del.), which *required* that aid be cut off until "substantial progress" had been made in obtaining an agreement regarding military forces on Cyprus. The Senate Appropriations Committee weakened the House language (cutting off aid until Turkey showed a "good faith effort" to reach an agreement), but the Senate adopted another Eagleton amendment barring military aid to any country which used it for any purpose other than internal security or self-defense.

As one would expect, President Ford opposed these attempts to restrict his flexibility in foreign affairs, but he said that he would

50. Fenno, op. cit., pp. 27–28.
51. See ibid., pp. 69–73, 212–26.
52. The material contained in the description which follows was taken from various issues of *Congressional Quarterly Weekly Report* from 1974 and 1975.

accept the cutoff with the "good faith" language. In response, the House-Senate conferees on the bill adopted this language, but the House (on a 69 to 291 vote) refused to accept the softening of the language and voted by voice vote for the "substantial progress" requirement. On October 9, the Senate adopted the conference report with the House version of the cutoff. On the same day, however, the Senate passed a resolution which provided for delay of the cutoff until December 15.

Ford had threatened to veto the continuing appropriations bill, and he did so on October 14th, after the House voted, 187 to 171, against the Senate-passed delay. The next few days were like a tennis match: October 15, the House sustained the veto, 226 to 135 (16 votes short of an override); October 16, the Congress cleared another continuing resolution with another, similar cutoff provision (it permitted a delay until December 10); October 17, Ford vetoed the second resolution, and minutes later the House sustained the veto, but only by two votes. Ford saw the handwriting on the wall. The last override vote was 161 to 83. The turnout was so low because members were anxious to get home to campaign, and the absentees were disproportionately Republicans because so many of them were in danger. Reluctantly, Ford agreed to the aid cutoff with the December 10 delay. This simply renewed the dispute in the context of the fiscal 1975 foreign aid authorization which was to be taken up after the election.

The Senate version of the bill included a required aid cutoff, but permitted delay until mid-February. The House International Relations Committee agreed to require a cutoff only until the president certified that Turkey was making "good faith effort" to reach a negotiated settlement, but Rosenthal offered another floor amendment (adopted 297 to 98 on December 11) requiring an immediate aid ban. The conferees on the bill agreed to permit the president to delay the cutoff until February 5, 1976, but adopted the "substantial progress" requirement for aid beyond that date. Both Houses adopted the conference report and Ford signed it.

When the February 5 deadline came, the president was unable to certify "substantial progress," and the aid was cut off. The administration's efforts then turned to attempts to get Congress to remove the ban, and on May 19, the Senate passed a bill (41 to 40) conditionally permitting the president to resume aid to Turkey. It was clear that the House would not agree to totally end the embargo, but on July 11 the administration's supporters on International Relations voted 16 to 11 to approve a partial resumption of aid. When, however, the bill reached the House floor on July 24, even this was rejected 206 to 223.

On July 31, the Senate passed (again by one vote, 47 to 46) another bill with language identical to that just rejected by the House. Parliamentary maneuvers delayed consideration of the bill until after the August recess. The International Relations Committee reported the bill on September 22, and on October 2, the House voted 237 to 176 for the bill.

There are a number of points to be drawn from these machinations. First, during the entire fight over aid, it was the Senate which was most responsive to the president's wishes, and the House that was most resistant. Indeed, while the Senate was willing to *totally* lift the ban in May, all the President could ultimately get from the House was permission to deliver equipment contracted for before February 5, to resume cash sales, and to give Turkey military aid required to meet its NATO responsibilities.[53]

Second, the fact that the aid cutoff was first approved in 1974 demonstrates that this resistance to the executive by the House was not simply a consequence of the election of a lot of liberal Democrats in 1974. While the support for Rosenthal's December 11 amendment was greatest among northern Democrats (9 percent), 85 percent of southern[54] Democrats and even 56 percent of Republicans supported it.

Third, within the House, a majority of members of the International Relations Committee were more supportive of and more responsive to the president than was the majority of the entire House.[55] Moreover, recognition of this fact by the committee affected its behavior (e.g., in adopting a partial lifting of the embargo rather than pressing for the Senate-passed provision permitting total resumption of aid).

Finally, analysis of the 1975 House votes on this issue indicates that senior members among both northern and southern Democrats are more responsive to the president than are their junior colleagues.[56] Table 9–21, which presents the votes by those groups on the July 24 rejection of the bill to partially lift the ban, demonstrates this point. It shows, moreover, that the difference in the responses of northern and southern Democrats is greatest among the senior members, and smallest among the freshmen.

Another important foreign policy development in 1975 involved the foreign economic aid bill. Indeed, perhaps the most significant aspect was the fact that the bill was limited to economic aid. For a number of

53. This last provision would not go into effect until adoption of the fiscal 1976 military sales bill.

54. Including Kentucky and Oklahoma.

55. And, as we noted above, [(note 49)], while Rosenthal was a member of the committee, the other main leaders of the anti-aid group (Sarbanes and Brademas) were not.

56. There are no substantial differences among Republicans along seniority lines.

Table 9–21. Democratic Votes on Resumption of Aid to Turkey (S 846, 1975), by Seniority (percent)

Congress in Which Service Began	Northern Democrats	Southern Democrats	Total
Before 92nd	32 (N=105)	83 (52)	49 (157)
92nd or 93rd	21 (39)	47 (15)	28 (54)
94th	13 (63)	23 (13)	14 (76)
Total	24 (207)	66 (80)	36 (287)

Note: Cells give percent of the members in that category (number in parentheses) who voted Aye on the bill.

years the Senate had attempted to separate economic from military aid, but the House had resisted the change. However, during consideration of the bill passed in 1973, House conferees had "agreed that they would no longer insist on one bill."[57]

The two kinds of aid had been linked in the past partly as an implicit "logroll"; some southern Democrats and Republicans would support the bill because of military aid and most northern Democrats would support it because of economic aid, and together these would produce a majority. In 1975, however, "the committee leadership felt that the economic portion could stand on its own merits,"[58] despite expected opposition from southern Democrats and Republicans.

The International Relations Committee included in the economic aid bill a number of significant changes in the Food for Peace program (PL 480). Many members had become concerned that the program was being used for political rather than humanitarian purposes. The committee, therefore, included in the bill a restriction which:

> required that no more than 30 percent of the food aid sold abroad under Title I of the program should go to countries that were not among the most seriously affected by food shortages. The president could waive the percentage limitation if he certified to Congress that the food assistance was for humanitarian purposes, and if neither house of Congress disapproved the assistance by resolution within thirty calendar days.[59]

57. *Congressional Quarterly Weekly Report* (August 9, 1975):1755.
58. *Congressional Quarterly Weekly Report* (September 13, 1975):1978.
59. *Congressional Quarterly Weekly Report* (August 9, 1975):1756.

Thus, the committee was attempting to place restrictions on the president in his operation of the program. Even these restrictions, however, were not enough for some members. When the bill came to the floor, freshman Tom Harkin (D., Ia.) offered an amendment that would prohibit U.S. aid being given to any country that consistently violated internationally-recognized human rights. The amendment permitted the president to waive the restriction if he certified that the aid would directly benefit the needy of the country and if either house of Congress didn't disapprove the waiver within thirty days. The House adopted the amendment 238 to 164, and then passed the bill 244 to 155.

This bill demonstrates again the greater willingness of a majority of the International Relations Committee to place restrictions on the president in foreign policy. It also demonstrates again that the House as a whole is willing to go further than the committee in such matters.

The passage of the Harkin amendment is another indication of the expanded role of junior members. In this case a freshman who was not even a member of the committee with jurisdiction was able to soundly defeat it on the floor.[60] Furthermore, the voting on the Harkin amendment again demonstrates the difference, along seniority lines, among members with respect to their willingness to restrict the president's freedom of action in foreign policy. (See Table 9–22.) This is even true of Republicans on this vote, although the relationship between support and seniority is not consistent for them. Indeed, it was members who entered the House through the 1970 election and later who were responsible for adoption of the Harkin amendment, since less than a majority of the holdovers from the Ninety-first Congress supported it.

As the International Relations Committee and the House have shifted their role, taking a more important and independent part in foreign policy making, the State Department, and particularly the Secretary of State, have reacted. A November 24, 1975, *Washington Post* article noted the difference, commenting that "Senate and House committee chairmen and individual members have replaced kings, presidents, and prime ministers" in Kissinger's shuttle diplomacy." The article continued:

60. Members of the committee voted 13 to 19 on the Harkin amendment. Democrats were split 11 to 11 and Republicans voted 2 to 8.

This vote also indicates how membership on a committee can lead one to behave differently from colleagues who are not members. Three freshman Democrats serve on International Relations: Meyner of New Jersey, Solarz of New York and Bonker of Washington. All three are liberal Northerners, and yet they all voted against the Harkin amendment. Among freshman northern Democrats who were not committee members, there were only two votes against Harkin. In addition, two of the three (Meyner and Solarz) voted for resumption of aid to Turkey on the July 24 vote discussed above. Among other freshmen Northerners there were only six aye votes.

Table 9–22. Votes on the Harkin Amendment to the 1975 Foreign Economic Aid Bill, by Seniority (percent)

Congress in Which Service Began	Northern Democrats	Southern Democrats	Republicans	Total
Before 92nd	61	47	29	48
	(N=99)	(47)	(65)	(211)
92nd or 93rd	79	67	50	64
	(38)	(15)	(46)	(99)
94th	92	85	39	80
	(61)	(13)	(18)	(92)
Total	74	57	38	59
	(198)	(75)	(129)	(402)

Note: Cells give percent of the members in that category (number in parentheses) who voted Aye on the amendment.

In six days between November 14 and 20, Kissinger appeared before three congressional committees to argue for approval of the president's $4.7 billion worldwide security assistance program, the bulk of which is the Middle East aid package. The secretary wants Congress to vote those funds and prepare itself for future large requests—steps that would affect his future negotiations in the Mid East.

While making the Capitol Hill appearances, Kissinger also had to handle senators and congressmen who wanted him to enforce old pieces of legislation on human rights and use of U.S.-purchased weapons or write new provisions—all of which affect the freedom he wants to carry on foreign policy.

If that were not enough, Kissinger also had to face questioning by the Senate intelligence committee on his past actions and subpoenas from the House intelligence committee for documents.

In past years, Kissinger—following presidential policy—treated, according to the view of people on the Hill, with some contempt attempts by Congress to play a role in foreign policy or intelligence operations. Information provided committees in those days was slim and tailored to support administration positions.

A Kissinger appearance was often ceremonial. Perfunctory questions often asked by Kissinger's supporters encouraged generalized answers that did not include all the facts available to the secretary.

Times have changed.[61]

61. Walter Pincus, "Kissinger Tries Shuttle Diplomacy on the Hill," *Washington Post* (November 24, 1975):A2.

The State Department has not capitulated to the Congress or even willingly cooperated with it; indeed, their cooperation has often been grudging. To one committee member,

> I think they tend to treat us with a little more deference. Not to a desired level, though. In fact, this exercise over the Sinai agreement is an example of that. They take the position that the written understandings with Israel should not be in the public domain. Despite the fact that the *New York Times* and the *Post* have already printed the text, they still adhere to that. It's not a response on their part to the wishes of Israel. This means that they really don't fully trust the committee. I'm not sure just what their reasoning is. They want to be the spokesmen for foreign policy, I'm sure of that, and to the extent that they can keep from the committee members the basic reasons, they reserve a lot of authority to themselves.

Paradoxically, both cooperation and hostility between the Department of State and the House International Relations Committee have increased in the Ninety-fourth Congress. This tension will likely continue into the future as the House committee tries to expand its scope.

V. Summary and Conclusions

In the preceding section we attempted to discern the impact that congressional change has had on the four committees we have selected for analysis. In this section we will attempt to offer some general conclusions from these individual analyses with regard to the questions with which we introduced the preceding section. We will also discuss the implications of these changes for the internal character of the House, the relationship of Congress to the executive branch, and the nature of national public policy. Certainly these judgments must be regarded as very tentative. Even if one concludes that the changes we have discussed have had substantial consequences, the resulting trends are just beginning, and developments in the future could substantially alter them. (For example, the election of a Democrat as president in 1976 or strong Republican gains in the congressional elections of that year would have an enormous potential effect on these matters.) We do believe, however, that some preliminary conclusions are possible.

Probably the least surprising generalization one can draw from the preceding analysis is that the impact of House turnover and reform has not been the same on all committees. The reason is that the committees were, as Fenno points out, themselves not all the same to begin with.[62] The differences which existed among these committees influenced the ways in which turnover and rules changes affected them. However, the major impact of the changes in the House in the early 1970s has been to make these differences less pronounced. House committees have not become, and almost certainly will not become, the same. They have become more similar in some salient ways.

First, the committees have become ideologically less disparate, with party contingents on them becoming more like that party's membership in the House. The most salient example is, of course, the change in Democratic representation on Agriculture, but (as Table 9–23 shows)

Table 9–23. Mean Conservative Coalition Support Ratios of Party Contingents on Committees, 91st and 94th Congresses

	Democrats		Republicans		All Members	
	91st Cong.	94th Cong.	91st Cong.	94th Cong.	91st Cong.	94th Cong.
Government Operations	27	29	58	72	40	43
Interstate and Foreign Commerce	38	34	85	81	58	49
International Relations	20	28	70	68	42	42
Agriculture	70	45	88	77	78	56
All House Members	41	37	77	80	57	51

this is only part of a larger pattern. Party contingents on committees are less deviant from chamber averages in both the liberal and conservative directions. For example, with regard to Democrats in the Ninety-first Congress, the mean conservative-coalition score for members in Agriculture was 29 points above the chamber average, and the mean for members on International Relations (then called Foreign Affairs) was 21 points below the average. Between the two was a range of 50 points. In the Ninety-fourth Congress, however, the range between the two was only 17 points.

Second, power within the committees has become less centralized. Many of the important preorgatives that chairmen of committees used to have at their disposal are simply no longer available under the rules.

62. See especially Fenno, op. cit., pp. 288–91, and his testimony before the Select Committee on Committees of the U.S. House of Representatives, Ninety-third Congress, Vol. 2, Part 1, pp. 5–8.

Thus individual members have an enhanced role both within committees and on the floor. This is particularly true of subcommittee chairmen, but the generalization also applies to members—even freshman members (e.g., Richmond on Agriculture and Krueger on Commerce).[63] By this process, some control over outcomes has been transferred from chairmen and full committees to subcommittees, and subcommittees have been given a great deal more autonomy in what they do.

On the committees we have examined, the chairmen for the most part have accepted the ascendency of subcommittees—if not enthusiastically, then at least as something about which nothing can be done. The one committee chairman who chose to resist the reforms saw them used against him to rewrite the committee rules to protect subcommittees *and* to deprive him of his own subcommittee chair. This revolt, however, was only possible when there was an influx of new members who provided sufficient votes, demonstrating the interaction of turnover and reforms.

Third, committee leaders (sub- and full-committee chairmen) have been made more responsible. Subcommittee chairmen can, as we have seen, be removed by the committee's Democratic caucus, and full committee chairmen can be removed by the House caucus. Moreover, both types of caucuses, in addition to their removal powers, can write rules which govern the behavior of these leaders.

In addition to these consequences, which pertain primarily to the internal operation of the committees, there is another related set of consequences that bear on the relationship between the committees and the House. Primary among these is that House committees today have less "decision-making autonomy."[64] This is in part due to the increased responsibility of committee leaders, but is also attributable to other matters. First, *committees* have been made more responsible. The Democratic caucus has seen fit on a number of occasions to direct committees to perform certain acts.[65] While it is unlikely that the caucus will exercise this prerogative very often, it has import as a potential control over committees. More important, however, is that committees are now more *vulnerable* on the floor. This seems to be

63. The enhanced role of the freshmen is not solely the consequence of the reforms or of the large class of 1974. It is part of a longer-run process which predated—and, in part, helped to produce—the reforms. See Herbert B. Asher, "The Changing Status of the Freshman Representatives," in Ornstein, *Congress in Change*, op. cit., pp. 216–39.

64. See Fenno, *Congressmen in Committees*, op. cit., pp. 137–38.

65. See Ornstein and Rohde, "Congressional Reform and Political Parties in the U.S. House of Representatives," op. cit., Section VII: "The Democratic Caucus as a Vehicle for Policy Making."

primarily due to the adoption of the recorded teller vote and a greater willingness on the part of members to fight committees on the floor. The adoption of the Harkin amendment is only a salient instance of a more general pattern. Committees are becoming, in Fenno's words, more "permeable" and less "corporate."[66]

This does not mean that all bills from all committees will consistently be rejected or extensively amended by the House. Indeed, some of the committees which Fenno identified as most fractionalized and permeable in the 1960s (such as Education and Labor) may have higher rates of floor success in the Ninety-fourth Congress than in previous years, because the ideological viewpoint of their majority is now more closely reflected by the views of the majority of the House. What the changes do mean, at least for the Ninety-fourth Congress, is that bills will be less likely to pass the House *solely* because prestigious committees have reported them, and legislation is more likely than in the past to be significantly altered on the floor.

Other consequences of congressional change are less directly committee centered. The increase in the strength of northern Democrats relative to Southerners, coupled with the moderate views of southern Democrats who have been elected, has decreased the ideological heterogeneity of the Democratic party in the House. This has facilitated the formation of partisan coalitions, particularly in the Ninety-fourth Congress when the number of Democrats was so great,[67] which has in turn left many Republicans frustrated because they have less influence over outcomes. One apparent expression of this is an increase in the conservatism of the voting patterns of moderate Republicans. Table 9–24 describes shifts in the conservative-coalition support ratios of members of the Ninety-fourth Congress who were also members of the Ninety-third. The only discernable pattern appears to be a fairly consistent increase, averaging about 10 points, in the scores of Republicans who had had scores of 80 or less in the Ninety-third Congress. This may be an indication that moderates, who used to be frequently allied with liberal Democrats, are not needed as often, and therefore increasingly align themselves with their more conservative colleagues.[68]

66. See Fenno, *Congressmen in Committees,* op. cit., especially pp. 276–79.

67. Of the 612 record votes taken in 1975, 296 (or 48 percent) were "party unity" votes on which majorities of both parties opposed each other. (See *Congressional Quarterly Weekly Report* (January 24, 1976):179–83. This is the highest proportion since 1965.

68. Even if this is not the reason for the statistical change, moderate Republicans are certainly frustrated. Representative Stewart McKinney (R., Conn.) recently said, "If you feel that the Republican party isn't going anywhere in Congress and you aren't going anywhere in the Republican party, how would you feel?" See Helen Dewar, "Rep. Gude Savors Retiring," *Washington Post* (February 26, 1976):B1.

Table 9-24. Changes in Conservative Coalition Support Ratios, 93rd-94th Congresses

Scores in 93rd Congress	Average Change in Score, 94th Congress		
	Northern Democrats	Southern Democrats	Republicans
0-20	+2.9 (N=78)	+1.2 (5)	+11.5 (2)
21-40	+0.7 (46)	+8.3 (4)	+9.9 (9)
41-60	−4.0 (12)	+4.3 (6)	+10.5 (17)
61-80	+0.4 (5)	+1.4 (21)	+9.2 (32)
81-100	+2.0 (3)	+0.3 (31)	+2.1 (67)
Total	+1.6 (145)	+1.5 (67)	+ 5.7 (127)

Note: Number of members in the category is in parentheses.

Another consequence of the increase in the liberalism of House Democrats in conjunction with the reforms is that the power of the old conservative coalition is waning. Northern Republicans are less numerous, and southern Democrats are less likely to be conservative. Those senior conservatives who remain have less formal authority than in the past. In 1975, the conservative coalition was victorious on only 52 percent of the votes on which it formed, the lowest proportion since the second session of the Eighty-ninth Congress. (Since the Eighty-ninth, the average proportion of victories during a session was 71 percent.[69])

While, as we have seen, the independent power of committees and their chairmen has declined, no new individual or group has become dominant. Majority-party leadership has remained weak despite the increase in the formal powers of the Speaker. In the view of some members this is due at least in part to an unwillingness on the part of Speaker Albert to take certain risks. As one committee chairman commented:

As we have torn down a little bit of the edifice of seniority—not altogether, but at least in part—we've raised very serious doubts about

69. *Congressional Quarterly Weekly Report* (January 24, 1976):170.

whether anybody would be likely to claim an office simply by divine right. Speakers are elected every two years, and you know one time it was said "no bishop, no king." So the chairman is subjected to interruption in his seniority; that makes the Speaker's election less certain. Or his reelection less certain in an absolute way.

What I'm saying is that the Speaker is now reluctant to say "bite the bullet," for fear he will go the way of the chairman.

It is especially difficult to speculate about what patterns of influence will exist in the House in future Congresses. Like actors in any large institution, legislators have a way of creating stable bases of authority regardless of either formal rules or reformers' intent. It would not be completely surprising to see the House of the 1980s built around subcommittee hegemony, with subcommittee chairmen controlling the legislative output of committees and members deferring to the subcommittee chairmen's expertise on the House floor.

Beyond the question of power relationships, the changes in the House in the 1970s have created a major upswing in legislative activity. Electronic voting, the recorded teller vote, and the subcommittee reforms have contributed to the tremendous increase in record votes in the Ninety-second to Ninety-fourth Congresses (see Table 9–25).

Table 9–25. Record Votes in the House, 1961–1975

Year	Record Votes	Year	Record Votes
1961	116	1969	177
1962	124	1970	266
1963	119	1971	320
1964	113	1972	329
1965	201	1973	541
1966	193	1974	537
1967	245	1975	612
1968	233		

Sources: 1961-1969, *Congressional Quarterly Almanac, 1969* 25 (Washington, D.C.: *Congressional Quarterly, Inc.*, 1970), p. 85; 1970-1975, *Congressional Quarterly Weekly Report* (December 27, 1975):2841.

The subcommittee reforms and ascension to subcommittee chairmanships of many activist liberal Democrats have led to many more committee and subcommittee meetings and hearings. The increase in various forms of legislative activity have affected all House members, spreading them thinner, and forcing them to depend more and more heavily on their staff resources. In a dramatic change from the past, virtually every House member now uses some of his personal staff for legislative (as opposed to clerical and constituent service) tasks. And many members, of course, now have subcommittee professional staff to help them meet their legislative responsibilities.

As the increase in demands on House members' time becomes more and more of a problem, we may see attempts to reform the scheduling process of the House, and perhaps some strong efforts by a future Speaker to streamline or restrict subcommittee or floor activity. This would very likely meet with much resistance from activist subcommittee chairmen, and a possible result would be an increasing fragmentation of legislative activity—like the Senate, House subcommittee hearings in future Congresses may be characterized by the appearance of the chairman and the absence of the rest of the membership.

Moving from internal House procedures to relationships between Congress and the executive branch, the Ninety-fourth Congress has seen an increasing aggressiveness by Congress towards the executive and correspondingly greater friction between the two branches. As we have seen, activist subcommittee chairmen, unleashed by the reforms, have investigated federal agencies like the IRS, the Federal Reserve Board, the CIA, and the Federal Trade Commission; subpoenaed executive and presidential documents, and moved to cite a number of cabinet members for contempt of Congress. Recent congressional activity and aggressiveness has been particularly marked in foreign affairs, where the House's role has traditionally been weak.

The major question to consider here is: To what extent will congressional aggressiveness in overseeing and investigating the executive branch waver if a liberal Democratic Congress is matched by a liberal Democratic president? Undoubtedly, some of the friction between the two branches will disappear, as the issue of partisanship disappears. But subcommittee chairmen like Benjamin Rosenthal, John Moss, Donald Fraser, Bella Abzug, and Robert Bergland are not likely to be subservient to departments, agencies, or the White House even with a Democratic president—in part because of their loyalty to congressional prerogatives, in part because their own personal interests would not be served by passive acceptance of presidential and bureaucratic initiatives and policy administration. But Congress' success in effective oversight of the executive branch remains spotty, and would certainly become no better with the president and Congress sharing policy outlooks and party affiliation.

What about the future role of Congress in the policy process? We have seen conflicting evidence in our detailed examination of four committees. Following the Vietnam experience and the revelations about CIA activities in Chile, Cuba, and elsewhere around the world, the House almost certainly will play a larger and more direct role in making foreign policy. Congress' actions on questions like Korean foreign aid and aid to Angola are examples of the new congressional viewpoint and behavior in the international arena.

From the comments of our interviewees, the House is likely to expand its role in the agricultural arena, perhaps creating a less limited food policy with emphasis on the whole food chain and on the international implications of food. The nature of House turnover combined with reforms encouraging activity and innovation are responsible; they have created an environment which will allow these new policy possibilities to germinate.

With more congressmen in positions to have an effect on public policy, as subcommittee chairmanships have expanded in number and in influence, policy innovation has become more likely in a number of different areas, including consumer affairs, environmental protection, and mass transportation. The House may well become a major congressional *incubator* of policy initiatives in the society, a role which, until now, has been played much more frequently by the Senate.[70]

Unfortunately, this sanguine view of future congressional performance is an indication of what is *possible* within the current framework, and is not based on a great deal of concrete evidence from the first session of the Ninety-fourth Congress. The increase in congressional activity which has been evident has certainly not produced a great deal of immediate satisfaction with the Congress' behavior or its policy outputs, either among elites or the mass electorate. Indeed, much of the increased activity has come about because reforms have created overlap and fragmentation of policy areas in House subcommittees. Defining proper jurisdictional authority—subcommittees' protecting their respective turfs—has consumed a good deal of energy in this House.

This spreading out of legislative opportunities gives more members an incentive to contribute to policy formulation in a particular area at an earlier stage in their House careers, but it also may preclude Congress from dealing with such intricate problems as energy, health, economic productivity, or transportation in any comprehensive way. The policy process has been greatly decentralized, without a corresponding coordination of the activities and deliberation of subcommittees or committees.[71] Units which could possibly provide the

70. See Nelson W. Polsby, "Strengthening Congress in National Policymaking," in Polsby (ed.), *Congressional Behavior* (New York: Random House, 1971), pp. 3–13.

71. We should note that the main reason that the Bolling Committee on Committees was formed in the Ninety-third Congress was so that these jurisdictional conflicts could be rectified and some coordination could be provided. Perhaps this effort will be revived in the future.

necessary coordination—the majority party caucus, or the Speaker of the House—have not done so, in spite of the fact that the reform process blessed them with more formal authority.

Thus, the changes in the House which have, through a decentralization of power, encouraged innovation and broad participation also run the risk of so fractionalizing the policy process so that nothing gets done. Only time will tell which of these effects will be dominant.

Part Three |

LEADERSHIP
AND THE
LEGISLATIVE PROCESS

10

Leadership and the Committee System

Louis P. Westefield

Students of congressional behavior are interested in party leadership, leadership management strategies, and the committee system.[1] Such themes are the concerns of this paper. Party leadership strategies and the committee system of the House are examined in concert to provide a very elementary, yet explicit, theory about one strategy of the majority party leaders with respect to a simple but largely ignored phenomenon, change in size of the standing committees of the House.[2]

Reprinted by permission of the author and publisher from Louis P. Westefield, "Majority Party Leadership and the Committee System in the House of Representatives," *American Political Science Review* 68:4 (1974):1593–1604. Copyright © 1974 by the American Political Science Association. I would like to express my gratitude to James W. Davis, Adam Przeworski, Robert Salisbury, Kenneth Shepsle, and John Sprague for their advice and helpful comments. In addition, I owe a very special and substantial debt to John Sprague who gave freely of his time and insight throughout this project. And while none of these individuals may wish to be associated with the arguments and interpretations of this paper, much of what may be useful is the result of their efforts. Finally, I would like to thank the two anonymous referees for their suggestions.

1. See, for example, Randall B. Ripley, *Party Leaders in The House of Representatives* (Washington: Brookings Institution, 1967); Charles O. Jones, *The Minority Party in Congress* (Boston: Little, Brown, 1970); Randall B. Ripley, *Majority Party Leadership in Congress* (Boston: Little, Brown, 1969); and Lewis A. Froman, Jr. and Randall B. Ripley, "Conditions for Party Leadership: The Case of the House Democrats," *American Political Science Review* 59 (March, 1965):52–63.

2. Gawthrop is one of the few scholars to point out this phenomenon. However, his primary concern was to describe the changing patterns of multiple committee assignments in the House. See Louis C. Gawthrop, "Changing Membership Pat-

The theory deals with the use of the committee system as a resource by the party leaders. Briefly, the argument is that the leaders pursue a strategy of accommodation. That is, the leaders attempt to accommodate member demands for committee positions in order to gain leverage with the members. To gain leverage the leaders must guarantee a steady supply of resources—i.e., party positions on committees.

The theory builds on several relatively clear concepts such as compliance, quality of assignment, expectation, and scarcity. The resulting argument orders and provides an interpretation for some elementary observations of leadership behavior. Furthermore, it is shown that distinguishing between the short-run and the long-run is useful theoretically, i.e., short-run decisions have long-run consequences.

Theory

Consider the majority party leaders.[3] What part do they play in the establishment of the sizes of the standing committees? Formally the task of making committee assignments falls to the respective party committee on committees. Since the Democrats, by virtue of their majority status, organized most of the Congresses in the period we shall examine, the responsibility for majority-party assignments has most often fallen upon the Democratic members of the Ways and Means Committee.[4] In practice the literature on committee assignments suggests that the position of the party leaders determines the outcomes (the assignments), should they, the leaders, choose to exercise their influence.[5] Their position is prominent particularly in assignments to the better committees. Very little, however, is known about the process of determining party ratios on committees and

terns in House Committees," *American Political Science Review* 60 (June, 1966): 366–73.

3. For the purposes of this paper, "majority-party leaders" will mean the Speaker, the majority leader, and the majority whip.

4. Their decisions are voted on by the Democratic Caucus. This final approval, however, is most often a pro forma action. See David W. Rohde and Kenneth A. Shepsle, "The Committee Assignment Process: A Case Study of Social Choice" (paper presented at the sixty-seventh annual meeting of the American Political Science Association, Chicago, 1971).

5. Nicholas A. Masters, "Committee Assignments in the House of Representatives," *American Political Science Review* 55 (June, 1961):345–57; Ripley, *Party Leaders in the House of Representatives*, pp. 57–61; Charles L. Clapp, *The Congressman: His Work As He Sees It* (Washington: The Brookings Institution, 1963), pp. 183–212; and John F. Manley, *The Politics of Finance: The House Committee on Ways and Means* (Boston: Little, Brown, 1970), p. 24.

committee size.[6] Therefore, we are forced to infer from the literature on committee assignments that the majority-party leaders also make the decisions about the sizes of the commitees. That is, leaders of both parties may negotiate about the establishment of party ratios and size, but the positions of the majority party leaders are preeminent and decisive.[7] Consequently, assume:

The majority party leaders are decisive in decisions about committee size.

This assumption is a necessary condition for the remainder of the argument. To be sure, the Legislative Reorganization Act of 1946 provides guidance about matters of committee size and the party ratios on committees. But the sizes of committees may be altered and still satisfy the condition that a division on committees should reflect the party ratio in the chamber. Furthermore, the argument will be evaluated in terms of a long-time series, a substantial part of which predates the 1946 reorganization.

Our theory has congressmen in it, and we must specify what they want, i.e., provide a motivation for the actors. Since we are dealing with majority-party strategy, the universe is the members of the majority party in the House. We partition these members into two groups, the party leaders and the rank-and-file members. What is it, then, that these actors want? We shall impute the following motivation to the followers:

The members want "good" assignments. Because the demand for "good" assignments most often exceeds the supply, these resources are scarce. The members want these scarce resources.

This assumption provides a motivation for the members which establishes an economic condition: "good" positions are scarce; the demand for these positions exceeds the supply. The status of this assumption, and of the other assumptions of the theory as well, is that of a statement asserted to be true for the purposes of the argument. However, these assumptions of motivation are plausible and correspond to what is known from the literature.[8] (The crucial shortage of desirable positions will be considered more fully later in the text.)

With respect to this first assumption, Masters's study of the commit-

6. On the temporal sequence of the assignment process, see Kenneth A. Shepsle, "A Model of the Congressional Committee Assignment Process: Contrained Maximization in an Institutional Setting" (paper presented at the sixty-ninth annual meeting of the American Political Science Association, New Orleans, 1973).

7. Democratic vacancies on Ways and Means are filled by the Democratic caucus. Ways and Means has been included as a committee to be observed because we assume the preeminent position of the leaders also applies to this committee.

8. The intent is not to raise the issue of the "realism" of the assumptions. Two classic statements by Friedman and Koopmans take opposite positions on this

tee assignment process can aid intuition. In discussing the Democratic Committee on Committees, he observes that committee positions are indeed scarce: "The volume of work before the committee varies, depending chiefly on the changes resulting from the preceding election. Almost always, however, there are more applications than vacancies; in the Eighty-sixth Congress 124 applications were made for 75 places to be filled."[9] Thus, there is evidence for assigning to committee positions an economic quality, namely scarcity.

We also furnish the majority party leaders with a motivation:

The majority party leaders want compliant behavior on the part of the members. They perceive that by accommodating the followers (dispensing "good" assignments) they, the leaders, can reward past loyalty or encourage such behavior in the future.

We elect to deal with party leaders in terms of their perceptions because we are not concerned at this point whether, in fact, this strategy does lead to compliant behavior on the part of the members. Nor are we concerned with the strategies the members might pursue to gain desirable assignments. True, a motivation is provided for the followers, but the theory is one of strategies of the party leaders. Therefore, we merely assume the leaders believe in such a strategy and act on the basis of this belief. (It should be emphasized that this argument treats the goal of the party leaders as general control over the members or at least over a large number of members and not policy-specific control.) Once more Masters's study is instructive, for it asserts that bargaining and rewards for compliance characterize the assignment process: "Party leaders, working in conjunction with their committee on committees, use assignments to major committees to bargain with the leaders of party groups or factions in order to preserve and fortify their leadership positions and conciliate potential rivals, as well as to reward members who have cooperated."[10] Randall Ripley, sorting out the Democratic committee assignments in the Eighty-eighth Congress, reaches much the same conclusion.[11] Thus, this motivational assumption also is plausible and it accords with what is known from the literature.

---

issue. See Milton Friedman, *Essays in Positive Economics* (Chicago: University of Chicago Press, 1953), pp. 3–43; and Tjalling C. Koopmans, *Three Essays on the State of Economic Science* (New York: Mcgraw-Hill, 1957), pp. 129–66.

9. Masters, p. 346. On scarcity of positions also see Richard F. Fenno, Jr., *The Power of the Purse: Appropriations Politics in Congress* (Boston: Little, Brown, 1966), Table 2.8 at p. 64; and Charles S. Bullock, III, "Committee Transfers in the United States House of Representatives," *Journal of Politics* 35 (February, 1973): footnote 39 at p. 101.

10. Masters, p. 357.

11. Ripley, *Party Leaders in the House of Representatives*, p. 60. Also, see Manley, *The Politics of Finance*, p. 24.

One qualitative distinction has been posited for the political actors and a motivation provided for each—the leaders and the followers. In this argument, committee positions are given the status of a currency, a basis of exchange between the leaders and followers. The leaders desire compliant behavior on the part of the members. By dispensing committee assignments the leaders believe they encourage compliance. Thus, having resources to allocate benefits the leaders; indeed, more resources provide more opportunities to gain leverage with the members. Furthermore, the perceived marginal cost of increasing the supply of seats is always less than the perceived value of the expected increase in compliance. That is, there is always some committee which if increased in size would increase expected compliance for some members.

What, then, are the consequences of these premises? First consider the supply of seats. Recall that the majority party leaders can increase their resource base, i.e., they can fix the size of the standing committees. Therefore:

Proposition I: The leaders expand their resource base by increasing the number of committee positions they can dispense.

Empirically, then, we are interested in the time path of the total number of committee seats in the House. Given the theory, this time path will be some monotonically increasing function of time. This theoretical relationship is displayed in Figure 10–1.

Evaluation

Are the data consistent with the theory? The data consist of the number of committee positions during the period 1927 to 1971.[12] We begin with 1927 because the number of standing committees in the House remained relatively unchanged from that date until the Legislative Reorganization Act of 1946. And except for the creation

12. All the data come from the available *Congressional Directory* closest to the opening of each Congress which lists committee assignments. In some cases it was necessary to use the *Congressional Directory* for the second session of a Congress. Since the committee system was reorganized in 1946, beginning with 1927 also provides two distinct time periods of approximately the same length. A list of the standing committees and their respective sizes may be found in *Cannon's Precedents of the House of Representatives,* vol. 3 (Washington: Government Printing Office, 1935), pp. 8–9. The Congresses listed there include the Sixtieth to Seventy-third Congresses. The Committee on Memorials (three seats) was created in the Seventieth Congress. The Committee on Un-American Activities has been excluded from the period preceding the Legislative Reorganization Act of 1946. Prior to 1927, the number of positions grew even in the midst of periodic adjustments in the committee system.

Figure 10–1. Representation of the Supply of Committee Seats: Dynamic on Time.

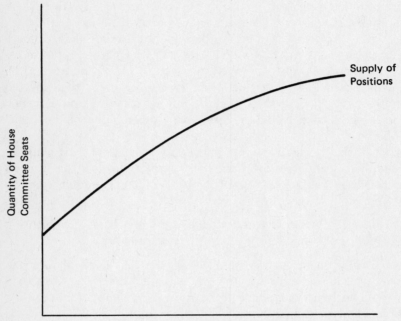

of the Committee on Science and Astronautics in 1959, the number of committees remained unchanged from 1947 to 1971. (The Committee on Standards of Official Conduct is excluded.)

Now let us evaluate this theory first for the period following the Legislative Reorganization Act of 1946. Figure 10–2 displays the time path of the total number of committee seats for the period 1947 to 1971. Even if the twenty-five seats created by the establishment of the Committee on Science and Astronautics are removed, the pattern is clear. The number of committee positions has increased since 1947 as an increasing function of time.[13]

Looked at from a slightly different perspective, the data again show

---

13. It is worth noting that alteration of committee size occurred prior to the time period examined in this paper. "In making committee assignments for Republicans in the Fifty-ninth Congress, Cannon was faced with a problem of too few choice seats for too many Republicans. He finally reached an agreement with the Democratic minority leader, John Sharpe Williams of Mississippi, that would increase the size of the committees and leave the Democratic representation undisturbed" (Ripley, *Majority Party Leadership in Congress*, p. 28).

Figure 10-2. Increase in Seats of the Standing Committees of the House, 1947–1971

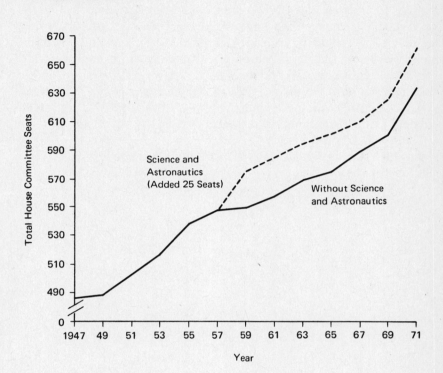

a systematic pattern. The total number of committee seats at any point in time is obtained by aggregating over committees. The product of the number of committees at a point in time and the number of Congresses observed in a time period provides the total number of "opportunities" to observe a change in the size of each committee. Of the total "opportunities" in the period 1947 to 1971 there were less than a dozen instances (3.8 percent of the total "opportunities") of a reduction in size of a standing committee. Furthermore, only one committee, Veterans' Affairs, experienced a net loss of seats during this period. Thus, aggregation does not obscure the results. The interpretation is straightforward; the data are consistent with the argument.[14]

14. One potential source of measurement error can be disregarded. The sizes of the committees may be altered during a Congress. However, the committee rosters for the second session of each Congress indicate that generally the size of committees is not altered within a Congress. And where an increase or decrease does occur, the committee is not changed to its former size at the beginning of the next Congress.

The Legislative Reorganization Act of 1946 forces us to deal separately with the period 1927 to 1945, but for the purposes of this analysis the reorganization is advantageous. We can extend the observations back in time and examine two distinct periods. Intuitively this earlier period should provide a much more difficult test of the argument. We know that there were a great many more committees and committee positions in the system during this period. Indeed, more than 830 positions existed in 1927 as opposed to slightly more than 480 in 1947. And with a large number of positions already in a system we might expect to find no evidence to support the argument

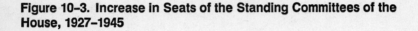

Figure 10–3. Increase in Seats of the Standing Committees of the House, 1927–1945

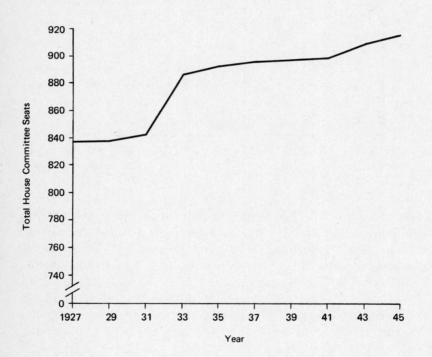

Figure 10–3 displays the time path of the total number of committee seats for the period 1927 to 1945. Note again that the number of committee seats is an increasing function of time.[15] Thus, even in the midst

15. There is an interesting interpretation to be made from the data of Figure 10–3. Note the rate of change in the interval 1931 to 1933. A party, long out of power and suddenly gaining majority status with an overwhelming numerical advantage, may have strong incentives to expand rapidly the number of rewards

of an abundance of positions, the leaders increase their resource base. And consider the "opportunities" to observe a reduction in committee size during this period. Again, there were less than a dozen cases of such reductions (1.4 percent of the "opportunities"). Moreover, no committee experienced a net loss of seats during this period. Taking the two periods together, we note that there were less than twenty instances of reduction in the number of seats on committees; these cases represent 2.3 percent of the total "opportunities."

An elementary economic argument about one leadership strategy has been constructed. The demands of the theory have been compared with observations for the two periods of time, and the data were found to be consistent with the argument.

Differential Valuation and the Distribution of the Increase in Seats Across Committees

Suppose the members prize assignments to some committees more than others. While the currency remains committee assignments, we now introduce *explicitly* the notion of differential valuation of committees.

The differential prestige of committees is established by at least two conditions: (1) formal rules and (2) the transfers of members from one committee to another. Transfers of members from one committee assignment to another have been used frequently to establish the hierarchy of committee prestige. And, as Bullock and Sprague point out, the formal rules dealing with privileges of committees and restrictions on multiple committee assignments recognize at least ordered classes of committees.[16] That committees are stratified in terms of prestige or desirability is significant because the leaders can be expected to add positions to committees in some nonrandom fashion. What is the advantage to the leaders of creating new positions on those committees which are not valued by the members? Having desirable assignments to allocate is what brings leverage to deal with members.

---

early in the game. Were the Republicans suddenly to achieve majority status by a large margin the same phenomenon may occur. Note, however, that this interpretation does not fall out of the argument. The argument presupposes only a weak condition (an increasing function of time) on the time path of the total number of committee positions.

16. Charles Bullock and John Sprague, "A Research Note on the Committee Assignments of Southern Democratic Congressmen," *Journal of Politics* 31 (May, 1969):493. For one example of the use of committee transfers, see George Goodwin, Jr., *The Little Legislatures: Committees of Congress* (Amherst: University of Massachusetts Press, 1970), pp. 114–5. And the positions on desirable committees are scarce. See footnote 9 above.

Thus, we move from the consideration of aggregate change (the time path of the total number of committee positions) to an examination of the distribution of the increase in positions across the hierarchy of committee prestige.

First, some method of ordering the standing committees in terms of desirability or prestige is required. In order to produce such an ordering conveniently, we shall adopt the convention of Bullock and Sprague.[17] Their measure expresses the number of transfers to a committee relative to the number of departures plus transfers. Since desirable committees draw members from other committees and lose few members to other committees, the higher the value of the index, the more prestigious the committee. Bullock, using this method, provides a measure of committee prestige for the period 1947 to 1967.[18] This same method can be employed to produce a committee prestige ordering for the earlier period. Only the prestige ordering for the majority party during each period will be used, because this theory accounts only for accommodation within the majority party.[19]

The prestige rankings for the two periods are displayed in Tables 10–1 and 10–2. Although there may be some quarrel with the ranking

Table 10–1. Prestige Ranking of Committees for House Democrats, 1947–1967

Ways and Means	1.000	Government Operations	.371
Rules	1.000	District of Columbia	.273
Appropriations	.983	Education and Labor	.250
Foreign Affairs	.852	House Administration	.243
Armed Services	.750	Interior	.241
Commerce	.743	Banking and Currency	.231
Judiciary	.708	Merchant Marine	.222
Agriculture	.541	Veteran's Affairs	.075
Public Works	.485	Post Office	.050
Science and Astronautics	.480	Un-American Activities	.000

Source: From Charles Bullock, "The Committee Assignments of Freshmen in the House of Representatives, 1947-1967" (Ph.D. dissertation Washington University, St. Louis, Missouri, 1968), Table 3, p. 35.

17. Bullock and Sprague, pp. 496–501.

18. Charles Bullock, "The Committee Assignments of Freshmen in the House of Representatives, 1947–1967" (dissertation, Washington University, St. Louis, 1968), p. 35.

19. As we have noted, the Democrats controlled most of the Congresses during this time period. Hence, for our purposes, the majority party empirically will mean the Democrats. Furthermore, the prestige rankings of committees for Democrats and Republicans are empirically distinct. See Bullock and Sprague, pp. 496–501. Although theoretical reasons dictate the use of majority-party rankings, use of

Table 10–2. Prestige Ranking of Committees for House Democrats, 1935–1945

Ways and Means	1.000	Immigration	.259
Rules	1.000	Coinage	.250
Appropriations	.989	Labor	.250
Agriculture	.915	Flood Control	.222
Commerce	.877	Accounts	.200
Naval Affairs	.867	Irrigation	.192
Judiciary	.841	Expenditures	.174
Banking and Currency	.836	Insular	.174
Military Affairs	.800	Indian	.167
Printing	.750	Territories	.167
Foreign Affairs	.588	Enrolled Bills	.143
Election of President	.556	Public Lands	.130
Rivers	.550	Elections #1	.111
Executive Papers	.500	Pensions	.105
Library	.500	Civil Service	.100
District of Columbia	.440	Elections #2	.100
Merchant Marine	.421	World War Veterans	.069
Memorials	.333	Public Buildings	.031
Patents	.333	Claims	.000
Roads	.333	Elections #3	.000
War Claims	.333	Invalid Pensions	.000
Post Office	.317	Mines	.000
Census	.292	Revision of Laws	.000
Education	.263		

Source: *Congressional Directory.* 73rd-79th Congresses (Washington, D.C.: Government Printing Office, various dates).

of several minor committees in the earlier period (Printing and Library, for example), these rankings correspond to other evaluations of the committee prestige.[20] Therefore, assume the following:

A single ordering of committee prestige can represent the "average" preferences of the members, and this measure generally will be stable through each time period.

This assumption presupposes two conditions: (1) "average" prefer-

---

rankings for Republicans or House members as a whole, both distinct from Democrats alone, will not dramatically alter the results reported below. This occurs because there is a correspondence between the rankings for the more desirable committees, the ones I shall argue take up most of the overall expansion in seats.

20. For the modern period see Goodwin, pp. 114–16. For the earlier period see George B. Galloway, *The Legislative Process in Congress* (New York: Thomas Y. Crowell, 1955), p. 128; Floyd M. Riddick, *Congressional Procedure* (Boston: Chapman and Grimes, 1941), pp. 115–16; Chang-Wei Chiu, *The Speaker of the House of Representatives Since 1896* (New York: Columbia University Press, 1928), p. 69; and George B. Galloway, *Congress at the Crossroads* (New York: Thomas Y. Crowell, 1946), p. 90.

ences of the members can be assigned and (2) the "average" committee prestige ranking will be stable over time. It is clear that partitioning the members of the House into various groups will produce somewhat different prestige orderings. Nevertheless, the correspondence between committee-prestige rankings of various groups of House members is quite high.[21] Therefore, it is assumed that a single ordering of committee prestige can represent the "average" preferences of the members.

The second condition, in effect, eliminates any consideration of change in preference over time. Of course, the longer the time period the more dubious is the standing of this assumption, for the probability of obscuring changes in preference surely increases as the time period lengthens. In practice this assumption demands the stability of each ordering over approximately a twenty year period, 1927 to 1945 and 1947 to 1971. The prestige measure for the Seventy-fourth to Seventy-ninth Congresses will represent the ordering in the former period, and the measure for 1947 to 1967 will represent the prestige hierarchy in the latter period.

We now need to specify the particular set of members for whom the measures are said to hold. Because this is a theory of majority-party leadership behavior, we assume the following:

The leaders of the majority party are concerned, first and foremost, with the committee preferences of their party members.

This assumption seems quite reasonable and needs little further comment. To be sure, the leaders may consider the needs of their calleagues in the minority party, particularly on a case by case basis. Still, we offer as a rule the notion that majority-party leaders are more interested in the desires of their party's rank and file.[22]

One final assumption is required; it specifies the amount of information in the system:

The majority party leaders know the committee preference ordering of their party members.

The leaders, though most often not the most senior members of their party, nevertheless have accumulated many terms of service and generally have had ample opportunity to learn the relative desirability of the various standing committees. Thus, we demand of the leaders of the majority party the ability to reproduce the "average" committee prestige ranking of their party members.

As we have seen, reductions in the sizes of the standing committees

21. See Bullock and Sprague, pp. 496–501.

22. It is impossible to reconstruct the particular circumstances of the creation of each new seat. For example, a new minority position might be created to reflect a new party ratio and to prevent a reduction in majority positions. Such an action is consistent with the argument.

have been most infrequent. Thus, given the notion of differential valuation of committees by the members, we can now examine the distribution of the total increase in committee positions across the prestige ranking of committees.

Suppose the leaders estimate expected compliance on the part of a member as a function of the prestige of the *new* seats to be created. We can suppose that expected compliance varies directly with prestige of the new seat. That is, the leaders expect greater compliance as the prestige of the new seats to be created increases. But increasing the number of positions reduces the total value of seats as resources. Specifically, the total value of these resources declines as a function of the prestige of the newly created seat. Adding seats to the very best committees reduces the value of total resources more than does adding positions to somewhat less prestigious committees. Thus, benefits (member compliance) increase with the expected prestige of the new position. But costs (depletion of seat value) also increase with the prestige of the new seat to be created. The economic interpretation, involving exchange and scarcity, is crucial. If the currency (the assignments) were not scarce and if anyone could have the assignment he desired, then seats would not constitute leadership resources.

On this argument, then, we can anticipate where the growth in committee positions will occur:

Proposition II: The leaders, in expanding their resource base, will concentrate the increase in the middle to upper range of the committee prestige ordering.

Empirically this means that a relative frequency distribution of the total increase in seats across committees will take the form displayed in Figure 10–4. This form results from the preceding argument and from the process of aggregating over a number of leaders and members. That is, a leader's estimate of the average minimum price in prestige to secure minimally acceptable expected compliance varies from one member to another. And one leader's estimates are likely to differ from those of another leader. Rayburn's estimates may not be the same as Albert's estimates. Hence the empirical distribution should have a mean at the higher prestige level with values distributed around that mean.

The interpretation is straightforward. Why increase the number of positions on committees that are not valued by the members? After all, such committees earn their low prestige standing through their inability to hold current members and attract new members from other committees. Moreover, why dispense more of the most prized positions? Expanding only the very best commitees rapidly depletes the value of

Figure 10–4. Expected Distribution of the Total Increase in Committee Seats

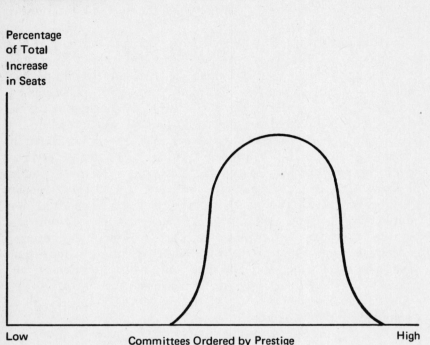

Percentage
of Total
Increase
in Seats

Low   Committees Ordered by Prestige   High

these leadership resources. In short, the leaders try to buy cheap and sell dear.[23]

Figure 10–5 displays the empirical distribution of total seat additions for the period 1947 to 1971. Notice that the bulk of the increase does occur at the higher prestige levels. Moreover, at the highest level of prestige the distribution does indeed tail off. At the other end of the distribution, however, several low-prestige committees have gained seats. Still it seems fair to conclude that the data are consistent with the argument.

Figure 10–6 displays the distribution of committee seat additions for the earlier period, 1927 to 1945. It is clear that the distribution takes the general form specified by the theory. In this case the fit is much closer to the theoretical prediction. It may be that the propensity to

23. One might suppose there is interdependence here. That is, adding positions to a committee may increase the number of transfers to that committee and hence affect the prestige measure. But prestige is also influenced by departures from a committee. Therefore, in principle it is possible to observe low-prestige committees increasing in size.

Figure 10–5. The Distribution of the Total Increase in Committee Seats, 1947–1971

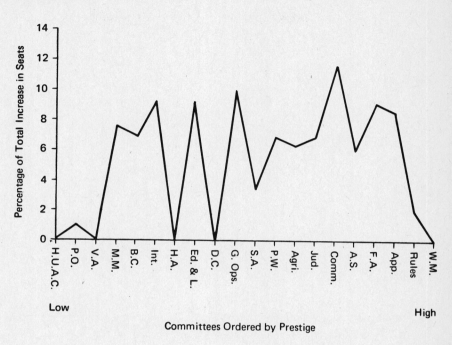

Note: Veterans Affairs suffered a net loss of one seat during this period; it has been counted as a zero increase in size.

limit the increase in seats to the best committees is particularly strong when there already are substantial numbers of committee positions in the system.

In this period, however, the distribution does not tail off at the high-prestige level as the theory demands. Undoubtedly this is due in large part to the confounding influence of the size of the Appropriations Committee. For both time periods, this committee consistently has been one and one-half to two times the size of the other committees in the House. An increase of five seats on a large committee probably does not have the same substantive meaning in terms of the argument as an increase of five positions on a much smaller committee of comparable prestige. Therefore, let us reexamine the increase in committee size. We will look at the increase in positions on a committee relative to the size of that committee.

Figure 10–7 contains the data for the modern period; Figure 10–8

Figure 10-6. The Distribution of the Total Increase in Committee Seats, 1927-1945

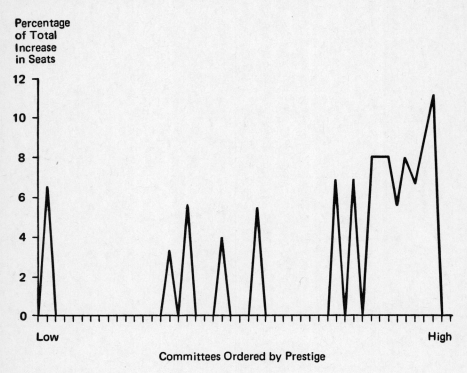

Percentage
of Total
Increase
in Seats

Low   High

Committees Ordered by Prestige

displays the data for the period 1927 to 1945. With the data ordered in this way note the tendency for the increases in size to tail off at the very-high-prestige level. The effect of taking into account the size of the Appropriations Committee is particularly noticeable in Figure 10–8. Therefore, both the time path of the total number of committee seats and the distribution of the increases in size across committees are consistent with the theory.

A Long-Run Consequence of a Short-Run Strategy

In evaluating the argument to this point we have confined our attention to the supply of committee positions, which is a directly observable variable. This leadership strategy, however, is likely to have other important consequences. Indeed, these decisions to expand positions at particular points in time have a cumulative effect. This

Figure 10-7. Increase in Size of the Standing Committees, 1947–1971

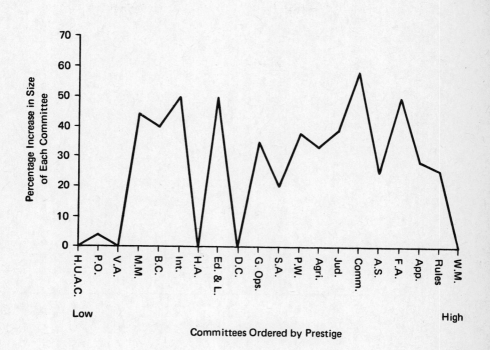

Note: Veterans Affairs suffered a net loss of one seat during this period; it has been counted as a zero increase in size.

consequence can be best examined by turning to the expressed demand for additional positions and considering the relationship between the supply of and demand for positions through time. We ask, in other words, what does the theory tell us about the long-run consequence of this particular leadership strategy?

Scarcity makes committee positions valuable leadership resources. The preceding argument provides an interpretation for the growth in the number of committee seats. But as the supply of committee positions increases, scarcity declines, thereby altering the relationship between the demand for and the supply of positions, i.e., the gap between demand and supply decreases. Thus, as currency becomes more and more plentiful, the basis of exchange is impaired. The leaders must revalue the currency or turn to another medium of exchange.[24]

24. The crucial notion of this argument is the *relative* time rate of change of supply and demand. We might consider the demand for positions to be fixed and constant over time. Alternatively, we may assume that interests proliferate as

Figure 10-8. Increase in Size of the Standing Committees, 1927-1945

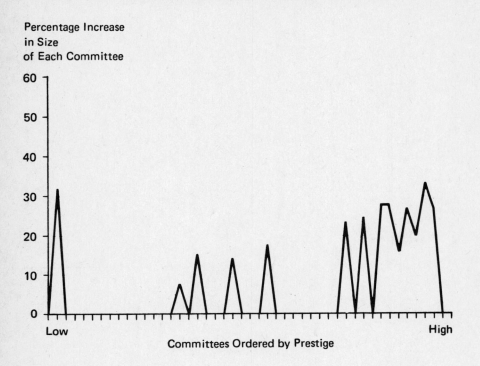

Percentage Increase
in Size
of Each Committee

Committees Ordered by Prestige

This reasoning leads to a third proposition:

Proposition III: In time the currency (committee positions) will be devalued to the point where the system of resources must be overhauled.

The interpretation is straightforward.[25] Short-run decisions designed to gain leverage with the members in time seriously erode the value of the leadership's resource base. Clearly the argument provides an

---

social, political, and economic systems become more complex, thereby increasing the demand for positions. Or demand for positions may decline through time. As long as the time rate of change of supply is greater than the time rate of change of demand, the basis of exchange between the party leaders and followers is impaired.

25. Clearly this proposition, the long-run consequence of a leadership management strategy, cannot be evaluated empirically in the same manner as the earlier portions of the argument. It takes time for the process to work itself out. Nonetheless, this argument can easily be formalized. Specific rate of change assumptions for D_t (demand) and S_t (supply) would make it possible to estimate at what point the committee system would be under stress, i.e., at what point conditions favorable to reorganization are likely to occur.

economic interpretation for periodic readjustments in the committee system or committee reorganization. Short-run decisions do indeed have long-run consequences: inflation brings impairment of the leadership resource base. Thus, another major reorganization of the committee system similar to that of 1946 should come as no surprise, i.e., there is a theoretical predicition that it will occur and a theoretical interpretation for its occurrence.[26]

Conclusion

An elementary theory of leadership expansion of committee positions has been presented. The data, the time path of the total number of committee positions, and the distribution of the increase in seats across the prestige hierarchy of committees are consistent with the argument. (And more than a dozen *new* committee positions were added at the opening of the Ninety-third Congress.) Furthermore, it has been shown that quite reasonable short-run decisions have a significant long-run consequence.

Possible alternative explanations of this phenomenon have not been examined. One such explanation, however, can be rejected. The House relies extensively on an elaborate division of labor, in committees and subcommittees, to conduct its business. The volume and technical complexity of legislation has increased through time. With this growth in workload has come an increase in the legislative budget.[27] Congressional staffs have grown as have funds for committee operations. To cope with the increased burdens on the work groups (the committees), one might suppose that increasing the number of committee members would be an appropriate management response: more members to deal with the increasing work load. Such a response might account for the growth in committee positions after World War II. But prior to 1946 an abundance of positions existed. And surely the volume and technical complexity of legislation from the 1920s to the

26. The leaders may also increase the size of a committee in order to reshape its composition for policy reasons. A good example would be the expansion of the Rules Committee. See Milton C. Cummings and Robert L. Peabody, "The Decision to Enlarge the Committee on Rules: An Analysis of the 1961 Vote," in *New Perspectives on the House of Representatives*, [First Edition], ed. Robert L. Peabody and Nelson W. Polsby (Chicago: Rand McNally, 1963), pp. 167–94. In such cases the leaders' desire for compliance is directed at a work group rather than a specific individual. Although this theory consists of assertions at the level of individuals, leadership decisions directed at work groups are not at odds with the argument. As long as scarcity of positions is important in the relations between leaders and followers, the argument holds.

27. See Nelson W. Polsby, "The Institutionalization of the U.S. House of Representatives," *American Political Science Review* 62 (March, 1968):158–60.

1940s was less than after 1946. Yet, even with a large number of positions in this earlier period, the leaders continued to create additional committee positions.

But is the creation of additional positions to meet an increasing workload a reasonable management strategy? Adding staff positions and funds for committee operations may be. But additional positions for the members must be filled from a constant membership base.[28] More positions, then, require more multiple memberships, more demands on a member's time and energy. And although members with multiple assignments have some freedom to choose where to concentrate their committee efforts, surely some committee responsibilities must suffer in the process. Thus, increasing committee positions as an organizational management strategy to cope with a growing workload seems to be neither a plausible nor compelling alternative explanation.[29]

Finally, although the phenomenon examined in this paper is but one aspect of congressional behavior, the argument presented is not at odds with other research on Congress. Indeed, it is quite reasonable in light of the discussions of the institutionalization of the House.[30]

With the rise of the seniority system, a committee position in practice has become a property right of the individual member. That is, leaders cannot arbitrarily move members from one committee to another. A member, as long as he remains in the House, is entitled to retain his present assignment. And as House service becomes more attractive and House turnover declines, a rigidity develops in the committee system. The leaders are constrained in the use of assignments as a resource, a means to gain leverage with the members. Vacancies alone determine

28. As we have seen, new positions on some committees are not matched by a reduction in size of other committees. In the period examined prior to 1946 almost half the members held multiple assignments. And the number of multiple memberships has steadily increased since 1946. See Gawthrop, "Changing Membership Patterns in House Committees," pp. 366–67.

29. There are other data which suggest the process discussed in this paper may be a general leadership management strategy, i.e., not confined solely to the House of Representatives. From 1927 to 1945 the time path of the total number of Senate committee positions is an increasing function of time. And this growth took place in the midst of an abundance of positions; the ratio of the number of seats to the number of senators was more than four to one. After the Reorganization Act of 1946, the number of positions once more steadily increased. After 1969 the time path begins to oscillate slightly. But some departure from the House pattern is not surprising. Inflation of seats has been much more pronounced in the Senate; even after 1946 the ratio of seats to members exceeded two to one.

30. See Polsby, pp. 148–68; Nelson W. Polsby, Miriam Gallaher, and Barry Spencer Rundquist, "The Growth of the Seniority System in the U.S. House of Representatives," *American Political Science Review* 63 (September, 1969):787–807; and Michael Abram and Joseph Cooper, "The Rise of Seniority in the House of Representatives," *Polity* 1 (Fall, 1968): 52–85.

the size of this leadership resource base. Hence the leaders, quite plausibly, can be expected to make their resource base more flexible, larger, and more responsive to their needs. Resorting to "manufacturing" committee positions, then, is a not surprising leadership response to the conditions of the modern House.

We might also speculate about the particular conditions under which the leaders would choose to add to the existing supply of committee positions. One such condition involves the magnitude of House turnover. Presumably there is little need to increase resources available for allocation when House turnover produces a number of vacancies. Rather it is when there is little House turnover, when deaths, retirements, and decisions at the polls do not produce a number of vacancies, that the leaders need to *create* vacancies, i.e., add positions. Thus, all other things being equal, the level of House turnover should vary inversely with the number of newly created positions. And, for the periods examined in this paper, this negative relationship does occur. More new seats are created when House turnover itself fails to produce the needed vacancies. (See Appendix.) The leaders are free from dependency on House turnover alone to produce committee vacancies for resource creation to gain leverage with the members is possible. In sum, this additional datum is consistent with the argument of this paper which, in turn, complements other research on Congress.

Appendix

The relationship between the creation of new seats and the magnitude of House turnover can be shown in the following manner. Resources (committee seats) can be expressed as the ratio of committee positions to the number of House members at the beginning of each Congress. Call this measure L_t. The change in resources, ΔL_t, may be defined as $\Delta L_t = L_t - L_{t-1}$. ΔL_t then represents short-run leadership decisions to alter the supply of positions. House turnover can be measured by the common convention, the proportion of first-term House members. Call this measure H_t. Committees frequently have been partitioned into three classes, Top, Service, and Duty. This partitioning generally coincides with the prestige hierarchy of committees. The most prized committees fall into the Top Committee class. Service Committees are somewhat less prized than Top Committees but are more prestigious and desirable than Duty Committees, the least-valued positions. Since we have seen that the number of positions on the least-prized committees is seldom increased, we can confine our attention to the Top and Service Committees. The regression of ΔL_t on H_t illustrates that more new seats are created when House turnover itself fails to produce the needed vacancies:

Table 10-3. New Seat Creations and House Turnover: The Regression of ΔL_t on H_t

Top Committees	Intercept	Slope	R^2
1935–1971	.038	−.140	.163
1949–1971	.044	−.177	.149
Service Committees			
1935–1971	.030	−.121	.342
1949–1971	.033	−.133	.317

The modern period has been considered separately to take into account the effects of the vastly greater number of committee positions prior to 1946. By the criterion of fit, substantial variation remains statistically unexplained; the correlations range between —.39 and —.58. Yet the relationships are in the expected direction and easily interpretable. They are consistent with the argument of this paper.

11

Committee Assignments

David W. Rohde and
Kenneth A. Shepsle

Since Woodrow Wilson wrote *Congressional Government,* the dominance of the standing committees in the House of Representatives in determining legislative outcomes has been accepted by students of Congress. In light of recent studies of groups of House committees[1] and in-depth studies of individual committees,[2] the generalization

Reprinted by permission of the authors and publisher, from David W. Rohde and Kenneth A. Shepsle, "Democratic Committee Assignments in the House of Representatives: Strategic Aspects of a Social Choice Process," American Political Science Review 67:3 (1973):889–905. Copyright © 1973 by the American Political Science Association. We would like to express our gratitude to Richard Fenno of the University of Rochester and John Manley of Stanford University for making available to us the request data for the Eighty-seventh, Eighty-eighth, and Ninetieth Congresses, and to Robert Salisbury of Washington University, St. Louis, for the request data from the Eighty-sixth Congress. We also wish to acknowledge the research assistance of Robert Delgrosso of Michigan State University. We finally want to thank Richard Fenno, Morris Fiorina of the California Institute of Technology, and the two anonymous referees for their helpful comments on previous versions of this study. An earlier draft of this paper was presented at the Sixty-seventh Annual Meeting of the American Political Science Association, Chicago, September 7–11, 1971.

1. Richard F. Fenno, Jr., "Congressional Committees: A Comparative View," a paper presented at the Sixtieth-sixth Annual Meeting of the American Political Science Association, Los Angeles, September 8–11, 1970; George Goodwin, Jr., *The Little Legislatures* (Amherst: University of Massachusetts Press, 1970).
2. Richard F. Fenno, Jr., *The Power of the Purse: Appropriations Politics in Congress* (Boston: Little, Brown and Co., 1966); John Manley, *The Politics of Finance: The House Committee on Ways and Means* (Boston: Little, Brown and Co., 1970).

about the central role of committees in the legislative process remains intact. These studies, however, indicate that there are major differences among these "little legislatures" in regard to their organization and behavior, and that these differences are in part a function of differences in their memberships. Furthermore, as Charles Clapp has said,

> Not only is the fate of most legislative proposals determined in committee: to an important degree the fate of individual congressmen may be decided there too. A person's congressional career may rest largely on the kind of committee post he is given.[3]

Therefore, given the importance of committee membership, both in policy-making and in determining the success of individual congressmen's careers, the process by which members are assigned to committees is of the greatest importance.

A good deal of research has been devoted to the committee assignment process in the House.[4] Most of this research, however, has been based on the *results* of the process, i.e., the committee assignments that were actually made. For example, the desirability of committees has been measured in terms of the proportion of the freshmen on each committee, or the number of transfers from a committee versus the number of transfers to it. The variable missing from such treatments has been the desires of the members. Also, success in achieving committee assignments has been treated in only the most general terms, again because of the absence of data on what committees members requested.

The purpose of this paper is to analyze committee assignments by focusing on this "missing link." Our subject will be the committee

3. *The Congressman: His Work as He Sees It* (New York: Doubleday and Co., 1963), p. 207.

4. The classic treatment of the process is Nicholas A. Masters, "Committee Assignments in the House of Representatives," *American Political Science Review* 55 (June, 1961):345–57. Assignments are discussed at length in Clapp, *The Congressman*, pp. 207–40, and Goodwin, *The Little Legislatures*, pp. 64–79. Some recent studies include Louis C. Gawthrop, "Changing Membership Patterns in House Committees," *American Political Science Review* 60 (June, 1966):366–73; Charles Bullock and John Sprague, "A Research Note on the Committee Reassignments of Southern Democratic Congressmen," *Journal of Politics* 31 (May, 1969):493–512; Charles Bullock, "Correlates of Committee Transfers in the United States House of Representatives," a paper delivered at the Annual Meeting of the Midwest Political Science Association, Chicago, April 29 to May 1, 1971; Charles Bullock, "The Influence of State Party Delegations on House Committee Assignments," *Midwest Journal of Political Science* 15 (August, 1971):525–46; and Charles Bullock, "Freshman Committee Assignments and Reelection in the United States House of Representatives," *American Political Science Review* 66 (September, 1972):996–1007.

assignments of Democratic members of the House of Representatives. Committee assignments, as Clapp's observation above suggests, are valued, are in limited supply, and are allocated by rather well-defined mechanisms and procedures. By viewing committee assignments as the culmination of a special sort of allocation process, we shall be in a position to *explain* the results of this process, the *descriptions* of which have constituted the bulk of research on this topic to date. It is explanations we seek, and we find more general theories of social choice particularly well-suited for this purpose. More specifically, we examine the data of committee assignments in terms of actors in pursuit of personal goals, constrained only by scarcity and institutional procedures. We will consider the process from the point of view of the members requesting assignment and the members who make the assignments: who wants what committees, and whose requests are satisfied. The basic data which will be employed are the requests for committee assignments, by all House Democrats, made to the Democratic Committee on Committees in the Eighty-sixth to Eighty-eighth and Ninetieth Congresses.[5]

Democratic Committee Assignments

In the House, the Democratic Committee on Committees is made up of the Democratic members of the Ways and Means Committee.[6] At the beginning of each Congress they are faced with the task of filling vacancies on the other standing comittees on the House. Each member of the committee is assigned a geographic zone, containing his own state and perhaps others, and he is responsible for handling requests for assignments from members in his zone.[7]

Some time after the November election, new Democratic congress-

5. In addition to our own data, this description relies heavily on Masters, "Committee Assignments," and on Clapp, *The Congressman*, ch. 5.

6. The Democratic delegation on Ways and Means is made up almost entirely of members drawn from the southern and border states and from the large industrial states. They are elected to membership by a vote of the full Democratic caucus. During the period covered by this study the committee was dominated by the southern and border state group, who were greatly overrepresented compared to their proportion of the Democratic delegation in the House. In the Eighty-sixth to Eighty-eighth Congresses, they had eight members out of the total of fifteen, and in the Ninetieth Congress they had seven of fifteen. For a discussion of assignments to Ways and Means, see Manley, *Politics of Finance*, pp. 22–38.

7. Zone assignments in the Eighty-sixth Congress are listed in Masters, "Committee Assignments," p. 347. The number of states represented varies greatly, with Keogh of New York, for example, representing only his own state, while Metcalf of Montana represents seven small Western and Midwestern states.

men submit to the Committee on Committees their requests, in order of preference, for committee assignments. At the same time, returning congressmen may submit requests for second assignments or for transfers from committees they held in the previous Congress.

After members submit requests, lobbying for assignments begins. Many representatives seeking assignments write letters to some or all members of the Committee on Committees, setting forth arguments on their own behalf. Many also pay personal visits to the members of the Committee (especially their zone representative), to the Democratic leaders, and to the chairmen of the committees they are requesting. Often letters are written to members of the Committee on Committees to support the cause of some requesters. Typically these letters came from the deans of state delegations (either from themselves alone or on behalf of the whole delegation), from party leaders or officeholders outside the House, from committee chairmen and from leaders of interest groups relevant to the work of the committees requested.

At the beginning of the Congress, the size of committees as well as party ratios are set by negotiation between the leaders of both parties. Thus the members of the Committee on Committees are faced with the task of filling the vacancies on the standing committees which have resulted either from the failure of some Democratic members to return or from the creation of new positions. The committee meets in executive session, and each of the committees is called up (usually alphabetically). For each committee the members proceed in order of seniority to nominate candidates from their zone.[9] The names of nominees are written on a blackboard, and they are discussed by the members. After nominations are completed, the members vote by secret ballot.

Finally, after the Committee on Committees has filled all the vacancies, their decisions are placed before the Democratic caucus for ratification. This is, however, almost always a pro forma action.

For our purposes, then, the time sequence of the committee assignment process, which culminates in the creation of a committee structure for a new Congress, may be characterized by the following stages:

(1) the committee configuration in the previous Congress;

(2) an election;

(3) requests for assignments by newly elected members and by

8. While party ratios usually reflect the partisan division in the House, it is **not** unlikely that decision on both these questions are influenced by the leadership's knowledge of the requests of the members of their party.

9. It is important to note that the only way a requester can be nominated for a committee post is to be nominated by his zone representative.

returning members who held assignments in the committee configuration of the previous Congress;

(4) the establishment of size and party ratios for committees in the new Congress;

(5) committee assignments by the Democratic Committee on Committees for the new Congress.

Stage 1 provides initial conditions which are "disturbed" by an election (stage 2). The election disturbs the initial committee structure in several obvious ways. First, aggregate party proportions in the chamber are altered, requiring the renegotiation of the committee structure by party leaders: committee sizes and party ratios are fixed at this stage (stage 4). Second, individual and aggregate election results effect a change in the opportunity structure in the chamber. Individual defeats of party members in the election create party committee vacancies, which may or may not be lost to the party depending on the aggregate election results and its effect on stage 4. At the outset of the new Congress, then, there are unfilled committee vacancies and demand for those slots by newly elected and returning members (as expressed at stage 3).

Our concern in this paper is with the process of committee assignments for the Democrats. We take the first, second, and fourth stages of the process as exogenous to our concerns (though, as we suggested earlier, stage 4 may well be conceived as as endogenous, since it is probable that deviations from the aggregate party ratio on any given committee are partly a result of the configuration of requests at stage 3). Before getting into the details of our analysis, we should first outline the general theoretical context within which we view the requests of the members and the decisions of the Committee on Committees.

Member Goals and Committee Assignments

As the title of this paper implies, we view the committee assignment process as an instance of "social choice" (or "collective decision-making"). That is, a group (the Committee on Committees) is charged with allocating the valuable resources (places on committees) of the collectivity (the Democratic members of the House). We view the participants in the process as rational actors, that is, actors who have goals that they want to achieve, and who, when confronted with a decision-making situation, examine the available alternatives and choose the alternative which seems most likely to lead to the achievement of those goals.

On the question of goals, Richard Fenno has argued that "of all the goals espoused by members of the House, three are most basic. They are reelection, influence within the House, and good public policy. There are others; but research on the House acknowledges these to be the most consequential."[10] If this view is accepted, we may now consider each of the participants in the assignment process and show how the outcomes of that process affect their goals.

(1) REQUESTERS. The impact of committee assignments on the members requesting those assignments is so obvious that it hardly needs to be discussed. If a congressman holds any or all of the goals mentioned above, his committee assignment will have a substantial impact on the probability of achieving them.

> A "good" assignment may greatly enhance his value to his constituents and provide unusual opportunities to publicize his activities in Congress; here he can develop the expertise and the reputation as a "specialist" that will enable him to influence his colleagues and important national policies.[11]

(2) THE COMMITTEE ON COMMITTEES. The interest of members of the Committee on Committees in what assignments are made is less direct than that of the requesters, but important nonetheless. If a member has a general interest in the policy area of a particular committee, he may support the assignments of congressmen whose views are most congruent with his own. Furthermore, when a piece of legislation important to a member of the Committee on Committees comes before the House, he may call in debts owed to him by congressmen he has sponsored for committee assignments in order to influence such legislation.[12]

(3) THE LEADERSHIP. The filling of committee vacancies is also important to the Democratic leadership, for much the same reasons as it is to the members of the Committee on Committees.

> Committee assignments are vital to the leadership in two ways. First, to the degree that the leadership affects assignment it has an important

10. Fenno, "Congressional Committees," p. 3.
11. Clapp, *The Congressman*, p. 207.
12. It is clear that such debts are recognized, and that they are called in. One member, commenting on the influence another member had within the House, said, "Much of his power rests with the fact he is on Ways and Means. Since that committee determines committee assignments, he is in a very important and strategic spot. He makes his deals with various groups as to which people he will support for certain spots. Naturally when the time comes that he wants something, he can make a request and people reciprocate." Quoted in Clapp, *The Congressman*, pp. 29–30.

resource for doing favors for members, for rewarding members for past favors, and for establishing bonds with members that may provide some leverage in future legislative situations. Second, committee assignments are vital to the policy for which the leadership is responsible.[13]

(4) STATE DELEGATIONS. Members of a state delegation serving on committees which affect the interests of their state. Such members serve as a source of information about the committee's business and a resource for influencing the course of legislation on that committee.[14]

This discussion could be extended to include the committee chairmen and persons outside the House (e.g., interest groups), but the essence of our point is established. How committee slots are assigned is of vital interest to many individuals and groups, because those assignments will have an impact on the achievement of their goals within the House.

Data and Analysis

The empirical analysis, which constitutes the bulk of this current study, employs *request* data from four Congresses. In all, we have data on the committee requests, in order of preference, of 106 freshmen and 89 nonfreshmen Democratic representatives. It is important to reiterate the distinctiveness of these data. Ordinarily, analyses of committee assignments are based on the *results* of the process, from which inferences about the process are drawn.[15] By using request data, however, we are in a position to assess the extent to which the process links requests on the one hand with final assignments on the other. Moreover, we may now determine who benefits and who is harmed by the assignment process, not in terms of so-called objective standards of "good" and "bad" assignments, but rather in terms of the subjective preferences of the actors affected. All these possibilities permit somewhat keener insights into the characteristics of this important internal process.

The first aspect of the assignment process we will consider is the requests themselves: what committees are requested most often, and how many requests are made. For this part of the analysis we will consider only the requests of freshman congressmen. Nonfreshmen

13. Manley, *Politics of Finance*, p. 24.
14. See Bullock, "The Influence of State Party Delegations."
15. Most of the individual committee studies (e.g., Fenno, Manley) also draw on interviews with committee members to generalize about what led them to seek assignment to the committee and why they were successful.

already hold committee assignments and, because of service restrictions,[16] are prevented from applying for certain committees (unless they are trying to transfer from the committee they hold).[17]

Table 11–1 presents these data on freshman requests. The first column gives the total number of requests for each of the standing committees. The second column gives the percentage of all requesters who applied for a slot on each of the committees. The last column indicates the percentage (and number) of all requests that were the requesters' first choices. Thus, fifteen congressmen (nearly 14 percent of all freshmen) requested Agriculture Committee slots. It may be further noted, however, that of these fifteen requests, seven were first-preference requests.[18]

Although this table does indicate the distribution of preferences for the various standing committees, consideration of aggregate demand to determine committee desirability is potentially misleading. First, the distribution of preferences reflects the *opportunity structure* as well as the preference structure, so that observations about committee popularity on this basis are necessarily ambiguous.[19] Second, even if we discount the effects of opportunity, the aggregate demand for a

16. The standing committees of the House are divided into three classes: exclusive, semiexclusive, and nonexclusive, and there are rules which govern assignments to each class. Members of exclusive committees may serve on no other committee. Members of semiexclusive committees may be given a second assignment only on a nonexclusive committee; and members of nonexclusive committees may be given second assignments on any semi- or nonexclusive committee. During the period covered by this study the committees in these classes were: *exclusive:* Appropriations, Rules, and Ways and Means; *semiexclusive:* Agriculture, Armed Services, Banking and Currency, Education and Labor, Foreign Affairs, Interstate and Foreign Commerce, Judiciary, Public Works, and Science and Astronautics; *nonexclusive:* District of Columbia, Government Operations, House Administration, Interior and Insular Affairs, Merchant Marine and Fisheries, Un-American Activities, and Veterans Affairs. In addition, Post Office and Civil Service was changed from semiexclusive to nonexclusive status at the beginning of the Eighty-eighth Congress. Finally, the twenty-first standing committee, Standards of Official Conduct (established in 1967) seems to occupy a special status since it is a third assignment for a number of members.

17. We do, however, include the requests of two nonfreshmen who were first elected in special elections near the end of a Congress. They were not assigned to any committees then, and thus they are in the same position as freshmen.

18. The reader will note that only eighteen committees are listed in Table 11–1. Ways and Means is excluded here, and throughout the rest of the analysis, because its vacancies are filled by the caucus. Rules, and Standards of Official Conduct are excluded because they were never requested, by either freshmen or nonfreshmen. In regard to Rules, this absence of requests probably reflects the special importance this committee has to the leadership, since almost never is a vacancy on Rules filled by a member not first sponsored by the leadership. See Clapp, *The Congressman*, p. 218; and Manley, *Politics of Finance*, p. 77.

19. Thus a problem with using requests or appointments as a measure of committee desirability results from anticipated reactions. A freshman will probably

Table 11–1. House Committee Requests and First-Choice Preferences of Freshmen

Committee	Total Requests	Percentage Requesting[a]	Percentage of Requests First Choice (N)[b]
Agriculture	15	14	47 (7)
Appropriations	12	11	42 (5)
Armed Services	26	24	26 (12)
Banking and Currency	34	32	41 (14)
District of Columbia	3	3	0 (0)
Education and Labor	17	16	29 (5)
Foreign Affairs	23	21	61 (14)
Government Operations	8	7	13 (1)
House Administration	1	1	0 (0)
Interior and Insular Affairs	20	19	50 (10)
Interstate and Foreign Commerce	34	32	38 (13)
Judiciary	25	23	36 (9)
Merchant Marine and Fisheries	5	5	20 (1)
Post Office and Civil Service	13	12	23 (3)
Public Works	29	27	31 (9)
Science and Astronautics	15	14	33 (5)
Un-American Activities	2	2	0 (0)
Veterans Affairs	8	7	13 (1)

Note: Number making requests = 108.
[a] Since requesters submitted multiple requests, this column sums to more than 100 percent.
[b] The number totals to 109 because one requester asked for "Foreign Affairs or Agriculture," and so both requests were considered first choices.

committee vacancy may not accurately reflect the intensity of preference for that vacancy. To take one example, although aggregate demand for Agriculture and Post Office-Civil Service is approximately the same (14 percent and 12 percent, respectively), there is a great difference in the proportion of those requests that are first choices (47 percent and 23 percent, respectively).

More important than the two previous points, however, is that attempts to provide an aggregate measure of committee desirability are inconsistent with the conception of the legislator's behavior as

refrain from requesting the committee he most wants if he believes there is no chance of getting it. Table 11–1 seems to support this view in regard to requests for Appropriations, which (along with the other two exclusive committees) is generally recognized to be the most sought-after committee. It is, however, also recognized that freshmen have little chance to be appointed. (Indeed, in the four Congresses analyzed here, no freshman was appointed.) There does not, however, seem to be any evidence of anticipated reaction in regard to requests for other committees.

goal-directed. All congressmen are not the same. Their goals differ, and the kinds of constituencies they represent vary. Thus, we would expect committees to have *differential* appeal to different types of congressmen.

The next two tables lend credence to this expectation. While it is difficult to measure the personal goals of legislators, it is probably safe to assume that most freshmen are initially concerned with firming up relationships with their constituencies. This is probably a minimal requirement for the pursuit of policy goals and internal House influence, and is, of course, directly relevant to the goal of reelection. Thus, we can classify members according to the kinds of districts they represent in order to demonstrate the extent to which "committee popularity" varies with constituency types.

In Table 11–2 we have classified districts according to region and population per square mile. Although the classification is crude and the

Table 11–2. House Committees Most Requested by Freshmen, Controlling for Region and Population Density

Region	Density[a]	Committee	Percentage Requesting
South (N = 18)	Sparse	Interstate Comm.	45
		Banking and Curr.	39
		Public Works	33
Midwest (7)	Sparse	Interior	57
		Interstate Comm.	57
		Public Works	43
West (16)	Sparse	Interior	75
		Public Works	38
East (8)	Medium	Armed Services	50
South (9)	Medium	Interstate Comm.	44
		Foreign Affairs	33
Midwest (9)	Medium	Judiciary	44
		Public Works	44
		Ed. and Labor	33
		Interstate Comm.	33
East (15)	Concentrated	Banking and Curr.	40
		Interstate Comm.	40
		Judiciary	33
West (7)	Concentrated	Banking and Curr.	71
		Interstate Comm.	71
		Ed. and Labor	57
		Foreign Affairs	43

[a] See footnote 20 for definitions

choice of variables somewhat arbitrary,[20] this scheme suffices to exhibit the very real differences in committee appeal. We have listed those committees requested (at any preference level) by 30 percent or more of the members in each category containing at least seven requesters.[21] Immediately one notes that committees differ greatly in their relative attractiveness to the various groups of representatives. Interior is one striking example. That committee was the most requested for both midwestern and western congressmen from sparsely populated districts. These members, moreover, accounted for 80 percent of the total requests for that committee (sixteen of twenty). The reason is clear: Congressmen from these constituencies can probably serve the interests of their districts better on that committee than on any other. In the words of one western representative on the committee:

> I was attracted to it, very frankly, because it's a bread and butter committee for my state. I guess about the only thing about it that is not of great interest to my state is insular affairs. I was able to get two or three bills of great importance to my state through last year. I had vested interests I wanted to protect, to be frank.[22]

Other specific examples may be cited. Public Works is requested by seventeen of the forty-one representatives from sparsely populated districts in the South, Midwest, and West, and they account for 59 percent of the requests for that committee. Banking and Currency, part of whose jurisdiction includes housing legislation, was the most re-

20. Differences among districts on a regional basis are well known, hence the selection of that variable. Regions are defined as follows: *Northeast:* Conn., Del., Me., Mass., N.H., N.J., N.Y., Pa., R.I., Vt.; *Border:* Ky., Md., Mo., Okla., W.Va.: *South:* Ala., Ark., Fla., Ga., La., Miss., N.C., S.C., Tenn., Tex., Va.; *Midwest:* Ill., Ind., Ia., Kan., Mich., Minn., Neb., N.D., Oh., S.D., Wisc.; *West:* Alaska, Ariz., Calif., Colo., Haw., Ida., Mont., Nev., N.M., Ore., Utah, Wash., Wyo.

Population per square mile was selected to tap the relatively urban or rural nature of districts. While percentage urban would have been a preferable measure in this regard, such data were available on a district basis only for the Eighty-eighth and Ninetieth Congresses. To operationalize this variable the districts were divided into three categories: sparse (less than 100 persons per sq. mi.), medium (100 to 999 persons per sq. mi.), and concentrated (1,000 or more persons per sq. mi.). Population data were obtained from *Congressional District Data Book: Districts of the Eighty-seventh Congress* (for the Eighty-sixth and Eighty-seventh Congresses) and from *Congressional District Data Book: Districts of the Eighty-eighth Congress* and its supplements (for the Eighty-eighth and Ninetieth Congress). Both books and the supplements are published by the Bureau of the Census.

21. The excluded categories and the number of members in each were: East, sparse (3); Border, sparse (4); Border, medium (5); West, medium (3); Border, concentrated (0); South, concentrated (0); Midwest, concentrated (4).

22. Quoted in Fenno, "Congressional Committees," p. 6.

quested committee by members from districts with concentrated populations in both the East and West.

Thus, as these data demonstrate, there is indeed a difference in the attractiveness of committees to various groups of representatives, and in most instances there is a clear relationship between the type of district represented and the committees most requested.

Table 11–3 provides even more direct evidence on this score. For five selected committees, we partitioned members into two groups—interesteds and indifferents—depending on constituency characteristics.[23] Although the relationship between ascribed interest and request

Table 11–3. Requests by Freshmen for Selected House Committees, Controlling for Interesteds and Indifferents

	Requested		Not Requested		Total		Percentage of Requests by Interesteds
	N	Percent	N	Percent	N	Percent	
Banking and Currency							
Interesteds	17	47	19	53	36	100	
Indifferents	9	20	36	80	45	100	65
Total	26	32	55	68	81	100	
Education and Labor							
Interesteds	11	30	25	70	36	100	
Indifferents	3	7	42	93	45	100	79
Total	14	17	67	83	81	100	
Interior and Ins. Aff.							
Interesteds	11	65	6	35	17	100	
Indifferents	5	8	59	92	64	100	69
Total	16	20	65	80	81	100	
Armed Services							
Interesteds	9	30	21	70	30	100	
Indifferents	9	18	42	82	51	100	50
Total	18	22	63	78	81	100	
Agriculture							
Interesteds	11	33	22	67	33	100	
Indifferents	1	2	47	98	48	100	92
Total	12	15	69	85	81	100	

Note: See footnote 23 for definitions [of "interested" and "indifferent."]

23. These committees were selected because of the availability of constituency data which seemed reasonably related to representatives' probable interest in the committee. We borrowed the terms "interested" and "indifferent," and the basic ideas on measuring interest, from Charles Bullock (see "Correlates of Committee Transfers," pp. 22–23), although our specific measures are somewhat different.

behavior varies from committee to committee, it is always in the predicted direction and quite strong. The ratio of the proportion of interesteds applying for a committee to the proportion of indifferents applying varies from a low of nearly two to one (Armed Services) to a high of more than sixteen to one (Agriculture). Moreover, a high proportion of requests for each committee is accounted for by interested requesters.[24]

These findings lead us to the following conclusions: Since the attractiveness of a committee does vary from member to member, a broad-gauged, systematic property like "committee desirability" may not be appropriate for an understanding of congressional behavior. A few committees (e.g., Appropriations, Ways and Means) may be almost universally desired, but beyond these few, the attractiveness of a committee, and the value of an assignment to it, may depend solely on the interests and preferences of the member under consideration. While to an urban congressman an assignment to Agriculture might be viewed as disastrous, a farm belt member might prefer it second only to an appointment to Appropriations.

To this point we have been characterizing the empirical request configuration. Before we turn to the data on assignments proper, we should report several additional features of this configuration as it relates to the opportunity structure of the House.

Clearly the decision about *which* committees to request is a complex

---

Bullock, in turn, adopted the terms from David R. Mayhew, *Party Loyalty Among Congressmen* (Cambridge: Harvard University Press, 1966).

Data on constituency characteristics were obtained from the *Congressional District Data Book: Districts of the Eighty-eighth Congress* and its supplements. In this source data were available on freshmen representatives in the Eighty-sixth and Eighty-seventh Congress only if they came from states which were not redistricted after the 1960 census. Therefore the number of members considered in Table 11–3 is 81 instead of 108.

For each committee a constituency measure was selected, and each representative's district was ranked as either above or below the national average on that measure. If the district was above the national average, the congressman was classed as an interested; if the district was below the national average, the congressman was classed as an indifferent. The measures of the committees are as follows (national averages are in parentheses); Banking and Currency and Education and Labor, percentage of population residing in urban areas (69.9 percent); Interior and Insular Affairs, land area of district (8,159 sq. mi.); Armed Services, percentage of the total labor force who are members of the armed forces (2.5 percent); and Agriculture, percentage of the employed civilian labor force employed in agriculture (6.6 percent).

24. The proportion of Armed Services requests made by interesteds is by far the lowest. This is probably because interest in this committee is determined by other things besides a relatively large number of servicemen in a district (e.g., large defense plants or a hope of attracting defense bases or plants to a district in the future).

strategic one for a member to resolve. Additionally, however, he must decide the strategic question of *how many* committees to include in his preference ordering. In many instances (at least with regard to freshmen) the final preference ordering submitted comprises the entire "information environment" of the Committee on Committees. In any event, it does provide one of the few pieces of hard data on members' desires. The extent to which a goal-directed member chooses to vary that information environment, then, becomes an important strategic consideration. (Shortly we examine the relationships among length of preference ordering, assignment success, and other features of the opportunity structure.)

Initially we consider this decision as faced by freshmen and non-freshmen. The strategic problems facing these two groups are very different. The freshman has no committee assignment at all. He desires a good committee, but he knows for certain that he will be assigned to *some* committee. That is, any committee assignment is possible, the range of alternatives open to the Committee on Committees is maximal, and the member is entirely at the Committee's mercy. The nonfreshman, on the other hand, already has a committee, one which he may keep as long as he wishes. Thus, he need not worry about being given a committee less desirable than the one he holds.

Therefore, if the member assumes that, circumstances permitting, the Committee on Committees will attempt to satisfy his request (obviously he must assume this, or else it would be irrational to bother making any requests at all), the two groups are likely to follow different strategies regarding the number of requests they make. Freshmen are likely to offer the Committee on Committees a wider range of alternatives (i.e., make more requests), while nonfreshmen will probably be much more specific in their requests. As Table 11–4 shows, the data

Table 11–4. Number of Requests by Freshmen and Nonfreshmen

Number of Requests	Freshmen		Nonfreshmen	
	N	Percent	N	Percent
1	24	22	71	82
2	15	14	9	10
3	49	45	3	3
4 or more	20	19	4	5
Total	108	100	87	100

Note: Here also the two unassigned nonfreshmen are included with the freshmen (see note 17)

are in accord with these expectations. Only 22 percent of the freshmen make only one request, while 82 percent of the nonfreshmen do so.

Within the freshman category in Table 11-4, there is considerable variation in the number of requests.[25] Some of this variation in request behavior reflects variations in opportunities confronting members.[26] The data of Table 11-5 are wholly consistent with this hypothesis. In this table we look at two features of the opportunity structure (unfortunately, our total N is too small to permit the meaningful introduction of other relevant features). The first is whether a member is confronted by competition for his first-choice committee by another member of his state delegation. Since the only way a member can get assigned to a committee is to be nominated by his zone representative, a member's probability of getting a particular assignment is substantially reduced if the zone representative or the Committee on Committees must choose among two or more members from the same state. Therefore, we would expect a member to "hedge his bets"—that is, make a greater number of requests—if another member from his state is requesting his most-preferred committee.

Table 11-5. Number of House Committee Requests by Freshmen, Controlling for State Vacancy and State Competition on First-Choice Committee

| Number of Requests | State Vacancy | | | | No State Vacancy | | | |
| | State Compet. | | No State Compet. | | State Compet. | | No State Compet. | |
	N	Percent	N	Percent	N	Percent	N	Percent
1	0	0	5	42	1	9	18	26
2	0	0	4	33	3	27	7	10
3	8	67	1	8	4	36	32	47
4 or more	4	33	2	17	3	27	11	16
Total	12	100	12	100	11	99[a]	68	99[a]

Note: Five members whose most-preferred committee had no vacancies are omitted here.
[a] Error is due to rounding.

25. We restrict the following discussion to freshmen because the argument about a nonfreshman's ability to be more specific in his requests applies as well here as it did above.
26. Here we consider opportunities to depend upon certain objective conditions, such as number of vacancies for a given committee (supply), number of requests (demand), and service restrictions regarding dual requests (formal rules), and upon informal norms which may guide the allocation of committee vacancies, such as "same-state" norms for appointment.

The second feature of the opportunity structure that may influence the decision concerning the number of requests a congressman makes is the source of vacancies. It is apparent that at least the large states regard themselves as entitled to one or more seats on important committees, and that members, when requesting assignments, feel that a claim made on "their state's" vacancy is a persuasive argument in their favor.[27] Thus a member whose most preferred committee (as revealed by him in his preference ordering) contains a state vacancy may be more likely to list few options, *ceteris paribus*, than other members.

As Table 11–5 reveals, when a state vacancy exists, the presence of state competition makes a great deal of difference in the number of committees requested. With state competition, no member makes fewer than three requests, but without state competition, 75 percent do so. When no state vacancy exists, state competition has no effect; 36 percent make fewer than three requests with state competition, and 36 percent make fewer than three requests without it. (There is a large difference, in the predicted direction, in the number that make a *single* request.) Furthermore, in the absence of state competition, a member is much more likely to submit fewer than three requests if there is a state vacancy than if there is not (75 percent versus 36 percent). Thus, as we expected, both the existence of state competition and the presence of a state vacancy exert an independent impact on the number of committees requested by freshmen.

So far, we have examined the committee assignment process from the point of view of the requester. We now consider who is successful in getting the assignments he requests, viewing the process in terms of the goals of the members of the Committee on Committees and the leadership.

Above we stated that the member must assume that, if circumstances permit, the Committee on Committees will try to satisfy his request. We also argued that the number of requests a member makes depends on certain strategic considerations, and thus we implicitly argued that a member would think that his probability of getting *some* requested committee depends (at least in part) on the number of requests made. In Table 11–6 we present data relating to these points. Freshmen and nonfreshmen are treated separately to prevent seniority from contaminating the results.

When the data are examined we find that in regard to freshmen our first statement is more correct than our second. That is, almost three-

27. See Bullock, "The Influence of State Party Delegations," and Clapp, *The Congressman,* pp. 220, 238.

Table 11–6. Number of House Committee Requests and Assignment Success, Freshmen and Nonfreshmen

	A. Freshmen Member Received:							
Number of Requests	First Choice		Other Choice		No Choice		Total	
	N	Percent	N	Percent	N	Percent	N	Percent
1	18	75	—	—	6	25	24	100
2	6	40	5	33	4	27	15	100
3	16	34	15	32	16	34	47	100
4 or more	9	45	8	40	3	15	20	100
Total	49	46	28	26	29	27	106	99[a]

	B. Nonfreshmen Member Received:							
Number of Requests	First Choice		Other Choice		No Choice		Total	
	N	Percent	N	Percent	N	Percent	N	Percent
1	32	45	—	—	39	55	71	100
2	1	11	5	56	3	33	9	100
3 or more	2	22	5	56	2	22	9	100
Total	35	39	10	11	44	49	89	99[a]

[a] Error is due to rounding.

fourths of the freshmen do get *some* committee that they requested, and the probability of getting *no* choice is affected little by the number of requests. For nonfreshmen, on the other hand, more requests do increase chances of some success.

The most striking finding in Table 11–6, however, results from our treating freshmen and nonfreshmen separately. Contrary to what one might expect in a body in which seniority is often important, freshmen are much more successful in getting requested assignments than are nonfreshmen. This finding is reinforced by the data in Table 11–7, which shows assignment success by amount of seniority. We find that the probability of receiving *no* request monotonically *increases* as seniority increases.

This result should not be entirely unexpected, for many references in the literature on committee assignments claim that seniority is often ignored when circumstances dictate. For example, Clapp claims that

given a contest for an important committee assignment, in which returning members of Congress may wish to transfer from another com-

Table 11–7. Seniority and Success in Assignment to House Committees

	Member Received:							
Number of Previous Terms	First Choice		Other Choice		No Choice		Total	
	N	Percent	N	Percent	N	Percent	N	Percent
0	49	46	28	26	29	27	106	99[a]
1	19	41	8	17	19	41	46	99[a]
2	9	43	1	5	11	52	21	100
3 or more	7	32	1	5	14	64	22	100[a]
Total	84	43	38	20	73	37	195	100

[a] Error is due to rounding.

mittee and find themselves competing with each other and with freshmen congressmen, seniority is not infrequently brushed aside, if it will not bring about the outcome desired by those making the decisions.[28]

Another observer of the process stated:

> Seniority may control if all other things are equal. But other things usually are not equal. Sometimes you begin to think seniority is little more than a device to fall back on when it is convenient to do so.[29]

To assess the accuracy of this last statement, we examined a situation where it is more likely for "other things" to be "equal": the case when two members from the same state are competing for the same committee. We looked at all committees that had vacancies, and determined for each requester whether another member from the same state was applying for that committee, and if so, whether the other member was more senior. The relevant data are presented in

28. Clapp, *The Congressman*, pp. 226–27.
29. Quoted in Clapp, *The Congressman*, p. 226. We should note here that the data in Tables 11–6 and 11–7 indicate only overall success and not success in those instances where the requests of freshmen and nonfreshmen are in direct competition. Masters states that "when two or more members stake a claim to the same assignment, on the ground that it is essential to their electoral success both party committees usually, if not invariably, will give preference to the member with longer service" (Masters, "Committee Assignments," p. 354). We do not know what arguments were made about electoral success, but in our data fifty nonfreshmen were in competition with one or more freshmen for assignments to semi- or nonexclusive committees which had insufficient vacancies to satisfy all requests. Of these fifty members, twenty-three were passed over in favor of freshmen. This does not include instances where the passed-over members received another, more preferred, assignment.

Table 11–8. State Competition, Seniority, and Success in House Committee Assignments, in All Committees with Vacancies

	Member Assigned		Member Not Assigned		Total	
	N	Percent	*N*	Percent	*N*	Percent
No Same State Competition	103	36	187	64	290	140
Same State Competition; Competitor Not More Senior	20	26	56	74	76	100
Same State Competition; Competitor More Senior	1	7	13	93	14	100
Total	124	33	256	67	380	100

Table 11–8. It is clear that a request for which there is no same state competition has a likelihood of about one chance in three of being granted. When there is competition, however, a member has about one chance in four of success if his competitor is not more senior, while he has only one chance in fourteen if the competitor *is* more senior. Thus in this instance, where "other things" are more likely to be "equal," seniority may become very advantageous, although it is generally not.

What then are the things that in other situations are *not* "equal"? That is, in terms of the goals of members who determine committee assignments, what factors cause them to ignore seniority? Clearly, many kinds of interacting and even conflicting motivations may influence the members of the Committee on Committees. Thus it is dangerous to posit either a single motive for all members of the Committee on Committees or even for any one member. Still, it is not unreasonable to assess the extent to which the data support any of these motives.

The first motive or goal for Committee on Committees members we have posited might be termed the *management goal*. The Committee on Committees, in this view, is concerned solely with satisfying requester demands. Thus, it acts as an "impersonal" preference aggregation device in an effort to keep requesters happy. In reporting on this motive, we find it useful to contrast it with another, the *constituency interest goal*. According to this goal, committee makers ignore request data, concerning themselves instead with matching individual members to committee vacancies on the basis of constituency characteristics and interests.

The data relevant to this comparison are presented in Table 11–9. For the committees investigated in Table 11–3 we partitioned fresh-

Table 11-9. Interesteds, Requests, and Success in House Committee Assignments (Freshmen)

Interested[a]	Yes	Yes	No	No	
Requested	Yes	No	Yes	No	Total
Committee					
Banking and Currency	47	0	33	3	15
	(N = 17)	(19)	(9)	(36)	(81)
Education and Labor	64	4	67	2	14
	(11)	(25)	(3)	(42)	(81)
Interior and Ins. Aff.	64	17	20	3	14
	(11)	(6)	(5)	(59)	(81)
Armed Services	33	0	11	2	6
	(9)	(21)	(9)	(42)	(81)
Agriculture	27	14	100	4	11
	(11)	(22)	(1)	(47)	(81)

Note: Each cell gives percentage of N assigned to that committee (N in parentheses).
[a] See footnote 23 for definition of interesteds.

men[30] members according to two criteria: whether they qualify as interested and whether they requested the committee. The results suggest that the management goal dominates the constituency interest goal. In most instances (the small N's make firm conclusions difficult), interested-requesters get the nod. Moreover, for *every* committee, requesting-indifferents are more successful than nonrequesting-interesteds. Minimally, we conclude that committee makers do not take member requests lightly—that, in requesting a committee, a member is not waltzing before a blind audience.

A third obvious candidate as a motivational hypothesis for members of the Committee on Committee is *party maintenance*. Whether a member is interested in influencing policy outcomes or in influence for its own sake, one thing that in part determines the amount of such influence is the majority or minority status of his party. A member has more influence if he is Speaker than if he is minority leader, more

30. We restrict our attention here in freshmen not only because of the effects of seniority on both request behavior and success, but also because the situation is much more complex in regard to nonfreshmen. Minimally we would have to control for whether a representative is already a member of a committee for which he would be classified as an interested. Further, we would probably want to control for whether the requests made are for transfers or dual service assignments. Also we would want to exclude prestige committee requests. These controls would make the N's so small and would break them into so many categories that a meaningful test would be impossible.

influence if he is chairman of a committee than if he is ranking minority member, and probably more influence if he is on the majority side of the committee than if he is in the minority. Therefore it is in the interest of most Committee members to help insure the reelection of party colleagues. Thus the question arises, who needs the most help? Clearly, the members most in need of help are those who were elected by the smallest margin. *Ceteris paribus,* a member elected with 51 percent of the vote is more likely to be defeated than one elected with 61 percent. Thus, we would expect members from marginal districts to be more successful than members from safe districts. (We have termed a district marginal if the member was elected with less than 55 percent of the vote.)

As the data in Table 11–10 show, our expectations are correct. Marginal freshmen are slightly less likely to fail to receive a requested committee and are much more likely to receive their first choice than are safe freshmen.

Marginal nonfreshmen are *much* less likely to receive no choice than are safe nonfreshmen, but they are about equally likely to receive their first choice as are safe nonfreshmen. We also find that some of the difference in success between freshmen and nonfreshmen disappears

Table 11–10. Margin of Election and Success in House Committee Assignments, Freshmen and Nonfreshmen

	A. Freshmen Member Received:							
District is	First Choice		Other Choice		No Choice		Total	
	N	Percent	N	Percent	N	Percent	N	Percent
Marginal	31	56	10	18	14	25	55	99[a]
Safe	18	35	18	35	15	29	51	99[a]
Total	49	46	28	26	29	27	106	99[a]

	B. Nonfreshmen Member Received:							
District is	First Choice		Other Choice		No Choice		Total	
	N	Percent	N	Percent	N	Percent	N	Percent
Marginal	7	39	5	28	6	33	18	100
Safe	28	39	5	7	38	54	71	100
Total	35	39	10	11	44	49	89	99[a]

[a] Error is due to rounding.

here—that is, safe freshmen are treated about the same as marginal nonfreshmen. When one recalls that these nonfreshmen, even though they are marginal, have demonstrated (at least once) their ability to get reelected, it does not seem surprising that these two groups are about equally successful.

The perceived stand of the individual member on specific issues is yet another basis on which committee makers may determine assignments.[31] Their prime concern here is the degree to which members will support the party position on issues which come before the standing committees (*party support goal*). While detailed considerations of individual committees are beyond the scope of an initial study such as ours, two pieces of evidence may shed some light on this question. Generally speaking, southern Democrats are less likely to support their party's position than are northern Democrats. Therefore, whether we consider the granting of a specific request a reward for past behavior or an attempt to gain influence over future behavior, the leadership should be less likely to intervene with the Committee on Committees on behalf of a Southerner than a Northerner. Moreover, since the Democratic members of the Ways and Means Committee are more liberal and more supportive of their party than is the average House Democrat,[32] those members, even when acting on their own, are likely to be more favorably disposed toward the requests of northern Democrats than toward those of Southerners. Therefore, we would expect Southeners to be less successful than Northerners in obtaining requested committees.

As Table 11–11 shows, the data support this hypothesis. For both freshmen and nonfreshmen, Southerners are more likely than nonsoutherners to receive *no* request. They are less successful than their colleagues from other regions in getting their first choices as well. One might wonder, however, whether this finding of lesser success among Southerners does not simply repeat our finding concerning marginal versus safe districts. That is, since Southerners are more likely to come from safe districts,[33] they may be less successful than nonsoutherners simply because they are elected by larger margins. To examine the possibility we present in Tables 11–12 and 11–13 data on region,

31. In addition to our discussion of member goals above, see Masters, "Committee Assignments," pp. 354–55, and Clapp, *The Congressman*, pp. 228–30.

32. See Fenno, "Congressional Committees," pp. 33–34, and Manley, *Politics of Finance*, pp. 29–32.

33. Using a different definition of safe seats, Wolfinger and Hollinger found that while Southerners held only 38 percent of the Democratic seats in the Eighty-eighth Congress, they held 63 percent of the safe seats. See Raymond E. Wolfinger and Joan H. Hollinger, "Safe Seats, Seniority, and Power in Congress," in *New Perspectives on the House of Representatives* 2nd ed., ed. Robert L. Peabody and Nelson W. Polsby (Chicago: Rand McNally, 1969), pp. 60–61.

Table 11–11. Region and Success in House Committee Assignments (Freshmen and Nonfreshmen)

| | A. Freshmen Member Received: | | | | | | | |
| | First Choice | | Other Choice | | No Choice | | Total | |
Region[a]	N	Percent	N	Percent	N	Percent	N	Percent
South	8	31	7	27	11	42	26	100
Nonsouth	41	51	21	26	18	23	80	100
Total	49	46	28	26	29	27	106	99[b]

| | B. Nonfreshmen Member Received: | | | | | | | |
| | First Choice | | Other Choice | | No Choice | | Total | |
Region[a]	N	Percent	N	Percent	N	Percent	N	Percent
South	7	27	2	8	17	65	26	100
Nonsouth	28	44	8	13	27	43	63	100
Total	35	39	10	11	44	49	89	99[b]

[a] The South includes the eleven states of the Confederacy.
[b] Error is due to rounding.

Table 11–12. Region, Margin of Election, and Success in House Committee Assignments (Freshmen)

| | A. Marginal Districts Member Received: | | | | | | | |
| | First Choice | | Other Choice | | No Choice | | Total | |
Region[a]	N	Percent	N	Percent	N	Percent	N	Percent
South	1	25	0	0	3	75	4	100
Nonsouth	30	59	10	20	11	22	51	101[b]
Total	31	56	10	18	14	26	55	100

| | B. Safe Districts Member Received: | | | | | | | |
| | First Choice | | Other Choice | | No Choice | | Total | |
Region[a]	N	Percent	N	Percent	N	Percent	N	Percent
South	7	32	7	32	8	36	22	100
Nonsouth	11	38	11	38	7	24	29	100
Total	18	35	18	35	15	29	51	99[b]

[a] The South includes the eleven states of the Confederacy.
[b] Error is due to rounding.

Table 11–13. Region, Margin of Election, and Assignment Success in House Committee Assignments (Nonfreshmen)

	A. Marginal Districts Member Received:							
	First Choice		Other Choice		No Choice		Total	
Region[a]	N	Percent	N	Percent	N	Percent	N	Percent
South	0	—	0	—	0	—	0	—
Nonsouth	7	39	5	28	6	33	18	100
Total	7	39	5	28	6	33	18	100

	B. Safe Districts Member Received:							
	First Choice		Other Choice		No Choice		Total	
Region[a]	N	Percent	N	Percent	N	Percent	N	Percent
South	7	27	2	8	17	65	26	100
Nonsouth	21	47	3	7	21	47	45	101[b]
Total	28	39	5	7	38	54	71	100

[a] The South includes the eleven states of the Confederacy.
[b] Error is due to rounding.

margin of election, and assignment success for freshmen and nonfreshmen, respectively.

Since there are few marginal-freshmen Southerners and no marginal-nonfreshmen Southerners, we will focus our discussion on members from safe districts. As the data demonstrate, even when marginal members are removed, Southerners are less successful than are nonsoutherners. Among both freshmen and nonfreshmen, safe Southerners are more likely receive no request than are safe nonsoutherners, and are less likely to receive a first request. The evidence is unequivocal: Region has a strong, independent impact on committee assignment success, even when election margin is controlled.[34]

34. This finding is all the more striking in light of the southern Democrats' dominance of the Committee on Committees during this period (see footnote 6). It is, admittedly, dangerous to treat a variable like region as a surrogate for, in this case, expected policy behavior. Support for party policies clearly varies within regions. Moreover, other informal, nonpolicy, behavioral norms are likely to cloud the relationship between region and appointment success. A clear indication of this intraregional variation is the rather startling differential in success between members from the South and those from outside the South when we control for the state of their zone representative. As the data in Table 11–14 show, the southern member who is from the same state as his zone representative is much more likely

Table 11–14. Assignment Success, Region, and Zone Representative's State Delegation

	Member Received:							
	First Choice		Other Choice		No Choice		Total	
	N	Percent	*N*	Percent	*N*	Percent	*N*	Percent
			A. Freshmen, Nonsouth					
Same State[a]	16	52	8	26	7	23	31	101[b]
Not	25	51	13	27	11	22	49	100
Total	41	51	21	26	18	23	80	100
			B. Freshmen, South					
Same State	5	46	4	36	2	18	11	100
Not	3	20	3	20	9	60	15	100
Total	8	31	7	27	11	42	26	100
			C. Nonfreshmen, Nonsouth					
Same State	13	46	3	11	12	43	28	100
Not	15	43	5	14	15	43	35	100
Total	28	44	8	13	27	43	63	100
			D. Nonfreshmen, South					
Same State	3	30	2	20	5	50	10	100
Not	4	25	0	0	12	75	16	100
Total	7	27	2	8	17	65	23	100

[a] Same State means that the member making the request and his zone representative are from the same state.
[b] Error due to rounding.

The second piece of evidence bearing on the party support goal is presented in Table 11–15. To construct this table we examined the party support scores of nonfreshmen requesters[35] for each of the Con-

to secure a requested assignment than are his southern colleagues who are not from the same state as their zone representatives. Whereas 60 percent of the freshmen who are *not* from the same state as their zone representative fail to receive any committee request, only 18 percent of those from the zone representative's state delegation are in the same unenviable position. The differential is somewhat smaller for nonfreshmen (75 percent versus 50 percent receive no request), but the pattern is the same. For members from outside the South, however, this differential does not appear. There is virtually no difference between the success of members who are from the same state as their zone representative and that of members who are not.

35. We exclude the two nonfreshmen elected in special elections near the close of the preceding Congress for whom there was no party support score data. For each Congress, a member's party support score is tabulated from his voting behavior in the previous Congress. Party support data is found in the appropriate volumes of the *Congressional Quarterly Almanac,* vol. 14 (1958), pp. 124–25; vol. 16 (1960), pp. 140–41; vol. 18 (1962), pp. 764–65; vol. 22 (1966), pp. 1030–31.

Table 11–15. Party Support and Success in House Committee Assignments (Nonfreshmen)

	A. 86th Congress		
	Assigned	Not Assigned	Total
Supporter[a]	62	38	100
	(8)	(5)	(13)
Nonsupporter	40	60	100
	(2)	(3)	(5)
Total	56	44	100
	(10)	(8)	(18)

	B. 87th Congress		
	Assigned	Not Assigned	Total
Supporter	50	50	100
	(8)	(8)	(16)
Nonsupporter	45	55	100
	(5)	(6)	(11)
Total	48	52	100
	(13)	(14)	(27)

	C. 88th Congress		
	Assigned	Not Assigned	Total
Supporter	62	38	100
	(8)	(5)	(13)
Nonsupporter	40	60	100
	(4)	(6)	(10)
Total	52	48	100
	(12)	(11)	(23)

	D. 90th Congress		
	Assigned	Not Assigned	Total
Supporter	60	40	100
	(9)	(6)	(15)
Nonsupporter	0	100	100
	(0)	(4)	(4)
Total	47	53	100
	(9)	(10)	(19)

Table 11-15. (Continued)

| | E. All Congresses | | |
	Assigned	Not Assigned	Total
Supporter	58	42	100
	(33)	(24)	(57)
Nonsupporter	37	63	100
	(11)	(19)	(30)
Total	51	49	100
	(44)	(43)	(87)

[a] Supporters are members whose party support scores were above or equal to the mean for the party for the previous Congress. Cell entries are percentages; Ns are in parentheses.

gresses in the sample, and compared the assignment success of those whose support surpasses the mean for the party in the previous Congress with those who gave the party less than the mean support. In each of the four Congresses, high party supporters were more successful in securing assignments (i.e., being granted any one of their requests) than low party supporters. Part E of this table gives the aggregate totals: 58 percent of the high party supporters, as opposed to 37 percent of the low party supporters, secured a requested committee.

Summary and Conclusions

In this paper we have viewed the Democratic assignment process as an instance of social choice. We have examined the process from the point of view of the members requesting assignments and of the members making assignments. We have assumed that both groups are goal-directed and that an understanding of their behavior derives from an analysis of alternative goals and alternative means (behaviors) of achieving them.

In regard to those members requesting assignments, we have shown that their choice of committees is related to the type of district they represent. Also, the data indicate that the decision concerning the number of requests to make appears to be affected by certain strategic considerations such as whether the requester is a freshmen, whether there is a vacancy from his state on his most preferred committee, and whether another member from his state is competing with him for his most preferred committee.

We next considered the making of assignments. Here we found that about three-fourths of the freshmen are granted some committee they requested. The data showed, however, that nonfreshmen are much less successful. Indeed, the probability of success decreased as seniority increased; therefore other factors were sought in order to explain assignment success. We considered several alternative goals for committee makers—the management goal, the constituency interest goal, the party maintenance goal, and the party support goal—and found strong support in the data for most of them. However, the interaction (and collinearity) among goals precludes any unqualified conclusions.

The assignment process in the House of Representatives is obviously complex, and it is affected by a host of factors, some of them detailed in the body of this paper. Our purposes here have been severalfold. First, we believe it is useful to view the assignment process as an institutionalized allocation process involving goal-seeking actors, scarce but valued commodities, and behavioral constraints. Second, given this view, we have sought to supply a "missing link" in the literature on committee assignments, namely the preferences of committee requests. Not only does this link provide some interesting insights about one group of actors in the process (requesters); additionally, it provides empirical knowledge about the constraints and information confronting the other significant group in the process—the committee makers. Third, the heuristic use of a social choice construct and the new data on the preferences of committee requesters have brought into focus and provided some order to the complex of strategic factors involved in this process.

The questions for future empirical analysis appear to be almost limitless. For example, future research should consider, instead of surrogate variables like region, the position of members on specific issues before and after the assignment decision. Another aspect to be examined is the behavior of individual members of the Committee on Committees. What requesters from which zones are most successful? Do zone representatives appear to nominate members whose views are like their own? A third aspect of the process which deserves further consideration is the opportunity structure: Are members who are granted their first choice more likely to make further requests in the future, and if so are they very successful? Are members who receive no request initially granted a good assignment at some later time, or are they perpetually unsuccessful?

The research reported here is not distinctive in one respect: It raises as many questions as it answers. Nevertheless, we feel this study has provided some initial direction for a more comprehensive, formal understanding of the committee assignment process, and thus of internal relationships in the House as a whole. In this fashion, we believe, students of the public sector will begin to ascertain some of the operating characteristics of its institutions and thus be in a better position to make sound evaluations and prescriptions.

12

Two Strategies of Influence: Choosing A Majority Leader, 1962

Nelson W. Polsby

Political scientists seem to be fond of debating whether tradtional political theory in America is dead or only sleeping.[1] Either way, there is no argument that the speculations which occupied thinkers of other days have been little used to illuminate current political behavior. The argument, when there is one, concerns whether it is even possible to use traditional political theory in this way. Regrettably, optimists on this point have not always demonstrated that they were right in supposing that traditional political theory could contribute to the understanding of present-day politics. But this does not mean that they are wrong.

This paper was originally presented at the annual meetings of the American Political Science Association, Washington, D.C., 1962. Several members of Congress, who I am sure would prefer to remain anonymous, read an early draft of this chapter and made many useful comments. I should also like to thank Lewis A. Dexter, H. Douglas Price, and Robert L. Peabody. Others who have been helpful include Aaron B. Wildavsky, Lewis A. Froman, Jr., Norman O. Brown, Luigi Einaudi, Joseph Cooper, Alan L. Otten, and Neil MacNeil. Research assistance was provided by a Ford Foundation grant to Wesleyan University.

1. The phrase "traditional political theory" refers in this context to the history of political thinking rather than to any specific political doctrines. See, for example, David Easton, *The Political System* (New York: Knopf, 1953); Harry V. Jaffa, "The Case Against Political Theory," *Journal of Politics* 22 (May, 1960): 259–75; Robert A. Dahl, "The Science of Politics, New and Old," *World Politics* 7 (April, 1955):479–89; Dahl, "Political Theory, Truth and Consequences," *World Politics* 11 (October, 1958):89–102; Norman Jacobson, "The Unity of Political Theory," in R. Young (ed.), *Approaches to the Study of Politics* (Evanston: Northwestern University Press, 1958), pp. 115–24.

A major obstacle to the use of traditional political theory in modern political science has been theory's long-standing concern with prescriptive statements. Prescriptions are not necessarily the best instruments for organizing information about the empirical world, since the preferences which they assert may not correspond to any observed (or even observable) events. However, prescriptions may in fact point to quite interesting and genuine dilemmas in the real world. In these circumstances, we have the option of converting the language of prescription to that of description if we desire to put traditional political theory to more modern uses.

The possibilities of this device have lately been explored by a group of students of the legislative process, using as their text the celebrated speech to the Electors of Bristol by Edmund Burke.[2] In this speech, on the occasion of his election as Member of Parliament from Bristol, it will be recalled that Burke undertook to state and resolve a recurring dilemma of the representative:

> Certainly, gentlemen, it ought to be the happiness and glory of a representative to live in the strictest union, the closest correspondence, and the most unreserved communication with his constituents. Their wishes ought to have great weight with him; their opinion high respect; their business unremitted attention. . . . But his unbiased opinion, his native judgment, his enlightened conscience he ought not to sacrifice to you. . . . Your representative owes you, not his industry only, but his judgment. . . . Government and legislation are matters of reason and judgment, and not of inclination; and what sort of reason is that, in which the determination precedes the discussion; in which one set of men deliberate and another decide . . . Parliament is not a *congress* of ambassadors from different and hostile interests . . . but . . . a *deliberative* assembly of *one* nation. . . . We are now members for a rich commercial city; this city, however, is but part of a rich commercial nation, the interests of which are various, multiform, and intricate. . . . All these widespread interests must be considered; must be compared; must be reconciled if possible.[3]

Six years after Burke spoke these words, he stood for election once again, and on the same topic said:

> I could wish undoubtedly . . . to make every part of my conduct agreeable to every one of my constituents. . . . But . . . do you think,

2. Heinz Eulau, John C. Wahlke, Leroy C. Ferguson, and William Buchanan, "The Role of the Representative: Some Empirical Observations on the Theory of Edmund Burke," *American Political Science Review* 53 (September, 1959): 742–56.

3. "Speech to the Electors of Bristol," November 3, 1774, *Works,* vol. 2 (London, etc.: Oxford University Press, 1906), pp. 164–66.

gentlemen, that every public act in six years since I stood in this place before you—that all the arduous things which have been done in this eventful period, which has crowded into a few years' space the revolutions of an age—can be opened to you on their fair grounds in half an hour's conversation? . . . Let me say with plainness . . . that if by a fair, by an indulgent, by a gentlemanly behavior to our representatives, we do not give confidence to their minds, and a liberal scope to their understandings; if we do not permit our members to act upon a *very* enlarged view of things, we shall at length infallibly degrade our national representation into a confused and scuffling bustle of local agency.[4]

A brief historical detour will suggest certain empirical problems related to Burke's position. Shortly after the second speech quoted here, Burke withdrew his candidacy, feeling he could not win. He and his constituents had disagreed over several matters, in particular his vote to free Irish trade from restrictions operating in favor of Bristol. Burke remained in Parliament, however, representing a pocket borough thereafter.[5] Although acting on his principle of independence from constituent pressures was costly to him, Burke was clearly in a position to take a more luxurious stand on such a question than another member could who did not have the protection of a pocket borough and the party list.

This raises still a more general empirical point: Under what conditions will the representative be more likely to respond to the demands of "local agency"? When is he more likely to respond to a political situation as it appears to him in the light of his experience at the seat of government? Under what conditions will attempts to influence the representative through his constituency bring better results than attempts to influence him through the network of loyalties and affiliations he has built up through service in his deliberative body— and vice versa?

The United States House of Representatives is one laboratory for the exploration of questions such as these. Indeed, where the stakes are as high as they often are in House decision-making, it is not surprising that full-scale campaigns are mounted in order to sway sometimes no more than a handful of marginal votes. But are these votes swayed from the inside or the outside? Do constituencies matter more or less than colleagues?[6]

4. "Speech at Bristol," September 6, 1780 in ibid., vol. 3, pp. 2, 3, 4.
5. Ibid., and F. W. Raffety, "Preface" in *Works*, vol. 2, pp. xiv–xv.
6. One approach to some of these questions was made by Julius Turner, who used the analysis of roll calls as his major source of data in *Party and Constituency: Pressures on Congress* (Baltimore: Johns Hopkins, 1951). See also David B. Truman, *The Congressional Party* (New York: Wiley, 1959).

Sometimes the answer is reasonably clear and unequivocal. Here are examples of *inside* influences at work:

> Representative Cleveland Bailey is a genuinely dedicated opponent of reciprocal trade. . . . [He] is unusual among members—probably unique—in that protection is *the* most important issue to him and that he creates the sense of having a deep-felt conviction on the subject. In 1953 to 1954 he went around and pled individually with a number of members to vote against reciprocal trade and for the West Virginia miners. One member put it, "He was rough, real rough . . . I had to be rough with him." Another said, "In the 1954 vote, Cleve Bailey was worth fifteen votes to his side easily."[7]

> The morning of one of the key votes on reciprocal trade [1955], Speaker Sam Rayburn attended a breakfast of the freshman Democrats in the House. I asked one of the congressmen who was there about it. He chuckled: "Oh, you heard about that? . . . We'd just invited Mr. Sam to this breakfast. He turned it into a sort of speech and said he'd observed that *generally the new members got along better who went along,* but he didn't make any particular application—of course you could guess what he had in mind. . . ."[8]

On the other hand, it is sometimes possible to detect *outside* influences. The following example comes from the January, 1961, battle over the size of the House Rules Committee:

> It was learned that Representative Howard Smith, southern leader and Rules Committee chairman, has held several meetings in his office in recent weeks with representatives of the most powerful conservative lobbies in the country, trying to shape a campaign to beat Rayburn by applying pressure on members from home. The groups included the National Association of Manufacturers, the United States Chamber of Commerce, the American Medical Association and the American Farm Bureau. . . . Some members have reported heavy mail from business interests in their home districts. . . . On the other side, northern Democrats have sent out an appeal to organized labor for help. Yesterday, Andrew J. Biemiller, chief AFL-CIO lobbyist, was at the Capitol trying to line up votes. . . .[9]

> During the aid to education debate [a Roman Catholic congressman] threatened to kill the public school measure by tagging on to it a parochial school amendment. [Presidential Assistant Lawrence] O'Brien

7. Lewis Anthony Dexter, "Congressmen and the People They Listen To" (Cambridge: Center for International Studies, Massachusetts Institute of Technology, Ditto, 1955), ch. 2, p. 14; ch. 8, p. 7.

8. Ibid., chap. 5, pp. 4–5.

9. Richard L. Lyons, "Pressure Rises as House Moves to Vote on Rules," *Washington Post* (January 31, 1961).

appealed to [the congressman's home district party leader] who immediately telephoned [the congressman]. "Who sent you there, me or the Bishop?" he growled. "And who's going to keep you there, me or the Bishop?"[10]

At other times strong inside and outside influences are blurred together quite inextricably:

A newspaper correspondent told me: "Oh yes, you know those two boys [congressmen] . . . well, you know why Jack voted against the leadership? Just to oblige Joe to whom he's very close; Joe was afraid he'd be the only fellow from the state to vote against the leadership and he'd get into trouble with the leadership and the party organization so Jack went along with him to prevent his sticking his neck out all alone. . . ."[11]

The whip from the area told me . . . "Tom rather wanted to go along with the leadership, but he found Dave and Don and four other guys from surrounding districts were against the leadership, and he decided he'd better go along with them, because after all he's hearing a lot from his district against it, and how could he explain his being for it and Dave and Don and the rest being against it?"[12]

The recent contest for the majority leadership of the House provides, as it happens, a rather good contrast between the two strategies of influence. In turn, the close examination of this case may begin to suggest answers to some of the questions posed above.

I

On January 10, 1962, the Democratic members of the House met in caucus in the House chamber and nominated John McCormack as their candidate for Speaker. Immediately following the conclusion of this business, Richard Bolling of Missouri asked that the agenda of the caucus be expanded by unanimous consent to include the selection of a majority leader, and Carl Albert of Oklahoma, his party's whip and the only congressman put in nomination, was elected to that post. Thus ended a period of skirmishing for the majority leadership that

10. *Time* (September 1, 1961):14. The congressman is not identified here, as he was in the *Time* article, first because he denies the conversation took place (*Congressional Record*, 87th Cong., 1st sess. [August 29, 1961], p. 16318) and second, because the *Time* reporter's source for the quote told me that he had deliberately left ambiguous the identity of the congressman, and, while the event really happened, the *Time* reporter was misled about whom it happend to.

11. Dexter, op. cit., ch. 8, p. 4.

12. Ibid, pp. 4–5.

had principally engaged Bolling and Albert from the time of Speaker Rayburn's death on November 16 of the previous year.

Most newspaper coverage of this event gave the impression that the battle between these two men was drawn on liberal-conservative lines. In Bolling's press conference on January 3 announcing his withdrawal from the race, newsmen repeatedly suggested that the contrast between them was predominantly ideological. A newspaperwoman asked, rhetorically, "Don't the liberals *ever* win around here, Mr. Bolling?" Another widely quoted colloquy went:

Reporter: "Mr. Bolling, do you regard your withdrawal . . . as a defeat for liberalism?"

Bolling: "Well, I consider myself a liberal, and at the moment I certainly feel defeated."[13]

Close observation suggests that the liberal-conservative distinction has only a limited kind of utility for understanding the Bolling-Albert fight for the majority leadership.[14] It is not necessary to base this conclusion on a *Congressional Quarterly* tabulation showing that Albert supported the Kennedy program 91 percent of the time in the first session of the Eighty-seventh Congress and Bolling 94 percent—a fact continually cited by liberal supporters of Mr. Albert.[15] Equally significant are the facts, first, that Albert indeed had a great deal of support among members with impeccably liberal records of long standing and, second, that he was regarded at the White House as a genuine friend of the Kennedy program.[16]

13. The best news coverage by far of this press conference that I saw occurred in the *Baltimore Sun* (January 4, 1962). See Rodney Crowther, "House Race Dropped by Bolling."

14. Pursuit of this line of thinking at a McCormack-Albert press conference, January 9, visibly irked Mr. McCormack. "A reporter . . . caught [Mr. McCormack] at the door of the Speaker's lobby and asked him if he had asked for complete support of President Kennedy's program. The new Speaker drew back indignantly. 'I'm not trying to put words in your mouth,' said the reporter. 'Yes you are,' said Mr. McCormack, 'I've been voting for progressive legislation for thirty years. I'm not a one-year man. Why don't you wake up?'" Mary McGrory, "McCormack Speaks as His Own Master," *Washington Star* (January 10, 1962).

15. *Congression Quarterly* 19 (November 24, 1961):1893–94. This tabulation also shows that throughout their careers in Congress, the voting records of these men were quite close by several criteria.

16. These statements, and many others throughout this paper, are based on interviews and observations gathered during the summer of 1961 and from December, 1961, to February, 1962, in Washington. During these months I spoke on matters connected with the subject of this paper to over 100 congressmen, congressional aides, newspapermen, and others, and during the latter period, I conducted interviews with twenty-six Democratic congressmen from all sections of the country on the leadership selection process then going on. Quotations are from notes taken during these interviews, and are occasionally slightly altered so as to preserve the anonymity of the respondent. My work in the summer of 1961 was supported by a grant-in-aid from the Social Science Research Council, whose assistance is gratefully acknowledged.

If, then, the outcome of the Bolling-Albert contest cannot be explained by the usual ideological arithmetic one uses in analyzing the House, how can one explain what happened? In part, an explanation can be based on the strategies each of the main actors pursued. These strategies were in turn largely dictated by their respective positions and roles in the House during the final years of the Rayburn speakership.

Often great differences in resources between political actors are largely nullified by the fact that resources are generally employed at low levels of intensity and with indifferent skill. In this case, however, resources on both sides were employed with considerable skill and finesse, and hence the outcome comes closer to reflecting a commonsense notion of the logic of the situation than might otherwise have been the case. It makes sense to describe the "cards" that each man held because, in this instance, the man who held the better cards made no more mistakes than his opponent, and, in the end, he won.

It is worth stressing that only part of the explanation can be given by referring to the roles and strategies of the main participants and to the different ways in which their demands were communicated to other House members. Two other significant variables can be sketched in only very crudely. This battle took place in the very core of an institution about whose habits and practices precious little is known, and, second, it engaged the participation of a great many more facets of the human personality than political decisions in the House normally do. The mysteries of how men interact with one another, of what leads people into enmity, jealousy, friendship, all seem to me to have played a very significant part in this contest. Obviously, the extent to which the outside observer can detect and extract meaning from these relationships is extremely limited, and this must inevitably weaken the plausibility and also the generality of the case I am about to construct, using, for the most part, more readily accessible materials.

II

The realization that Speaker Rayburn's health was failing seriously dawned on different members of the House at different times during the summer of 1961. That summer happened to have been an extremely hot and humid one in Washington. The House stayed in session continuously through the summer, one of the longest, bitterest, and most grueling sessions in the memory of veterans on Capitol Hill.[17]

17. The session lasted 277 days, the longest in ten years. Late one especially debilitating August afternoon, an elderly southern congressman shuffled over

Over the course of this period, many members and observers, especially those who were close to the Speaker, could not help but notice the wasting of Mr. Rayburn's solid, imposing figure, the occasional, uncharacteristic wandering of his attention from the business of the House, his increased susceptibility to bouts of fatigue and irritability, the slowing of his gait.

The House is, in the words of one of its members, a "Council of Elders." It honors age and places much power and trust in the hands of its most senior and oldest men. One consequence of this fact is the necessary, calm preoccupation of members—especially those just below the top rungs of power—with the inevitable occurrence of death. To that large fraction of members for whom the House is a career and a vocation, the longevity of members above them in the many hierarchies of the House—not the entirely predictable congressional election returns in their home districts—is the key to the political future. This is not to say that members habitually rub their hands ghoulishly or enjoy the prospect of losing valued friends, but only that the norms and the rules of the House bring due rewards to men who accept the world as it is, who prudently make their plans and bide their time.

On the other hand, informal norms of the House also put constraints on members based on commonly accepted notions of decent behavior, decorum, and good taste. Hence it is impossible for an outsider to say when Mr. Albert and Mr. Bolling began thinking in any concrete way about the next step in their careers within the House. However, it seems safe to make two assumptions: First, that they each had entertained some general thoughts on the question of the majority leadership well in advance of the occurrence of an actual vacancy (on January 9) or probable vacancy (on November 16) in the position. Second, both men knew Speaker Rayburn well, and both undoubtedly guessed earlier than most members that his health had permanently disintegrated.

III

On Saturday, November 18, Sam Rayburn was buried in Bonham, Texas. Mr. Albert reports that he had planned to wait until the following Wednesday to begin his campaign for majority leader.

---

to where I was standing just outside the Speaker's lobby, and confided that he was going to sponsor a bill that would abolish the final month of each session of Congress.

"I was in my office in McAlester on Sunday night," Mr. Albert said, "when Charlie Ward [his assistant] came in and said, "Bolling has announced for majority leader.' I heard it on the radio that night and saw a copy of the press release from my hometown paper before I announced myself. It was an Associated Press report, and Bill Arbogast [who covers the House for AP] wrote the story."

As a result of this turn of events, Mr. Albert got into the race sooner than he had intended. Mr. Bolling had thrown down a challenge which he could ignore only at his peril. In addition, Mr. Bolling's action offered Mr. Albert an opportunity to run a campaign against him, rather than against any of the more popular or more senior members who had been mentioned for leadership positions.

To each side it appeared that the other had begun to make plans well before Mr. Rayburn's death. Observers partial to Mr. Albert noted that as long before as the previous spring, Mr. Bolling was being referred to in public as a prominent contender for a leadership post.[18] It was easy to infer that, at least in part, these references had been suggested or "inspired" by Mr. Bolling. On the other hand, observers partial to Mr. Bolling thought an alliance between Mr. Albert and the Speaker-to-be, John McCormack, was being announced when Mr. Albert, as his chief deputy, led the tributes on September 26, 1961, in honor of Mr. McCormack's twenty-one years as majority leader.[19]

It seems plausible to suggest that the signs and portents friends of both men were reading did not reflect conscious efforts by either man to organize a premature campaign for the majority leadership. Rather, each man appealed particularly to slightly different publics: Bolling to the press corps, Albert to various groups within the House itself. These groups may, without encouragement from either man, have initiated activity designed to facilitate their chances of advancement. "After Mr. Rayburn went home to Texas," Mr. Albert reported, "I had fifty or sixty members pull me aside and say to me, 'He's not coming back. Don't sit there and be done out of what you're entitled to.' But I refused to discuss the matter with them." Several members mentioned that they had volunteered their support to Mr. Albert, and some, apparently, had attempted to persuade him to run for Speaker. "I would never do that against John McCormack," Mr. Albert said. "Mr.

18. For example, Mr. Bolling was introduced to a large public meeting at the Midwest Conference of Political Scientists on May 11, 1961, as "the next Speaker of the House of Representatives."

19. Mr. Albert's tribute on this occasion was much more elaborate than that tendered by any other member—save by Mr. McCormack's Massachusetts colleagues. See the *Congressional Record* 87th Cong., 1st sess. (September 26, 1961), pp. 20084–96.

Rayburn and Mr. McCormack picked me and made me whip, and to run against Mr. McCormack would have been the act of an ingrate."

Two groups were especially partial to Mr. Albert: his deputy whip organization and colleagues in the Oklahoma delegation. "We make a fetish of the fact that if you scratch one Okie you've scratched all of 'em," one member told me. As soon as Mr. Albert announced that he would run for majority leader, the members of the delegation did whatever they could to help his candidacy. The deputy whips gave Mr. Albert a party after Mr. Rayburn had gone to Texas, and attempted, without success, to induce Mr. Albert to begin work on his candidacy at that time.

Mr. Albert's announcement to the press followed the report of Mr. Bolling's by several hours. As soon as the announcement was made, Mr. Albert sent off a telegram to all members asking for their support and began telephoning each of them individually. "I bet you he was on the phone four days running," one member said.

Mr. Albert's intensive telephone campaign began with the west coast members. "James Roosevelt [congressman from Los Angeles] was the first man I called outside my own delegation," he said. By the end of the first day of telephoning, Mr. Albert thought he had all but five westerners committed to him. "If I wasn't sure of a senior man in a delegation," Mr. Albert said, "I started with the most junior men and asked them directly to support me. Then I'd work my way up the line so that when the senior man said, 'I'll have to check with my delegation,' I would have something to report to him. Of course on a thing like this, you call your friends first, but I had no set, written-out plan. I don't work that way."

The reasons members gave for supporting Mr. Albert are quite illuminating. They reflect two dominant themes, both of which illustrate the "inside" quality of his influence. On the one hand, Mr. Albert was his party's whip. Although there is no tradition which dictates that the whip shall be advanced to the majority leadership (as there is in promoting the majority leader to Speaker) many members felt that Mr. Albert nonetheless was "entitled" to the job by virtue of his six years service in the leadership hierarchy of the House. Some of them said:

> [From a liberal leader:] I made a commitment to Carl based on his years of service as whip and the fact that he was in line for this job from the standpoint of his long service as whip.

> [From a southwesterner:] Because I feel that he was entitled to it by reason of his effective part in the leadership of the House along with the Speaker and Mr. McCormack, I promised him my support.

[From the elderly dean of a large delegation:] I am a firm believer in the rule that has governed the House for over 100 years, and that is that of seniority. If Congressman McCormack is to be promoted to the Speakership of the House on the premise of his seniority and being in line position, then obviously the majority leader and whip should pursue the same course.[20] I have had the honor of being a member of this great body for [many years] . . . and while I would be reluctant to say that the seniority process does not have some imperfections, nevertheless if any other procedure were to be applied, I am inclined to believe that rather a chaotic situation would immediately be evident.

A second theme illustrates Mr. Albert's personal popularity in the House. Many members could cite warm personal ties they had developed with Mr. Albert. The late John Riley of South Carolina said, "Carl Albert married a girl from Columbia, you know, and so he is practically a constituent of mine."

A northern liberal: "I'm in something of a special situation with Carl, since we're the only two members of the House who [belong to an exclusive, honorary organization]."

A congressman from a border state said, "In all good conscience, I had to agree to support Carl because of his great help and encouragement to me [on a pet bill]."

A southwesterner said, "As one of his deputy whips, I feel committed to Carl Albert."

A southerner: "I committed myself to Carl Albert, who is my neighbor in the House Office Building."

Another southerner: "My association with Carl Albert has been extremely intimate."

Three men who served with Mr. Albert on committees:

"Carl and I have sat side by side on [our] committee for fifteen years."

"Carl has been very kind to me in the committee work and has done several things for me which have been very important for my people. . . ."

20. Mr. Albert entered the House in 1947, Mr. Bolling in 1949, making them thirtieth (tied with nine others) and thirty-ninth (tied with nineteen others) in seniority respectively in the Democratic party in the House—not a very great difference. Mr. McCormack, on the other hand, was the beneficiary of a long tradition of advancement from majority leader to Speaker, and, in addition, after the death of Speaker Rayburn, was third in seniority. He had never served as whip, incidentally, before his election as majority leader, nor had Speaker Rayburn. Both Mr. McCormack and Mr. Rayburn had held office for so many years it is highly probable that most members were unaware of the differences in the customs pertaining to the advancement of the majority leader and the whip

"I sit right next to Carl Albert. . . . We have been close personal friends due to our connection on the committee. . . ."

Another member said, "Ordinarily I'm slow to make commitments, but due to a friendship with Carl which began when we were in the . . . Army together, I told him quite a while back that should he seek the position of Democratic leader, I would support him."

And some members, not unexpectedly, combined the themes. For example: "He is not only my neighbor but a member of my committee, and with it all a fine, able, conscientious man who has been doing the dirty work for the leadership for a long time. . . ."

It was characteristic of Mr. Albert's "inside" strategy of influence that he used the telephone energetically and extensively himself to make personal contacts with members as quickly as possible. As whip, he was the custodian of a complete set of home, office, and district telephone numbers for each member.[21] One member said:

> Albert got on the phone and tracked me down in the frozen wastes of northern Rockystate the first day after the speaker was buried. You wouldn't think politicians would fall for that, but many of them did. They were impressed by the fact that he'd called them first. As a result he was able to line up a lot of the members, including many northern bleeding-heart liberals, in the first few days.

The principal argument which Mr. Albert used in asking the support of almost all the members I spoke with was the fact that he had already received a large number of commitments. This is instructive, because it evokes the almost obsessive preoccupation of congressmen with "getting along" and not sticking their necks out unnecessarily. "This House gives out no medals for individual bravery," said one congressman, "except posthumously."

Mr. Albert had an important further asset—the apparent backing of John McCormack. "I have heard McCormack say again and again that we have got to have a team player," one congressman said. "I guess he means by that a member of his team, and I suppose he favors Carl Albert." I asked a newspaperman who was following the situation closely to tell me who the most important congressman on Mr. Albert's side was, and he replied, "John McCormack." However, I could find no evidence that Mr. McCormack gave Mr. Albert any public endorsement.

21. Mr. Albert's administrative assistant said that this list happened to be in the Washington office while the telephoning was being done from McAlester, Oklahoma, where only the House telephone directory issued to all members was readily available.

Describing his campaign, Mr. Albert said:

> I didn't want to hurt Mr. Bolling's fellings. I never once threw knives or wrote mean things, although plenty of knives got thrown at me. I never once got on television. The sum total of my national publicity was a release when I got into the race and a release when I got up to Washington saying I thought I had enough votes to win. I refused to go on television although I was invited to go on most of the news and panel shows. I never mentioned Bolling's name at all. I never mentioned issues or anything. . . .

IV

Mr. Bolling's campaign, in contrast, followed an "outside" strategy of influence. As in the Rules Committee fight at the opening of the Eighty-seventh Congress and on numerous other occasions where he had planned legislative strategy and tactics, he held aloof from direct contact with most members. "I seldom try to persuade people directly," he said. "Our districts persuade us—if we are going to be persuaded at all."

Bolling had an uphill battle on his hands. He was severely handicapped at the start by his unwillingness to do anything in his own behalf until well after the Speaker had died. "It's a funny thing that Dick was so dilatory," a friend said. Although he leaked an announcement of his candidacy for the majority leadership to the press on November 19, the day after the Speaker's funeral, it was not until November 28 that he sent a strikingly diffident letter to each of the Democrats in the House. This letter said:

> Just a note to confirm that I am running for Democratic floor leader and am seeking the support of my Democratic colleagues for that position. Reports during the past week have been encouraging and I am in this contest all the way.
>
> I am running on my legislative record and experience and hope that you will give my candidacy your consideration on that basis.

Several of his supporters expressed surprise at the mildness of this approach. The letter asked for "consideration," not support, and was not followed up by an energetic telephone campaign. Furthermore, Bolling had waited twelve precious days after the Speaker's death before making his move. Why?

Answers to a question of motive such as this one—even the answers given by Mr. Bolling himself—are bound to verge on speculation. My guess is that Mr. Bolling's hesitancy had something to do with the relationship he had had with Speaker Rayburn. According to the reports of numerous observers who had no axes to grind, Mr. Bolling and the Speaker had built a bond of affection between them that went well beyond the usual political alliance.[22] Mr. Sam, who had no immediate family, was well known for his habit of adopting political protégés with whom he could develop a relationship of warmth and trust similar to that found in the family situation. This was, apparently, Mr. Rayburn's way of overcoming the loneliness that otherwise might well have overtaken any elderly bachelor.

The need to overcome loneliness was strongly ingrained in Mr. Rayburn from childhood. Mr. Rayburn is quoted as saying:

> Many a time when I was a child and lived way out in the country, I'd sit on the fence and wish to God that somebody would ride by on a horse or drive by in a buggy—just anything to relieve my loneliness. Loneliness consumes people. It kills 'em eventually. God help the lonely. . . .[23]

Mr. Rayburn's advice to Presidents Truman, Eisenhower, and Kennedy reflect the same theme. As he reported afterward, on a conversation with Mr. Truman just after the latter had become president:

> "You've got many hazards," I said "One of your great hazards is in this White House," I said. "I've been watching things around here a long time, and I've seen people in the White House try to build a fence around the White House and keep the various people away from the President that he should see. . . ."[24]

His biographer and research assistant, D. B. Hardeman says, "Mr. Sam was . . . annoyed by inactivity. When he could think of nothing

22. Friends of Mr. Albert note that Mr. Albert was Speaker Rayburn's personal choice for whip in 1954 and further suggest that Mr. Albert was also a close personal friend of Mr. Rayburn's. One influential congressman said, "Mr. Sam thought the world of Carl Albert." But this same congressman indicated that he thought Mr. Bolling's relationship with the Speaker was unique. Without excluding the strong probability that Mr. Rayburn had a high personal regard for Mr. Albert (and, one supposes, several other members as well), the testimony of several knowledgeable and apparently unbiased observers was quite unanimous in indicating that for several years preceding his death Mr. Rayburn was particularly close to Mr. Bolling.

23. David Cohn, "Mr. Speaker: An Atlantic Portrait," *Atlantic Monthly* (October, 1942):73–78. The quoted portion appears on p. 76. Mr. Cohn was a personal friend of the Speaker's. He comments on the quoted passage, "As he spoke, Rayburn relived the long, lean, lonely years of his childhood, and it was clear that he wished other children might be spared the bleakness of his youth."

24. CBS News, "Mr. Sam: A Personal and Political Biography," telecast, November 16, 1961.

else to do at home in Bonham he would get out all his shoes and polish them. He dreaded holidays and Sundays because visitors were few."[25]

Mr. Rayburn found it particularly congenial to work with younger men. D. B. Hardeman says, "Lyndon Johnson once confessed, 'The Speaker and I have always been very close but if we are not as close as we were once, it is because I'm almost fifty. If you notice, he never has older men around him.' "[26]

"I always liked the House the best," Mr. Rayburn said. "There're more people there, usually they're younger people, and as I've advanced in years, I've stepped back in my associations, boys, young people ten, twenty years younger than I. Their bodies are not only resilient but their minds are too. They can learn faster than the fellow advanced in years."[27]

One of the things which no doubt drew Mr. Rayburn to Mr. Bolling was the exceptional resiliency and quickness of the latter's mind. On this quality, friends and political enemies of Mr. Bolling agreed. He is an extremely "quick study," and had several other things in common with the Speaker:

"Bolling loves the House," a judicious, slow-spoken southern congressman who knows him rather well told me. "He loves it and has studied it. He has read everything that has been written about the House and has studied its power structure. He has a brilliant mind."

Although nearly thirty-five years separated them, both Mr. Rayburn and Mr. Bolling were strongly committed emotionally to many liberal programs. Bolling refers to himself quite frankly as a "gut liberal"; *Time* magazine has aptly characterized Rayburn as a "liberal of the heart."[28] In addition, both men shared a high sense of rectitude in their work, treating the majority of their colleagues with reserve and judging them rather severely. This social distance which both men maintained was no doubt related in some complex way to the intensity of their feelings about political issues. It is instructive in this connection to note the tendency of both men to become laconic in public when dealing with problems with which they had great personal involvement. Compare Bolling's prepared statement of withdrawal from the majority leadership race in 1962 with Rayburn's statement of withdrawal in 1934 from an unsuccessful race for the Speakership.[29]

25. D. B. Hardeman, "The Unseen Side of the Man They Called Mr. Speaker," *Life* 51 (December 1, 1961):21.

26. Ibid.

27. CBS News, "Mr. Sam . . .," op. cit.

28. *Time* 77 (February 10, 1961):12. What is significant here, I think, is not the placement of either man on an ideological spectrum so much as the high degree of personal engagement which the references to parts of the body suggest.

29. I was a witness to the events surrounding the composition of Bolling's statement of withdrawal, and am quite convinced that Bolling had no knowledge of

In 1934 Rayburn said, "I am no longer a candidate for Speaker. There are no alibis. Under the circumstances, I cannot be elected."[30]

In 1962 Bolling said, "I am withdrawing from the race for leadership of the House. Developments of the last few days have convinced me that I don't have a chance to win."[31]

Bolling privately expressed an unwillingness amounting to an incapacity either to "do anything" until after a "decent" time had elapsed after the Speaker's death,[32] or to canvass for votes in his own behalf. The major portion of this burden within the House was carried by Representative Frank Thompson of New Jersey and a group of four or five others. The brunt of Bolling's campaign was, however, carried on from outside the House.[33] Initially, he had to decide whether to run for Speaker or majority leader—which no doubt also contributed to the quality of hesitancy in his campaign.

Rayburn's statement. Rather, the striking resemblance between the two seems to me to illustrate a remarkable similarity in the styles of the two men, not conscious imitation.

30. Bascom N. Timmons, "Rayburn" (ditto, n.d.), part 4, p. 1. This series was supplied to certain newspapers at the time of Speaker Rayburn's death. Mr. Timmons is a newspaperman accredited to the House Press Gallery from a string of newspapers in the southwest. He is a Texan and was a friend and contemporary of Mr. Rayburn's.

31. Rodney Crowther, *Baltimore Sun*, loc. cit. The psychologically-minded would also no doubt find it relevant that Mr. Bolling's father died when he was in his early teens. However, anyone concluding from data such as have been presented here that either Mr. Bolling or Mr Rayburn gave indications in their behavior of being emotionally crippled or lacking in control could not possibly be further from the mark. The point here is simply that certain easily verified events and patterns in the lives of each man may well have predisposed him to like the other.

32. Mr. Bolling's imputation of indecorousness (the news of which was communicated in such places as "Bitter Withdrawal," *Time* 79 [January 12, 1962, 12]) was resented in the Albert camp. In their view, Mr. Bolling had himself precipitated the battle by first permitting word to leak to the newspapers that he was a candidate for majority leader.

33. One index of this is the apparent fact that Mr. Thompson is generally not too popular in the House (a fact of which both he and Mr. Bolling are aware). Mr. Thompson is an able and gifted man with extremely good political connections outside the House, both "downtown" and in his home state. (See Richard L. Lyons, "Thompson Decision to Retain Seat Gives House Liberals Needed Lift," *Washington Post* [January 31, 1961].) But inside the House, he has a reputation for being sharp-tongued, supercilious, and too witty for his own good. He has a way of hanging nicknames that "stick" on friend and foe alike—to the delight of the former, the great chagrin of the latter. One political ally of Mr. Thompson's said, "He has got the reputation that whenever he is in favor of a bill, it is bound to lose. . . . Thompson is one of Bolling's major liabilities. I hear how the guys talk at the back of the room there [in the aisle behind the seats in the Hall of the House]. They say, 'Whose amendment is that? Thompson's? That guy? To hell with that' And they vote it down." Another ally of Thompson's said, "Frank's always trying to talk silly with you when you're talking serious, and trying to talk serious when you're talking silly."

Factors pointing to the Speakership included the relative unpopularity of Mr. McCormack (1) with members, and (2) at the White House; but against this had to be weighed (1) Mr. McCormack's generally blameless voting record (from the standpoint of a proadministration Democrat), (2) his long service in the second position, (3) the weight of a tradition which strongly favored the elevation of a majority leader, (4) Mr. Bolling's own relatively junior position, (5) the fact that Mr. McCormack, if he lost the Speakership, would remain as a majority leader not especially favorably disposed toward the program of an administration that had just done him in politically, and, (6) the fact that opposing Mr. McCormack would unavoidably exacerbate the religious cleavage in the House and the country which the fight over school aid in the last session had revealed.[34]

And so, Mr. Bolling decided to run for majority leader against the extremely popular Mr. Albert. In a straight popularity contest, Mr. Bolling knew he was "born dead." His role in the House had been quite unlike Mr. Albert's; indeed, several congressmen contrasted them starkly.

A close friend described Mr. Albert's approach to the job of whip:

> The whip is more the eyes and ears of the leadership than anything. On controversial matters, they like to know what the chances of success are. . . . So the deputy whips count noses, and the whip's job is to evaluate the count—especially to assess the doubtfuls. . . . Albert developed quite a genius for knowing what people would do. . . .
>
> Another service he performed endears him to people. Carl's the kind of a guy everybody could find. He would talk to the leadership for [rank-and-file congressmen].
>
> A lot of these eastern guys have a Tuesday through Thursday club. The whip takes the duty on of telling them if the signals change so they can get back here if they're needed.
>
> He's done so many things for people. They trust him. They think of him, "Here's a man I can talk to when I need help." When the members go about picking a leader, they want personal services, not intellectuals.[35]

I dare you to find a member of Congress who said Bolling had lifted a finger for him.

---

34. See H. Douglas Price, "Race, Religion and the Rules Committee" in Alan Westin (ed.) *The Uses of Power* (New York: Harcourt, Brace & World, 1962), pp. 1–71.

35. Mr. Albert's friend may, in reflecting unfavorably on Mr. Bolling, have done Mr. Albert a slight injustice. Mr. Albert was an honor graduate of the University of Oklahoma and a Rhodes Scholar—neither of which makes him an intellectual, but they clearly don't disqualify him either.

A supporter of Mr. Bolling's (for whom Bolling had, according to this member's testimony, lifted many a finger) saw the roles of the two principals in much the same light, although his evaluation of their roles was quite different:

> Albert's approach to legislative matters is, well, everybody ought to vote his own district. . . . He brings his friends and his enemies in [to vote] both. . . . Why the hell get [a certain southern congressman] out [to vote]? He doesn't vote with us on anything. And he's a deputy whip! It's ridiculous. . . . The function of the whip [under Mr. Albert] is room service to members.

> Albert was the whip, but Bolling was doing the whipping. . . . When the heat was being put on in the Rules Committee and all the other fights, it was Bolling putting it on, and he wasn't making any friends doing it.[36]

Mr. Bolling was, as a friend of his described it, a "hatchet man" for Speaker Rayburn. This entailed a variety of activities on the Rules Committee, including monitoring the attendance of friends and foes, arranging for the disposition of bills, and keeping track of the intentions of the various (and numerous) factions in the House with respect to important legislation in behalf of the Speaker. Occasionally, Mr. Bolling's job included putting the finger on members who were open to (or vulnerable to) persuasion, and he often had a crucial part in the process of persuading them—not always a pleasant task.[37]

Although Mr. Bolling is entirely in sympathy with policies espoused by liberals in the House, his position close to the Speaker precluded his joining in any formal way in the activities of the Democratic Study Group, the House liberal organization. As a friend of his put it, "Dick was aloof from the uprisings of the peasants."

"Bolling's got a sort of a chip on his shoulder," another member said.

"The thing you have to realize about Bolling," said an Albert backer,

---

36. There are now several accounts of the 1961 battle over the Rules Committee in print, including a treatment of the episode in Price, op. cit.; the analysis of the vote by Cummings and Peabody in Robert L. Peabody and Nelson W. Polsby, *New Perspectives on the House of Representatives*, 1st ed., (Chicago: Rand McNally, 1963), ch. 7, pp. 167–94; a long chapter by Neil MacNeil in *Forge of Democracy* (New York: McKay, 1963), pp. 410–88; and a forthcoming case study in the Eagleton series by William MacKaye.

37. See *Time* 77 (February 10, 1961); William S. White, "The Invisible Gentleman from Kansas City," *Harper's* (May, 1961); Neil MacNeil, "The House Confronts Mr. Kennedy," *Fortune* 65 (January 1962):70–73.

"is that he never bothers to speak to anyone else. I don't think Bolling understands politics."

Mr. Bolling's aloofness was, as I have suggested, probably something more than simply a reflection of his peculiar institutional position. A second friend of Bolling's said, "Despite a good deal of charm, Bolling just does not have a personality that inspires loyalty and friendship among men.[38] He's not a backslapping, how-the-hell-are-you type of guy. Bolling is personally quite pleasant, but reticent."

The late Clem Miller of California said, "Congress is a World War I rather than a World War II operation. You have to move huge bodies of men a few feet at a time. . . . Dick's spent the last few years divorcing himself from a base of fire. His job was right-hand man to the Speaker. He came to Democratic Study Group meetings but always identified himself as an observer, not as a participant. He came in a sense to lecture us like small children rather than lead us in our councils. There was a good deal of hostility toward him in the Study Group as a result of that. The Study Group was set up as a foil for the leadership. You can't have your foot in both camps, and so Dick alienated the base of support that he needed in the House."

Another member, often allied with Mr. Bolling, characterized him as "totally unfriendly."

Mr. Bolling's personal situation within the House was further complicated by a common enough phenomenon. As a relative newcomer, as an extremely able member performing difficult tasks well, and as an intimate of the Speaker, Mr. Bolling was, in the opinion of several observers, the victim of a certain amount of jealous resentment.

"Jealousy is a big factor," one congressman said. "Liberals have several characteristics that tend to make them ineffective, and vanity is one of them. They tend to be prima donnas."[39] Another said, "Dick is not a popular man in the House, no doubt a surprise to newsmen. For one thing, he's resented because of his ability."

Liberals were clearly not the only group of congressmen susceptible to jealous feelings toward Mr. Bolling. His relative youth was offensive to some of his seniors. Mr. Bolling had risen very fast in the House and had been given many advantages by his friend, the Speaker. The record he had made thus far also suggested that, if elected, he would take many more initiatives than Mr. Albert and would more decisively challenge the powers of committee and subcommittee chairmen to

38. Statements such as this one obviously are not intended to be taken with strict literalness. Most social scientists are agreed that the personal "qualities" of leaders vary according to the situation.

39. Cf. a similar comment on Senate liberals by Tristam Coffin, "The Well-Tempered Politician," *Holiday* (April, 1962):107.

control the flow and content of legislation—in behalf of programs for which many of these leaders had no particular liking.

Even to the superficial observer, Mr. Albert and Mr. Bolling are quite contrasting figures. Mr. Albert was fifty-three years old, exactly on the House median; Mr. Bolling was only forty-five. Albert is physically probably the shortest man in the House and looks nothing like the collegiate wrestler he once was. He has a softly lined, friendly, gentle face which, says a colleague, "always looks faintly worried." Bolling is a tall, husky, quite handsome and imposing-looking man who gives the appearance of great self-confidence and looks very much like the collegiate football player he was. Mr. Albert in conversation is homespun, soft-spoken, emotionally unengaged, and low-pressure. A colleague says, "You could vote impeachment of the president, and it wouldn't bother Carl." Mr. Bolling in conversation is articulate, expansive, sophisticated, intense; in short, one would surmise, a rather more threatening figure to someone of average inclinations than Mr. Albert.

Mr. Bolling has far greater acceptance in the higher echelons of the "downtown" bureaucracies and surely in the press corps than almost any other congressman, including Mr. Albert. Mr. Bolling is far more likely to spend his leisure hours among pundits, diplomats, and subcabinet officials than with congressmen, a pattern which Mr. Albert reverses. Mr. Albert prides himself, in fact, in spending a greater proportion of his time on the floor of the House than any other member, where he is continually accessible to his colleagues.[40]

To a great extent, Mr. Bolling understood that a variety of institutional and personal "inside" factors were working against him, and so he launched an "outside" campaign.

40. See John M. Virden, "Little Giant from Bug Tussle," *Saturday Evening Post* 235 (March 24, 1962):94–97; Paul Duke, "Albert's Soft Sell," *Wall Street Journal* (March 6, 1962); "Carl Albert, Nose-Counter from Bug Tussle," *Time* 79 (January 12, 1962):13.

Certain other characteristics place Mr. Albert closer to the rank and file of congressmen than Mr. Bolling. Mr. Albert was a small-town boy, the son of a farmer and laborer, educated in public schools, and is a Methodist. Mr. Bolling was born in New York City, the son of a well-to-do physician. He grew up in comfortable circumstances and socially prominent circles in Huntsville, Alabama, after his father's death went to Exeter and the University of the South, has a Master's degree from Sewanee, did further graduate work at Vanderbilt, and is an Episcopalian. If the script for this contest had been written by C. Wright Mills or one of his followers, Mr. Albert would have been the more "liberal" candidate and wouldn't have had a chance. (See Mills, *The Power Elite* [New York: Oxford University Press, 1956]). Mills carefully excludes Congress from his discussion of "the power elite" for reasons which seem to this reader designed to protect his thesis from evidence which would reject it.

V

Bolling's task, as he saw it, was divided into several phases of activity. First, he had to stall the Albert bandwagon. Then he had to receive enough commitments to win himself. His primary targets were the big state delegations of New York, California, Illinois, and Pennsylvania. Secondary targets included getting a firm grip on his home-state delegation and going after younger, liberal congressmen and congressmen who had substantial labor and civil-rights-minded constituencies.

His strategy for accomplishing these ends had two major features. First, he intended to draw as sharp a contrast as he could between himself and Mr. Albert on issues and sell the contrast as hard as he could through the mass media. Second, he set about "pulling strings" on members, a process which he had practiced before in legislative battles.[41] This entailed identifying the men and interest groups favorable to his candidacy who for various reasons could reach and persuade members of Congress. Naturally, the foremost among these would have been the president, but at no time was presidential aid offered, and none was requested by Mr. Bolling.

The position of the White House in this battle was a complex one. While the mass media, on the whole, bought Mr. Bolling's contention that substantial differences in public policy separated him and Mr. Albert, the White House never did. It regarded both men as good friends of the Kennedy program, each having personal and political strengths and weaknesses. To intervene in behalf of one friend would have meant sacrificing another. For the White House to intervene and lose would have been disastrous for its prestige and legislative program. To intervene and win would have been more satisfactory but still would have involved (aside from the making of enemies) great exertion, the distribution of indulgences and the "cashing in" on favors owed, all of which could otherwise be employed to improve the chances for passage of controversial reciprocal trade, medical aid, tax reform, and education bills. Several members of the president's official

41. An example of this process was given in *Time* 77 (February 10, 1961) at the time of the Rules Committee fight: "*Time* Correspondent Neil MacNeil listened as two Rayburn lieutenants were running down the list of doubtful members. On one: 'The General Services Administration ought to be able to get him.' On another: 'The Air Force can take care of him.' A third? 'If you can get the Post Office to issue that special stamp for him, you've got him.' And a fourth? 'The United Mine Workers can get him.' And a fifth? 'Hell, if we can't get him we might as well quit. Go talk to him.' A sixth? 'No, but I'll fix that bastard.' " *Time* gives the strong impression that the two lieutenants are Bolling and Thompson.

family were close to Mr. Bolling and were almost certainly partial to him, but none participated in the fight.

Mr. Bolling and his backers in the House concurred in the White House policy of nonintervention and in the reasoning behind it. The major inside advantage of their side, as they saw it, was a professional ability to predict outcomes accurately and to recommend appropriate strategies. They understood fully that the risks to the White House were great, the probabilities of success dubious. If they could come close to winning on their own, within perhaps five or ten votes, then their recommendation might change, since the White House could then probably put them over the top. But it is not at all certain that even then the White House would have been ready to move.

If the administration was inactive, other keenly interested bystanders were not. The AFL-CIO backed Mr. Bolling strongly and performed several notable services in behalf of his candidacy. Labor lobbyists made a complete canvass of possible supporters in the House and, in several cases, made representations in Mr. Bolling's behalf with members. The NAACP was also active. Roy Wilkins, national chairman, telegraphed 153 selected branches of his organization, "Bolling right on twenty-six civil rights votes, Albert wrong. Wire, write or call your Congressman. This could affect civil-rights legislation for years to come." The Democratic Reform Clubs of New York City were also interested in Bolling's candidacy, as were some local and national political leaders around the country and at least one farm organization.

An example of indirect influence in Mr. Bolling's behalf was described by an Albert supporter, "I heard that President Truman, a neighbor of Bolling's and a loyal Missourian, called Mayor Wagner of New York to try and get the New York delegation to support Bolling."

Mr. Bolling was especially successful in enlisting the aid of the mass media. Since the civil rights battle of 1957, when he anonymously kept newsmen briefed on the confusing tactical situation within the House, Mr. Bolling has been extremely popular with the Washington press corps.[42] He is asked to appear on broadcasts and telecasts much more often than the average member. He counts many Washington correspondents, including several famous ones, as close personal friends.

Hence, it is not altogether surprising that he was able to gain the

42. A Washington correspondent commented: "[Bolling] was a good news source and popular among newsmen from the time he first got on the House Banking Committee and became even more popular when he was moved to Rules as Rayburn's obvious protégé."

endorsement of the *New York Times* as early as December 11. On Sunday, December 24, the *Times* reiterated its stand, saying, "The conservative coalition of southern Democrats and northern Republicans would find it much more difficult to exercise its suffocating veto over forward-looking legislation with the imaginative and hard driving Mr. Bolling as majority floor chief."[43]

Five days previously, on December 19, James Wechsler, editor of the *New York Post*, gave a strong endorsement to Mr. Bolling, in which he printed a long verbatim extract of a letter endorsing Carl Albert which Bolling had received from Judge Howard W. Smith, leader of conservative southerners in the House.[44] Wechsler commented, "This is not to say Albert has faithfully followed Smith's gospel. He is a moderate, pleasant man whose voting record might be far more impressive if he came from a state more congenial to the advance of civil rights and less dominated by the natural gas interests. Despite their differences on a variety of matters, Smith is plainly confident that he can handle Albert; he is equally convinced that Bolling spells trouble. . . ."[45]

On December 29, Marquis Childs[46] and Edward P. Morgan both urged the selection of Mr. Bolling, referring once again to the Smith letter and to issues separating the two candidates. Mr. Morgan was especially vigorous in his commentary:

43. *New York Times* (December 24, 1961).

44. This letter was sent in response to Mr. Bolling's November 28 request for "consideration" from each Democrat. Supporters of Mr. Albert were dismayed by the fact that while they had not solicited Judge Smith's support and Mr. Bolling had, the Smith endorsement was being used by Mr. Bolling against Mr. Albert with the press.

45. James Wechsler, "Hill Battle," *New York Post* (December 19, 1961). Mr. Bolling's constituency is the Fifth District of Missouri, which includes most of Kansas City. Mr. Albert represents the thirteen counties of Oklahoma's Third District, an area known as "Little Dixie." This district is predominantly rural and is somewhat depressed economically. Its major products are timber, peanuts, cotton, and livestock. Several Albert supporters suggested that a generally liberal record such as Mr. Albert had made in the House was in some ways a more creditable performance for a man from a district of this kind than for a man from a big city. Although this argument has some plausibility, it should also be noted that several of the most respected southern liberals and moderates in the House have come from districts very similar to Mr. Albert's. Sam Rayburn himself was one such example. Others would be Carl Elliott of Alabama, Frank Smith of Mississippi, and James Trimble of Arkansas. This argument may, in other words, be an attempt to appeal to a popular stereotype which automatically classifies big-city districts as "liberal" and rural southern districts as "conservative." But it may be that on the vast majority of issues coming to a vote in Congress, representatives from southern, rural, economically depressed areas have constituencies as liberal as any in the country.

46. Marquis Childs, "The High Stakes in House Battle," *Washington Post* (December 29, 1961)—and elsewhere.

Where Bolling has been consistently for them, Albert has been basically against civil rights legislation, federal aid to education, full foreign aid and regulation of the oil and gas industry. It is reliably reported that one Texas congressman told a southern colleague that "with Albert in there, oil will be safe for twenty years."[47]

What of the outcomes of these activities? The relations between outside "pressures" and congressmen have been variously described in popular and academic literature. There is an old tradition which regards these relations as essentially nefarious.[48] Descriptively, the congressman is sometimes thought to be a relatively passive creature who is pulled and hauled about according to the play of pressures upon him and whose final decision is determined by the relative strength of outside forces.[49] More recently, political scientists have become preoccupied with the qualities of reciprocity in the relations of interest groups and politicians. This literature calls attention to mutually beneficial aspects of the relationship and lays stress on the ways in which politicians may act to govern the outside pressures placed on them.[50]

My information on the impact of Bolling's outside campaign is necessarily incomplete. It is apparent at a minimum that a sufficient number of congressmen were never reached by this campaign. One congressman said:

Bolling's best hope was forces outside the House—labor and civil rights groups. But I received not one communication in his behalf from

47. "Edward P. Morgan and the News," American Broadcasting Company (December 29, 1961). The documentation of this case has never, to my knowledge, been made. I suggest that at the least the reference to Mr. Albert's position on federal aid to education would be difficult to defend.

48. See, for examples of this tradition, H. H. Wilson, *Congress: Corruption and Compromise* (New York: Rinehart, 1951); Karl Schriftgiesser, *The Lobbyists* (Boston: Little, Brown, 1951).

49. An excellent example of this mode of thinking is contained in Max Lerner, *America as a Civilization* (New York: Simon & Schuster, 1957), pp. 415 ff. and especially p. 424. More generally, see Arthur F. Bentley, *The Process of Government* (Evanston: Principia, 1949); Earl Latham, *The Group Basis of Politics* (Ithaca: Cornell University Press, 1952); Oliver Garceau, "Interest Group Theory in Political Research," *The Annals* 319 (September, 1958), and David B. Truman, *The Governmental Process* (New York: Knopf, 1955). Truman explicitly rejects the notion that congressmen are wholly passive.

50. Lewis A. Dexter, op. cit., and Dexter, "The Representative and His District," *Human Organization* 16 (Summer, 1957):2–13, reprinted as Chapter 1 of the present volume; Dexter, "What Do Congressmen Hear: The Mail," *Public Opinion Quarterly* 20 (Spring, 1956):16–26. See also Donald R. Matthews, *U.S. Senators and Their World* (Chapel Hill: University of North Carolina Press, 1960), esp. chs. 8, 9.

anybody. There was nobody campaigning for him. Nobody knew if he was serious or not. Where was the heat?

Another congressman, from a heavily populated area, said:

> Our delegation was never put on the spot. Bolling never tried to wage a campaign in our delegation. Apparently he tried to get labor leaders to pressure Cautious [the state party leader] to put pressure on our congressmen. This is OK, but you really have to put the pressure on because if you know Cautious, he won't ever move unless he's really in a box.

In other cases, congressmen were able quite easily to *resist* pressure. "The word got around," one liberal congressman said, "that this wasn't like the Rules Committee fight, where there was a legitimate issue. Rather, it was all in the family, and any outside interference, even from the White House, would be resented."

Harlem's Representative Adam Clayton Powell, announcing his support of Albert, charged that some organized labor representatives were putting pressure on some Democratic members of his committee. He added, "I can't understand why labor union leaders would do this. Frankly, this is Democratic party business, not labor business."[51]

On the other hand, Bolling's campaign from the outside made several converts. Representative Leonard Farbstein of New York City, for example, announced that he would vote for Mr. Bolling on the basis of Mr. Wechsler's column.[52]

Another congressman, a conservative veteran, wrote Bolling and detailed the substantial political disagreements between them, concluding, "But Famous Farmer tells me he is supporting you, and if he is supporting you, I am supporting you."

A leader of another interest group, in another part of the country, wrote, "I have just been informed by Congressman Dean Delegation's home secretary that Dean will be supporting you for majority leader. If there are any particular targets in [this state], I'm still available to apply whatever other pressures I can."

In aggregate, however, the impact of this campaign was not sufficient to accomplish Mr. Bolling's major goal. Edward Morgan commented with some asperity on the failure of Mr. Bolling to consolidate his

51. Robert C. Albright, "Powell Backs Albert for House Post," *Washington Post* (December 1, 1961). Powell, unlike the congressman just quoted, checked with the White House before he made his announcement, obviously taking the position that the President had a legitimate interest in the outcome.
52. *New York Post* (December 21, 1961).

support on an ideological basis, and at the same time he renewed the plea that the battle be defined in ideological terms:

> If they voted . . . in support of their constituencies' needs for protect-tion on gas prices, housing, civil rights, and the like, the big city and industrial area representatives would have to come down almost unanimously for Bolling over Albert on their voting records alone and the man from Missouri would have it cinched. But he doesn't have it cinched. . . . At least one Massachusetts congressman has already committed himself to Albert in writing . . . Adam Clayton Powell is looking south . . . So are a couple of New Jersey Representatives. . . . Most surprisingly, perhaps, two leading California Congressmen, Holifield and Roosevelt, have not dashed to Bolling's aid.[53]

Over the long New Year's weekend, Bolling, Thompson, and Andrew Biemiller of the AFL-CIO met and assessed Bolling's "hard" strength at between sixty-five and seventy votes. Perhaps fifty more would have joined them if Bolling were going to win, but otherwise, they faded. A Bolling lieutenant said, "Everybody wanted to know, 'What's his chances?' The typical response was, 'I'll lie low. I'm with you if you've got a chance; otherwise, nix.'"

By the most realistic calculations, however, Mr. Bolling fell short of the 130 or more votes that he needed. He decided to withdraw his candidacy rather than embarrass his supporters in their state delegations and possibly jeopardize their future effectiveness in Congress.

VI

It is possible to identify at least four reasons why Mr. Bolling's attempt to win from the outside failed. The first two have already been mentioned: Mr. Albert's extreme popularity and Bolling's relative isolation provided little incentive for individual members to seek outside excuses of their own accord to do what they could more

---

53. "Edward P. Morgan and the News," American Broadcasting Company (December 29, 1961). This account may be contrasted with a column put out by William S. White, a former Capitol Hill reporter. White's explanation of what happened is: "Whatever chance [Bolling] might have had, however, was sunk without a trace by the ultraliberals themselves. They rushed forward to gather him into their arms, through zealous indorsements by such too-gooder groups as Americans for Democratic Action. No man in a House which—like the country itself—is essentially moderate could possibly have survived such embarrassing public embraces. So Mr. Bolling had to withdraw his candidacy. . . ." *Washington Star* (January 5, 1962)—and elsewhere. I could discover little evidence which would lend credibility to this analysis. Regrettably, Mr. White offers none.

conveniently do for inside reasons. Second, the hands-off policy of the White House deprived Mr. Bolling's campaign of what would have been a major outside weapon had the president chosen to come in on Mr. Bolling's side.

The third major obstacle to the success of the outside campaign was the fact that, through no fault of Mr. Bolling's, a few of his supporters unwittingly blunted one of his principal weapons, the ideological contrast between himself and Mr. Albert. Just before the opening of the second session of the Eighty-seventh Congress, and at the same time the struggle over the majority leadership was going on, a group of liberal congressmen proposed that a policy committee be created in the Democratic party to be elected by the members from each of the eighteen whip zones. This committee was to advise and counsel with the leadership, and it was contemplated that it would be "more representative" (and presumably more liberal) than the leadership, unaided, would be.

Congressmen favoring this proposal circulated it among their Democratic colleagues in an attempt to get the fifty signatures necessary to place it on the agenda of the caucus which was to elect a new Speaker. Several liberals favoring Mr. Albert promptly signed, thus furnishing themselves with an excellent alibi, if they were challenged on ideological grounds by constituents and interest groups. They could claim that the fight over the majority leadership was not really significant since Bolling and Albert were, in their voting records, so close. But on the basic issue, on the institutional structure of leadership in the House, they were, as always, for liberalization.

This proposal went through several stages. At one point, it was seriously proposed that Mr. Bolling accept the chairmanship of this committee as the price for withdrawing his candidacy for the majority leadership. This proposal implied that the new Speaker had accepted the policy committee in principle.[54] Mr. Bolling was himself dubious about the chances that such a committee could perform the tasks its supporters envisaged for it. Counterproposals and negotiations buzzed back and forth about the possibility of putting "teeth" into the com-

54. The rate at which tentative proposals and counterproposals of this sort fly around Washington is perfectly phenomenal. Theodore H. White rhapsodizes about the kinds of people who often act in the capacity of carrier pigeon: "Washington holds perhaps fifty or a hundred . . . men, lawyers all, successful all, who in their dark-paneled law chambers nurse an amateur's love for politics and dabble in it whenever their practices permit. Where, in the regions, cities, and states of the country, provincial lawyers love to counsel local politicians, promote names for the local judiciary, arrange the candidacies of lesser men, in Washington lawyers dabble in national politics, in appointments to places of high political destiny. Their influence, collectively, can never be ignored, because, collectively, they possess a larger fund of wisdom, experience, contacts,

mittee and about prior agreements as to its membership. At another level, Mr. Bolling and Mr. Thompson had to avoid being mousetrapped by the petition to put the policy committee on the agenda. To have signed the petition might have looked to Albert-McCormack forces like a proposal of terms and an acknowledgment of defeat. The fact that supporters of the Bolling candidacy were leading the fight for the policy committee was compromising enough as it was.

In the end, the whole idea came to nothing.[55] The proposal never received enough signatures to gain a place on the agenda, and at John McCormack's first press conference upon his nomination for the speakership, he said, "A policy committee is out."[56] But the policy committee plan served one significant purpose. It softened and blurred Bolling's attempt to define the issue between himself and Mr. Albert in such a way as to embarrass liberals who were not supporting him.

The fourth reason for the failure of the outside campaign is probably the most important. It has to do with the conditions under which the actual choice was going to be made. Normally, a congressman has considerable leeway in the casting of his vote because the issues are complex and technical, because the ways in which they are framed

---

memories, running back over thirty years of national politics, than most candidates on the national scene can ever hope to acquire on their own. . . ." *The Making of the President, 1960* (New York: Atheneum, 1961), p. 33.

Newspaper people also quite often undertake this sort of activity, and occasionally lobbyists do, too.

Fortuitously, much of the activity described in this paper took place during the Christmas-Debutante-New Year's social season in Washington. As a result, many of the participants in these events kept running into each other at parties. Political science may some day catch up with the slick magazines and novels in comprehending the true significance of Washington parties. In this case, it appear that much of the negotiating on whether or not Mr. Bolling would join the leadership group as head of the policy committee took place on an informal basis, through intermediaries and without any soul-stirring confrontations of rivals such as are found in Allen Drury's *Advise and Consent.*

55. That is, it came to almost nothing. In mid-March, 1962, three months after the events described here took place, the Democrats reactivated a "steering" committee along the lines of the "policy" committee proposed at the opening of the session. Mr. Bolling did not become a member. A leading Democrat in the House observed to me that the members of this committee, including James Davis of Georgia, William Colmer of Mississippi, Paul Kitchin of North Carolina, Clarence Cannon of Missouri, were likely, if anything, to be *less* liberal than the leadership they were supposed to advise. This was an outcome exactly opposite to the one envisaged by proponents of the policy committee idea.

56. For the story at various stages, see Robert C. Albright, "Drive is Begun for Democratic Steering Group," *Washington Post* (December 30, 1961); Mary McGrory, "McCormack Silent on Liberals Plan," *Washington Star* (December 31, 1961); Robert K. Walsh, "Party Harmony Setup Seen by House Liberals," *Washington Star* (January 5, 1962); Richard L. Lyons, "Liberal Democrats Defer Demands," *Washington Post* (January 9, 1962); Rowland Evans, Jr., "Democrats Unanimous," *New York Herald Tribune,* (January 10, 1962).

sometimes inspires no sharp cleavages of opinion, because interest groups are often disinterested and inattentive. But when an issue heats up and reaches the final stages of the legislative process, leeway dissipates. Interest groups become active. The mail begins to pour in.[57] Newsmen appear on the scene. Congressmen stick close to the floor, listen to debate, mill around, stand ready to answer quorum calls or to vote on amendments.

There are four procedures for voting in the House: voices, standing, tellers, and roll call, in the order in which they expose members to public view. In the Committee on the Whole House, only the first three types of votes are taken. A diligent reporter or lobbyist can, however, even without benefit of a roll call, usually find out how a given member votes. The procedure is not foolproof, but, from the gallery, an outsider can always keep his eye fixed on one or a few congressmen whose votes are of interest to him. Corroboration, if any is needed, can be obtained by asking around among other congressmen.

The caucus at which voting for majority leader was to have taken place provided no such opportunities for outside surveillance. No spectators were admitted. Congressmen were even protected from the scrutiny of their colleagues; Representative Francis Walter, chairman of the caucus, sent word that the balloting for majority leader, when the time came, would be secret. The rules of the caucus say nothing about a secret ballot; rather, general parliamentary law governs the caucus meetings, and there is a special provision that "the yeas and nays on any question shall, at the desire of one-fifth of those present, be entered on the journal"—all of which did not alter the fact that the balloting would be secret.

In spite of the interest which Mr. Bolling had stirred up among outside groups, these groups were operating under an insuperable handicap. The voting procedure maximized the chances that a congressman cross-pressured between the demands of "local agency" and his own personal feelings could vote his private preferences with impunity.

VII

What does this case suggest about the general relations between inside and outside influences in the decision-making processes of

---

57. Lewis Dexter makes the point that the mail usually comes too late to affect the substance of legislation. However mail is used here only as an index of attentiveness to issues on the part of publics. See Dexter, "What Do Congressmen Hear," op. cit.

the House?[58] Several things. First, it shows the extent to which inside and outside strategies tend to encourage different modes of communication among members and to evoke different definitions of the decision-making situation. The inside strategy is likely to define situations as "family matters," and to feature face-to-face interaction among members. The outside strategy is likely to evoke a more ideological, issue-oriented definition of the situation. Interaction among members is more likely to take place through third persons, lobbyists, and the press. Second, this case suggests conditions tending to promote the success of each strategy of influence. Inside strategies are favored when: (1) the matter to be decided can be rationalized as in some sense procedural rather than substantive; (2) there are great differences in the inside strengths of the two sides, but their outside strengths approach equality; and (3) members are protected from surveillance by outsiders. Outside strategies are favored, presumably, when these conditions are reversed.

Additional conditions bearing on the effectiveness of inside and outside strategies may be imagined. Presumably, the autonomy of a representative from constituent pressures diminishes as his constituency approaches unanimity in its preferences or as the intensity of preference for a given alternative by any substantial portion of his constituency increases. We know that few decisions before Congress are likely to unite constituencies in this way or to inflame their passions to such a great extent. In addition, Congress takes routine steps to insulate its decision-making from certain kinds of outside influences.

One such device is the consideration of business in the Committee of the Whole, where substantial revisions of legislation can be made on the floor without binding congressmen to a record vote. The committees—whose composition and behavior sometimes reflect outside interests[59] and sometimes inside distributions of influence[60]—mark up

58. Obviously, no real-world case will fit a typology perfectly. It may be well to remind the reader that the predominant strategies of the major actors were as I have indicated, but that Mr. Albert had some support from outside the House (such as from Senators Kerr and Monroney and Governor Edmondson of Oklahoma), and many of Bolling's supporters within the House backed him for reasons other than outside "pressures" which he might have been able to bring to bear on them. These included some members from the South whose position on civil rights was more accurately reflected by Mr. Albert.

59. As for example, the Agriculture Committee. See Charles O. Jones, "Representation in Congress: The Case of the House Agriculture Committee," *American Political Science Review* 55 (June, 1961):358–67 [reprinted as Chapter VIII of the present volume].

60. There are numerous examples of this—e.g., the operation of the seniority system. See George Goodwin, "The Seniority System in Congress," *American Political Science Review* 53 (June 1959):412–36. On the influence of state delegations on committee assignments and the force of tradition in determining the

bills and vote on them in executive sessions only. A third device favoring inside distributions of influence in the House is the Rules Committee. One of the prerequisites for appointment to service on this committee is ability to "take the heat" and resist constituency pressures to report out bills which the House leadership wants killed.[61]

The enumeration of these devices hints at some of the problems facing two significant groups of outsiders: presidents of the United States and political scientists. The president has a never ending battle of converting decisions in the House choices from inside ones to outside ones. Most of his attempts to influence decisions are direct, but his efforts to dramatize issues before relevant publics may also be interpreted as attempts to activate interest groups and unify constituencies so as to make the employment of inside strategies of influence in the House difficult.

For political scientists, the lesson is clear. In order to understand the context within which decisions in the House are being made sufficiently well so that we can identify the goals in terms of which outcomes may be seen as "rational," it will be necessary to study the House at close range. On the whole, political scientists have taken a somewhat Olympian view of congressional behavior. We have tended to organize our conceptions of rationality and legitimacy around presidential goals and presidential party platforms.[62] This has operated to obscure the constraints on the behavior of those in the House who share the policy preferences these political theories imply. It has also, I think, bred a kind of impatience with the study of strategies and tactics of House decision-making, which study, I believe, is a necessary step in understanding why the House operates as it does.

---

allocation of seats, see in general, Nicholas Masters, "Committee Assignments in the House of Representatives," *American Political Science Review* 55 (June, 1961):345–57.

61. On the Rules Committee, see Robert L. Peabody, "The Enlarged Rules Committee," [in Peabody and Polsby, *New Perspectives*, 1st ed., op. cit., ch. 6, pp. 129–64], and the following articles by James A. Robinson, "Organizational and Constituency Backgrounds of the House Rules Committee" in Joseph R. Fiszman (ed.), *The American Political Arena* (Boston: Little, Brown, 1962); "The Role of the Rules Committee in Regulating Debate in the U.S. House of Representatives," *Midwest Journal of Political Science* 5 (February, 1961), 59–69; "Decision-making in the House Rules Committee," *Administrative Science Quarterly* 3 (June, 1958): 73–86; "The Role of the Rules Committee in Arranging the Program of the U.S. House of Representatives," *Western Political Quarterly* 12 (September, 1959): 653–69.

62. This comment may be anachronistic, judging from much of the recent work on the House. It agrees with Ralph K. Huitt's similar judgment in "Democratic Party Leadership in the Senate," *American Political Science Review* 55 (June, 1961): 333 f.

13

Party Leadership Change
In the United States
House of Representatives

Robert L. Peabody

Long periods of one-party domination, increased average tenure in office for representatives, and the institutionalization of patterns of succession to the Speakership have all contributed to a tendency toward leadership stability in the twentieth-century House of Representatives. The elections of Sam Rayburn (D., Tex.) and John McCormack (D., Mass.) to the offices of Speaker and majority leader in 1940, of Joseph Martin (R., Mass.) to the office of minority leader in 1939, and of Leslie Arends (R., Ill.) to the position of Republican whip in 1943, mark the beginnings of the longest tenures in these four positions for any incumbents in the history of Congress.[1] When changes

Reprinted from *American Political Science Review* 61: 3 (1967). Copyright © 1967 by the American Political Science Association. The themes of this article are elaborated and extended in Peabody, *Leadership in Congress: Stability, Succession and Change* (Boston: Little, Brown, 1976).

This article was stimulated by an opportunity to study the 1965 Ford-Halleck minority leadership contest at first hand. The resulting case study led to speculation on the general problem of leadership change in the House of Representatives. I would like to acknowledge my indebtedness to numerous readers of earlier drafts, especially James D. Barber, Milton C. Cummings, Jr., Richard F. Fenno, Jr., Ralph K. Huitt, Charles O. Jones, Nelson W. Polsby, Randall B. Ripley, and Francis E. Rourke. Financial assistance was provided by grants from the Social Science Research Council Committee on Political Behavior and the Johns Hopkins University Committee on Public Affairs.

1. George B. Galloway, *History of the House of Representatives* (New York, 1962), pp. 287–92; Randall B. Ripley, "The Party Whip Organizations in the United States House of Representatives," *American Political Science Review* 58 (September, 1964): 563.

in top leadership occur—as with the overthrow of Minority Leader Charles A. Halleck by Republican Representative Gerald R. Ford, Jr., in 1965, or the succession of Majority Leader McCormack to the office of the Speaker in 1962 following the death of Rayburn—the consequences are considerable. In the case of revolt, individual careers are made and broken. The organization and policy orientations of a congressional party may be extensively altered. While orderly succession has less dramatic impact, it too has a significant effect on "who gets what, when, and how." Some members move closer to the seats of power and others fall out of favor. Key committee assignments, and hence the development of entire legislative careers, are likely to ride or fall on the outcomes. A congressional party's philosophical approach, the kinds of legislation it promotes, its strategies of implementation, all hinge to a considerable degree on the individual personalities, political backgrounds, and state and regional outlooks of its principal leaders. Only the contest for the control of the White House and the occasional elections which convert one party from a minority into a majority within Congress are likely to have a more significant consequence for party fortunes.

Despite its acknowledged importance, our overall understanding of the workings of congressional party leadership is rudimentary.[2] The day-to-day observations of newspaper reporters provide some insights, but journalists seldom generalize about their impressions.[3] With increasing frequency political scientists can profit from the writings of more analytically oriented congressmen.[4] Unfortunately, good biographies on House members are relatively rare compared with presidential, judicial, or even senatorial biography.[5] Most full-length

2. As David B. Truman observed in 1959: "Everyone knows something of leaders and leadership of various sorts, but no one knows very much. Leadership, especially in the political realm, unavoidably or by design often is suffused by an atmosphere of the mystic and the magical, and these mysteries have been little penetrated by systematic observation." *The Congressional Party* (New York, 1959), p. 94.

3. The most notable exceptions in recent years are William S. White, *Citadel: The Story of the U. S. Senate* (New York, 1956), and Neil MacNeil, *Forge of Democracy: The House of Representatives* (New York, 1963). A masterpiece from the past is Ben Perley Poore, *Pereley's Reminiscences of Sixty Years in the National Metropolis*, 2 vols. (Philadelphia: 1886).

4. Two of the best examples are Clem Miller, *Member of the House* (New York, 1962) and Richard Bolling, *House Out of Order* (New York, 1965).

5. Treatment of Speakers seems to be an exception. See, for example, James A. Barnes, *John G. Carlisle* (New York, 1931): James G. Blaine, *Twenty Years of Congress, from Lincoln to Garfield*, 2 vols. (Norwich, Conn., 1884); Samuel W. McCall, *The Life of Thomas B. Reed* (Cambridge, 1919); William A. Robinson, *Thomas B. Reed, Parliamentarian* (New York, 1930); L. White Busbey, *Uncle Joe Cannon* (New York, 1927); Champ Clark, *My Quarter Century of*

studies of party leadership have long been outdated.[6] Only within the past decade have political scientists begun to set forth propositions about congressional leadership developed from intensive field research.[7]

Much less is known about change in leadership. Newspaper accounts of all but the most recent contests are likely to be fragmentary and superficial. Biographies rarely describe leadership contests in any detail and usually these accounts are anecdotal and one-sided. Only two studies exist of contests analyzed in depth by political scientists on the scene.[8] Lack of knowledge about types, the conditions which promote one type rather than another, and the consequences of leadership change are further complicated by the hazards of generalizing from what must inevitably be a limited number of cases. Yet, research on congressional leadership must move in the direction of generalization over a series of Congresses if a theory of party leadership and its consequences for the legislative process is to be developed.

American Politics (New York, 1920); and Bascom N. Timmons, *Garner of Texas* (New York, 1948). A forthcoming political biography of the late Speaker Rayburn by his staff assistant, D. B. Hardeman, should correct the shortcomings of the only full-length existing biography, C. Dwight Dorough, *Mr. Sam* (New York, 1962), which tells us almost nothing about Rayburn, the legislative leader.

6. Chang-wei Chiu, *The Speaker of the House of Representatives Since 1896* (New York, 1927). This Columbia doctoral dissertation builds on a much better Radcliffe thesis first published in 1896: Mary Parker Follett, *The Speaker of the House of Representatives* (New York, 1909). Among the more useful older studies on party leadership, see DeAlva S. Alexander, *History and Procedure of the House of Representatives* (Boston, 1916); George R. Brown, *The Leadership of Congress* (Indianapolis, 1922); and Paul D. Hasbrouck, *Party Government in the House of Representatives* (New York, 1927).

7. See, for example, Truman, op. cit.; Donald R. Matthews, *U.S. Senators and Their World* (Chapel Hill, 1960); Ralph K. Huitt, "Democratic Party Leadership in the Senate," *American Political Science Review* 55 (June, 1961): 333–44; Nelson W. Polsby, "Two Strategies of Influence: Choosing a Majority Leader, 1962," in Robert L. Peabody and Nelson W. Polsby (eds.), *New Perspectives on the House of Representatives* (Chicago, 1963) [Chapter 12 in this volume]; James A. Robinson, *The House Rules Committee* (Indianapolis, 1963); Randall B. Ripley, "The Party Whip Organizations in the United States House of Representatives," op. cit., 561–76; Lewis A. Froman and Randall B. Ripley, "Conditions for Party Leadership: The Case of the House Democrats," *American Political Science Review* 59 (March, 1965):52–63; and Charles O. Jones, *Party and Policy-Making: The House Republican Policy Committee* (New Brunswick, 1964).

8. The analysis which follows is dependent upon Nelson W. Polsby's study of the Albert-Bolling contest, "Two Strategies of Influence: Choosing a Majority Leader, 1962," op. cit; and Robert L. Peabody, "The Ford-Halleck Minority Leadership Contest, 1965," Eagleton Institute Cases in Practical Politics (New York, 1966), No. 40. The latter study is based on eighty-five interviews with over forty Republican representatives and staff members during and immediately following the several contests which preoccupied House Republicans from early December, 1964, through February, 1965.

This article begins by outlining a scheme for classifying types of intraparty leadership change in legislatures. This scheme is illustrated with nineteen cases of change or attempted change taking place in the United States House of Representatives in the Eighty-fourth to Eighty-ninth Congresses (1955–1966). After noting the rather striking differences in the degree to which the Republican minority resorts to contested change as compared with relatively peaceful patterns of leadership succession in the Democratic majority, some of the conditions which seem to facilitate one type of change rather than another are discussed. Finally, some of the consequences of leadership change for individual careers, legislation, party fortunes, and the representative process are suggested.

I. Types of Intraparty Leadership Change

Change in party leadership in legislatures comes about in three principal ways. *Interparty turnover,* the replacement of one party's set of leaders by those of another party, occurs when the results of national elections convert a minority into a majority. Such changed is relatively rare. For example, in the United States House of Representatives, party control has switched but twenty-four times in the ninety Congresses elected every two years since 1788.[9] This article focuses upon a more common type, *intraparty change,* or the replacement of one or more incumbents within a party hierarchy by other members of the same party. A third type, *institutional reform,* is characterized not by the replacement of leaders but by alterations in party organization or the rules of a legislature which modify the powers of an existing office or create a new position. In the absence of interparty turnover and as an alternative to institutional reform, legislators frequently turn to intraparty change, both as a means of fulfilling vacancies and as a device to promote leadership more favorable to their own interests.

Three variables have been selected as a means of classifying types of intraparty leadership change: (1) whether or not a vacancy exists in a leadership position, (2) the presence or absence of an established pattern of succession, and (3) the extent to which the change is contested. When dichotomized these variables lead to a six-fold classification scheme as outlined in Table 13–1. The first variable is discrete: either a vacancy exists in a given position such as the Speakership, or

9. U.S. Bureau of the Census, *Historical Statistics of the United States, Colonial Times to 1957* (Washington, D. C., 1960), pp. 691–92.

Table 13-1. Types of Intraparty Leadership Change

	No Contest	Contest
No Vacancy	Status quo	(5) Revolt or its aftermath
Vacancy		
Established pattern of succession	(1) Routine advancement	(4) Challenge to the heir apparent
No established pattern of succession	(2) Appointment or emergence of a consensus choice	(3) Open competition

it does not. The vacancy may come about for a variety of reasons, including death, resignation, retirement, or election defeat. The remaining two variables are not as easily dichotomized. Patterns of succession may be quite firmly established, as with elevation from the minority or majority leader to the office of Speaker in the House of Representatives. Other patterns, such as succession to the majority leader from the position of party whip, are only tentative and emerging. The final variable, the extent to which a given change is contested, is even more difficult to define in operational terms. For purposes of this analysis, a "contest" takes place when two or more legislators announce their candidacies and work actively to align support. For simplicity of classification the "contest—no contest" variable has been dichotomized, although as with most variables in the social sciences it is continuous rather than discrete.[10] That is to say, there are a number of finer gradations along a continuum which a more fully developed scheme would have to take into account. For example, the "no contest" classification may include situations where a contest is considered but abandoned short of announcement because the dissident party faction decides it does not have the necessary votes to make a successful challenge.[11] Contests may range from (a) situations in which two or more candidates announce but all but one withdraw before the final

10. For discussion of this problem in the determination of causality, see Hubert M. Blalock, Jr., *Causal Inferences in Nonexperimental Research* (Chapel Hill, 1964), pp. 32–33.

11. The attention of journalists and political scientists is naturally drawn to instances of organized revolt. For newspapermen, it is conflict, of course, which makes news. But political scientists need to explore situations where the threatened change does not get beyond the discussion stage, as for example, threats to replace Thomas Kuchel, the incumbent minority whip in the United States Senate, at the opening of the Eighty-ninth Congress, and disgruntlement with Speaker McCormack's leadership at the beginning of the Ninetieth Congress.

vote; to (*b*) controversies which force concessions, although the leaders survive; or (*c*) instances of successful revolt.[12]

These distinctions will become more meaningful after discussion and illustration of the types of intraparty leadership change suggested by this classification scheme: (1) routine advancement, (2) appointment or emergence of a consensus choice, (3) open competition, (4) challenge to the heir apparent, and (5) revolt or its aftermath.

These types are ordered in terms of the amount of credit expenditure (time, energy, number of members involved, and so on) which each is likely to engender.[13] Routine advancement involves little or no expenditure of resources. Dissident members may invest some time conducting an informal poll of the membership to see if a contest has any chance of succeeding. Typically, no commitments are sought, and the campaign is never launched for lack of a single candidate which all opposing factions can rally behind. The second and third types usually involve lower party positions where the stakes are not as high. Leadership appointments may be challenged in a party conference or caucus, but at some cost. If no consensus choice emerges, several candidates may run. Friends, committtee associates, and state or regional delegations may be brought in on either side. When the party position is important for the resources it controls, such as the campaign committee chairmanship, or because it is seen as a stepping stone to higher office, then more members are recruited to work actively in behalf of the candidates. If the contest goes to a formal vote, the pressures to align uncommitted members become intense. The greatest credit expenditures are likely to occur in challenges to an heir apparent, or contests which attempt to remove incumbent party leaders. Revolts may end up involving the full time and energy of as many as a third of the party membership over periods of several weeks or longer.

The upper left-hand cell of Table 13–1 or the status quo is, of course,

12. In the Republican Party (*a*) is illustrated by the Miller-McCulloch contest of 1960; (*b*) by the unsuccessful challenge against Minority Whip Arends in 1965 as well as the famed "revolt" against Speaker Cannon in 1910; and (*c*) by the minority leadership contests of 1959 and 1965.

13. For general discussion of a theory of social exchange, see Talcott Parsons, "On the Concept of Influence," [and] James S. Coleman, "Comment on 'On the Concept of Influence,'" *Public Opinion Quarterly* 27 (Spring, 1963):37–62, 63–82; George C. Homans, "Social Behavior as Exchange," *American Journal of Sociology* 63 (1958), 597–606; and Peter M. Blau, *Exchange and Power in Social Life* (New York, 1964). For more specific applications of exchange theory to legislatures, see Robert L. Peabody, "Organization Theory and Legislative Behavior: Bargaining, Hierarchy, and Change in the U. S. House of Representatives" (paper delivered before the American Political Science Association, New York City, September 7, 1963); James S. Coleman, "Collective Decisions," *Sociological Inquiry* (Spring, 1964):166–81; and James D. Barber, "Leadership Strategies for Legislative Party Cohesion," *Journal of Politics* 28 (May, 1966):347–67.

the routine situation. No vacancy in a leadership position exists and no contest takes place. Continuity in office is the general practice in the House of Representatives, as in most organizations. For example, Representative Joseph Martin, Jr., of Massachusetts was first elected to Congress in 1924. He became Republican minority leader in 1939. He was reelected minority leader seven times and Speaker twice before the one instance of his defeat in 1959 by his former majority leader in the Eightieth and Eighty-third Congresses, Charles Halleck of Indiana. Halleck was twice reelected minority leader before his overthrow by Ford in 1965. Republican whip Leslie Arends, first elected whip in 1943, has maintained his position under three different minority leaders: Martin, Halleck, and Ford.

The late Speaker Sam Rayburn of Texas first elected to Congress in 1912. He became chairman of the Interstate and Foreign Commerce Committee in 1931. In 1934 he briefly challenged Joseph W. Byrns of Tennessee, the incumbent majority leader, for the nomination for Speaker. However, Rayburn withdrew from the race before a vote in the Democratic caucus. Rayburn went on to defeat Rules Committee Chairman John J. O'Connor of New York in a contest for majority leader in 1937. He was elevated to the Speakership in 1940. His occupancy of the top Democratic House position during the next twenty-one years was never challenged.

The ability of incumbents to retain office is not difficult to explain. Party leaders, particularly Speakers, have multiple opportunities to grant favors, create obligations, and build credit, all of which they can use to maintain a network of continuing support. A Speaker or floor leader has available, in addition, a number of sanctions, including the withholding of patronage and the vetoing of committee assignments, the threat of which can act as strong deterrents on contested change. In addition, there are a number of benefits to be gained from continuity of party leadership, not the least of which is experienced floor management. Contests, and particularly revolts against incumbent leadership, are likely to generate high costs in terms of subsequent party harmony. For all these reasons, the predominant pattern in congressional parties is the retention of incumbents rather than frequent leadership turnover.

II. Frequency of Change

Evidence of the frequency of change in five major party-wide positions in both the Democratic and Republican parties for a twelve-year period, 1955 to 1966, is presented in Tables 13–2 and 13–3. This period was selected because it encompasses the six complete Con-

Table 13–2. Democratic (Majority) Party Leaders, House of Representatives, 1955–1966

Congress	Speaker	Majority Leader	Majority Whip	Caucus Chairman	Congressional (Campaign) Comm. Chairman
84th: 1955 1956	Sam Rayburn,[a] (Tex.)	John McCormack,[b] (Mass.)	Carl Albert, (Okla.)	John Rooney, (N.Y.)	Michael Kirwan,[c] (Oh.)
85th: 1957 1958	Rayburn	McCormack	Albert	Melvin Price, (Ill.)	Kirwan
86th: 1959 1960	Rayburn	McCormack	Albert	Price	Kirwan
87th: 1961 1962	Rayburn McCormack	McCormack Albert	Albert Hale Boggs, (La.)	Francis Walter, (Pa.)	Kirwan
88th: 1963 1964	McCormack	Albert	Boggs	Walter Albert Thomas, (Tex.)	Kirwan
89th: 1965 1966	McCormack	Albert	Boggs	Eugene Keogh, (N.Y.)	Kirwan

Sources: George Galloway, *History of the House of Representatives* (New York: Crowell, 1961); Randall B. Ripley, "The Party Whip Organizations in the United States House of Representatives," *American Political Science Review* 58 (September, 1964); 561-76; *Biographical Directory of the American Congress, 1774-1961; Congressional Record; Congressional Quarterly Almanacs;* Michael J. Kirwan, *How to Succeed in Politics* (New York, 1964, p. 9.
[a] Rayburn was first elected Speaker in the 76th Congress on September 16, 1940.
[b] McCormack was first elected majority leader in the 76th Congress on September 25, 1940.
[c] Kirwan was first elected chairman of the Democratic National Congressional (Campaign) Committee midway in the 80th Congress (1948).

gresses since the last election bringing about interparty change in the organization of the House, the midterm election of 1954.[14]

14. Only one instance of leadership change took place at the opening of the Ninetieth Congress in January, 1967. Representative Dan Rostenkowski of Chicago was elected chairman of the Democratic caucus, replacing Eugene Keogh of New York, who had retired at the end of the Eighty-ninth Congress. All other incumbent leaders, Democrats and Republicans, were reelected to the positions they held in the previous Congress. In addition, House Republicans converted the chairmanship of their Committee on Planning and Research from an appointive to an elective position.

Table 13–3. Republican (Minority) Party Leaders House of Representatives, 1955–1966

Congress	Minority Leader	Whip	Policy Comm. Chairman	Conference Chairman	Congressional (Campaign) Comm. Chairman
84th: 1955 1956	Joseph Martin,[a] (Mass.)	Leslie Arends,[b] (Ill.)	Joseph Martin,[c] (Mass.)	Clifford Hope,[d] (Kan.)	Richard Simpson,[e] (Pa.)
85th: 1957 1958	Martin	Arends	Martin	Charles Hoeven, (Iowa)	Simpson
86th: 1959 1960	Charles Halleck, (Ind.)	Arends	John Byrnes, (Wisc.)	Hoeven	Simpson William Miller, (N.Y.)
87th: 1961 1962	Halleck	Arends	Byrnes	Hoeven	Bob Wilson,[f] (Calif.)
88th: 1963 1964	Halleck	Arends	Byrnes	Gerald Ford, (Mich.)	Wilson
89th: 1965 1966	Gerald Ford, (Mich.)	Arends	John Rhodes, (Ariz.)	Melvin Laird, (Wisc.)	Wilson

Sources: George Galloway, *History of the House of Representatives* (New York: Crowell, 1961); Randall B. Ripley, "The Party Whip Organizations in the United States House of Representatives," *American Political Science Review* 58 (September, 1964): 561-76; *Biographical Directory of the American Congress, 1774-1961; Congressional Records; Congressional Quarterly Almanacs;* Charles O. Jones, *The Republican Party in American Politics* (New York, 1965).

[a] Martin was first elected Minority Leader at the opening of the 76th Congress, January 3, 1939.

[b] Arends was first elected Minority Whip midway in the 78th Congress (1943).

[c] Martin served as both Minority Leader and Policy Committee Chairman from 1949 until 1959.

[d] Hope served as Conference Chairman from the 82nd Congress until his retirement at the end of the 84th Congress (1951-1956).

[e] Simpson served as Chairman of the Republican Congressional (Campaign) Committee from 1953 until his death on January 1, 1960. He was succeeded by Miller in late January, 1960.

[f] Wilson was elected Chairman of the Republican Congressional (Campaign) Committee on June 29, 1961 following Miller's selection as National Chairman of the Republican Party.

For the Democratic party, the majority party in the House of Representatives throughout this period, the five major party-wide leadership positions are the Speaker, the majority leader, the majority whip, the chairman of the Democratic caucus, and the chairman of the

Democratic National Congressional (Campaign) Committee.[15] With the exception of the whip, all of these positions are elective. The Democratic whip is appointed by the majority leader in consultation with the Speaker. Nominations to lesser party positions are largely controlled by the Speaker and majority leader, but their choice must be ratified by the Democratic caucus, composed of all Democratic House members. Table 13–2 lists the incumbents for these five positions since 1955.

For the Republican party, the minority party throughout this period, the five major party positions are minority leader, minority whip, chairman of the Republican conference, chairman of the Republican Policy Committee, and chairman of the Republican Congressional (Campaign) Committee. All of these positions are elective in the sense that the nominees must ultimately be approved by the Republican conference, counterpart to the Democratic caucus. For two offices during most of this period the selection process has been made by separate committees. From 1919 until 1963 the choice of the Republican whip was formally made by the Republican Committee on Committees, acting on the recommendation of the Speaker or minority leader. In 1965 the Republican whip was directly elected by the Republican conference. The chairman of the Republican Congressional Committee, the counterpart to the Democratic National Congressional Committee, is elected by that committee. As with the Republican Committee on Committees, each state with Republican members is entitled to one Representative with as many votes as there are Republican House members in his state delegation. Table 13–3 lists the incumbents for these five Republican leadership positions for the Eighty-fourth to Eighty-ninth Congresses.

As Tables 13–2 and 13–3 suggest, the prevailing practice is continuity in office rather than leadership change. At first glance, Republicans are no more susceptible to change than Democrats. Of the thirty changes in each party which could be hypothetically expected (a change in each position with each Congress) each party has made but nine.[16] It should be noted, however, that five of the nine Demo-

15. A sixth leadership position, chairman of the Democratic Steering Committee, has been omitted from consideration. This committee, the counterpart to the Republican Policy Committee, was largely dormant throughout this period. Reactivated briefly in 1962 and again in 1965, its chairman is thirteen-term Representative Ray Madden of Indiana, senior administration supporter on the Committee on Rules.

16. For the Democrats these nine changes consist of the choice of McCormack for Speaker in 1962; Albert for majority leader in 1962; Albert and Boggs for whip in 1955 and 1962; and the five choices for chairman of the Democratic caucus (see Table 13–2). The nine Republican changes in leadership would in-

cratic cases are accounted for by the practice of rotating the largely honorary position of caucus chairman among senior Democrats who have not yet become chairman of standing committees. As will become more apparent, the way in which change comes about has far more important consequences than the number of changes per se.

III. Leadership Change, Eighty-fourth to Eighty-ninth Congresses

The utility of a classification scheme is demonstrated both by its ability to order phenomena as well as the fruitfulness of the hypotheses it generates. Before suggesting why one party resorts to conflict as a means of change more frequently than the other party, each of the five types of intraparty leadership change needs further elaboration. Four of the five types are illustrated by nineteen cases of change or attempted change which took place during the Eighty-fourth to Eighty-ninth Congresses (Table 13–4). Two earlier contests for the nomination for Speaker within the Republican party in 1919 and 1931 provide more clearcut cases of the remaining type, challenge to an heir apparent.

(1) Routine Advancement

This first type of intraparty leadership change takes place when a vacancy occurs in a top leadership position, a clear pattern of succession exists, and the next-ranking member in the party hierarchy is elevated without challenge. One index of the increasing institutionalization of the House has been the development of patterns of succession to top leadership. Eleven of the twelve Speakers in the twentieth century have been elevated from either the majority leadership or from the minority leadership following congressional election victories. The one exception to this established pattern was Gillett's defeat of Minority Leader Mann for the Republican nomination for Speaker after Republicans regained control of the House in 1919.

McCormack's succession to the Speakership in January, 1962, following the death of Rayburn, illustrates the prevailing practice of

---

clude the selections of Halleck and Ford for minority leader in 1959 and 1965; Byrnes and Rhodes for Policy Committee chairman in 1959 and 1965; Hoeven, Ford, and Laird for chairman of the Republican conference in 1957, 1963, and 1965; and Miller and Wilson for chairman of the Campaign Committee in 1960 and 1961 (see Table 13–3). In the following section one further case is added, the unsuccessful attempt to remove Arends as Minority whip in 1965.

Table 13-4. Types of Intraparty Leadership Change, House of Representatives, 84th–89th Congresses (1955–1966)

	No Contest		Contest[a]	
	Democratic Majority	Republican Minority	Democratic Majority	Republican Minority
NO VACANCY	Status quo		(5) Revolt or its aftermath	Minority Leader Halleck vs. Martin, 1959; Ford vs. Halleck, 1965; Conference Chairman Ford vs. Hoeven, 1963; Minority Whip Arends vs. Frelinghuysen, 1965[b]
VACANCY Established pattern of succession	(1) Routine advancement Floor leader to Speaker McCormack, 1962		(4) Challenge to heir apparent	
No established pattern of succession	(2) Appointment or emergence of a consensus choice Majority Whip Albert, 1955; Boggs, 1962; Caucus Chairman Rooney, 1955; Price, 1957; Walter, 1961; Thomas, 1964; Keogh, 1965	Conference Chairman Hoeven, 1957; Policy Comm. Chairman Byrnes, 1959; Rhodes, 1965	(3) Open competition Majority Leader Albert vs. Bolling, 1962	Conference Chairman Laird vs. Frelinghuysen, 1965; Congressional (Campaign) Comm. Chairman Miller vs. McCulloch, 1960; Wilson vs. McCulloch, 1961
Total number of changes	8	3	1	7

a In cases of contest, the winning candidate is listed first.
b Strictly speaking, the Arends-Frelinghuysen contest is not an illustration of a change in leadership since the incumbent whip Arends withstood the challenge.

routine advancement. Rayburn and McCormack had served together in the principal Democratic leadership positions in the House since September, 1940. When Speaker Bankhead of Alabama died in 1940, Majority Leader Rayburn was elevated without contest. McCormack, with White House backing, defeated Clifton Woodrum of Virginia for the office of majority leader by a vote of 141 to 67. Prior to his selection, McCormack was chairman of the Democratic caucus and fourth-ranking member on the Ways and Means Committee. His northern background, which complemented Rayburn's, was a strong factor in his election. The two men served in tandem throughout the 1940s and 1950s, dropping down to minority leader and minority whip, respectively, during the two Republican-controlled Congresses, the Eightieth and Eighty-third.

Rayburn's health began to fail in the summer of 1961. Before he left for his home in Bonham, Texas, in late August he designated Majority Leader McCormack as Speaker pro tempore. McCormack served out the remaining month of the session in that capacity. Rayburn died on November 16, 1961.

None of McCormack's possible liabilities—his age, religion, or lack of popularity with some elements of the House, particularly Democratic Study Group members—proved serious enough to bring on a challenge. Some members feared that McCormack, at 71, was slowing down and would not provide the strong leadership necessary to get the Kennedy legislative program enacted. Others were hostile to the elevation of another Roman Catholic to a position of national leadership along with President Kennedy and Senate Majority Leader Mansfield. Although not particularly popular with northern liberals and some southern members, McCormack had the support and respect of a number of the senior oligarchs of the House, especially Carl Vinson of Georgia and Howard W. Smith of Virginia. The inability of his opponents to rally around one of the several possible candidates and the hands off policy adopted by President Kennedy and his White House assistants made McCormack's election inevitable. On January 10, 1962, he became the forty-fifth Speaker of the House.

(2) Appointment or Emergence of a Consensus Choice

This second type of change is illustrated by a number of appointments or unchallenged elections at the lower levels of the party hierarchy where patterns of succession are not yet established. The appointments of Majority Whips Carl Albert in 1955 and Hale Boggs in 1962 are illustrative. When the Democrats regained control of the

House in the Eighty-fourth Congress (1955–1956), a vacancy had been created in the whip position by Tennessee Representative Percy Priest's elevation to the chairmanship of the Committee on Interstate and Foreign Commerce. Albert, who was beginning his fifth term, had come to Rayburn's attention as the representative of the Oklahoma district adjacent to Rayburn's own Texas district and through parliamentary skills displayed in floor debate. At the same time that Rayburn and McCormack were appointing Albert as majority whip they created a new position of deputy whip for another talented young representative, Hale Boggs of Louisiana. In January, 1962, after Albert was elected majority leader, he appointed Boggs as majority whip. John Moss of California advanced from a regional whip position to deputy whip at the same time.

The selection of the chairmen of the Democratic caucus for these six Congresses also illustrates this second type. Since the principal responsibility of this party official is to preside over the party caucus at the opening of each session of Congress, a caucus which seldom meets again, the position is primarily honorary. By tradition, incumbents serve for one or at the most two terms. They are nominated by the leadership and selected from a pool of loyal senior members who are not yet chairmen of standing committees.

Until 1963, the chairman of the Republican conference was also an honorary title with few duties beyond presiding over infrequent meetings of House Republicans. Unlike the Democrats, the Republicans have not rotated the position. Thus, Clifford Hope of Kansas served in this capacity from 1951 until his retirement in 1956. Charles Hoeven of Iowa, first selected in 1957, served until his defeat by Gerald Ford at the opening of the Eighty-eighth Congress. Since Ford's election in 1963, and particularly since Melvin Laird's election in 1965, the responsibility of the Republican conference chairman has undergone considerable reorganization and upgrading.

Two uncontested choices for chairman of the Republican Policy Committee also illustrate emergence of a consensus choice. In response to the disastrous 1948 election, Republicans seeking to improve their organizational structure converted a defunct steering committee into a policy committee. Little was made of it, however. Republican Minority Leader Martin served as chairman of a largely inoperative committee for the next ten years. In 1959, following Charles Halleck's overthrow of Martin, the chairmanship was given independent status. John W. Byrnes of Wisconsin, the most senior available member save for Halleck among several members considered as possible challengers to Martin, was elected without opposition.

The selection of John Rhodes of Arizona as Byrnes's successor in 1965 is a less clearcut case of a consensus choice. Byrnes resigned from the chairmanship of the Republican Policy Committee in late January, 1965, in order to devote his full time to serving as ranking minority member of the Ways and Means Committee. With Byrnes's endorsement, the Republican conference adopted a resolution on January 14, 1965, which prohibits its five principal party leaders from serving as chairman or ranking minority member on standing committees. Byrnes's intention to resign had cleared the way for another Wisconsin Republican, Melvin Laird, to be elected chairman of the Republican conference. The selection of Rhodes was not challenged, even though he was not the new Minority Leader Ford's first choice. Rhodes, first elected to Congress in 1952, had served as chairman of the Policy Committee's subcommittee on special projects since 1961. A friend of Ford's, he had nevertheless backed Halleck in the 1965 contest against Ford. After Rhodes announced his candidacy, Ford considered putting up a candidate of his own choice, but because of the potential costs to his own prestige and to party harmony, he decided to avoid a direct confrontation. With the support of Laird and Arends, he created a separate Committee on Planning and Research to coordinate the task forces. Ford's first choice to head the Republican Policy Committee had been four-term Representative Charles Goodell of New York. Goodell, comanager of Ford's successful challenge to Halleck, was appointed chairman of the newly created Committee on Planning and Research. His appointment was confirmed on February 23, 1965, the same day that Rhodes was unanimously elected chairman of a restructured Republican Policy Committee.

(3) Open Competition

When a vacancy occurs in a party leadership position which is not appointive and where no pattern of succession has been established, open competition between two or more candidates may take place. The two contests for chairmanship of the Republican Congressional (Campaign) Committee in 1960 and 1961 illustrate this type. Richard Simpson of Pennsylvania, chairman from 1953 to 1960, died on January 7, 1960. Many of the Republican members who had backed Martin against Halleck in 1959 aligned themselves behind William McCulloch of Ohio. On January 20, 1960, the Halleck forces won a further victory when their candidate, William E. Miller of New York, was elected chairman. Miller had behind-the-scenes support from Vice-President Richard M. Nixon, and was also acceptable to another prospective presidential candidate, Governor Nelson Rockefeller of New York. When Miller was elevated to chairman of the Republican National Committee in June, 1961, another nonmidwesterner, Bob Wilson of California, emerged from a field of potential candidates which included Laird of Wisconsin, Rhodes of Arizona, and Ford of Michigan in addition to McCulloch. While the selection of Miller and Wilson cannot be divorced from prior House contests and political maneuvering on the national scene, they also reflected successful efforts to widen geographical and expand suburban representation within the House Republican leadership.

Both regional and ideological differences were at issue in another example of open competition, the contest between Laird of Wisconsin and Peter Frelinghuysen of New Jersey for chairman of the Republican conference in 1965. Ford, the chairman in the previous Congress, had announced his intention to resign regardless of the outcome of his open challenge to Minority Leader Halleck, Laird, sympathetic to Ford's candidacy, announced his own independent bid for the conference chairmanship on December 29, 1964, the week before the Eighty-ninth Congress convened. First elected to Congress in 1952, Laird had risen to fourth-ranking Republican on Appropriations and served as chairman of the Republican Platform Committee at San Francisco in 1964. His firm management of the drafting of the platform, which Goldwater and Miller later campaigned on, led to intensified criticism of Laird from eastern seaboard liberals such as John Lindsay of New York and Bradford Morse and Silvio Conte of Massachusetts. Together with some twenty House colleagues organized as the Wednesday Club, they decided to field a last-minute candidate of their own. Meeting on Sunday night before the January 4, 1965, vote, the Wednesday Club selected Frelinghuysen as their choice. He had only recently joined their group but he was one of the few members with a seniority equivalent to Laird's. Despite Frelinghuysen's late announcement he received sixty-two votes to seventy-seven cast for Laird.

Richard Bolling's abortive effort to prevent Carl Albert's advancement from Democratic whip to majority leader at the opening of the second session of the Eighty-seventh Congress in 1962 represents still another example of open competition. Following Rayburn's death in 1961, Bolling at first considered a challenge to McCormack. He finally concluded he would have a better chance to defeat Albert, although he realized that in both cases the odds were severely stacked against him. Strong support for Bolling's candidacy failed to materialize at sixty-five to seventy votes, far short of the 130 votes needed to win in the Democratic caucus. Bolling announced his withdrawal on January 3, 1962.

One week later at the opening caucus Carl Albert was unanimously elected majority leader.[17]

(4) Challenge to an Heir Apparent

This fourth type of contest takes place when a vacancy occurs through death, defeat, or retirement, but the apparent successor's claim is contested. No clearcut case took place in the House during the Eighty-fourth to Eighty-ninth Congresses. Several earlier contests in this century, the Gillett-Mann struggle over the nomination for Speakership in 1919 and the upset of former Majority Leader Tilson by Republican Rules Committee Chairman Snell in 1931 just prior to the organization of the Seventy-second Congress, are illustrative examples. The Republican party had endured minority status and the rather arbitrary rule of Minority Leader James R. Mann of Illinois, successor to Speaker Cannon, for eight years before they regained control of the House in the election of 1918. Favorable election results did not inhibit national party leaders and House opponents of Mann from putting together support within the Republican conference to win the nomination, and ultimately, the Speakership, for Frederick H. Gillett of Massachusetts. Gillett, first elected in 1892, was one of two Republicans in the House who had served longer than any other member, save for ex-Speaker Cannon. Gillett, the ranking Republican member on the Committee on Appropriations, had few personal enemies. Mann, in contrast, had antagonized many members in both parties with his relentless and caustic criticisms of legislation. In addition to his strong identification with the Cannon regime, his opponents accused him of conflict of interest in his relations with the Chicago meat packing industry. On February 27, 1919, Gillett defeated Mann by 138 votes to 69 with three other candidates receiving 18 votes.[18] Gillett served

17. This contest comes close to qualifying as the fourth type, *challenge to the heir apparent*. Excerpts from the interviews reported in Polsby's detailed study of this contest clearly reveal the extent to which members perceived Albert as "'entitled' to the job by virtue of his six years' service in the leadership hierarchy of the House," op, cit., p. 247. But while the pattern of succession from floor leader to Speaker has been firmly established, there is only limited precedent for elevating the party whip to floor leader. Oscar Underwood of Alabama served briefly as minority whip in 1900 to 1901, but ten years intervened before he became majority floor leader in 1911. With the possible exception of John Garner of Texas, no other floor leader save for Albert had previously served as whip *prior* to his first selection as floor leader (Ripley, op. cit., p. 563, p. 564, n. 19). Albert, however, was able to capitalize on McCormack's two related experiences of serving as minority whip and then moving back up to majority leader following the Eightieth and Eighty-third Congresses. Boggs's elevation from deputy whip to whip in 1962 was further evidence of a developing pattern.

18. *New York Times* (February 28, 1919):1; Chiu, op. cit., pp. 25–27.

as a rather ineffective Speaker from 1919 to 1924, when he resigned to run for the Senate.

In 1931, Halleck's predecessor, Joseph Martin of Massachusetts, backed Bertrand H. Snell of New York in a bitter conference struggle resulting in the overthrow of Republican Speaker Nicholas Longworth's apparent successor, seventy-three year old John Q. Tilson of Connecticut.[19] Longworth had died on April 9, 1931, before the Seventy-second Congress convened. Tilson had served as Republican majority leader under Longworth since 1925, the year in which Martin was first elected to the House. This contest followed a forty-nine–seat election setback for the Republicans in 1930. The deaths of several Republican incumbents before December, 1931, allowed the Democrats to gain control of the House and frustrated Snell's ambitions to be Speaker. Snell voluntarily retired from the House in 1938. Martin, the eastern assistant whip and the Republican campaign chairman in a year in which the Republicans won back eighty seats, was elected minority leader in 1939 without any serious challenge.[20]

(5) Revolt or its Aftermath

This last type, usually the most costly in terms of the investment of resources required, takes place when: (1) no vacancy in a leadership position exists, (2) the incumbent cannot be persuaded to step aside, and (3) an intraparty contest ensues. The Halleck-Martin struggle for the minority leadership in 1959, the Ford-Hoeven fight over the chairmanship of the Republican conference in 1963, and the Ford-Halleck contest for the minority leadership in 1965 all illustrate this type of intraparty change. Ford's unsuccessful attempt to remove incumbent Minority Whip Arends represents a quite different form of revolt.

In the late 1950s, when Martin's health began to fail, a number of younger Republicans sought more vigorous party leadership. The election disaster of 1958 provided a further impetus for change. In mid-December, more than a dozen Republicans met in the office of Representative Bob Wilson of California to discuss what could be done to improve party fortunes. While they were agreed that new leadership was needed, they were divided in their choice among

19. Snell moved from 55 votes on the first ballot to a 96 to 64 lead over Tilson on the seventh ballot, but still one short of a majority. Before the eighth ballot began, Tilson moved to make the nomination unanimous. *New York Times* (December 1, 1931):1, 4; (December 8, 1931):1, 16.

20. Joe Martin, *My First Fifty Years in Politics* (as told to Robert J. Donovan) (New York, 1960), pp. 81–82.

Halleck of Indiana, Byrnes of Wisconsin, Ford of Michigan, and Simpson of Pennsylvania. In an informal poll of members, they found widespread sentiment for change, but only one active candidate, former Majority Leader Halleck. After determining that the White House would remain neutral, Halleck announced his candidacy. On the eve of the vote, his backers estimated they had more than eigthy votes of the 154 Republican representatives-elect. Martin, like Halleck six years later, did not take the challenge seriously until it was too late.

At the afternoon conference on Tuesday, January 6, 1959, the Martin forces led by Richard Simpson of Pennsylvania, Leo Allen and Leslie Arends of Illinois, and Clarence Brown of Ohio, lost a move to avoid a secret ballot by a vote of 96 to 50. Halleck edged Martin on the first ballot by a vote of 73 to 72 with one ballot rejected as illegible. Since neither candidate received a majority another ballot was necessary. Halleck won on the second ballot by a vote of 74 to 70.[21]

The Ford-Hoeven contest of 1963 was an important precursor of the 1965 minority leadership struggle. It was initiated at the opening of the Eighty-eighth Congress by two junior members on the House Education and Labor Committee, Robert P. Griffin of Michigan (first elected in 1956) and Charles E. Goodell of New York (first elected in a special election on May 26, 1959). After considering and rejecting challenges to either Halleck or Arends, Griffin and Goodell decided to go after the Republican conference chairmanship as a further step toward revitalizing party machinery. With the active support of most of the House members elected in 1958, 1960, and 1962, and the tacit approval of many of the same activists who had promoted the Halleck upset of Martin, they launched an over-the-weekend campaign against Hoeven, the incumbent conference chairman since 1957. On January

21. The best single review of this contest is Jones, op. cit., pp. 29–38. His summary contains one questionable statement: "A poll of members showed that John W. Byrnes of Wisconsin had the most support, Gerald R. Ford, Jr., of Michigan was second, and Halleck was third." (p. 35). A more plausible interpretation is that the informal polls taken in late December and early January were too indefinite to do much more than suggest that there were several possible candidates with Halleck and Byrnes the front-runners. The insurgents discussed going with Byrnes, but found him reluctant to step out in front of Halleck, an experienced floor leader. When one of their group, former Representative Jack Westland of Washington, discussed the possibilities of a revolt with Halleck in Florida, Halleck insisted on his right as the former majority leader to make the challenge. Other contemporary accounts seem to support this interpretation. See, for example, Richard Fryklund, "Story of GOP Revolt Has Varied Chapters," *Washington Star* (January 11, 1959):A1; John L. Steele, "GOP Tactics That Toppled A Veteran Leader," *Life* (January 19, 1959); and Martin's own version, op. cit., pp. 3–19. I am indebted to Representative Bob Wilson for making available a sixty-nine-page scrapbook of clippings and other materials which he kept on this contest.

8, 1963, their candidate, the forty-nine-year-old Ford, defeated the sixty-seven-year-old Hoeven by a secret ballot vote of 86 to 78.[22]

A necessary, but not sufficient, cause of the 1965 revolt was the Republican election disaster of November, 1964. The Goldwater defeat and the net loss of thirty-eight Republican House seats created a psychological climate within which revolt flourished. But the seeds of dissatisfaction with Halleck's leadership extended back to bitterness engendered by Halleck's defeat of Martin in 1959. This irritation and unrest was compounded by the continuing frustrations of minority status. Agitation for change, only temporarily dampened by Ford's defeat of Hoeven in 1963, intensified throughout the long and trying sessions of the Eighty-eighth Congress.

A postelection House Republican conference held on December 16, 1964, put Halleck to test. Although called to evaluate Republican party organization and policy positions, its principal consequence was to bring back to Washington a diversified group of younger activists who were convinced that the first step toward achieving majority status was new leadership. Two likely challengers emerged, Gerald R. Ford, Jr., of Michigan and Melvin R. Laird of Wisconsin. Ford, with four more years of seniority, was selected as the candidate with the best chance of defeating Halleck.

Ford announced his candidacy on December 19, 1964. By dint of superior organization and hard campaigning the young activists, led by Griffin of Michigan, Goodell of New York, Quie of Minnesota, Ellsworth of Kansas, and Rumsfeld of Illinois, got off to an early lead which they never relinquished. Halleck's counterattack was a classic illustration of "too little and too late." Only a few members worked actively in his behalf. Most of his contacts were made in the final week of the campaign. Only in the closing days did he begin to cash in on his credits outstanding. On January 4, 1965, at the opening of the Eighty-ninth Congress, Ford defeated Halleck by a secret ballot vote of 73 to 67. In the final analysis, it was the two-thirds of the House Republican party in the five most junior classes which made victory possible for Ford. The bulk of his support, and certainly the organizational nucleus of his campaign, came from members elected in 1956 and subsequent elections.[23]

A fourth contest, New Jersey Representative Frelinghuysen's unsuccessful challenge to the incumbent minority whip, Leslie Arends of

22. "Ford's Election Sparks Shifts in GOP House Strategy," *Congressional Quarterly Weekly Report* 21 (February 8, 1963):149–56.
23. Peabody, "The Ford-Halleck Minority Leadership Contest, 1965," op. cit., pp. 32–35.

Illinois, ten days after Ford's defeat of Halleck in 1965, came about as an aftermath of revolt. In this instance, the challenger ran with the new minority leader's endorsement in a losing effort to consolidate the revolt and provide wider geographical and ideological representation within the minority leadership. Arends's early start in the defense of his incumbency, his more than twenty years of service as party whip, and his widespread personal popularity proved to be too strong. He won by 70 votes to 59. Frelinghuysen's personal reserve and rather aristocratic background cost him some support. So did his identification with the Wednesday Club. Conservatives, already smarting under National Chairman Burch's resignation, found Frelinghuysen's stand on the nuclear policy plank at San Francisco and his general liberal voting record on foreign affairs further reasons for opposing Ford's choice. In any event, Ford, like Martin and Halleck before him, came to understand more fully that members are more hesitant to reveal their true preferences to an incumbent minority leader.

IV. Conditions Which Facilitate or Inhibit Change

The differences between the dominant types of intraparty change adopted by the two parties are quite striking. As Table 13–4 illustrates, all but one of the nine instances of leadership selection in the Democratic majority were uncontested. Even in this one instance —the Albert-Bolling fight for Majority Leader in 1961 to 1962—the challenger withdrew before the contest reached the voting stage in the Democratic caucus. In contrast, seven of the ten Republican leadership changes were decided by intraparty combat. Four of the seven contests involved challenges in incumbents.

Why has the Democratic majority developed patterns of succession and utilized relatively peaceful means of leadership change? What causes the Republican minority to seldom resort to change short of contests? Among the most important factors which combine to facilitate or inhibit one type of change rather than another are (1) the skill of the incumbent, (2) majority-minority status, (3) election results, and (4) differences in hierarchy and structure in the two congressional parties.

(1) Skill of the Incumbent

The age, personality, and skill of the incumbent in contrast to his potential or actual challengers are clearly among the most crucial factors affecting patterns of leadership change. In contrast to their Democratic counterparts, first Martin and later Halleck seemed to have lost touch with their colleagues, particularly junior Republicans. Halleck and his supporters used this criticism to telling advantage in the 1959 minority leadership contest. The same charge was leveled against Halleck in 1965. As one of his supporters admitted: "I don't know anyone who was really close to him. That was one of Charlie's problems—communication. I presume he ate by himself. He didn't show up at the Republican luncheon in the Capitol. He shielded himself from other members. He was out of touch with the team to an unnecessary degree." Truman's analysis of voting patterns in an earlier Congress, the Eighty-first, provides some corroborating evidence. Neither Martin nor Halleck appeared to be very influential with the more junior members of the Republican minority; Democratic junior members were much more likely to vote in accordance with their party floor leader, McCormack.[24]

One characteristic of successful leadership is an ability to recruit and develop younger talent for positions of future leadership, Rayburn had this reputation. One of Ford's principal campaign themes was his promise to be accessible to all and to make sixty-minute ball players out of all 140 House Republicans. Assessments of personality played a prominent role in the outcomes of other contests, for example, Albert's popularity and Bolling's relative estrangement in 1962.

Leadership contests are won by the side which can mobilize the greatest number of members who are willing to work long and intensively in an effort to convert their fellow congressmen. Here, more than in typical battles over legislative issues, personal loyalties and animosities developed over a series of Congresses are crucial. Respect, trust, and affection are usually more crucial than explicit bargaining based on such tangible objects of exchange as committee assignments or the promise of additional patronage. Over the long run, however, the majority leadership enjoys greater stability, in part, because of its superior resources, both tangible and intangible.

(2) Majority-minority Status

Congressional leaders have many opportunities to help their colleagues achieve their personal and legislative objectives. A leader's endorsement frequently decides which one of several candidates will receive a preferred committee assignment. A floor leader may interrupt a freshman member's speech to argue in favor of his public works

24. Truman, op. cit., pp. 212–27.

project and, in the process, convert enough wavering members to make the difference. Party leaders appear at fundraising dinners. They provide the kind of personal endorsement which will enhance a member's chances for reelection. Both majority and minority party leaders are constantly involved in such credit-building endeavors. But majority party leaders enjoy superior resources. They work within a climate of expanding rather than contracting credit.

Credit expands because of the multiple benefits which accrue with majority status. There are more committee assignments and appointments to prestige boards and commissions to be distributed. It is the majority which receives most of the credit when legislation is passed. Their projects receive higher priority. Majority members chair the committees and subcommittees. With position comes staff, superior access to executive officialdom, and greater influence on legislative outcomes. Since there are more benefits to go around, majority members are more satisfied and less critical of their leadership. Majority status promotes a search for compromise, accommodation, and the acceptance of the established patterns of succession.

In contrast, the minority party operates in an environment of continuing frustration and increasing discord. There are fewer choice committee assignments to go around. The majority controls most of the prestige appointments. Political patronage and staff assistance are not as abundant. Opportunities for constructive participation in the drafting and implementing of major legislation are more limited. Limited resources, contracting credit, an inability to adequately reward the party faithful, the prospects of continuing defeat in floor struggles—all foster internal dissension and further undermine the leadership. If election results continue to run against the minority party, as they have with House Republicans during this period with the single exception of 1960, then party juniors are motivated to take their frustrations out through change in leadership.

(3) Election Results

Party structure and leadership change in the House of Representatives are intimately related to congressional election results. In the first place, the party which wins a majority of the 435 seats earns the right to organize the House, choose the Speaker and select the committee chairmen. What has not been so clearly understood is the relationship between the aggregate size of the net gain or loss and its implications for intraparty leadership change. Strong victories promote good will and generally reflect to the benefit of party leaders. Conversely, defeat results in pessimism, hostility, and a search for scapegoats. If the net losses are particularly severe, as many as thirty to fifty seats, then the possibilities of minority leadership change through revolt are greatly enhanced.

Table 13–5 summarizes the congressional election results and party lineups from 1954 to 1964. This period was a particularly trying one for House Republicans. Eisenhower was in the White House from 1952 to 1960, but Republicans lost control of Congress after 1954. They continued as a minority party through the mid-sixties. Halleck apparently considered the possibility of a contest against Martin after the elections of 1954 and 1956, but did not make a bid because White House neutrality was not forthcoming. At least three and perhaps all four cases of revolt were preceded by election disappointments. In the 1958 election, House Republicans suffered a further net loss of forty-seven seats. Halleck's defeat of Martin followed. Under Halleck's leadership and with Nixon at the head of the ticket, House Republicans made moderate gains in 1960.

Table 13–5. Party Lineup, House of Representatives, and President, 1954–1964

Election Year	Congress	House of Representatives				President
		Members Elected		Gains/Losses[a]		
		Dem.	Rep.	Dem.	Rep.	
1954	84th	232	203	+19	−18	Eisenhower (R)
1956	85th	234	201	+ 2	− 2	
1958	86th	283	154	+49	−47	
1960	87th	263	174	−20	+20	Kennedy (D)
1962	88th	259	176	− 4	+ 2	
1964	89th	295	140	+38	−38	Johnson (D)

Source: *Congress and the Nation* (Washington: Congressional Quarterly Service, 1965), p. 63.
[a] Gains and losses do not always balance because of independent candidates or increases and decreases in the size of the House as a result of the admission of Hawaii and Alaska and reapportionment.

When traditional midterm gains were not forthcoming in 1962, junior Republicans led by Goodell and Griffin took out their frustrations on Republican Conference Chairman Hoeven. In 1964, with Goldwater at the head of the Republican ticket, House Republicans lost forty-eight House seats and picked up only ten seats previously held by Democrats. Ford's defeat of Halleck and the attempt to remove Arends followed. A senior Republican, who played a prominent role in both the 1959 and 1965 minority leadership contests, summed up the climate created by election defeats:

> Such elections normally make minorities anxious. A climate is created. Members are seeking some way to make a change. It is in the nature of things. If the results are downhill, you make the change. If you hold your own or win, you don't. The election defeat creates an environment which makes members look for some change. It's a sense of unrest, a subconscious searching for something to ease individual consciences. The result is often "let's change our leadership."

The Democratic majority fared far better throughout this period, a factor which contributed to stable leadership. After regaining control of the House in 1954, Speaker Rayburn and Majority Leader Mc-Cormack picked Albert as whip and created the new position of deputy whip for Boggs. In the face of Eisenhower's overwhelming victory in 1956, the Democratic leadership was content to hold its own. Inability to capitalize on large Democratic majorities achieved in 1958 led to the formation of the Democratic Study Group.[25] Composed of mostly northern moderates and liberals, the DSG played a crucial role in the 1961 fight to enlarge the principal scheduling body of the House, the Committee on Rules. But Rayburn also needed 22 Republican votes to offset 1960 election losses in his narrow 217 to 212 win.[26] After Rayburn's death, McCormack, Albert, and Boggs each advanced one step in the party hierarchy. Following decisive election gains in 1964, the DSG promoted caucus action which stripped two southern Democrats of their committee seniority and brought about further liberalization of the House rules.

Election defeat tends to produce party leadership conflict within the Republican minority. Conversely, election successes have enhanced leadership stability in the House Democratic majority.[27] But it is not

25. Kenneth Kofmehl, "The Institutionalization of a Voting Bloc," *Western Political Quarterly* 17 (June, 1964):256–72.

26. Milton C. Cummings, Jr., and Robert L. Peabody, "The Decision to Enlarge the Committee on Rules: An Analysis of the 1961 Vote," in Peabody and Polsby, op. cit., [1st ed.], pp. 167–94.

27. The impact of the midterm election of 1966 on prospective leadership change at the beginning of the Ninetieth Congress adds further support to these generalizations. Republicans made a net gain of fourty-seven House seats, but fell thirty-one seats short of winning control. The party breakdown for the Ninetieth Congress was 248 Democrats and 187 Republicans. A principal effect of the election was to consolidate Ford's position as minority leader. Although the House Democratic majority leadership came in for some criticism and floor setbacks in the opening months, their leadership positions were not directly contested.

just the climate created by the election, but its impact on hierarchy and party structure within the two House parties which promotes or deters change.

(4) Hierarchy and Party Structure

The Republican minority has been more prone to leadership change through contested means for two further reasons. First, unlike the Democratic majority, Republicans in recent Congresses have suffered from a disproportionate number of junior members to senior members. This problem becomes particularly acute after major election defeats, such as 1958 and 1964. For example, following the Goldwater disaster, 93 of the 140 House Republicans (66.4 percent) were members of the five most junior classes (1956, 1958, 1960, 1962, and 1964). Even with the large class of entering freshmen, the comparable figure for Democrats was 169 members out of 295 (57.3 percent). What was more striking, however, was not relatively greater average seniority among Democrats, but much more depth among its senior members. Of seventy-two members in the Eighty-ninth Congress who had served ten terms or more, only eleven (15.6 percent) were Republicans. Just as Martin before him, it was Halleck who suffered most from the loss of loyal senior supporters in 1964.

Conversely, it was the very existence of this pool of senior Democrats, many of them committee chairmen and heads of state delegations, which helps to explain the development of hierarchical patterns of leadership succession and the reluctance to challenge incumbents characteristic of the Democratic majority. A Representative must have substantial service, a minimum of five terms, before he can be considered a candidate for leadership. Seniority is not the only factor. The dissident factions must settle on a candidate capable of winning. When a vacancy occurs there are likely to be two or three equally plausible prospects, no one of whom is preferable to all of the factions within the party. Hierarchical balance is bolstered by traditions of the majority party which foster moderation and acceptance of the existing leadership. "Above all, in the House, one must *last*. If one does last, influence will accure, but this power is diluted with any defeat. So a congressman, however strong or senior, does not commit himself carelessly. He waits."[28]

Differences in party structure also contribute to the pronounced variations in types of leadership change characteristic of the two

28. Excerpt from an unpublished newsletter of the late Representative Clem Miller (January–February, 1962):3.

House parties. At the risk of oversimplification and ignoring variations from Congress to Congress, the Democratic majority is composed of more than two northern moderates and liberals for every southern conservative. Urban machine Democrats and border state congressmen, epitomized by Speaker McCormack and Majority Leader Albert, have traditionally formed a moderating nucleus between the ideological extremes of the party. Neither wing can organize the House nor reap the benefits of majority status without the other. Although this dominant cleavage makes House Democrats less cohesive than Republicans in their voting patterns, majority status and the need to promote a presidential program lead to greater accommodation among elective leaders and seniority leaders than is the case among minority Republicans.[29]

In contrast, the Republican minority, although characterized by greater voting cohesiveness, is less susceptible to compromise and accommodation. Its rather monolithic voting structure is skewed heavily in the conservative direction. There appears to be little attempt by conservatives, who outnumber liberals by six or seven to one, to tolerate dissent or accord liberals positions in the party leadership. If the activities of the Wednesday Club in a series of contests taking place at the opening of the Eighty-ninth Congress are at all characteristic, liberals have seldom been cohesive enough to form a balance of power between personal or sectional interests within the predominantly conservative Republican ranks.

Lacking a better historical perspective, the full import of party structure for leadership change must remain speculative. But it would appear that the basic bimodal distribution within the Democratic majority is a strength as well as a weakness, since it promotes compromise and a trading off of major leadership positions between North and South. The relatively monolithic structure of the House Republican party may lend itself to party harmony and centralization of leadership when the GOP controls Congress, but this same structure seems to discourage accommodation and the selection of its leaders short of contests in times of minority status.

V. Consequences

What difference does it make when a Halleck upsets a Martin or a McCormack succeeds a Rayburn? More broadly, what are the

29. For evidence of such effects in an earlier Congress, the Eighty-first, see Truman, op. cit., pp. 231–46.

consequences when one party, the Democratic majority, develops patterns of succession to top leadership, while the other, the Republican minority, seldom stops short of contests in the selection of its party leaders? As Truman, Huitt, and others have pointed out, the discretionary aspects of congressional leadership are considerable.[30] Their personalities and backgrounds not only shape the positions they occupy, but also have important implications for the careers of their supporters and the success or failure of legislation. The predominant mode of change adopted by the two House parties has additional consequences for national elections, the two-party system, and representative government.

Within the confines of this article it is impossible to assess fully the impact of even the most important leadership choices made by the two House parties during this twelve year period. It is possible, however, to use two examples—Halleck's defeat of Martin in 1959 and McCormack's elevation to the Speakership in 1962—to briefly illustrate some of the most important kinds of consequences of replacing one incumbent leader by another.[31]

Revolt, by its very nature, results in more wholesale change than orderly succession. Following his defeat of Martin, Halleck brought new vigor to the Republican party leadership. A canny, aggressive "gut-fighter," he was at his best in the give-and-take of floor debate and behind-the-scenes maneuvering. In contrast to Martin, he seldom cooperated with Rayburn, McCormack, and the more liberal wing of the Democratic majority, but instead actively cultivated ties with conservative southern Democrats. Moderate Republicans on the Committee on Rules who had retired or advanced to the Senate were replaced with solid conservatives. The dormant Republican Policy Committee was reinstituted, John Byrnes of Wisconsin was elected chairman, and arrangements were made to provide professional staff. Under Byrnes and John Rhodes of Arizona, task forces were created to investigate problems which cut across committee lines or which might serve as the basis of campaign issues. Freshman members were given representation on the executive subcommittee of the Republican Committee on Committees.

When Halleck took over as minority leader in 1959, Republicans had 154 House members. At one time during the Eighty-eighth Congress, the number increased to 178. For a majority of 140 Republicans-

30. Truman, op. cit., p. 245; Huitt, op. cit., pp. 336–37.
31. For an attempt to more fully analyze the consequences of Ford's defeat of Halleck in 1965, see Robert L. Peabody, "House Republican Leadership: Change and Consolidation in a Minority Party" (paper delivered before the American Political Science Association, New York City, September 9, 1966).

elect at the beginning of the Eighty-ninth Congress, however, Halleck's ability to promote party solidarity and to administer defeat to Democratic proposals was not enough. Ford's promise to "promote and communicate the image of a fighting, forward-looking party seeking responsible and constructive solutions to national problems" struck a receptive chord. The intensive efforts of some thirty members working in Ford's behalf led to Halleck's defeat only six years after his own coup.

Peaceful succession brings on more incremental change, but the impact of such different personalities as Rayburn and McCormack on the office of the Speaker is considerable. McCormack's style is both more institutional and partisan than Rayburn's. He calls more meetings to discuss legislative strategy and involves the majority leader and whip to a much greater extent than Rayburn did. Under his leadership, the Democratic Steering Committee has been revived and the caucus has come into greater use. The telephone is one of McCormack's most effective weapons—"I'd call the devil if I thought it would do any good." In contrast, Rayburn operated on a more independent and personal basis. He preferred the intimacy and informality of after-the-session gatherings of the "Board of Education."[32] The whip organization was used less frequently and Rayburn almost never called a party caucus beyond the opening meeting.

McCormack's shift from partisan majority leader to impartial presiding officer was not an easy transition. His strong partisan identifications reflect his South Boston organizational ties. Rayburn's rural Texas background and more conservative political outlook made him more acceptable to most southern Democrats. He was more inclined to cooperate with Republicans, a relationship facilitated by his close friendship with former Minority Leader Martin.

With the selection of a new Speaker or minority leader, some congressmen exercise more influence and others fall out of favor. The relationship of members of the Committee on Rules to the new Speaker provides an illustration. The influence of Bolling of Missouri and Thornberry of Texas declined; O'Neill of Massachusetts and, to a lesser extent, Madden of Indiana, gained influence. Committee assignments in 1963 also reflected the composition of the new leadership. For example, McCormack was instrumental in packing the Committee on Appropriations with five northern liberals over the objections of its conservative chairman, Cannon of Missouri.

Leadership change also has a direct impact on legislation. Certainly

32. For a discussion of Rayburn's use of this informal institution, see MacNeil, op. cit. pp. 82–84.

a bill to enlarge the House of Representatives to 438 members by adding one additional member from Massachusetts, Missouri, and Pennsylvania would not have advanced as far as it did without the new Speaker's support.[33] McCormack's Catholicism made it even more mandatory that any federal-aid-to-education bill be accompanied by some resolution of the church-state issue. The possibilities of strong civil rights, medicare, and mass transit legislation improved as a more sympathetic leader advanced to the Speakership. Since ideological differences between Martin, Halleck and Ford were less pronounced and the minority has far less control over scheduling, the impact of leadership change on Republican legislative goals is more difficult to trace.

The relatively peaceful modes of leadership change practiced by House Democrats in recent years have promoted party harmony, facilitated the passage of legislation, and thus aided the reelection of Democrats. But the development of patterns of succession is by no means universally endorsed by House Democrats. A junior member, a potential candidate for leadership, summed up some of the disenchantment:

> A man shouldn't become a leader just because sometime fifteen or twenty years ago somebody made an obscure decision to put someone in as whip or deputy whip, and then he advances up the hierarchy. There's a real problem in the House. It's a kind of hardening of the arteries, too much bureaucracy. We're beginning to be more like the people we criticize downtown. Leadership should come from a man's proven ability, not just because he got started on the ladder. . . .
>
> I think what the Republicans have done is a healthy development. If Joe Martin were a Democrat, we'd still have him as our leader.

Change through contested means has a number of opposite consequences. Few House Republicans are complaining about bureaucratized patterns of succession since none exist. In any future change, the incumbent whip would be bypassed as he has been in the past. Should Ford falter, the closest approximation to an heir apparent is Conference Chairman Laird. But other potential candidates—among them Wilson, Rhodes, and Goodell—wait in the wings. House Republicans can take some consolation from one byproduct of overwhelming election defeats—it moves able younger members into

33. McCormack disavowed his support of HR 10264 after an uneasy bipartisan coalition came apart on the floor of the House during the amendment stage: *Congressional Quarterly Weekly Report* 20 (March 16, 1962):429.

positions of high rank far quicker than any other means. The overall costs to internal party harmony from frequent contests are difficult to estimate. More latent than manifest, they seldom reveal themselves in legislative voting patterns. But the animosities and bitterness flowing from leadership contests remain an underlying source of tension and distrust. One contest tends to promote another. Continuing frustrations at the polls will quite likely lead to further contests.

To an extent not adequately stressed, congressional leadership change has important consequences for national politics and the strength of the two-party system. The House provides a pool of talent for nominations to the Senate or state-wide offices. The Senate has produced more presidential candidates in recent years, but the House is frequently a mid-career stage for aspiring national leaders. House members continue to participate intensively in the selection of candidates, the writing of party platforms, and the management of national conventions. The party which does not control the White House turns to its congressional leaders for the nucleus of opposition party leadership. As leaders of the congressional majority, Rayburn and Johnson had more resources at their command, including better press coverage, than Republican minority leaders like Dirksen, Halleck, and Ford. Currently the Joint Senate-House Republican Leadership and the Republican Coordinating Committee play dominant roles in the selection of domestic campaign issues and the structuring of debate on foreign policy. Thus, a change in House leadership has implications far beyond the internal activities of Congress.

VI. Conclusions

Collective decisions made by the electorates of 435 House districts have a number of important consequences for representative government in the United States. First, the election results advance or limit the careers of some 800 promising politicians, not a few of whom are destined for national leadership as party spokesmen, committee chairmen, and presidential aspirants. Second, the aggregate outcome of seats won and lost determines which congressional party shall be the majority with the right to organize the House of Representatives. Third, the size of the majority sets the limits for success or failure of the president's legislative program. If Congress is controlled by the opposition party, or if his own party does not have a working majority, then a president's expectations as to what is politically feasible must be lowered. He may even have to shift from a policy largely oriented toward passing legislation to one primarily designed to promote campaign issues two or four years hence. Finally, as the findings of this article suggest, the size of the net gain or loss sets the climate for continuity or change in House party leadership. These aggregate election results provide the clearest instruction offered by the electorate in what is at best a generalized and largely uninformed evaluation of administration and congressional performance.[34] Congressmen translate these instructions into mandates for continuing support or opportunities for change in congressional party leadership.

This analysis began by distinguishing three basic kinds of leadership change in legislatures: interparty turnover, intraparty change, and institutional reform. After noting that continuity rather than change is the predominant pattern of congressional leadership, five types of intraparty leadership change were set forth: (1) routine succession; (2) appointment, or the emergence of a consensus choice; (3) open competition; (4) challenge to an heir apparent; and (5) revolt, or its aftermath. All but one of these types were illustrated by nineteen instances of leadership change or attempted change which took place in the five top party-wide leadership positions in both House parties during the Eighty-fourth to Eighty-ninth Congresses (1955–1966). The remaining type, challenge to an heir apparent, was illustrated by two earlier contests in 1919 and 1931.

Some rather striking differences were revealed in the predominant mode of change practiced by the two House parties during this twelve-year period. The Democratic majority was able to resolve its problems of leadership change through relatively peaceful means in eight out of nine cases. In contrast, the Republican minority resorted to contested means in seven out of ten cases. In four instances, most

34. "In Detroit in January, 1957, only 18 percent of the people could correctly name the congressman from their own district, and only 13 percent knew the names of both United States Senators from Michigan. . . . The world of the political activists and the newspapers which report political events is much more remote from the world of the average citizen than is generally realized." Daniel Katz and Samuel J. Eldersveld, "The Inmpact of Local Party Activity Upon the Electorate," *Public Opinion Quarterly* 25 (Spring, 1961):1–24 and 20. "The electorate sees very little altogether of what goes on in the national legislature. Few judgments of legislative performance are associated with the parties, and much of the public is unaware even of which party has control of Congress. As a result, the absence of party discipline or legislative results is unlikely to bring down electoral sanctions on the ineffective party or the errant Congressman." Donald E. Stokes and Warren E. Miller, "Party Government and the Saliency of Congress," *Public Opinion Quarterly* 26 (Winter, 1962):531–46, at 545. It seems clear that the electorate does not bring down electoral sanctions upon the ineffective party in the sense of the responsible party doctrine. However, members of Congress, particularly Representatives in the minority party, seem to interpret large-scale shifts in seats won or lost as a judgment on their party image and the calibre of its leadership.

notably the minority leadership contests of 1959 and 1965, change in Republican party leadership was sought through organized revolt. Two sets of findings emerge from analysis of these cases:

1. Democratic majority:
   A. The Democratic majority is much more likely than the Republican minority to resolve questions of leadership change through noncontested elections or appointments.
   B. The longer the period of majority status, the more likely the majority party is to develop established patterns of succession.
   C. When contests take place in the Democratic majority, they will most likely occur at the middle or lower levels of the party hierarchy.

2. Republican minority:
   A. The Republican minority is more prone to intraparty leadership change through contested means.
   B. The longer the period of minority status, the more prone the minority party is to leadership change through revolt.
   C. Revolts are most likely to occur following congressional election disasters (the net loss of thirty or more seats).

Further historical research is needed to determine the extent to which these findings are limited to this twelve-year period or have broader applicability. In order to prove or disprove hypotheses relating party differences and majority-minority status to types of leadership change, it will be necessary to examine in detail the periods 1894 to 1930 and 1931 to 1954. During the earlier period the Republican party was in the majority save for a Democratic interlude from 1910 until 1918. To what extent were the Cannon revolt and the Gillett-Mann and Snell-Tilson contests the exceptions rather than the rule? How was the Democratic party, as the minority party, able to avoid leadership contests during the 1920s? Were the series of leadership contests which preoccupied the Democratic majority in the 1930s a spilling over of the frustrations of minority status in the 1920s and a reflection of its new and unwieldy party structure? What other factors were at work in the selection of party leaders throughout these periods?

The outcome of future leadership change in both parties will provide a further test and opportunity for modification of these findings. Given the high component of chance, prediction in politics is always hazardous. Yet, in the long run, a science of politics is as dependent upon its ability to predict as on its capacity for explanation.[35] When

35. Abraham Kaplan, *The Conduct of Inquiry* (San Francisco, 1964), pp. 346–51.

change comes about in the Democratic party, it is most likely to occur through the death or retirement of the seventy-five-year-old Speaker, John W. McCormack of Massachusetts. The incumbent majority leader, Carl Albert of Oklahoma, should routinely advance to the Speakership, contingent upon his full recovery from a September, 1966, heart attack. If a contest develops in the majority party, it is most likely to occur when and if the incumbent whip, Hale Boggs of Louisiana, attempts to move up to majority leader. The problem for his opponents, just as it was in the 1959 and 1965 minority leadership contests, will be to agree upon a candidate with sufficient seniority, demonstrated leadership skills, and popularity around whom a majority might coalesce. Should Boggs succeed, and should the incumbent deputy whip, John Moss of California, be appointed whip, then leadership succession in the House of Representatives, at least as it reflects majority practices, will have undergone further institutionalization. The return in 1968 of a sizeable number of the Democratic freshman members who lost in 1966 could sufficiently strengthen the Democratic Study Group so as to give it a decisive voice in subsequent leadership contests.

Leadership change in the Republican minority party will depend heavily upon the results of the presidential election of 1968 and the congressional election of 1970. Minority Leader Ford needed a substantial victory in 1966 to consolidate his leadership. He got it—a net gain of forty-seven House seats. But should his party stumble in the next two campaigns, then he, like Martin and Halleck before him, is likely to be asked to step down or face the consequences of further revolt.

Studies in depth of past and future leadership change in the House of Representatives, as well as the modification of these hypotheses as they apply to other legislatures such as the United States Senate or the British House of Commons, should improve our understanding of the workings of legislative parties. They would also provide an opportunity for further examination of such important explanatory variables as the personality and skill of party leaders, majority and minority status, and the impact of election results on party structure and hierarchy.

14

Congressional Leadership
Then and Now

David W. Brady

Of the Congresses for which we have information on levels of party voting, the Fifty-fifth and Fifty-sixth United States House of Representatives stand out for their high levels of party voting. Table 14–1 shows the proportion of party votes in the House of Representatives for selected Congresses from 1845 to 1966. The criterion for a party vote in this table is 90 percent of one party voting against 90 percent of the other party.

If the criterion for characterizing a roll call as a party vote is reduced to a majority of one party voting against a majority of the other party, then the percentages of party votes in the Fifty-fifth and Fifty-sixth House rise to 93.9 percent and 92.2 percent respectively. No matter how party voting is defined, it is clear that party voting was more visible at the turn of the century than at any other time in the known history of the House.

The two variables which have been most consistently related to high levels of party voting in American legislatures are a strong centralized leadership and ideological parties representing distinct poles

Reprinted by permission of the author and Wayne State University Press, from David W. Brady, "Congressional Leadership and Party Voting in the McKinley Era: A Comparison to the Modern House," *Midwest Journal of Political Science* 16:3 (1972):439–49. Copyright © 1972 by the Wayne State University Press. I would like to thank two anonymous *Journal* critics for their cogent comments on the original manuscript for this article.

Table 14-1. Party Voting in the U.S. House of Representatives

Year	Congress	President	Percentage of Party Votes
1845–47	29th	Polk	10.7
1863–65	38th	Lincoln	30.2
1887–89	50th	Cleveland	13.6
1897–99	55th	McKinley	50.9
1899–1901	56th	McKinley	49.3
1921	66th	Harding	28.6
1928	70th	Coolidge	7.1
1930–31	71st	Hoover	31.0
1933	72nd	Roosevelt	22.5
1937	74th	Roosevelt	11.8
1944	78th	Roosevelt	10.7
1945	79th	Roosevelt-Truman	17.5
1946	79th	Truman	10.5
1947	80th	Truman	15.1
1948	80th	Truman	16.4
1953	83rd	Eisenhower	7.0
1959	86th	Eisenhower	8.0
1963	88th	Kennedy	7.6
1964	88th	Johnson	6.2
1965	89th	Johnson	2.8
1966	89th	Johnson	1.6

Sources: W. Wayne Shannon, *Party, Constituency, and Congressional Voting*, p. 42; and Julius Turner and Edward Schneier, Jr., *Party and Constituency: Pressures on Congress*, p. 17.

of a continuum—normally a socioeconomic class continuum.[1] Comparing the House of Representatives at the turn of the century to the modern House leads to the conclusion that the House in the 1890s had a centralized leadership and congressional parties representing separate

1. Malcolm Jewell and Samuel Patterson, *The Legislative Process in the United States* (New York: Random House, 1966), p. 425; Duncan MacRae, Jr., "The Relation Between Roll Call Votes and Constituencies in the Massachusetts House of Representatives," *American Political Science Review* 46 (December, 1952): 1046–55; Thomas A. Flinn, "Party Responsibility in the States: Some Causal Factors," *American Political Science Review* 58 (March, 1964):60–72; Thomas Dye, "A Comparison of Constituency Influences in the Upper and Lower Chambers of a State Legislature," *Western Political Quarterly* 14 (June, 1961):473–80; Malcolm Jewell, "Party Voting in American State Legislatures," *American Political Science Review* 49 (September, 1955):773–91; and Nelson Polsby et al., "The Growth of the Seniority System in the U. S. House of Representatives," *American Political Science Review* 63 (September, 1969):787–807.

ends of an industrial-agricultural continuum.[2] The Speaker of the House in the Fifty-fifth and Fifty-sixth Houses (1897–1901) appointed the committees, was chairman of the Rules Committee and generally had at his command more sanctions to invoke against dissenting members than does his modern counterpart.[3] The combination of these characteristics as shown in the research of Ripley and others demonstrates convincingly that the House leadership in the 1890s was both powerful and centralized.

The electoral realignment of the 1896 period led to the formation of two congressional parties located at distinct ends of an industrial-agricultural continuum.[4] Table 14–2 shows the dispersion of the two congressional parties along an industrial-agricultural and a sectional continuum.

Thus we can conclude that relative to the modern House the Fifty-fifth and Fifty-sixth Houses were characterized by centralized leadership and congressional parties representing distinctly different constituencies. However, the connections between party voting, centralized leadership and the constituency bases of congressional parties remains problematical.

This paper examines three aspects of the relationship between leadership structure and levels of party support. First, an overview of the level of party support among congressional leaders in the Fifty-fifth and Fifty-sixth Houses is given. Second, the leadership of the 1890s Houses is compared to the leadership of a modern House in regard to levels of party support. Third, the causes of the high levels of party support among leaders in the 1890s Houses are analyzed, and the contrast between levels of support among leaders in the two eras is examined.

2. In regard to the structure of leadership in the U. S. House in the 1890 to 1910 period, see Randall Ripley, *Majority Party Leadership in Congress* (Boston: Little Brown and Company, 1969), pp. 2–4; Randall Ripley, *Party Leaders in the House of Representatives* (Washington, D.C.: Brookings Institute Press, 1967), ch. 2; Lewis Froman, Jr., Randall Ripley, "Conditions for Party Leadership: The Case of the House Democrats," *American Political Science Review* 59 (March, 1965):52–63; Nelson Polsby, "The Institutionalization of the U. S. House of Representatives," *American Political Science Review* 62 (March, 1968):144–69; Nelson W. Polsby, et al., op. cit.; DeAlva Stanwood Alexander, *History and Procedures of the U. S. House of Representatives* (Boston: Houghton Mifflin Company, 1916), ch. 4; and Lauros McConachie, *Congressional Committees* (New York: Thomas Y. Crowell Company, 1898), pp. 154–71.

3. McConachie, op. cit., pp. 197–98; George Galloway, *History of the House of Representatives* (New York: Thomas Y. Crowell Company, 1968), pp. 52–53 and 134–38; Ripley, *Leadership in Congress*, pp. 2–5.

4. Walter A. Burnham, "The Changing Scope of the American Political Universe," *American Political Science Review* 59 (March, 1965):7–29; V. O. Key, Jr., "A Theory of Critical Elections," *Journal of Politics* 17 (February, 1955):3–18.

Table 14–2. Occupational and Regional Composition of the Congressional Parties in the 55th and 56th Congress (percent)

Congress and Party	Type of District[a]			Region				
	Industrial	Mixed	Agricultural	East	Midwest	South	Border	West
55th House								
Democrats	14	24	65	10	25	87	65	50
Republicans	86	76	35	90	75	13	35	50
Total	100	100	100	100	100	100	100	100
56th House								
Democrats	38	30	62	33	26	98	70	25
Republicans	62	70	38	67	74	2	30	75
Total	100	100	100	100	100	100	100	100

[a] Of the 300 districts for which occupational data were collected, 51 were industrial [(less than 25 percent farming)], 123 were mixed [(26 to 70 percent farming)], and 126 were agricultural [(more than 70 percent farming)]. In percentages, 17 percent of all districts for which data were available were industrial, 41 percent were agricultural.

Measuring the Party Vote in the Fifty-fifth and Fifty-sixth House

Before the question of leadership effect on the vote can be ascertained it is necessary to discuss the method used to measure the party vote. The first test used to measure the party vote was to run a Q-analysis on all roll call votes in both Houses. Q-analysis runs each roll call against every other roll call, thus providing a measure of association between all pairs of votes. The value of Q ranges from —1.0 to 1.0. The higher the Q value, the greater the association of the roll calls. The analysis of all the roll calls determines which roll calls cluster together. MacRae, in his study of the Eighty-first Congress, fed different voting clusters into a Guttman scalogram analysis, thereby generating the issue dimensions in that Congress.[5] For the present study, the same type of Q-analysis was run on the Fifty-fifth and Fifty-sixth Houses of Representatives.

There were 182 roll-call votes taken in the Fifty-fifth Congress. Since eighteen of these votes were unanimous or nearly unanimous (less than 10 percent voting negative), they were deleted. Members of the Fifty-sixth House answered the roll call 146 times, with ten of these being unanimous or nearly unanimous; they also were dropped. Thus the Fifty-sixth House is analyzed on the basis of 136 roll-call votes.

The Q-formula requires that a minimum Q-value (Q-min) be selected for purposes of eliminating roll calls from clusters with which they are only loosely associated. That is, one does not wish to include in a set of related roll calls votes which are likely to be only minimally related to the dimension the researcher is seeking to separate out from the universe of roll calls. Anderson, Watts, and Wilcox suggest that if errors (including minimally associated roll calls in a dimension cluster) are to be extremely small, then the criteria or value of Q should be set high, at .8 or above.[6] My purpose is to determine the pervasiveness of party voting in the Fifty-fifth and Fifty-sixth House of Representatives and to exclude from the party votes those roll calls which are only minimally associated with the party votes. Therefore, the minimum Q-value accepted as showing association between two roll calls was .8, the values suggested by Anderson, Watts, and Wilcox. Setting the Q-value at .8 insures that the roll calls which cluster together are highly related.

5. Duncan MacRae, Jr., *Dimensions of Congressional Voting* (Berkeley: University of California Press, 1958), pp. 315–23.
6. Lee F. Anderson et al., *Legislative Roll Call Analysis* (Evanston: Northwestern University Press, 1966), p. 103.

Since the analysis seeks to discern the strength of the party vote in these two nineteenth-century Houses, it is necessary to identify a party vote to which all other roll calls can be compared. The vote on the election of the Speaker of the House traditionally has been, and still is, a straight party vote. By comparing all other roll calls to this party vote, choosing a Speaker, the extent of party voting should be ascertained. In short, if a large number of the remaining roll calls are highly related, .8 or above, to the straight party vote the pervasiveness of the party factor will have been demonstrated. In the Fifty-fifth House of Representatives the vote on election of a Speaker was related to 148 of the remaining 163 roll calls at a level of .8 or above. Of the sixteen roll calls unrelated to the initial party vote, six of these were related to other bills which were part of the original cluster, leaving only ten roll calls not directly related to the initial party vote. These unrelated roll calls did not ostensibly fit into any coherent issue dimension.

The scheme used in analyzing the Fifty-fifth Congress was also applied to the Fifty-sixth Congress. The initial party vote was used as the key variable. One-hundred and eleven of the 135 roll calls were related to the adoption of the rules vote at a level of .8 or above. Of the twenty-four remaining votes, nineteen were related to at least five other roll calls which in turn were related to the party vote, leaving only five votes which did not fall into the original cluster.

Thus the conclusion that party was pervasive in these two Congresses seems inescapable. The Q-analysis over all roll calls showed less than 10 percent of the votes unrelated to the party vote. Those roll calls which did not relate to the initial party vote were found to be issues on which either a direct state or district vote replaced the party loyalties.[7]

The party support scores for the representatives of the Fifty-fifth and Fifty-sixth House were calculated over the roll calls which were strongly related (.8 or above) to the vote for the Speaker. Thus, in the Fifty-fifth House there were 148 party-related roll calls and in the Fifty-sixth House 111 party-related roll calls. A support score for each representative was calculated on the basis of the percentage of times the representative voted with a majority of his party. In short, a representative's support score measures the percentage of times a congressman voted with a majority of his party on 148 party votes in the Fifty-fifth House and 111 party votes in the Fifty-sixth House. Table 14–3 shows the dispersion of party voting.

7. A set of Varimax rotated factor analyses was performed on all roll calls in both Houses and the results showed a one factor solution for both Houses; the roll calls that loaded significantly (.5 or above) on the first factor were discovered to be party votes where 75 percent or more of one party opposed 75 percent or more of the other party.

Table 14–3. Party Support in the 55th and 56th House of Representatives by Party

	Percent of times voted with party majority	55th House		56th House	
		D	R	D	R
Strong Republican Support	85+	0	34	0	50
Moderate Strong Republican Support	70 to 84	0	149	0	121
Republican Supportive	60 to 69	0	21	0	8
Mixed	40 to 59	2	2	6	2
Democratic Supportive	60 to 69	17	0	32	0
Moderate Strong Democratic Support	70 to 84	72	0	84	0
Strong Democratic Support	85+	36	0	30	0
Total		127	206	152	181

Leadership Effects

Truman, in his study of the Eighty-first Congress, discovered that "just as a floor leader's influence may be augmented by the assumption that he will one day be Speaker, and correspondingly diminished if the feeling gets around that he is not first in the line of succession, so it seems likely that the 'Speaker's boys,' especially the older ones, may have their informal followings which help to knit the party together . . . Informal, and in gross probably immeasurable, these ties are part of the stuff of party leadership in the House as they are in the Senate."[8] Given the informality of the decisional process in the Fifty-fifth and Fifty-sixth Houses, such ties probably were more important then than they are in the modern House. In an attempt to discern the effects of such ties, the leadership will be separated from the membership and a comparison of voting scores will be run. In order to conserve space wherever the results for both Houses are nearly identical, extensive remarks will not be made in regard to the Fifty-sixth House. However, the tables which present the data for the Fifty-sixth House are given.

Ripley and others have shown that in the 1890s party and committee leadership were fused; that is, the party leaders were also the chairmen of the important committees, so that Speaker Reed was the

8. David B. Truman, *The Congressional Party* (New York: John Wiley and Sons, 1959), pp. 205–6.

chairman of the Rules Committee and Cannon was chairman of Appropriations and floor leader.[9] Given this arrangement, it is relatively easy to separate the leadership in the House from the membership by selecting the most important committees and their most important members. Selecting the top leadership in the House does not pose a serious problem since all of the historical sources agree on which committees were the most important, namely: Rules, Appropriations, and Ways and Means.[10] Thus, the Republican members of the Rules Committee, the chairman and ranking majority member of the Ways and Means Committee, and the chairman and ranking majority member of the Appropriations Committee plus Representative Tawney of the Judiciary Committee were separated out as the top leadership of the Republican party. Representative Tawney was included because Tawney was the Republican whip in both the Fifty-fifth and Fifty-sixth Houses of Representatives. The ranking Democratic members of Ways and Means, Rules, and Appropriations Committees were selected as the Democratic top leadership. The number of representatives selected as composing the top leadership by this method resulted in eight Republican and six Democratic top leaders in the Fifty-fifth House, and seven Republican and seven Democratic top leaders in the Fifty-sixth House.

A second set of criteria was used to select the secondary leadership in the House. The rules of the Fifty-fifth and Fifty-sixth House revealed that fifteen committees had the right to report to the House at any time, so these committees were used as the basis for identifying the secondary leadership. The selection of these committees is based on McConachie's analysis of committee importance and the assumption that the right to report at any time signified importance.[11] Of the fifteen committees with the right to report at any time, Elections, Territories, Invalid Pensions, and Printing were dropped because their right to report appears to have been an historical right rather than of contemporary political importance.[12] Those committees which had won the right to appropriate funds on their own accord rather than through the Appropriations Committee were added to the eleven

9. Randall Ripley, "Party in Congress: Whip Organizations in the United States House of Representatives," *American Political Science Review* 58 (September, 1964):561–64 and McConachie, op. cit., pp. 180–85.

10. Alexander, op. cit., pp. 230–36; McConachie, op. cit., pp. 175–91. For committee rankings from 1914 to 1947, see John B. Everhart's rankings, which are quoted in George Galloway, *Congress at the Crossroads* (New York: Thomas Y. Crowell Company, 1963), p. 90.

11. McConachie, op. cit., pp. 173–75; Alexander, op. cit., p. 230 corroborates this point.

12. McConachie, op. cit., pp. 173–200 and Appendix 6.

important committees which had the right to report at any time, and these eighteen committees constitute the important House committees.[13] The total membership of the Rules, Appropriations, and Ways and Means Committees, other than those in the top leadership group, was selected as secondary legislative leaders. The chairman and ranking minority members of the remaining fifteen committees were added to the members of the three most important committees, and for the purpose of this study those members were the secondary leaders. In short, the secondary leaders were the chairmen of the important, but not top-rank, committees plus the regular members of the Rules, Appropriations, and Ways and Means Committees. The number of secondary leaders in both Houses was as follows: twenty-four Democratic and thirty-four Republican secondary leaders in the Fifty-fifth House and twenty-three Democrats and thirty-two Republicans in the Fifty-sixth House. Members of these two Houses who were not selected in either the top or secondary leadership groups were placed in the membership category.

The partisan nature of the McKinley Congresses plus the analysis of leadership structure leads to the hypothesis that the congressional party leadership in these Congresses will have been more supportive of the party position than were the members, and to a secondary hypothesis that both leaders and members of the Fifty-fifth and Fifty-sixth Houses will have shown higher party support scores than their modern counterparts. That is, the House leadership in the 1890s was hierarchical, informal, and centralized, which resulted in policy formation by the leadership. It should be noted that one major reason why the centralization of leadership produced more party support is that committee chairmen and members of key committees were often picked because of loyalty or allegiance to the leadership and not because of seniority. Further, even if seniority was not violated in choosing chairmen and making committee assignments, the Speaker had the power to remove dissenting members in the next session. If the policy was formulated by the leadership and the leaders had more sanctions to invoke against dissenting members, then the leaders should have the highest party support scores within the Fifty-fifth and Fifty-sixth Houses, and the overall level of party support should be higher than is the case in the modern House.

In contrast, the modern House is characterized by a decentralized leadership structure in which the party and committee leaders are not

13. The committees are: Rules, Ways and Means, Rivers and Harbors, Appropriations, Naval Affairs, Military Affairs, Militia, Agriculture, Foreign Affairs, Indian Affairs, Post Offices and Road, Banking and Currency, Industry, Public Lands, Enrolled Bills, Accounts, Commerce, and Coinage, Weights, and Measures.

fused but conspicuously separated.[14] Further, in the modern House both party and committee leaders orient themselves to the presidential program and are, relatively speaking, less autonomous in regard to the president than were their counterparts in the 1890s. On this basis then, the leadership of the Eighty-ninth House of Representatives ought to be less supportive of the party position than were the leaders of the Fifty-fifth and Fifty-sixth U.S. House of Representatives.

In order to test this hypothesis, the top and secondary leaders were separated from the membership in the Eighty-ninth House. The top congressional leaders were the majority and minority leaders, the whips, and the chairman and ranking members of the Rules, Ways and Means, and Appropriations Committees. The secondary leaders were the chairman and ranking members of the remaining standing committees, the regional whips in both parties, and the remaining members of the Rules, Ways and Means, and Appropriation Committees. Those members not falling into either of the above two categories were classified as rank-and-file members. The party support score for each representative was taken from the *Congressional Quarterly Almanac* for the Eighty-ninth House. The *Congressional Quarterly's* party support score measures the number of times a representative voted with a majority of his party on 185 party-related roll calls. The hypothesis is that congressional leaders in the Fifty-fifth and Fifty-sixth House will show greater support for their party than will the congressional leaders in the Eighty-ninth House. Table 14–4 shows the levels of party support by categories of leadership and Congresses.

The results clearly substantiate the hypothesis. Both top and secondary leaders in the Fifty-fifth and Fifty-sixth House were more supportive of their party than were their equivalents in the Eighty-ninth House, and the overall level of party support was higher in the two 1890s Houses than was the case in the Eighty-ninth House. In the two nineteenth-century Houses there is a progression of levels of support as one moves from top leaders to rank-and-file members, with the top leaders being more supportive of the party position. In the Eighty-ninth House this pattern does not obtain. That is, top leaders were not significantly different from secondary leaders or rank-and-file members in terms of their levels of party support; and it is interesting to note that the Eighty-ninth House has been interpreted as one of the more partisan in modern times. The only exception to this general finding is that 100 percent of the Republican leaders in the Eighty-ninth House supported their party on at least 70 percent of all roll calls. However,

14. Ralph Huitt, "Democratic Party Leadership in the Senate," in Ralph Huitt and Robert Peabody, eds., *Congress: Two Decades of Analysis* (New York: Harper and Row, 1969), pp. 140–42.

Table 14-4. Leaders and Members of the 55th, 56th, and 89th House Compared on Party Support (percent)

Party Support	Democrats			Republicans		
	Top Leaders	Secondary Leaders	Rank-and-file Members	Top Leaders	Secondary Leaders	Rank-and-file Members
55th House Support Scores						
Strong	50	29	29	63	24	15
Moderately Strong	50	50	57	37	74	72
Supportive	0	17	13	0	2	12
Mixed	0	4	1	0	0	1
	100	100	100	100	100	100
56th House Support Scores						
Strong	43	22	19	71	47	23
Moderately Strong	57	56	55	29	44	72
Supportive	0	22	22	0	6	4
Mixed	0	0	4	0	3	1
	100	100	100	100	100	100
89th House Support Scores						
Strong	27	17	22	20	22	20
Moderately Strong	27	25	37	80	45	42
Supportive	19	19	11	0	18	18
Mixed	27	39	30	0	15	20
	100	100	100	100	100	100

Note: Strong=voted with party majority on 85 percent+ of roll calls. Moderately strong=voted with party majority on 70 to 84 percent of roll calls. Supportive=voted with party majority on 60-69 percent of roll calls. Mixed=voted with party majority on less than 59 percent of roll calls.

it should be noted that only 20 percent of the Republican leaders in the Eighty-ninth House were supportive of the party position on 85 percent or more of party-related roll calls. One way to account for the differences noted in this table is to divide the leadership of the Eighty-ninth House into party organizational leaders and committee leaders. In the Eighty-ninth House Democratic party leaders voted with a party majority 88 percent of the time while committee chairman voted with a party majority 59 percent of the time on the same roll calls. For the Republicans, the pattern was the same. Party organization leaders voted with a party majority more often than did committee leaders.[15]

Causes of the Leadership's Extreme Support

Part of the reason for the leader's strong support of the party in the two turn-of-the-century Houses was due to the fact that the leadership of the House determined the party position on issues. The House leaders determined which issues were to have legislative priority, and also on which issues the full weight of the congressional party would be brought to bear. For instance, in the Fifty-sixth House the Republican leaders decided that the currency question would have top priority, and that Negro voting rights were not a party issue. The leaders, then, set the party position by farming policy and the membership either supported or rejected their position. The data for the Fifty-fifth and Fifty-sixth Houses revealed that the party rank-and-file seldom, if ever, went against the party leaders' position.

Demonstrating that the congressional parties in the McKinley era were cohesive does not, of course, prove that the leaders of the parties formulated policy. The assertion is that if the congressional parties' leadership structure was centralized and did set the parties' positions, then one would expect that the leaders strongly supported their own policies. Further, the leaders could have been expected to be more supportive of their policies than was the rank-and-file. The data have shown that precisely this pattern of support occurred in both the Fifty-fifth and Fifty-sixth Houses. Further evidence is needed, however, to indicate that the leaders made their policy the equivalent of party policy.

Professor Shannon, in his book on party voting in the House, asks why party voting dropped from 85.7 percent in the first session to

15. In regard to the distinction between party and committee leaders, see Barbara Hinckley, "Congressional Leadership Selection and Support," *Journal of Politics* 32 (May, 1970):268–87. She shows that there behavioral differences between committee and party leaders in terms of liberal-conservative support.

20 percent in the second session of the Fifty-fifth House.[16] The answer to his question sheds light on the process whereby party leaders made their policy position the congressional party's position. The leaders of the Fifty-fifth House, assured of reelection, met in Washington months before the House convened, decided on legislative priorities, and formulated specific policy proposals. Many of the bills before the first session of the Fifty-fifth House had been formed in the Fifty-fourth House, but not voted upon.[17] The point is that because the leaders were assured of reelection, they were able to bring continuity to the House's legislative business. Thus the leaders of the Fifty-fourth House decided what legislation would have priority before the Fifty-fifth convened. Before committees were appointed, the top priority legislation was presented to the House for passage. In the Fifty-fifth House, Speaker Reed refused to appoint committees for 131 days. During this period, on 85.7 percent of all votes 90 percent of one party opposed 90 percent of the other (a party vote). Given the large number of first and second term congressmen (over 60 percent), a majority of representatives were voting on specific and technical legislation with which they were entirely unfamiliar.[18]

In this situation, the rank-and-file of the congressional party had only leadership cues to guide their vote, and the analysis of the data demonstrates the extent to which they accepted the leadership's position as their own. During the passage of the Dingley Tariff in the opening days of the first session of the Fifty-fifth House, Representative Bailey (D., Tex.) voiced his objections to the style of the Republican leadership outlined above. He said: "It [the Dingley committee] met and submitted, in hot haste, its bill on Tuesday. Then one day to look at 162 pages and a final vote."[19] The complicated Dingley Tariff bill was presented, discussed, and passed within fourteen days of the opening of the Fifty-fifth House. Unlike the modern House, where there is a flurry of business before the closing of the final session, the House in the McKinley era was not pressed in the final session. Indeed, the number of members voting in the later sessions was 25 percent less than the average for the first sessions, and most of the official business consisted of voting on motions to adjourn. In contrast, the modern House normally is pressed with business at the end of a session and relatively unencumbered at the opening of a session. The reason for the press of business at the end of a session of the modern House is

16. W. Wayne Shannon, *Party, Constituency, and Congressional Voting* (Baton Rouge: Louisiana State University Press, 1968), p. 42.
17. McConachie, op. cit., p. 139.
18. Polsby, op. cit., p. 146.
19. *Congressional Record,* 55th Cong. 1st Sess., 1897, 30, p. 17.

that legislation is hammered out in committee while the House is in session, and a significant number of committees report bills in the final days of a session. The difference between the modern House and the 1890s House is a stylistic difference between a relatively hierarchical centralized leadership and a decentralized leadership. Part of the reason for the leaders' strong party support is surely the centralized and unified structure of leadership in the House in the 1890s. The second part of the answer to the "extremity" lies in the nature of the leadership's constituencies.

From previous research it is known that at the turn of the century a typical Republican district was mixed agricultural-industrial, located in the East or Midwest and modified competitive, while the typical Democratic district was agricultural, located in the southern or border regions and usually safely Democratic.[20] In what follows it will be shown that both the top leaders and secondary leaders of both parties were drawn from districts which overemphasized the critical features of typical districts. The importance of this fact is that the very constituency factors which best account for party differences are accentuated in the leadership of both parties. The critical elements in defining the typical districts of each party were: (1) Democrats tended to be elected from agricultural districts while Republicans represented industrial districts; (2) Democrats tended to come from the southern and border states while Republicans came from the eastern and midwestern states. The argument being made is that the leaders of the two congressional parties represented districts which accentuated the differences between the parties. That is, Republican leaders came from highly industrial districts while Democratic leaders came from highly agricultural districts. Further, Democratic leaders came exclusively from the southern and border regions with southern leaders predominant, while Republican leaders came exclusively from the eastern and midwestern states with eastern leaders predominant. The fact that the leaders of the parties represented districts at opposite ends of the industrial-agricultural continuum and came from separate regions which were solidly one-party in nature meant that the leaders in both parties came from noncompetitive districts. Thus, the hypothesis is Republican leaders represented safe eastern and midwestern industrial districts while Democratic leaders represented safe southern and border agricultural districts.

If this hypothesis is correct, then the congressional leadership was not affected by constituency cross-pressures, and as a result the leaders

20. David W. Brady, *Party Voting in the McKinley Era*, unpublished Ph.D. dissertation, University of Iowa (1970), ch. 5; and see Table 14–2 of this paper.

of both parties were totally opposed on the central economic questions of the day. Given their constituencies, Republican leaders could strongly support a holding action unfavorable to the industrial interests in America. Table 14–5 compares the leaders of the Fifty-fifth and Fifty-sixth House with the rank-and-file members on districts, number of terms served, and region where the districts are located.

The pattern revealed by the data in the table is clear. The top leaders of both parties are drawn from districts which accentuate the differences between the parties. That is, Republican leaders came from highly industrial districts while Democratic leaders represented agricultural constituencies. Both parties' top leaders came from noncompetitive districts and were experienced hands in the legislative process. Republican top leaders came from eastern states and Democratic top leaders came from the southern states. The critical difference between the leaders of the two parties is that they represented districts whose economic interests were perceived as opposites. Republican leaders represented industrial constituencies for whom the continued expansion of American industry was a necessity. Democratic leaders represented agricultural constituents who perceived the continued growth of American industry as inimical to their well-being. The "safeness" of the leaders' seats was due to homogeneity of interests within the districts and the region. That is, industrial districts favored industrial growth and agricultural districts favored agrarian growth. The Republican party was the party of industry, while the Democratic party was the party of the small cash-crop farmer. Moreover, the most heavily industrial districts were in the East while the South was entirely agricultural. Thus, the Republicans were *the* party of the East and the Democrats *the* party of the South. Given the simple fact that seniority and specialization were necessary conditions for obtaining leadership positions, the safeness of Eastern industrial and Southern agricultural districts insured representatives from these districts positions of leadership. And, as we have seen, the leadership in the House during the 1890s was capable of exercising great control over what legislative issues would receive priority and the substantive nature of priority issues.

In contrast to this pattern in the Fifty-fifth and Fifty-sixth House, the top leaders of the Eighty-ninth House were not drawn from homogeneous districts. Table 14–6 compares the top leaders in the Fifty-fifth House with the top leaders in the Eighty-ninth House.[21]

21. The breakdown of district classifications was compiled by the author from the *1890 Census* and the *Congressional District Data Book* for the Eighty-ninth House.

Table 14–5. Leaders and Members of the House: A Comparison of Constituencies for the 55th and 56th Congresses (percent)

Constituency Characteristic	Top Leaders				Secondary Leaders				Members Rank-and-File			
	Democrats 55th	Democrats 56th	Republicans 55th	Republicans 56th	Democrats 55th	Democrats 56th	Republicans 55th	Republicans 56th	Democrats 55th	Democrats 56th	Republicans 55th	Republicans 56th
Competitiveness of District[a]												
One-party (100% ≥ V ≥ 71.0%)	75	66	50	63	49	52	13	10	25	20	5	7
Modified one-party (70.9% ≥ V ≥ 61.0%)	25	34	50	37	17	26	27	30	24	16	13	12
One-party competitive (60.9% ≥ V ≥ 56.0%)	0	0	0	0	17	13	27	23	8	7	23	27
Competitive (55.9% ≥ V ≥ 49.0%)	0	0	0	0	17	9	33	37	43	57	59	54
Total	100	100	100	100	100	100	100	100	100	100	100	100
Occupational Composition of District												
Industrial (Less than 25% farming)	0	0	25	25	20	15	21	15	4	17	27	17
Mixed (26% to 70% farming)	0	0	63	75	5	15	48	55	29	26	49	50
Agricultural (More than 70% farming)	100	100	12	0	75	70	31	30	67	57	24	33
Total	100	100	100	100	100	100	100	100	100	100	100	100

Number of Terms

Less than 2	0	0	0	0	17	12	6	12	85	76	61	53
2 through 4	0	0	0	0	56	50	68	61	13	21	37	44
5+	100	100	100	100	27	38	26	27	2	3	2	3
Total	100	100	100	100	100	100	100	100	100	100	100	100

Region of District

East	0	0	57	75	13	16	44	50	22	7	34	42
Midwest	0	0	43	25	9	8	47	41	23	26	50	42
South	86	83	0	0	61	63	0	0	36	43	3	5
Border	14	17	0	0	13	13	6	6	18	18	6	8
West	0	0	0	0	4	0	3	3	1	6	7	3
Total	100	100	100	100	100	100	100	100	100	100	100	100

a Computed over a 10 year, 5 election period. The numeric formulas read (For one-party (100% $\geq$ V $\geq$ 71%). Average percentage of victory margin less than 100 percent but greater than 71 percent.

Table 14–6. A Comparison of Constituency Characteristics of Top Leaders in the House of Representatives of the 55th and 89th Congresses (percent)

	55th House		89th House	
	Democrats	Republicans	Democrats	Republicans
Competitiveness of Districts				
One-party	75	50	55	20
Modified one-party	25	50	45	40
One-party competitive	0	0	0	40
Competitive	0	0	0	0
Total	100	100	100	100
Occupational Composition[a]				
Industrial	0	25	45	20
Mixed	0	63	36	40
Agricultural	100	12	19	40
Total	100	100	100	100
Region				
East	0	57	0	10
Midwest	0	43	18	60
South	86	0	54	10
Border	14	0	9	0
West	0	0	0	20
Total	100	100	100	100

[a] For the 89th House, districts where over 60 percent of the work force was blue collar were classified as industrial; districts with from 35 to 59 percent blue collar were mixed, and districts with less than 35 percent blue collar and more than 30 percent engaged in agricultural were classified agricultural. For the 55th House the criteria are the same as in Tables 14-5 and 14-6.

The table reveals that the top leaders in the Eighty-ninth House represent a greater range of district types than did their counterparts in the Fifty-fifth House. Democratic top leaders represented districts which ranged from the heavily blue-collar industrial district of Representative Madden of Indiana to the essentially rural agricultural district represented by William Colmer of Mississippi.[22] Further, the regional dispersion of Democratic top leaders in the Eighty-ninth House was greater than was the case in the Fifty-fifth House. The

22. The districts for the Eighty-ninth House were classified according to percentage white collar, percentage urban population, and percentage urban-suburban population. However, no classification would yield a bipolar distribution similar to that discovered for the Fifty-fifth House.

pattern for the Republican top leaders in the Eighty-ninth House was somewhat similar to the homogeneity found in the Fifty-fifth House. The top Republicans represented primarily white-collar and agricultural districts located in the Midwest. However, even though the Republican top leaders in the Eighty-ninth House came from more homogeneous districts than did their Democratic counterparts, the district types represented were not as homogeneous as was the case in the Fifty-fifth House. The most obvious explanation for the differences found in Table 14–6 is that in the Eighty-ninth House the congressional Democratic party as a whole was composed of members from both industrial northern districts and relatively rural southern districts. Thus, the top leadership of the party reflected these disparate elements within it. In the Fifty-fifth House the regional and industrial continuum was for all practical purposes the same; thus, the terms of East and Industrial, South and Agricultural were interchangeable. In short, the differences found in the types of districts represented by the top leaders in the two eras is a reflection of the occupational and regional bases of the entire congressional parties.

Comments

The primary finding of this paper is that both the leadership and membership of the late 1890s Houses were more supportive of the party position than are their modern counterparts. This was shown to be related to two structural characteristics of the Fifty-fifth and Fifty-sixth Houses. First the top and secondary leadership were selected in a fashion which contributed to the centralization of leadership, by melding the party and committee leadership. Second, the fusion of party and committee leadership insured that the committee system would be controlled by the party leaders. Thus, representatives in these two Houses were not cross-pressured by both party and committee leadership cues. That is, of course, in contrast to the modern House where committee leadership cues often outweigh party cues. The fact that the leadership in the two nineteenth century Houses were more supportive of the party position than are their modern counterparts is also partially attributable to the relative autonomy in policy matters enjoyed by the centralized leadership in the late 1890s. The other major factor which accounts for the higher support scores of both the leaders and members of the Fifty-fifth and Fifty-sixth Houses is the much greater homogeneity of the constituencies represented by each party.

The results of this study seem to indicate the essential correctness of Polsby's assertion that a large part of the behavior of the House is affected by the structure of the House.[23] In short, different leadership structures have differing effects on voting behavior. In the case of the Fifty-fifth and Fifty-sixth Houses the pattern of leadership reinforced rather than moderated basic cleavages.[24]

23. Polsby, op. cit., pp. 165–66.
24. John Wahlke, Heinz Eulau, et al., *The Legislative System: Explorations in Legislative Behavior* (New York: John Wiley and Sons, 1962), pp. 414–31 and 343–76.

Index